# KEY CONCEPTS OF
# CULTURAL ANTHROPOLOGY

## ARI ARIYARATNE

**Kendall Hunt**
publishing company

www.kendallhunt.com
*Send all inquiries to:*
4050 Westmark Drive
Dubuque, IA 52004-1840

Copyright © 2020 by Kendall Hunt Publishing Company

ISBN 978-1-7924-0764-2

Published in the United States of America

# BRIEF CONTENTS

# CONTENTS

## Chapter 7 Kinship, Descent, and Marriage: Comprehending Relatedness 147

## Chapter 13 Globalization: Making Sense of the Culture of Capitalism 319

# PREFACE

Every year I teach cultural anthropology to hundreds of undergraduates in two Illinois colleges. Most of them include students in their first two years of college, and although having little or no familiarity with anthropology, still grow an interest and appreciation for the subject itself. My experience in dealing with these students helped me to set my objective straight as an educator: delivering cutting edge knowledge of anthropology while making my students feel that it is accessible, applicable, and relevant as they navigate through everyday affairs of ordinary life. This textbook is written with the above objective in mind.

## Organization of the Book

This textbook is designed in a way that professors and students alike will find that it is usable with equal ease and comfort either by following the given arrangement of chapters fully or by preferring an order that suits their own options and interests.

*Key Concepts of Cultural Anthropology* consists thirteen chapters covering the breadth of the discipline of cultural anthropology. The first four chapters provide the foundation for the study of human culture. **Chapter 1** presents an overview of anthropology, introducing the guiding principles of its perspective and its main subfields, and referring to anthropology as a discipline located on the edge of the sciences and the humanities. **Chapter 2** focuses on fieldwork, by which cultural anthropological knowledge is produced. It discusses common fieldwork situations, where issues, concerns, and problems common to all ethnographic fieldworkers twine together, describes fieldwork techniques and some of the new approaches to fieldwork, and traces the processes involving the production of ethnographic monographs. The chapter also refers to an array of ethical considerations pertaining to fieldwork. **Chapter 3** introduces culture, cultural anthropology's key concept, with which human condition may be distinguishable. It examines some of the salient characteristics of culture which can be recognizable universally, and explains how culture unites all subfields of anthropology with its all-encompassing theme. **Chapter 4** situates the concept of culture on firm theoretical footing, and reviews the growth of cultural anthropological theory. In so doing, it intends to assist students to get a sense of how the texts they are reading fit into a wider theoretical context of cultural anthropology.

**Chapter 5** concentrates on language, with which humans encode and communicate about their experiential world. The chapter reviews linguistic researches that recognize language as a mode of thinking and expression unique to humans as a symbolic species. It also introduces linguistic anthropology's subdisciplines, focusing on each field's scope, core themes, and methods of investigation. **Chapter 6** proceeds to explore another very distinctive aspect of being human: artistic expression and appreciation or symbolic creativity seen across cultures. The chapter deals with art's biological origins and formal qualities, as well as the salient aspects of the anthropological perspective of art. It also explores the themes of art and power, art and media, and art and globalization.

**Chapter 7** focuses on kinship, the system of meaning and power with which humans construct some of their most stable, reliable, enduring, and distinctive relationships. The chapter examines the various strategies people use to form kinship ties through descent, marriage, and family cross-culturally, discussing the implications of kinship's changing expressions in the twenty-first century.

**Chapter 8** on economic anthropology delves into the themes of subsistence strategies through which people across cultures sustain themselves. **Chapter 9** concentrates on some of the main themes in economic anthropology as well. Specifically, it investigates the patterns of economic exchange and distribution, and the anthropological theories pertaining to them.

**Chapter 10** concentrates on social stratification based on class, caste, race, ethnicity, gender, and the like in the contemporary world, examining how hierarchical relationships commensurate with culturally institutionalized inequality.

Focusing on the nexus of power and culture, **Chapter 11** on political anthropology probes the exercise of social power. The chapter discusses how a state exercises power, referring to related concepts such as structural power, hegemony, and governmentality.

Adopting a historical perspective, **Chapter 12** examines the growth of the modern world order over the course of last five centuries. It investigates into the motives for European expansion and the methods used to accomplish it, exploring its impact on native populations around the world from the sixteenth through the eighteenth centuries. The chapter proceeds to delve into colonialism of the nineteenth and the early twentieth centuries, the decolonization process in the aftermath of the Second World War, and the predicaments borne of neocolonialism. The chapter also critically examines the critiques of modern world order, primarily focusing on the theoretical positions of the dependency theorists and the subscriptions to the world-system analysis.

**Chapter 13**, the final chapter of the book, concentrates on the complex processes that lead to globalization. It provides an overview of the theoretical approaches to cultural globalization that lays stress on homogenization and heterogeneity, and takes up the complexity of the new global cultural economy recently analyzed through anthropological models such as global cultural flows or landscapes, changing modalities of governance, and friction or awkward interconnection across difference.

## Pedagogy

*Key Concepts of Cultural Anthropology* contains the following supportive features: A wide array of carefully chosen, color and black-and-white photographs are included to enhance visual appeal and enliven textual material; a number of diagrams and maps are added as the text warrants; a summary of the main points are added to the end of each chapter; the key terms bolded within the text are listed alphabetically in the glossary at the end of the book together with their definitions; a standard bibliography and an index are given at the end of the book.

## Supplements

As an attractive, convenient, and economical alternative, *Key Concepts of Cultural Anthropology* is also available as an electronic text.

## Acknowledgments

The writing of this book has truly been a self-effacing experience. I have been awed by encountering the gilt-edged scholarly work dedicated to the anthropological ideal of gaining insights into people of all variety, in all places, and at all times. I have also been equally moved by the passion, energy, and commitment of my fellow anthropologists to invest in that holistic understanding with the resolve of making the world a better place for living. On this excursion, I became humbler and wiser in the best possible sense of the word. Along the way it has been my privilege to have the assistance and encouragement of a range of people. Without them this book would not have been possible.

I would like to begin this brief note by remembering late professor Senaka Bandaranayake who encouraged my interest on anthropology during my undergraduate years in Sri Lanka. I was taught anthropology at University of Illinois by Professors Harold Gould, Kris Lehman (late), Edward Bruner, Clark Cunningham, David Plath, Mahir Saul, Janet Keller, Bill Kelleher (late), and Alma Gottlieb, to all of whom I am truly grateful. In my time at Graduate School, I was also greatly benefited from having the company of many energetic colleagues with a wide range of theoretical pursuits. Indeed, some of them have now blossomed into brilliant scholarly minds.

Sometime back in my college teaching, I began to notice that my cultural anthropology students lean more on the class notes I have circulated among them than on the textbook assigned for the class. It was a gesture powerful enough in instilling in my mind the idea of writing a textbook someday. However, that initial thought was morphed into a full-fledged plan only when Keely Newton, my acquisition editor at Kendall Hunt Publishing Company, approached me with the suggestion to write an original textbook for college-level cultural anthropology beginners. Bev Kraus of Kendall Hunt Publishing, the coordinator of this book project, and her staff diligently tended to every step in the process turning the manuscript into a book.

Among the many people who saw me through this book, I would like to extend my gratitude to the following scholars, colleagues, and friends for offering me varying degrees of advocacy, assistance, and intellectual comfort at various stages of this book project: Paul Streumer, Alex Bolyanatz, Laura Gonzalez, Sherry Harlacher, Raheel Dhattiwar, Padriac Shinville, Sarah Diel-Hunt, Somasiri Munasinghe, Upasena Hewage, and Joni Jecklin. A special thank must be made to Mahir Saul, one of my professors at University of Illinois, who also offered to write the blurb for the back cover of this book.

Gajaba Naraddage, my son, has not only been my most candid and constructive critic, but also most unwavering source of encouragement. He also assisted me by editing drafts of chapters in this book and preparing diagrams (Tables and Figures) diligently even though it surely sucked up numerous hours of his valuable time at University of Illinois. Samudrika Weeraratne, his mother, has been providing moral support steadfastly. Lee Naraddage, my elder brother, has been perseveringly supportive of this endeavor as well.

I would like to dedicate this textbook to my students who unceasingly convince me the following in every class I teach: Anthropology's ability and potential to delve deep into humanity with the hope of building a better world is such that it is well worth spending time for.

# ABOUT THE AUTHOR

Source: Ari Ariyaratne

Ari Ariyaratne is Distinguished Adjunct Professor of Anthropology at Heartland Community College, Bloomington, IL. He is also anthropology faculty at College of DuPage, Glen Ellyn, IL. Before coming to HCC in 2005, Ariyaratne taught at University of Illinois at Urbana-Champaign, IL, Eureka College at Eureka, IL, and Parkland College at Champaign, IL. He teaches courses on cultural anthropology, general anthropology, ancient civilizations and societies, and people and cultures of the world.

Professor Ariyaratne has conducted extensive ethnographic fieldwork in Sri Lanka. His doctoral dissertation is a comprehensive ethnography of the Sinhalese peasants in central Sri Lanka woven against the backdrop of a major dispute unraveled during the 1990s. It discusses the predicaments of the Sri Lankan state from a theoretical standpoint stemming mainly from Antonio Gramsci's notion of cultural hegemony. Ari's current research interests include critical pedagogy, globalization, nation-state, South Asia, and Sri Lanka.

Professor Ariyaratne received his B. A. from University of Kelaniya, Sri Lanka, with First Class Honors. He received his M. A. and Ph. D. in cultural anthropology from University of Illinois at Urbana-Champaign, IL.

# Perspectives: Introducing Anthropology

© Andrea Izzotti/Shutterstock.com

Broadly stated, anthropology is the study of humankind in all its facets, times, and places. The etymology of the term **anthropology** shows the breadth of its perspective unmistakably: The Greek words of *"anthropos"* (man or human beings) and *"logia"* (the study of) join to denote that anthropology is the study of human beings, literally. The broadness is also evident in the question that captures the discipline's main theme: What does it mean to be human? The exploration of being human takes one to a vast array of study topics, ranging from human evolution and variation, culture and social relations, language and communication, and vestiges of human habitation. A fascination on human similarity and difference transforms one from an indifferent individual to an excursionist to humanity. Anthropological gaze that helps to make sense of human similarity and difference transforms one from a globetrotter to a native of humanity.

# Guiding Principles

So broad in its scope, anthropology has adopted several guiding principles fundamental to its perspective: holistic approach, comparative method, and fieldwork.

## Holistic Approach

**Holistic approach** stresses seeing the human condition in its broadest possible context. Having a highest possible level of inclusion makes it possible to delineate human situations together with their interconnections and interdependence, and thereby, to forge a deeper understanding. Holism in anthropological perspective is easily palpable. As stated earlier, anthropology is a discipline that studies humans of all variety, everywhere, throughout time. Many other subjects in sciences and humanities also study something about humans. However, anthropology is perhaps the only contemporary discipline that studies all types of people around the world within a highest possible stretch of time, and from an integrative perspective of all biological, archaeological, linguistic, and cultural dimensions. Holistic approach gives anthropology a synergistic strength by helping to understand how the above dimensions of humanity are distinct and special in their own way, yet still interrelated.

## Comparative Method

In its characteristic interest in human biocultural variation and change, anthropology finds a natural ally in comparison. **Comparative method**, the methodological approach in examining data for the purpose of noting similarities and differences, is a key element in anthropological perspective. Without relying on the data gleaned from a single source, anthropologists strive to collect comparative evidence from a wide array of human societies and cultures before analyzing and interpreting the human condition.

## Fieldwork-Based Data Collection

**Fieldwork-based data collection** or gathering primary evidence in natural field contexts is common to practitioners of various subdisciplines in anthropology. In biological anthropology, for example, primatologists often study primates such as chimpanzees and gorillas in their habitats and in captivity. In much the same vein, paleoanthropologists collect fossil evidence when they examine their actual field locations. Likewise, biological anthropologists who study human biological diversity gather data in appropriate field settings such as population segments in neighborhoods and laboratories. Much like paleoanthropologists, archaeologists gather material evidence on the past human cultures through excavations in archaeological sites. Some archaeological research steps such as dating artifacts, taking measurement, and recording are also taken before removing such evidence from the ground and taking to the laboratories for further analysis. More to the point, cultural anthropologists gain insights into people and their life ways primarily by doing fieldwork. This process of learning about a culture through immersion and producing written, visual, or virtual accounts of such fieldwork, known as ethnography, is the hallmark of cultural anthropology. Additionally, linguistic anthropologists learn about the various aspects of language and communication by conducting fieldwork among specific speech communities. All in all, fieldwork-based data collection is, and always has been, an essential part anthropology.

## The Subfields of Anthropology

Anthropology has four main subdisciplines or areas of specialization. They are cultural anthropology or sociocultural anthropology, biological or physical anthropology, anthropological linguistics or linguistic anthropology, and archaeology or archaeological anthropology.

### TABLE 1.1   Subfields of Anthropology

**Biological or Physical Anthropology**
- Paleoanthropology
- Primatology
- Human Biological Variation

**Archaeology or Archaeological Anthropology**
- Prehistoric Archaeology
- Historic Archaeology

**Linguistic Anthropology or Anthropological Linguistics**
- Structural Linguistics
- Historical Linguistics
- Sociolinguistics

**Cultural or Sociocultural Anthropology**
- Ethnology
- Ethnography

**Applied or Practicing Anthropology**

Source: Gajaba Naraddage

## Biological Anthropology

**Biological anthropology,** also known as *physical anthropology,* is the subfield of anthropology that studies human biology from an evolutionary perspective, with a stress laid on the interaction between biology and culture.

© Usagi-P/Shutterstock.com

It is composed of three subdisciplines. The first, **paleoanthropology**, is the study of the complex course of human evolution, specifically as evidenced in the fossil record. In their aim of gaining insights into how and when human beings came into being, paleoanthropologists seek to identify the various early hominid species, establish a chronological sequence of links among them, and learn about their process of adaptation and behavior.

The second subfield of biological anthropology is **primatology**, the study of nonhuman primates such as prosimians, monkeys, and apes in their habitats or in captivity. Primatologists believe that, because primates are the closest living relatives of human beings, locating the underlying factors on their social behavior, communication, infant care, reproductive behavior, and so on, helps to understand many aspects of human adaptation and behavior better.

The third subfield concentrates on salient aspects of **human biological variation** to clarify the evolutionary factors contributing to generate variation. Anthropologists working on human biological diversity often collaborate with geneticists, the scientists who examine how traits are transmitted from one generation to the next. This field of inquiry, known as molecular anthropology, is closely related to two areas of specialization. The first of them, population studies, examines topics such as the connections between physical traits specific

© GUDKOV ANDREY/Shutterstock.com

to certain populations and environmental conditions including infectious disease. The second of them is nutritional studies. It examines the possible links of dietary elements, physiology, and cultural practices, to health and disease. The latter is also closely related to the studies of human fertility, growth, and development.

## Archaeological Anthropology

**Archaeological anthropology** or *archaeology* concentrates on reconstructing, describing, and interpreting human life ways and patterns through the study of material remains of prehistoric and historical populations. In pursuit of evidence on past human cultural activity, archaeologists examine **archaeological sites** or locations where material evidence of past human activity is present, while focusing on four kinds of remains. They are artifacts, eco-facts, features, and fossils. **Artifacts** are anything made or altered by past humans—they are blandly said, ancient garbage. These material evidences, if necessary, can be removed from the sites and taken to the laboratory for further examination and analysis. For instance, lithic or stone tools, ceramics or earthenware made from baked clay, and the tools made from wood and animal bones, are artifacts. **Eco-facts** are a variety of objects found in natural environment ranging from animal bones, plant seeds, and wood, to the remains of insect and animal pests. They are somewhat like artifacts, but distinguishable for an important reason: These are the objects that have been used and discarded by past humans, but never modified. The animal bones eaten and discarded by humans, pollen originated from various plants brought to their dwelling by humans to use, and the remains of pests and rodents in archaeological sites, such as ancient cockroaches and mice, are some of the examples to eco-facts. **Features**, like artifacts, are the objects of human manufacture or modification. Unlike artifacts however, they cannot be readily removed from the archaeological site and carried away to the laboratory for further study. In a site, features represent some nonportable activity by past humans. This is because features are the objects stretching both vertically and horizontally over a very deep and large area by becoming intrinsic *features* of the site. Most common features include pits, ditches, house foundations, fireplaces, and middens or dump deposits. **Fossils** are hardened remains and impressions of ancient life forms including humans preserved under the conditions favorable for fossilization. Such conditions include the presence of limestone, volcanic ash, or highly mineralized groundwater. Given the fact that fossil evidences are specifically useful to understand human biological evolution, often, archaeological anthropologists work collaboratively with paleoanthropologists in dealing with fossils.

© Openfinal/Shutterstock.com

Archaeologists often concentrate on specific time periods, distinct cultural zones, or specific geographic regions of the world. Archaeological specificity may also be based on the context in which archaeological research activity takes place. For instance, maritime or underwater archaeology studies submerged sites of archaeology such as shipwrecks. Likewise, virtual archaeology has to do with archaeological research involving cyber space, such as computer graphics–aided 3D models, computer-built topographical models, and computer-simulated past living conditions. However, a crucial factor on which most archaeological research is based is the existence or nonexistence of written records of history. Accordingly, archaeology has two principal forms of investigation: prehistoric archaeology and historical archaeology. **Prehistoric archaeology** focuses on the preurban societies in the world for which historical records literally do not exist. In its effort to reconstruct the ecological settings of prehistoric societies, prehistoric archaeology follows a distinctive set of procedures with which fossil evidence may be carefully identified, documented, and analyzed. **Historic archaeology** deals with the past human societies that left behind historical records. These records are usually written materials, but oral traditions are also admissible as they can equally inform and contextualize cultural evidence. Historic archaeologists are always keen to know whether the archaeological evidence found at a site is in concert with or in conflict with the written records and oral traditions.

© krugloff/Shutterstock.com

While understanding historical and prehistoric cultures remains their primary objective, some archaeologists today are also keen to use the methods of archaeology to study the aspects of contemporary material culture with the hope of resolving human predicaments and accomplishing policy goals. Indeed, the time range for archaeological research encompasses not only the earliest human ancestors who inhabited in this world millions of years ago and the archaeological populations in historic times, but also the people who live even today. The study of garbage middens or **garbology** commenced by the archaeologists at the University of Arizona at Tucson was significant in this regard. By excavating part of the Fresh Kills landfill on Staten Island, New York City, these archaeologists intended to explore the links between material culture and consumer behavior among the urbanites (Rathje and Murphy 1992). Indeed, the study of the contemporary life has gained currency among some archaeological practitioners in recent years.

Identifying, conserving, and managing archaeological sites and monuments of cultural value threatened by current human activity has been another salient area in which archaeologists work as the specialists of **Cultural Resource Management (CRM)**.

## Cultural Anthropology

**Cultural anthropology,** sometimes called *social* or *sociocultural anthropology,* is the study of similarities, differences, and change among contemporary and recent human societies across the globe as they are fashioned by culture. The term **culture** refers to a series of beliefs and practices humans acquire as constituent parts of society through learning and sharing (discussed in Chapter 3). Cultural anthropologists study culture by engaging in two types of activity: ethnology and ethnography. **Ethnology**, in its current usage, is the comparative study of two or more cultures. This comparison, often selective in nature, makes ethnologists essentially cross-cultural researchers. **Ethnography** refers to extended, up-close, and personal fieldwork-based anthropological monographs produced in written, visual, or virtual forms (discussed in Chapter 2).

The concept of culture being the central organizing construct of anthropology, cultural anthropologists are well aware that understanding cultures of the people whose backgrounds and histories are different from their own demands an emphatic rejection of **ethnocentrism**, the tendency to judge the aspects of other cultures from the vantage point of one's own culture. It is an intellectually unsound notion in that it tends to drive any attempt at comprehending other cultures to an inevitable dead end. If one assumes that she or he has all the correct explanations for human condition as one belonging to the superior culture, one's study of other cultures simply becomes a study of other people's blunders! Ethnocentrism is not merely an abstract concept of fallacy, however. As several centuries of Western colonialism had brought to bear, when accompanied by the forces of power, ethnocentrism can generate realities mostly unfavorable to weaker human communities.

© Suiyobish/Shutterstock.com

Identifying and getting rid of ethnocentrism is easier said than done. Its overt forms may be readily apparent, and their links with power may be easily located. However, its covert forms may not be that unambiguous, and their power connections may not be conveniently traceable. For instance, like any ideology, ethnocentrism operates behind one's back, making one often unaware of its existence within one's own thought and action. Fully aware of such complexities, cultural anthropologists have proposed to apprehend the beliefs and behavior of another culture within the context of that culture, and not within the cultural setting of one's own. This perspective is known as **cultural relativism**. It reminds one to recognize the significance of cultural similarities and differences, and to appreciate them outside of one's ethnocentrism to relax opinion and to give weight to unbiased appreciation. Relativistic approach, in its strict sense, can be problematic, nevertheless. Because it can facilitate the view that it is simply not possible to question the rationale behind the thoughts and actions of any culture, including one's own. Notwithstanding such limits, cultural relativism has been a guiding principle in much of cultural anthropology's history. It reminds the researchers to be mindful of the existence of different viewpoints. It also alerts to the fact that one's ethnocentric predispositions may blind one to alternative views.

## Linguistic Anthropology

**Linguistic anthropology** or *anthropological linguistics* is the subfield of anthropology concerned with the systems of human communication and languages in time and space. Language being the cornerstone of human culture and being a primary means of interaction in doing ethnographic fieldwork, anthropological interest on language and linguistics is well understood. Anthropological linguistics comprises three subfields: **structural linguistics** or *descriptive linguistics* focuses on documenting, describing, and analyzing structural features of language; **historical linguistics** concentrates on studying the links between earlier and later forms of language; **sociolinguistics** focuses on investigating language in its social and cultural context (discussed in Chapter 5).

© kathrinerajalingam/Shutterstock.com

Of late, linguistic anthropologists have stretched their research interests to accommodate the themes such as linguistic features of popular culture and social media, advertising, emoticons, and netiquette. Critical Discourse Analysis (CDA), another trending research area, concentrates on examining the relations between power and stretches of everyday communication, or discourse.

When taken as a whole, anthropology is a holistic field of study consisting of the four main subdisciplines—biological, archaeological, cultural, and linguistic anthropology—known as four-field anthropology or **general anthropology**. Four-field anthropology approaches the human condition from a perspective capable of clearly articulating all biological, archaeological, cultural, and linguistic aspects.

## Applied Anthropology

**Applied anthropology** or *practicing anthropology* is increasingly regarded as a main subfield of general anthropology as well. It is the use of existing anthropological knowledge to determine, evaluate, and resolve or prevent problems in the contemporary world, while fashioning and accomplishing policy objectives. Academic and applied anthropology are not mutually exclusive perspectives by any means. However, applied anthropologists are more explicit and conscious about their practical goals and public role. They are keen to accommodate any theoretical perspective or methodological approach from general anthropology for applied purposes. Academic anthropological researchers almost always work in universities, colleges, and museums, the traditional settings of academia. By contrast, applied anthropologists are usually employed or involved in a vast array of settings outside of traditional educational communities, ranging from government agencies, consulting firms, business entrepreneurs, offices of law and enforcement, medical schools, public health organizations, charitable foundations, social service agencies, to international development agencies. Today, nearly a half of all anthropology professionals from all four subfields of general anthropology are engaged in applied anthropological research. For instance, some biological anthropologists work as forensic anthropologists while helping law enforcement authorities to solve crimes. Moreover, biological and cultural anthropologists do collaborative work in studying health and illness while seeking solutions to problems arising out from the areas such as epidemiology, public health, nutrition, ethnomedicine, and maternal and child health. This vibrant branch of applied anthropology is known as medical anthropology. Furthermore, working with some of the last speakers of dying languages around the world, and methodically collecting such language-specific local knowledge, linguistic anthropologists are active in the area of salvage ethnography and language revitalization. Meanwhile, some applied archaeologists, also known as public archaeologists, conduct archaeological research, survey, and excavation on behalf of government agencies, private organizations, or individual landowners. These professional archaeologists are known as the practitioners of contract archaeology.

**TABLE 1.2    Some Examples for Applied Anthropology**

**Biological/Physical Anthropology**
- Forensic Anthropology
- Genetic and Biomedical Research
- Evolutionary Medicine
- Ethnomedicine
- Primate Conservation
- Museum Studies
- Zoology

**Archaeology**
- Cultural Resource Management (CRM)
- Public Archaeology
- Contract Archaeology

**Linguistic Anthropology**
- Study of Linguistic Diversity in Classroom
- Preservation of Dying Languages

**Cultural Anthropology**
- Development Anthropology
- Business Anthropology
- Embedded Anthropology
- Advocacy Anthropology

Source: Gajaba Naraddage

# Anthropology, the Sciences, and the Humanities

Anthropology is situated on the edge of the sciences and the humanities. Academic fields have been customarily and broadly categorized as natural sciences, social sciences, and the humanities. The natural sciences, such as physics and chemistry, seek to establish general rules by constructing empirically falsifiable theories. The social sciences, or the fields of inquiry concerned with society and human behavior, generally try to develop methods similar to those used in the physical and biological sciences with the aim of establishing generalizations on social phenomena. They encompass a number of fields including economics, political science, geography, criminology, psychology, and sociology. The humanities study the subjects pertaining to human thought and culture such as languages, literature, philosophy, the arts, and history by employing qualitative research methods. Different subfields of anthropology draw on one or more of these realms of knowledge. However, anthropology is not a subject fitting well into any one of them. It is a distinctive discipline located at the nexus of the natural sciences, social sciences, and the humanities.

## Positivist Approach

At the beginning of the twentieth century, like most of their colleagues in other fields of social sciences, many anthropologists treated their discipline as a science. Their quest for science in its stricter modern sense, as explainable, predictable, empirically verifiable, value-neutral, and universal knowledge pursued through the unity of scientific method, was heavily influenced by **positivism**, a school of modern Western thought that advocated such pursuits. Assuming that the natural laws of the physical world and the laws governing society were identical, these anthropologists used the methods resembling those used by natural scientists for understanding society. Alternatively, a physicist conducting experiments in a laboratory was what they tried to emulate in their own research on human societies while treating field sites as living laboratories. The emulation of the aforementioned prototypical research scenario seemed plausible because the main trend among these anthropologists coming from complex and industrial societies of the West has been to study the people in less complex societies in remote regions of the world, known then as the "primitive people" or the "savages" (discussed in Chapter 2).

In their attempt of putting anthropology in firm scientific footing, anthropology professionals in the four subdisciplines never deviated from the established tenets of the scientific inquiry such as: employing research methodologies, formulating and testing hypotheses, developing extensive sets of data, and applying theories. However, the debate over anthropology's links with the sciences and the humanities has been evident during the first half of the twentieth century and afterward. For example, A. R. Radcliffe-Brown (1881–1955), one of the founders of British school of social anthropology, was firm on his belief that social anthropology, like natural sciences, strives to build generalizations with which specific social institutions can be discerned. By contrast, E. E. Evans-Pritchard (1902–1973), one of Brown's Oxford anthropology colleagues, maintained that social anthropology is a discipline of the humanities for its focus of combining pertinent social phenomena without resorting to establish universally applicable laws. In much the same vein, the physicist-turned-anthropologist Franz Boas (1858–1942), a pioneer in American anthropology, was convinced on the scientific nature of anthropology. He was a main proponent for applying the scientific method to the study of human societies and cultures. Nevertheless, his student Ruth Benedict (1887–1948) held a point of view different from her mentor in this regard. Conscious about boundary bridging across the academic disciplines, she advocated anthropologists to espouse the methods of both the sciences and the humanities, which in her view, are entirely complementary.

## Postmodernism

From the 1970s onward, and especially during the 1980s and the 1990s, discussion over the purview of anthropology assumed a new level of salience. This was partly due to the critique by a number of anthropologists who referred to themselves as postmodernists. **Postmodernism**, in general, is a style and movement in architecture, art, literary criticism, and many other fields, and a related theoretical perspective that came into being as a severe critique of modernist enterprise and its ideals, including scientific objectivity and the scientific method. According to the postmodernists, the modernist project of the past two centuries was launched through a strong bias toward science, and uneven power relations between the affluent countries (the colonizers) and the poorer countries (the colonized). The post-modern anthropologists were deeply skeptical on building generalizable theories on human cultures since such theoretical tools seek to construct abstract principles at the expense of the living qualities of cultures and their intricacies. In pursuit of meanings in cultures, they advised to switch from the methods of experimental sciences such as the search for general laws to interpretation. Anthropology, in this sense, is a more humanistic enterprise than a scientific project. The postmodernists also viewed all anthropological accounts as subjective. The established tenet of ethnographic objectivity is an elusive concept given the fact that ethnographic observations are conditioned by the anthropologist's social, cultural, gender orientations, personal experiences, and feelings. As such, the postmodernist anthropologists favored a more inclusive approach to the study of cultures and advocated an active collabo-ration between anthropologists and the people they intend to study. Today, anthropologists of all theoretical orientations are far more conscious of the links between the knowledge that they produce on human beings and power. They are also more receptive to the postmodern-ist call for humanism, native collaboration, and reflexivity.

In the age of **Anthropocene**, during which human activity (*anthropogenic disruptions*) has been the dominant influence on global climate, ecosystems, and sociocultural environment, anthropology has become more relevant to humans than ever. Anthropology's holistic approach, long engagement in questions of society and culture, and in-depth fieldwork methodology yields insights invaluable for the future of humanity.

© Ekaphon maneechot/Shutterstock.com

## Chapter Summary

This chapter presents an overview of anthropology, introducing the guiding principles of its perspective and its main subfields, and referring to anthropology as a discipline located on the edge of the sciences and the humanities.

- Anthropology is the study of human beings of all variety, everywhere, throughout time.
- Anthropological perspective is comprised of holistic approach, comparative method, and fieldwork-based acquisition of data.
- The four subfields of anthropology are biological anthropology, archaeological anthropology, cultural anthropology, and linguistic anthropology.
- Increasingly, applied anthropology is also considered as a main subfield of anthropology.
- The discipline of anthropology is located at the nexus of the natural sciences, social sciences, and the humanities.

# Fieldwork: Producing Cultural Anthropological Knowledge

© Suiyobish/Shutterstock.com

Fieldwork is the central ritual of the tribe of cultural anthropology. In documenting, describing, and analyzing the vast variety of life ways found among the people across the globe today, cultural anthropologists rely primarily on experiential engagement in fieldwork. They gather their field data mainly by living among the people being studied, participating in their daily rounds of activities and special events, and learning from them for an extended period of time. In other words, in order to collect research findings, cultural anthropologists prefer to immerse in the culture and society that they are trying to make sense of. This method of research data gathering that emphasizes on-site engagement in fieldwork and experiential learning is also known as **ethnographic fieldwork**, and it is a necessary and distinctive part in cultural anthropologists' rites of passage.

## From the Armchair and the Verandah to the Tent

However, ethnographic fieldwork has not always been so central to cultural anthropological practice. In the second half of the nineteenth century, the first Western scholars who turned to study the then little known subject of anthropology did not think that, gaining some firsthand experience of the specific people being studied was necessary to write about their beliefs and behavior. For intellectual aspiration, they were heavily leaning on the school of thought known as **social Darwinism**, in vogue at the time. Social Darwinists believed that Darwin's theory of evolution was applicable to society and culture. As these theorists viewed, specific societies and cultures were recognizably located within a hierarchical order according to their level of progression from savagery to barbarism, and eventually to civilization. Whereas their own Western societies were at the zenith of the aforesaid hierarchy (i. e., civilization), the small-scale societies that they were studying and writing about were still at the very bottom (i. e., savagery). More to the point, in popular thought at the time, the savages or the primitive people were subhuman creatures who were at the mercy of their emotions, weren't in control of their rational thought, and were sort of blown here and there by changing emotional forms.

Adherents to such views, earlier anthropologists believed that the people in the small-scale societies have to be studied from a distance, and not by having direct contact with them. Therefore, to gain insights on such people, they entirely rely on sources which were available at their arm's length: the writings of travelers, explorers, missionaries, colonial officers, and the likes. This nineteenth-century practice of doing anthropology by sitting comfortably at home in their leather armchairs, reading amateur reports about their exotic subjects, and compiling descriptive accounts on them is known today as *armchair anthropology*.

In the late nineteenth and early twentieth centuries, some anthropologists, hired by European colonial governments, traveled to European colonies and began to study the native people by living close to them and talking to them. However, they preferred to talk to the natives only in the verandah of their abodes, and the talking was more or less closer to interrogation. Nevertheless, by staying away deliberately from the armchair for the verandah, these anthropologists have signaled that they were almost ready for firsthand fieldwork experience. Their practice is referred to as *verandah anthropology*.

In the early twentieth century, the innovative approaches introduced by two anthropologists have changed the way of studying people and their ways of life. They were German-born American anthropologist Franz Boas and Polish-born British social anthropologist Bronislaw Malinowski. Boas, who spent a considerable time studying the Kwakiutl Indians in the Pacific Northwest, insisted on carefully studying a culture for an extended period of time while living among the people being researched, and examining specific cultural traits such as beliefs, behaviors, and symbols in their local context.

Science History Images/Alamy Stock Photo

Malinowski is credited for introducing participant-observation, the core ethnographic technique of researching about a culture through up-close, on-sight, personal observation, and active participation (discussed below). Malinowski used this technique during his fieldwork among the Trobriand islanders of the Western Pacific from 1915 to 1918.

© Joyce Mar/Shutterstock.com

By camping and living right in the village, learning local language and nuances to communicate, seeing the daily life and specific occurrences, and dealing with natives intensely, Malinowski was able to articulate well some of the basic tenets of practicing cultural anthropology more than any other anthropologist before or during his time. Without a doubt, that's why he is canonized today as the anthropologist who brought cultural anthropology "off the verandah" and placed firmly in the ethnographer's tent.

Chronicle/Alamy Stock Photo

## Common Fieldwork Situations

Any ethnographic fieldwork experience is a snapshot of a specific life way shared by a people in a specific time and place. As **restudies** or fieldwork research carried out in previously researched communities have shown time and again, no fieldwork situation is comparable on equal grounds with any other. Over the years, the scope of cultural anthropological fieldwork has expanded to include the city and urban life in industrial societies. However, research on traditional, small-scale societies has been remaining as a well-established practice of cultural anthropology. This aspect of field research has to be understood within the context that the anthropological paradigm of fieldwork experience as a cultural encounter between the researcher and a specific group of people (whose way of life unfamiliar to the researcher) remains largely unchanged.

This is why common fieldwork situations are recognizable, regardless of the uniqueness of each fieldwork situation. **Common fieldwork situations** refer to instances in which fieldworkers consistently face intertwining issues, concerns, and problems common to all ethnographic fieldworkers as they begin and proceed through the fieldwork process. They include selecting a research problem, choosing a research location, doing a literature review (and, if possible, a pilot study), securing funds to conduct the research, obtaining language training, arriving at the field site and settling there, rebounding from culture shock (sense of alienation for being outside of one's comfort zone), gaining rapport, locating cultural consultants, gathering data, and producing ethnographic accounts (See TABLE 2.1).

| TABLE 2.1   Some of the Common Fieldwork Situations | |
| --- | --- |
| Selecting a Research Problem | Rebounding from Culture Shock |
| Choosing a Research Location | Gaining Rapport |
| Doing a Literature Review | Locating Cultural Consultants |
| Securing Funds | Gathering Data |
| Obtaining Language Training | Producing Ethnographic Accounts |
| Arriving at the Field Site | |

Source: Gajaba Naraddage

## Fieldwork Techniques

Given that each field situation, each culture being studied, and each ethnographer is like no other, it is hard to pick the most appropriate field technique(s) for each field situation with pin-point accuracy. Cultural anthropologists who strive to study the vast spectrum of ways of life found among people around the world have a number of field techniques at their disposal to choose from. Most of these field techniques have originated when doing fieldwork among a culturally and linguistically unfamiliar group of people from a distant land was the norm. The quest for exotic wonder and savagery is now largely sidelined as the condition within which fieldwork has been carried out has been changed. Whereas, the fieldwork techniques used in that quest are still being used by anthropologists since the intrigue over human similarity and difference, a central motivating factor of doing anthropology remains intact.

Depending on a number of reasons, cultural anthropologists tend to focus on research techniques more useful in collecting qualitative or quantitative data. These reasons range from the theoretical orientation, the nature of research problem, research goals, the receptivity of the people being studied, time constraints, the priorities put forth by the funds providers, and to the resources at the researchers' disposal. The qualitative fieldwork techniques used in ethnography include participant-observation, the ethnographic interview, life history research, working with key cultural consultants, the genealogical method, ethnographic photography, ethnographic filming, ethnographic videography, and ethnographic audio recording.

| TABLE 2.2    Some of the Common Fieldwork Techniques | |
|---|---|
| Participant-Observation | Eliciting Devices |
| Ethnographic interview | Ethnographic Photography, Filmmaking, |
| Key Cultural Consultants | Videography, and Audio Recording |
| Life History Research | Ethnographic Mapping |
| Genealogical Method | Critical Ethnography |
| Reflexive Ethnography | Multisited Ethnography |

Source: Gajaba Naraddage

Techniques such as taking field notes, using eliciting devices, charting (comparative charts/tables, network charts, and genealogical charts), mapping, are used by researchers who favor both qualitative and quantitative data gathering. In addition, cultural anthropologists seek consultation of archival and previously published materials, and tap into Internet-based research materials. Oftentimes, they employ manifold field methods to provide extensity and profundity to ethnographic data acquisition through cross-checking of the field findings.

Typical quantitative research techniques include sampling, surveying, questionnaires, and opinion polls. Sometimes, ethnographic fieldworkers use these techniques for their projects. However, they do not rely exclusively or, at times, even primarily on such techniques.

## Participant-Observation

Ever since its introduction by pioneer anthropologists such as Bronislaw Malinowski and Franz Boas, **participant-observation** has been the hallmark of ethnographic field research. This technique, considered as one of the main requirements in the ethnographic research method, is very useful when immersing in the culture being studied for an extended period of time. It involves two intertwining processes of learning a people's way of life through personal observation and social participation. It seeks to study people at the grassroot level by actively involving in ordinary affairs of everyday life and special events, and putting that experience-based knowledge into perspective. This is done while doing away with the reduction of meanings to what is observable. Basically, the participant-observation is a fieldwork technique of an experiential cultural learning that requires eating food of the people being studied, dwelling like they do, learning to speak their language, experiencing their customs, and behaving accordingly.

Synthesizing participation and observation, and thereby, finding ways of comprehending the research experience from a perspective more close to an insider's view, and describing that experience from a position nearer to an outsider's view can be a difficult challenge to overcome. But the dividends are impressive. For example, the participant-observer is likely to do better than a mere observer in bridging cultures; her or his manifest interest in learning local culture, and the earnest efforts to reach out local people in doing so, is likely to increase her or his ability to improve rapport. And, that can create an environment quite conducive for gathering qualitative field data. Moreover, the ethnographer's participation in daily round of activities could make his presence almost ordinary to the local people. Once the initial curiosity on the ethnographer is submerged in familiarity and fade to the periphery of consciousness, they may go about their business as usual in the presence of the ethnographer. This approach to fieldwork can minimize the *Hawthorne effect,* or the local people's tendency of adopting a behavior more accommodative of what they perceive to be the expectations of the anthropologist.

When people begin to behave in a way they would usually behave in the absence of the anthropologist's presence, it helps a great deal for the anthropologist to differentiate what people say they do, from what they do.

The lengthy time usually consumed to gather research data, the problems it poses when recording and comparing the findings, and the difficulties it can cause when gaining access to individuals or events due to the ethnographer's gender orientation are cited as some among the possible shortcomings of the participant-observation as a fieldwork technique.

## Ethnographic Interview

Much of what cultural anthropologists do in the field, and indeed much of what they do as participant-observers, is based on the **ethnographic interview**. Although the researchers of many disciplinary backgrounds use the interview as a main technique to solicit information, the ethnographic interview is unique in several salient respects. First and foremost, it is primarily used by anthropologists to gain

Polynesian Tattoo

© Vectors by Skop/Shutterstock.com

Science History Images/Alamy Stock Photo

insights on every possible aspect of a particular way of life found among a particular group of people. In this sense, the breadth and the depth of its scope is unparalleled by any other interview type. The ethnographic interviewers are certainly interested in knowing the extents of difference between what people say what they do, and what they actually do. They are also keen in treating the data related to both of the above ends as equally significant in understanding a specific culture in all its facets. Second, the ethnographic interviewers consider building rapport between them and the interviewees as vital to the quality of their ethnographic findings. Keenly aware of the fact that their worldview and interpretive frameworks are largely fashioned by the people that they listen to and converse with, ethnographic interviewers take extra care to build mutual trust and understanding. Unlike the researchers in other social and behavioral sciences, and unlike even the practitioners in the early days of their own discipline, current anthropologists do not treat their interviewees as *subjects.* These networks of friends and contacts are known today as cultural consultants, *respondents, coauthors, interlocutors,* or *collaborators.* More to the point, the ethnographic interview is a domain where, almost always, two or more people who speak different native languages meet, greet, and exchange ideas. Although eliciting information remains the prime motive, in this domain, the ethnographic interviewers pay special attention to the nuances of language that need delicate and careful probing. They know that their sensitivity toward the concerns of local speech community and their expertise in the local language(s) have a considerable bearing on the quality of the interview findings. In other interview types, language does not play a role as crucial as in the ethnographic interview.

Ethnographic interviews are in two types: *formal* or **structured interviews**, and *informal* or **unstructured interviews**. Ethnographers oftentimes select the type of ethnographic interview or a combination of the types that is most appropriate to the purpose of the ethnographic project, amount of time they have, and language fluency. The extent of control retained by the interviewers during the process is also one of the deciding factors as to whether the interviews maybe structured or unstructured.

In an unstructured interview, the interviewers maintain minimum control over the process; the interviews can take place wherever and whenever possible. The interviewees have ample space to choose the themes or the topic(s) and talk at their own pace in an open-ended conversation. Effective ethnographic interviewers learn early on how to organize unstructured interviews and conversations artfully, by creating a respectful space for the interviewees through careful listening and delicate probing. In other words, the structure of the "unstructured" interviews is less rigid and designed to maximize the potential of learning about culture as it is manifested in people's daily round of activities, not as it is given in cultural ideals. The difficulty of recording, quantifying, and comparing the research data are regarded as some of the deficiencies in unstructured interviews. The specific cultural information elicited from unstructured interviews is frequently used to form questions for structural interviews. Hence, unstructured interviews are mostly conducted in the early paces of fieldwork.

In a structured interview, the interviewers maintain considerable control over the process; usually, the interviews take place under the same set of conditions. The interviewees have to respond to the same set of scripted and follow-up questions given in the same sequence. In following this close-ended format, structural interviewers try to get rid of distracting variables, and thereby, reduce situational bias stemming from social situation in which the interviews take place. The field data collected through structural interviews are mostly quantifiable, verifiable, and easy to record. Structural interviews are mostly conducted in late paces of fieldwork.

Ethnographic interviews may be limited to two participating individuals (the interviewer and the interviewee) or may be open to several individuals. The interviews with more than two participating individuals are referred to as **group interviews** or *focus group.*

## Key Cultural Consultants

In every human community, there are individuals who are more knowledgeable, coherent, and articulate than others about the aspects of their society and culture. Upon identification through the initial paces of fieldwork, anthropologists tend to stick and work with them more often than they do with the others within the same community. Seeking consultation of such people in gaining insights on a specific society and culture is the technique known as working with **key cultural consultants**. In my own fieldwork in a central Sri Lankan village for example, I met a village elder named Charles Appuhamy who knew a great deal about village history, family genealogies, and the agricultural practices of the people who live there. I found myself spending many useful hours in conversing with him on the aforementioned and related topics, and transcribing the taped interviews afterward (Ariyaratne 2000).

## Life History Research

**Life history research** is a technique used by ethnographic fieldworkers to gain an in-depth understanding on the life of one or several individuals, and thereby to gain insights into the specific society and culture in which the individual(s) is a member. The individual's narrative of his or her experiences, gleaned through extensive interviews and conversations, is presented by the researcher as an in-depth description of a life history. In early days of life history research, anthropologists preferred to present a life experience of an individual, who, in their view, was typically representative of his or her culture. Today however, life histories tend to describe life experiences of individuals that can be helpful to learn about the specific social and cultural niches in which they inhabit. They also tend to illustrate specific individuals' perceptions, reactions, and contributions to ongoing change as the individuals experience the way change affects their lives.

## The Genealogical Method

Kin ties being at the core of human relations in foraging and horticultural societies, early anthropologists who began doing fieldwork on them spent considerable time systematically collecting data on kinship, descent, and marriage. They developed a system of notation and symbols in doing so, and this system is known as the **genealogical method**. Today, anthropologists find that this technique is useful in tracing "family tree," in learning about interactions between family members and their behavioral expectations, and documenting the vicissitudes of change in family, descent, and marriage, as well as other networks of human connections even in industrial societies (discussed in Chapter 7). Hence, the genealogical method is a well-established technique in ethnographic fieldwork.

## Eliciting Devices

The use of numerous **eliciting devices** (activities or objects) to persuade people and intimate them to recollect or share information has been a research technique frequently used by ethnographic fieldworkers ever since the adoption of ethnography as a main research methodology in anthropology. For instance, when conducting fieldwork that led to his ethnographic account *Argonauts of the Western Pacific* (Malinowski 1922), Malinowski has used an incidence of sudden illness (caused, according to natives, by the work of a female witch) to be asked from the Trobriand Islanders about their association with the sea, shipwreck, and magic. In the same vein, upon seeing what was happening in the village from the door of his tent in the Nuerland, Sudan, anthropologist E. E. Evans-Pritchard has used the opening strategically to spend time in the villagers' company and seek details of their lineage, as described in his ethnographic text *The Nuer* (Evans-Pritchard 1967 [1940]).

## Ethnographic Photography, Ethnographic Filmmaking, Ethnographic Videography, and Ethnographic Audio Recording

Recording images for ethnographic fieldwork purposes has been among anthropologists' repertoire of fieldwork devices from the early on. For example, even in his first field expedition to the Canadian arctic region in the 1880s, Franz Boas used **ethnographic photography** to visually capture the Inuit way of life. In the same vein, Bronislaw Malinowski used his camera to record the affairs of the Trobriand life when conducting fieldwork among the islanders. His ethnographic monograph contained 66 photographs. In much the same way, their coauthored photographic ethnography entitled *Balinese Character: A Photographic Analysis* (Bateson and Mead 1942), anthropologists Gregory Bateson and Margaret Mead extensively used the photographs they took during their ethnographic fieldwork in Bali, Indonesia, from 1936 to 1938.

Soon after the technology of cinematography became available in 1894, anthropologists found that **ethnographic filmmaking** was very helpful for salvage ethnography, the practice of documenting exotic people's way of life supposedly threatened with extinction by the sheer forces of Westernization. For example, British social anthropologist Alfred C. Huddon, who led the Torres Strait expedition in 1898, reportedly made the first ethnographic film in the field. Furthermore, Robert Flaherty's *Nanook of the North* (1922) and John Marshall's *The Hunters* (1958) were two of the well-known feature-length ethnographic documentaries in which, visually capturing and representing the Inuit way of life in the Canadian arctic region and the !Kung way of life in the Kalahari, Africa, was intended for respectively.

Visual anthropology (or ethnographic photographing and ethnographic filmmaking) has now gradually stepped into new territories as evident in the practice of **ethnographic videography** and in the increasing use of digital images for ethnographic fieldwork.

The frozen images (photographs) and the images in motion (film and video images) are capable of registering the everyday life of the people in all its mundane aspects, as well as the specific events more powerfully than what the scratch notes jotted down in the field can do. Oftentimes, anthropologists find a surprising amount of field materials left unnoticed by the field notes when they review snapshots or video footage of the same fieldwork situation later on. Additionally, ethnographic photographs and ethnographic video recordings are immensely

Historic Collection/Alamy Stock Photo

helpful field techniques when dealing with **proxemic analysis** or the study of the ways with which people in different cultures perceive and use space, and **event analysis**, or the documentation of notable episodes in a cultural landscape such as rituals, ceremonies, and festivities.

Whereas photographs, film, video, and digital images have an uncanny ability to humanize people with whom the ethnographic fieldworker has lived and worked with, they also have the unbounded capacity to exoticize the people in them. Moreover, they have an unmistakable ability to eavesdrop on people's lives and leave lasting records when left unguarded. The ethnographic fieldworkers should be sensitive to such issues and their ethical dimensions when using these field techniques.

Just like its visual counterparts, **ethnographic audio recording** is an important technique used in cultural anthropological fieldwork for its ability to document the salient aspects of culture and communication in audio format. It has become an essential tool in recording ethnographic interviews, conversations, and specific events. It can be particularly salient to researchers, who deal with topics related to ethnomusicology, oral texts, language, performance, and the likes. Usually, ethnographic fieldworkers spend considerable time in transcribing or typing up the materials collected through ethnographic audio recording in the field.

## Ethnographic Mapping

This data gathering technique helps the ethnographic fieldworkers to move beyond the regional maps of the cartographers, and focus on culturally distinctive, geographically relevant, and ethnographically specific features of the local landscape, instead. **Ethnographic mapping** became increasingly relevant and significant since the early 1970s, with the steady anthropological involvement on indigenous land use and occupancy studies. Ethnographic fieldworkers certainly find that advanced mapping techniques such as aerial and panoramic photographs, geographic information system (GIS), and remote sensing are useful in this regard. The data on a particular ethnographic locality collected through such mapping techniques are useful in discussing themes such as population expansion and density, land ownership, resource depletion, kinship, and other social networks more meaningfully.

Ethnographic fieldworkers use multiple techniques of charting or diagramming to codify the ethnographic findings, and thereby, to streamline their analyses, as evident in the use of comparative charts/tables, network charts, and genealogical charts.

# New Approaches to Ethnographic Fieldwork

As the condition under which ethnographic fieldwork has been conducted in the early years of anthropology has been considerably transformed, a whole host of interrelated questions and issues is being raised on field research in cultural anthropology. They range from the field worker's identity, power relations, native versus outside fieldworker, reflexivity, ethical challenges, and to the validity of using classic anthropological techniques in doing fieldwork in the twenty-first century.

## Reflexive Ethnography

Today, most anthropologists have begun to look at ethnographic fieldwork as a continuing process of mutual discovery on the part of the anthropologist and members of the host community. By getting clues from literary conventions and strategies, some anthropologists attempt to unfreeze ethnographic narratives through adding multiple voices and layers, and thereby, making them more dialogic and thick.

Cultural anthropologists also respond positively to the postmodern call for reflexivity. Reflexive ethnography takes fieldworker's cultural identity and personal characteristics into account in constructing ethnographic narratives. By acknowledging their own role in the field as individuals and socially situated actors, ethnographic fieldworkers can reflect on their personal feelings, actions, and reactions, and the responses these interactions brought forth from the people under study, in constructing ethnographic narratives.

## Critical Anthropology and Multisited Ethnography

While textual and literary approaches to ethnography are meaningful, critiques contend, the need to reach beyond the limits of such perspectives has become imperative. These critical anthropologists, Marxian in theoretical orientation, stress the validity of focusing on themes such as contexts of power inequality, resistance, and institutional constraints. Although pivotal to make ethnographic fieldwork meaningful, such themes have gone unheeded for so long, critical anthropologists point out further.

© Anton_Ivanov/Shutterstock.com

They have also been harshly critical of the established anthropological practice of treating ethnographic localities (i. e., specific societies and cultures being studied by ethnographers) as internally homogeneous, externally distinctive, and bounded entities. Some in particular advocate that ethnographic fieldwork should move from its long-standing practice of conducting fieldwork in single-site location to multiple sites of ethnographic observation and participation. In this research method, known as **multisited ethnography**, the fieldworker tracks a cultural phenomenon such as a people, an object, a metaphor, a narrative, a biography, across spatial and temporal boundaries. According to the anthropologists who favor multisited ethnography, such an investigative move helps immensely to grapple macroconstructions of a global social order to which cultures are embedded in. Moreover, they believe, it helps to gain better insights on the impact of the world-systems on global and local communities (Marcus 1995; Guest 2003).

## Producing Anthropological Accounts

The primary aim of the ethnographic fieldwork is to produce descriptive accounts on the social and cultural thoughts and practices of a particular group of people.

# Ethnography

These accounts, mostly in written form, and occasionally in visual form (as ethnographic films), are sometimes referred to as *ethnographies*. They are also known as *ethnographic monographs* owing to the fact that they usually describe a single culture and society based on ethnographic fieldwork. Without some form of materialization as such, an ethnographic project is bound to remain an unfinished business, to say the least. The ethnographies, the products of the ethnographic research strategy, are important as much as the ethnographic strategy is, if not more, in doing cultural anthropology. This aspect is stressed even in the etymology of the term ethnography. It originates from the two Greek words of *ethnos* (people) and *graphos* (writing) to denote that, it is literally writing about people. Ethnography, therefore, is both a distinctive strategy cultural anthropology uses to collect fieldwork-based information on an identifiable group of people, and the ethnographic texts produced in written, visual, or virtual form by drawing from such fieldwork data.

# Ethnology

Whereas ethnography focuses on describing a specific culture and society, ethnology attempts to look beyond the specificity to the more general. By using the data gleaned from existing ethnographies and other sources (such as historical documents, for example), it concentrates on comparing and contrasting two or more cultures to draw out general laws or principles governing the cultural phenomena. Ethnology, therefore, is both a research strategy in cultural anthropology and its products: It is an anthropological research schema to compare many different cultural practices. The products of that research schema, or *ethnologies* as they are referred to sometimes, are anthropological accounts in which cross-cultural comparison is intended for.

Some anthropological writings, mainly theoretical and historical in nature, do not fit to any of the above categories. These writings tend to address a vast array of themes ranging from retrospective critiques of anthropological conventions, current possibilities, and future directions.

# Ethnographic Monographs

The ethnographic writing process begins early on. The ethnographers jot their observations, experiences, and reflective thoughts extensively in field journals and personal diaries. Nowadays they increasingly type their field notes by using computers as well. The indexing of notes, entering quantitative data into spreadsheets, transcribing tape-recorded ethnographic interviews and conversations, preparing maps and charts, and analyzing photographs and video-recorded materials are mostly done after leaving the field site, and when the analysis of gathered data begins in earnest. Often, ethnographers spend considerable time working with their ethnographic data, and in writing up, revising, and rewriting their analyses both in and out of the field. All of the above activities are important paces in the process of producing the ethnographic monographs.

Cultural anthropologists present the data they accumulate during ethnographic fieldwork in a variety of ways. These anthropological accounts may be published to be used in anthropology classes as ethnographic texts, as scholarly articles to appear in professional journals of anthropology, as nontechnical and brief pieces written to reach out for wider audience, and as papers to be read at professional conferences of anthropology. The ethnographic data may also be presented in the format of ethnographic film to be viewed in anthropology classes as visual supplements, to be directed at groups of visual media prodding cultural materials, and research academicians of anthropology and other social sciences. In addition, some anthropologists increasingly choose to present their ethnographic materials today as online articles or e-books targeting anthropology readers in the virtual world.

Ethnographic monographs are a specific genre of written (or visual) representations of realities, and not documents with which unequivocal reporting of information is intended for. They are hybrid texts capable of traversing through genres as diverse as colonial administrative reports, travel writing, memoirs, and novels, and disciplines as varied as history, geography, literature, psychology, economics, and political science. The way they register cultural phenomena is affected by, among other things, literary processes such as metaphor, figuration, and narrative.

The classical ethnographies, based on fieldwork on a geographically and culturally remote society from that of the anthropologist, were accounts attempting to describe every aspect of that culture and society. In other words, they were holistic descriptions on a particular way of life in a distant locality. Today however, most ethnographies concentrate on exploring a specific problem of anthropological significance from the insights of the people that the ethnographers have become familiar with.

Regardless of this shift of emphasis, there exists a recognizable order and style common to both classical ethnographic monographs (written mostly through the mid-twentieth century) and their present counterparts. The following structure is noticeable in most of the ethnographies: the introductory chapter, the body of ethnographic evidence, and the concluding chapter. The introductory chapter introduces the reader to the ethnographic setting while situating the ethnographic description within the current theoretical discussions of anthropology. Typically, the chapter begins with a small ethnographic vignette illustrating the anthropologist's point of entry to the ethnographic setting, and giving an early glimpse on what were to follow. This **arrival trope** (central theme on entry), at once personal, contrastive, and dramatic, has been one among several stylistic features ethnographers used to convince the reader that their presentation is authoritative and reliable. In the other part of the introductory chapter, ethnographers review the existing theoretical and regional literature in adequate detail, and attempt to place their own thesis in firm theoretical footing. Some anthropologists choose to extend theoretical confessions to the second chapter as well. Following the first chapter are the chapters with which the ethnographers present the data gathered in the field in support of the thesis or the main argument. In most canonical ethnographic texts written with the holistic approach in mind, the sequential arrangement of chapters shows a plausible pattern. These ethnographies usually begin with descriptions on the ecological and historical background, strategies of sustenance, and then, gradually proceed to explore aspects of the sociocultural world of the people whose way of life they attempt to portray. The latter aspects are addressed through the topics such as kinship and social organization, religious beliefs and ritual, and the arts and crafts. The concluding chapter is usually comprised of a summary of the ethnographic materials presented, and a discussion on how they are relevant to the theoretical issues raised both in the ethnographic account and in ongoing anthropological debates.

The production of ethnographic accounts is not merely an act of reporting data. Rather, it is a process with which the presentation of data and their interpretation takes place simultaneously. It involves watchful and purposeful choosing, arranging, and emphasizing of fashions or structures the ethnographic account to its final shape.

## Fieldwork and Ethical Considerations

Cultural anthropological fieldwork consists of human beings, the members of the anthropologists' own species. For example, unlike physicists experimenting in the laboratory with a research matter having no inherent power of action, motion, or resistance, cultural

anthropologists conduct research on individuals just as curious as themselves. In the field, they must fathom with the unmistakable realization that, social scrutiny is not a one-sided affair; when they are looking, they are being looked at, and when they are talking, they are being talked too, simultaneously. As individuals and socially situated actors having complex connections and commitments with various involving parties (such as their own discipline, professional colleagues, funding agencies, their own governments, and host governments), ethnographic fieldworkers are prone to face ethical dilemmas when they make choices from a host of conflicting values and interests. However, cultural anthropologists must be sensitive to the effects of their presence and their work on the people being studied and prioritize ensuring the well-being of the people accordingly.

As a discipline developed during the late nineteenth and early twentieth century, early practitioners of cultural anthropology, Caucasians of European descent, were scholars either working for or under the colonial governments and the people they were researching on were non-Western, colonial subjects.

There have been several instances in recent history such as Project Camelot and Project Minerva, instances in which anthropologists have reportedly become active collaborators of their own governments as well. **Project Camelot** was an aborted research program funded by the U. S. Army to study the possible causes for civil unrest and violence in developing countries. When it was made public in 1965, it was implicated in using enlisted anthropologists and other social scientists as cultural means to suppress insurgency movements and support pro-American governments. Similarly, **Project Minerva** was a project launched in the 1980s to seek social science expertise to counter actual and potential threats to U. S. national security.

© Vadim Petrakov/Shutterstock.com

There have also been other occasions in which anthropologists have allegedly worked on an individual basis, prioritizing their own interests at the expense of the well-being of the researched people. Moreover, questions have been raised over the role of many applied anthropologists, whose prime motive oftentimes have been to protect and promote the interests of the organizations or institutions from which they receive funds for research, even when they are at odd with the interests of the affected communities.

By acknowledging the need to address questions of the sort pertaining to professional ethics of anthropology, American Anthropological Association (AAA), the foremost organization for anthropology professionals in the U. S., adopted its "Principles of Professional Responsibility," in 1971. According to AAA ethical code, it is among anthropology researchers' main areas of responsibility to protect the physical, psychological, and social well-being of the people being researched. Furthermore, it is emphatic on the point that, participation in research projects has to be voluntary, and be based on the truthful disclosure of the aims, nature, and anticipated consequences of the research project, known as the principle of **informed consent**.

On this point, many cultural anthropologists today write collaborative ethnographies, acknowledging their cultural consultants as equal partners, collaborators, or coauthors. There are others who call for advocacy in anthropology or active engagement in voicing native concerns and working toward achieving their goals.

## Chapter Summary

This chapter focuses on fieldwork, by which cultural anthropological knowledge is produced. It discusses common fieldwork situations, where issues, concerns, and problems common to all ethnographic fieldworkers twine together. It describes fieldwork techniques and some of the new approaches to fieldwork, while also tracing the processes involving the production of ethnographic monographs. The chapter also refers to an array of ethical considerations pertaining to fieldwork.

- Ethnographic fieldwork is the central method of research data collection in cultural anthropology. Its predecessors were the nineteenth and the early twentieth-century practices of armchair anthropology and verandah anthropology. In the early twentieth century, some of the main features of ethnographic fieldwork were introduced by, among others, anthropologists Franz Boas and Bronislow Malinowski. Malinowski is credited for introducing participant-observation as the core ethnographic technique of researching.

- Common field situations are indicative of issues, concerns, and problems common to all ethnographic fieldworkers as they commence their fieldwork process and proceed through.

- The qualitative techniques used in ethnographic fieldwork include participant-observation, the ethnographic interview, life history research, key cultural consultants, the genealogical method, text analysis, ethnographic photography, ethnographic filming, and ethnographic audio recording. Field notes, eliciting devices, charts, and maps are used by both qualitative data collectors and quantitative data collectors alike. Reflexive ethnography and multisited ethnography are two among the new approaches to ethnographic fieldwork.

- Ethnography refers to both a strategy used in cultural anthropology to collect data, and ethnographic accounts produced by drawing from such fieldwork findings. Ethnology is both a research strategy in cultural anthropology, and its products.

- Ethnographic field findings are published as ethnographic texts, scholarly articles, non-technical and short papers, ethnographic films, ethnographic videos, virtual texts, and digital images.

- Most ethnographic accounts have common and recognizable structural features. They are the following: the introductory chapter, the body of ethnographic evidence, and the concluding chapter.

- According to the AAA code of ethics for anthropology, the paramount responsibility of all practitioners of anthropology should be to safeguard the physical, psychological, and social well-being of the people under study. Native participation in research, it states further, should be based on informed consent.

# Culture: Distinguishing Human Condition

© Asia Images Group/Shutterstock.com

Culture, the most pivotal aspect of being human, is consisted of a series of beliefs and practices that human beings gain possession of through learning and sharing, as members of a species accustomed to collective social life.

When anthropology gained recognition as a discipline about humanity in the late nineteenth century, anthropologists were attempting to define culture in holistic terms. For example, Edward B. Tylor defined culture holistically and qualitatively while equating it with **civilization** (Tylor 1871). According to his definition, all human groups possessed culture in varying degrees.

Since then, there have been a number of ambitious attempts at expanding the definition further, as well as refining it by giving a less totalizing meaning. For instance, in 1945, George Peter Murdock presented a collection of what he considered to be universal cultural traits shared by human societies and cultures around the world (Murdock 1945, 124). In the 1970s, several anthropologists followed Murdock's lead in their quest for cultural universals, including, Lionel Tiger and Robin Fox (Tiger and Fox 1971), as well as Charles Hockett (Hockett 1963). Even today, there are anthropologists who keep their focus on the universal aspects of different cultural features, as evident in Donald Brown's work (1991 and 2004).

© hiv360/Shutterstock.com

In another significant attempt to expand the meaning of culture, Raymond Williams, an early pioneer in the field of cultural studies, referred to the symbolic dimensions of human life ways. He contended that, in every society and every mind, culture is ordinary (Williams 1958). Williams' was a conscious attempt to wrest culture from its elitist space of "**high culture**" (Arnold 1869), characterized by artistic consummation and epistemic (knowledge-related) perfection, and situate within the experience of the ordinary affairs pertaining to everyday life. His notion of culture was reminiscent of the views of literary theorists such as T. S. Elliot who saw high culture, as well as **popular culture** (sometimes referred to as *mass culture*) as inseparable parts of the cultural totality (Elliot 1948).

In 1952, Alfred Kroeber and Clyde Kluckhohn presented a list of 164 definitions of culture that they have collected (Kroeber and Kluckhohn 1952). These definitions have

© 8th.creator/Shutterstock.com

been used to stress different aspects of culture, including its historical, behavioral, normative, functional, structural, and symbolic aspects. The existence of such definitions is merely reflective of different theoretical approaches, positions, and methods adopted by anthropologists in exploring human condition. Nevertheless, all such definitions acknowledge culture's preeminent position as the central organizing construct of anthropology.

© Spotmatik Ltd/Shutterstock.com

Of late, there have been certain meaningful efforts made by some anthropologists to reevaluate the notion of culture against the backdrop of how it has been used in anthropology as a device to separate other from self, and place in a hierarchical order. During a better part of the twentieth century and continuously in the twenty-first century, many anthropologists have been acknowledging *Culture* (with an upper case "C") as distinguishable from *culture(s)* (with a lower case "c" with a possibility of a final "s"): whereas Culture has been used to refer to universal human capacity for learned and shared life ways, cultures have been used to indicate specific, learned, and shared ways of life by specific groups of people. This latter plural usage of culture has become controversial the most (discussed in Chapter 4).

© Kartinkin77/Shutterstock.com

# Cultural Characteristics

Anthropologists have identified several salient characteristics of culture with which the nature of culture is explainable. Accordingly, culture is learned, shared, symbolic, patterned, dynamic, and adaptive.

**TABLE 3.1  Some of the Main Characteristics of Culture**

Culture Is Learned

Culture Is Shared

Culture Is Symbolic

Cultural Is Patterned

Culture Is Dynamic

Culture Is Adaptive

Source: Gajaba Naraddage

## Culture Is Learned

Unlike most animals born equipped with biological instincts, humans are not born with the skills required for survival, but they acquire them through learning after birth. Cultural acquisition makes human behavior starkly different and distinguishable from the behavior of most other animals, and to a considerable extent, even from apes and monkeys, their closest biological relatives. Humans learn culture by growing up in it; cultural knowledge is gained in the course of ordinary affairs of everyday life and special events. From the moment of birth, children begin to internalize, incorporate, and modify cultural beliefs and behavior through observation, advice (gained mostly from family members), and practice, as well as through unconscious absorption. Cultural learning helps individuals to adapt and transform the environment in which they live. A moment of concentration on what we think, say, and do on every day basis, anything and everything from talking, drinking, bathing, eating, mating, and sleeping, to eliminating makes us realize that we do not spare even a single moment in our lives totally separated from cultural beliefs and practices.

© Dietmar Temps/Shutterstock.com

If, for example, we focus on everyday dining experience, that is, what we eat, how we obtain it, how we prepare it, when, where, and how we eat, we begin to recognize that our act of eating has a great deal to do with cultural perceptions and prescriptions. This complex social process with which culture is gradually learned and transmitted across generations is known as **enculturation**. Culture, through enculturation in specific cultural traditions, sets guidance for specific groups' perceptions and behavior; it shapes the way humans think and behave by providing, as anthropologist Clifford Geertz characterizes it, "sets of control mechanisms—plans, recipes, rules, instructions, what computer engineers call 'programs'" (Geertz 1973).

© Melinda Nagy/Shutterstock.com

## Culture Is Shared

It is because cultural knowledge is shared, cultural learning and transmission becomes possible, and vice versa. Although every living culture keeps changing constantly, its shared nature is capable of generating a certain amount of consistency, endurance, and predictability in cultural behavior, and thereby, mapping the boundaries for behavioral expectations.

Nevertheless, culture is not shared by all members of a particular society, and cultural behavior is, therefore, not fully harmonious. Societies are generally diverse and segmented by an array of divisions such as class, race, ethnicity, age, gender, and so on. This makes cultural sharing incomplete. Also, it makes possible for collective cultural identities, notably different from that of the core culture within a society, nevertheless capable of carving their enclaves within the same space where the core culture inhabits, to thrive. These latter are palpable as instances of **subculture**.

© hans engbers/Shutterstock.com

Cultural differences stemming from sorts of social divisions are also the sources of tension, discord, and change. Therefore, cultural norms (commonly held behavioral expectations), cultural values (shared behavioral norms, attitudes, and ethics), and worldviews (comprehensive ideas based on sets of shared assumptions over how the world works) are not harmonious and fixed categories, but discursive spaces within which, their legitimacy is being constantly negotiated, contested, and resisted.

© Sergio Rojo/Shutterstock.com

## Culture Is Symbolic

It is an intricate and pervasive system filled with symbolic meanings with which humans organize, codify, streamline, and comprehend their world. A symbol is something (a word, a sound, an object, or an action) that stands for or represents something else (an idea, an event, a sentiment, or a meaning), to which it is not intrinsically related. Symbolic mode of thought is an unparalleled human ability, and it is also pivotal to cultural learning.

Symbolic representations are oftentimes linguistically oriented. Human language is an inexhaustibly rich and extraordinarily complex system of symbols with which an infinite number of expressions and representations can be made. Symbols saturate culture through nonlinguistic ways (nonverbal) as well however, making objects, events, and actions symbolically meaningful. For instance, an object such as a national flag, an event such as the celebration of Independent Day, and an action such as hoisting the national flag or burning it in public can generate staunch meanings within a culture.

© arindambanerjee/Shutterstock.com

## Culture Is Patterned

Culture is thought of, to a certain extent, as a system in which its various parts are intermingled to form a complex or unitary whole, not as a random assemblage of thoughts and activities. Culture's interrelated nature generates a pattern. This means, within a culture, similar traits tend to show up in a variety of cultural domains leaving a recognizable consistency. Anthropological endeavor has always been to sort, analyze, and interpret this pattern. The late nineteenth-century sociologists such as Herbert Spencer (discussed in Chapter 4) and the early twentieth-century functionalist anthropologists such as A. R. Radcliffe-Brown and Bronislaw Malinowski used the organic analogy as a useful model to explain how society and culture should be understood as an integrated whole. They would argue that, just as organisms comprised of myriad parts that were functional and consistent, cultures had various parts that were closely intertwining and functionally contributing to the cultural whole. Accordingly, beliefs and behavior in one cultural realm, such as economy, for instance, would necessarily become compatible with and supportive of the ideas and behavior in other realms such as social organization and political system.

Critiques point out however, seeing a culture as fully functional, coherent, and patterned whole often tends to ignore the reality that, there always exist certain dysfunctional, inconsistent, and disorderly parts within a culture causing discord, conflict, and change.

## Culture Is Dynamic

Whereas conventional wisdom often tends to characterize culture as a frozen set of rules that people merely enact, the surest aspect of culture is that it is constantly changing. Culture does not change overnight. Nor does it change in such a way that the young people in every generation have to learn a culture entirely different from what their parents had acquired and perfected; certain core cultural beliefs and practices have their endurance, and that makes culture cross-generational. However, whether it comes in snail pace or in revolutionary bursts, whether it is internally born, externally influenced, or conjunctionally produced, cultural change is always present in every society, regardless. Moreover, owing to culture's systemic nature, a change in one cultural facet is highly likely to bring about changes in other facets as well.

The dynamic processes leading to change in some of the main components of culture (what people think, do, and produce) are traditionally identified by anthropologists as diffusion and invention. Today however, globalization is being broadly discussed as among the leading causes of cultural change.

**Diffusion**, sometimes referred to as *borrowing* is the transmission of discrete cultural traits in the form of objects, ideas, and behaviors from its original culture to another through migration, trade, intermarriage, warfare, or other means of contact and interaction. An essentially two-way process, diffusion is likely to bring changes to each involving culture. However, it is also a process both contingent and arbitrary. The impact of diffusion is well documented in the realms of business and industrialization. For instance, Japanese business historians have shown a keen interest in finding the role diffusion has played in transforming the traditional Japanese society into what it has become today, a leading industrial nation. Diffusion's contributive role in shaping the growth of industrial societies in the United States and the continental Europe has attracted the attention of several business historians as well.

© milatas/Shutterstock.com

**Acculturation** or *forced borrowing* is a specialized form of cultural diffusion. Under this process of the intermingling of cultures, firsthand contact and forced borrowing take place generating profound changes in either or both involving cultures. The sort of change that acculturation brings forth may be reciprocal, and that could increase similarity between the two cultures. Oftentimes however, acculturation is a process with which a dominant culture systematically and aggressively forces a dominated culture to borrow alien cultural traits. Therefore, the process frequently turns to be an asymmetrical one.

© Everett Historical/Shutterstock.com

While acculturation refers to the sorts of change a specific culture experiences when dominant cultural traits overwhelm it, **assimilation** is the process by which individuals of foreign or minority origin become integrated with the standards of the dominant culture. They learn language, adopt life ways, and acquire social, political, and economic standards of the dominant culture in the process of assimilation. Acculturation and assimilation have frequently been studied within the context of Caucasian immigrants coming from continental Europe to the United States during the nineteenth and early twentieth century, as well as the minority groups already existing in the United States at the time. Acculturation and assimilation studies of the sorts have pointed out a number of cross-cultural generalizations in this regard. For example, through coercive practices, dominant cultures force individuals of minority and foreign origin to acculturate and assimilate. However, the latter groups may resist and try to take the steam out of such efforts by forming occupational or territorial enclaves within the dominant culture where they can be numerically and culturally significant. Similarly, acculturation ought to take precedence over assimilation. In the same vein, acculturation of the members of minority groups does not make certain that they would eventually assimilate. Regardless, acculturation and assimilation serve primarily to homogenize minority or alien individuals to dominant cultures. Acculturation studies have thus shown how certain factors such as age, ethnic origin, language, economic status, and religious or political affiliation of the individuals have been facilitating assimilation of minority groups, or preventing them from becoming integrated within the dominant culture (Thompson 1996, 113–14).

**Invention** or **innovation** is the emergence of qualitatively advanced and ideologically or technologically oriented cultural forms (such as material objects, thoughts, or behavioral patterns) as a result of a synthesis taking place in between such existing features within a culture. Invention of mathematical methods such as algebra and calculus, creation of parliament democracy to replace autocracy, or application of dialectic thinking to society are some instances of ideological inventions. Much discussed technological inventions are ranged from energy sources, transportation methods, information and media technologies, medical discoveries, to tools and weaponry. In addition, style and fashion brings forth ephemeral and frivolous, yet faddist and notable inventions to culture.

Contrary to popular belief that inventions and innovative ideas are born as chance occurrences and accidental discoveries relating to random individuals, they emerge against the backdrop of myriad previous efforts that eventually lead to new and fruitful combinations of existing cultural forms. Isaac Newton's apple and the discovery of gravity or Alexander Fleming's contaminated bacteria samples and the discovery of penicillin, for instance, have to be appreciated within the context of the scientific knowledge and requisites provided for Newton and Fleming by the previous researches conducted on the same area. Put another way, inventions are culminant parts of the structures constructed by cultural building blocks.

Invention is regarded as an internally born process with which members of a specific culture seek solutions to problems by becoming apt at inventing, devising, or contriving. Due to the comparability of the sorts of the predicaments humans confront everywhere in the world, arriving at similar, yet independent, solutions is possible. For example, the development of intensive agricultural practices and the rise of state systems were observable in the Middle East, Indus River Valley, Northern and Southern China, and Mexico, roughly some 10,000 years ago. However, the lack of archeological or historical evidences on contact

© Martchan/Shutterstock.com

in between these early civilizations suggests that, in each region, agriculture had originated independently.

**Globalization**, one of the most important sources of cultural change, is the intense interconnectedness and movement, evident in the massive global flow of natural resources, trade goods, human labor, information, technology, and finance capital to literally all areas of the world, as well as the proliferation of global institutions and organizations that structure those flows (discussed in Chapter 13). The world has been linked and interdependent ever since the sociopolitical and economic changes that swept through Europe in the sixteenth century paving the way for the capitalist world economy to emerge. This systemic process was previously identified through various terms such as modernization, commercialization, mercantilism, industrialization, colonialism, and imperialism. The successor to the above world-system under which a small number of powerful, mainly European, capitalist regimes were able to expropriate world resources, globalization is a new mold of capitalism having a wide range and building on earlier cultural structures pertaining to the global systems of trade.

Anthropological interest on globalization is influenced, in large part, by the magnitude of its impact on numerous local cultures around the world. Anthropological approaches in this regard notably shift away from the modernist focus on the West, and instead concentrate on transnational processes, the processes pervading throughout cultures, countries, and regions. These approaches often stem from two theoretical standpoints: one of them views globalization as a process of increasing **homogeneity**, whereas the other sees it as a process of increasing **heterogeneity**.

According to the first school of thought, cultural globalization is seen as the transnational expansion of common codes and practices; it generates a global culture while minimizing

© Laboo Studio/Shutterstock.com

cultural diversity simultaneously. Global culture, this perspective assumes further, is a result of transnational flow of various cultural traits from an extensive cultural origin, mainly from the Euro-American cultural complex. The dominant global presence of a specific culture or **cultural imperialism** is understood in this view as a trend associated with homogeneity. The dominant roles played by American culture (Kuisel 1993; Ritzer 1995, 2000), the West (Giddens 1990), or the core countries (Hannerz 1990) in spreading Euro-American capitalist life ways and expressive culture throughout the world are often cited as ubiquitous evidence for cultural imperialism. The global spread of Western consumerism through a variety of U.S. dominated channels of corporate culture and the resultant increasing rationalization of everyday routine tasks are often dubbed as **McDonaldization** (Ritzer 2004), *Wal-Marting*, or *Disneyfication* coining the American business and cultural icons of consumerism (Farrell 2003). Moreover, the Corporate media giants based in the West hold an enormous power in cultivating consumer-driven cultural habits, and thereby, creating a culture of discontent all over the world.

Those who focus on economic issues generally tend to stress their significance and homogenizing effects on the world—they often view globalization as the global expansion of market economy. For example, in a critical analysis, Stiglitz points out the key role global financial institutions such as World Bank (WB) and International Monetary Fund (IMF) play in homogenizing world economy (Stiglitz 2002). More to the point, the rise of Multi-National Corporations (MNCs) in the latter half of the twentieth century and their on-going, phenomenal growth cutting across the international boundaries between nation-states has propelled these global corporations to the forefront of global homogenization.

While stressing the homogenizing effects of globalization, Hobsbawm (1997), Appadurai (1996), Robbins (1999), and French (2000) contend that the growth of transnational institutions (e. g. MNCs) and transnational organizations (e. g. Non-Governmental Organizations or NGOs, Transnational Treaty Organizations such as World Trade Organization [WTO]) is greatly diminishing the power of the existing nation-states and local social structures worldwide.

The proponents of the second school of thought maintain that globalization is a process in which many global and local cultural inputs interact to generate something distinctive—a blend. This complex process is referred to as *syncretism, hybridization, creolization*, or *glocalization*. Globalization facilitates the proliferation of cultural hybrids (Canclini 1995, Pieterse 1995) or glocals (Robertson 1992). Nevertheless, globally disseminating dominant cultural traits are rarely incorporated into local cultures in a way equally beneficial to everyone in that, global changes are abetted by powerful interests. This is the reason that the synthesis between the global and the local cultural traits tends to generate instances of *cultural pastiche* or irregular cultural blend (Friedman 1994). Within this context, the members of the local cultures may selectively incorporate hegemonic cultural practices originating from the West into their own culture in such a way that they eventually develop something of their own in the process: *alternative modernities* (Gaonkar 2001).

Critiques on the economic front point out that, the economic policies in the globalized world have aggravated environmental pollution, widespread poverty, hunger, obesity, and gender inequality. In search of cheap labor, for example, MNCs often seek to recruit women in developing countries for low-skilled assembly jobs. By so doing, they have increasingly become some of the main contributors to the global emergence of a marked

© Sk Hasan Ali/Shutterstock.com

gender-segregated division of labor. This is a phenomenon in which women represent disproportionate percentages of the poor in the globalizing world. It is sometimes referred to as the *feminization of poverty* (Martha et al 2005, 36–57).

The local people around the world deal with the agents of change representing global systems by devising various strategies, including alternative forms of cultural expression and political mobilization. Ethnic resurgence and the splintering tendency of multiethnic states, the rise of resistant political movements such as the Arab Spring, and the Taliban movement in Afghanistan, indigenous political activism that led to the creation of organizations like The World Council of Indigenous Peoples in 1975, and political protest movements such as Occupy Wall Street, and Greenpeace protests against French nuclear tests, as well as Japanese commercial whaling are some of the examples to the point.

## Culture Is Adaptive

In their continuing struggle to survive and reproduce, humans rely on culture as the primary mean to contend with their environmental stresses successfully. It is this reliance that has been furnishing human species with a prodigious adaptive advantage over all other forms of life. Culture has been instrumental for humans in their effort of developing myriad forms of knowledge and technology as the strategy for sustaining themselves, as the measure of curing and preventing diseases, as the way of fulfilling sociopsychological needs, and as the mode of transmitting learned skills for successive generations. In this respect, instances such as gaining the knowledge of tool making, learning how to domesticate plants and animals,

© Maria Oleinikova/Shutterstock.com

and taking revolutionary steps to industrialize the production and the services strongly testify to the fact that culture has been the most salient adaptive mechanism for human beings in the past.

In much the same way, nurturing skills for symbolic mode of expressible thought, and crafting sociocultural life ways through institutions such as kinship and family have been conspicuous evidences to culture's vital adaptive role. In brief, human versatility, a hallmark of being human, is made possible by culture.

Whereas human cultural traits have been mostly adaptive throughout, there have been notable instances in which some cultural traits becoming adaptively neutral, dysfunctional, or even turning into outright maladaptive. For example, large-scale industrial farming introduced over the last century with petrochemicals usage and the mechanization of production process enabled humans to increase production substantially and thereby, to enhance their capacity to feed large population segments. However, this same adaptive trait also spurred unintended and negative consequences such as environmental degradation, (natural) resource depletion, overpopulation, monotonous dietary habits, overconsumption, and malnutrition leading some critiques to characterize that turning to agriculture as a catastrophic mistake from which the members of human species have never recovered (Diamond 1987).

© Carl Forbes/Shutterstock.com

# Culture and Its Evolutionary Roots

Human condition is easily distinguishable from the conditions of the other living species, mainly due to humans' total dependence on culture for survival. Humans are truly bio-cultural beings. Biological anthropologists refer to several key attributes as the defining developments in the six millennia of hominine evolution, the evolution of the ape-like ancestors that lead to humans, excluding primate relatives. They are as follows:

- walking in two feet or bipedalism (six million years ago),
- nonhoning chewing (five and a half m. y. a.),
- tool making (two and a half m. y. a.),
- speaking (two and a half m. y. a.),
- hunting (one m. y. a.), and
- domesticating plants and animals (ten to eleven thousand y. a.) (Larsen 2010).

These attributes clearly indicate the extent, to which humans depended on culture, as culture facilitated human survival by enabling human beings to adapt to different and changing settings and conditions. Moreover, they show how the current human capacity for culture evolved throughout human evolutionary history.

Human dependence on culture has become even more relevant and intriguing theme as some biological anthropologists have been seeking to place emphasis on **versatility** or the ability to adapt, in studying human evolution. Versatility has been, according to the Smithsonian anthropologist Rick Potts, a hallmark of human evolution. Proposing that environmental fluctuations were the driving force in human evolution, Potts argues that it was not by "fitting" into a specific environment that humans were able to survive and reproduce better than other hominid species. Rather, it was by being versatile or being able to adapt to the changes brought forth by environmental fluctuations and instability, human species prevailed. Human evolution has not been an instance of the "survival of the fittest," as traditionally understood by scientists, but one of the "survivals of the versatile," as "you can't have the survival of the fittest when the definition of fittest keeps changing," contends Potts (Potts 2010).

Seen in this light, with firm legs to walk upright habitually, a large brain to think symbolically, dexterous hands to manipulate matter comfortably, and the eyes to appraise the surroundings penetratingly, hominines have elaborated their capacity to adapt in changing and different surroundings. The growth of their capacity for culture was evident in the aptitude they have displayed in stone tool making. Elements of material culture, amply evident in such attempts by hominines to manipulate environment, testify to the fact that culture or learned beliefs and behavior was already becoming a complex human characteristics that facilitated human survival. Given what is known about the simple tool usage and manufacture by monkeys and apes (e. g. fishing termites with twigs, as well as cracking palm nuts to open them with stones by chimps, washing food to get rid of dirt by Japanese macaque monkeys, aiming and throwing objects by chimps and orangutans, and building nests by gorillas), it is certain that early hominids possessed these skills in rudimentary proportions as well.

© Danny Ye/Shutterstock.com

Rick Potts stresses the prudence in seeing the present human capacity for culture within the context of human evolutionary past; rather than thinking about it in terms of a block of stone having a uniform and intractable character, it has to be understood as a structure that has gleaned its distinct elements at various times in human evolution.

Recent researches on how Darwinian processes underlie the brain's growth, function, and evolution, focus on the salience of explaining what made *Homo sapiens* different from other species within the context of the evolutionary circumstances that brought forth human difference. On this point, by drawing on his research in comparative neuroscience, biological anthropologist Terrance Deacon points out that, humans are the only species in the animal kingdom who are capable of **symbolic representation**, an ability they have acquired by internalizing the intricate process of symbolism that underlie human language. According to Deacon, human language is not simply a mode of communication, but a pervasive mode of thought that has fashioned and streamlined, literally, every aspect of human intellect; it is due to this reason, language has become one of the most striking features of human culture (discussed in Chapter 5). No other species, Deacon maintains, has the outwardly expressible, symbolic mode of thought that human species has, in that, without symbolization, symbolic thinking becomes something unfathomable. "Symbolic thought," Deacon writes, "does not come innately built in, but develops by internalizing the symbolic process that underlie language" (Deacon 1997). He characterizes that the experience of being human, in real sense of the term, is the profound ability to live and share the virtual world. This is a characterization resonated in recent anthropological research, including in an ethnographic account precisely based on virtual or online communities (Boellstroff 2008).

Deacon believes that the significance of human symbolic thinking has to be understood within the context of the coevolutionary exchange between language and brain over millennia of hominid evolution (evolution of the members of the zoological family Hominidae that includes the groups that lead to humans, living humans, and their primate relatives). To varying degrees, the primate relatives of humans such as chimps, gorillas, and monkeys show an embryonic, nonetheless remarkable, capacity for symbolic codification and representation, a capacity unmistakably possessed by early bipedal hominines as well. How has symbolic representation grown from such rudimentary levels to assume unprecedented heights among living humans? By way of answering the above question, Deacon uses the metaphors of parasite and host, while explaining the nature of interaction and dependence between language and brain respectively. He contends that the structural features of language have coevolved to adapt to their host, the brain, and vice versa. Humans are, therefore, the members of the "symbolic species," and their capacity for culture is as old as humanity itself (Deacon 1997).

## Culture and Anthropology Subfields

Culture unites all subfields of anthropology with its all-encompassing theme.

Biological anthropology, for instance, tries to explain how defining features of human species are codetermined by biological and cultural factors. It considers every individual as a product of evolutionary history while also pondering every person as the product of her or his own individual life history. In these intertwining considerations, the crucial role culture played as a primary adaptive mechanism for early humans, their ape-like ancestors, and members of their hominine lineage is well recognized. Put another way, biological anthropology advocates a bio-cultural approach to the understanding of human evolution, adaptation, and variation; it studies the coevolving relationship between genetic inheritance of humans and their culture.

Similarly, anthropological linguistics concentrates on language, the most striking cultural feature of human beings. Language being largely instrumental for sharing and learning cultural features, making sense of a particular culture without learning its language, as well as learning a specific language without paying heed to its cultural context are utterly impracticable tasks. Cultural anthropologists are well aware of the fact that a working knowledge of language is essential to conduct meaningful ethnographic fieldwork. Likewise, it is a prerequisite for linguistic anthropologists to be attentive to the beliefs and practices of people since they are often reflective of peculiar features of language. Indeed, social linguistics (cultural linguistics), one of the main branches of linguistic anthropology, focuses precisely on this theme, the nexus of language and its sociocultural context.

In the same vein, archaeological anthropologists focus on material evidence of past human culture. By examining archaeological sites or locations where material remains of past human activity are present, they attempt to gain insights into the processes of past cultural transformation. As they excavate sites looking for signs of early tool making in association with fossil evidence, archaeologists oftentimes find that their research interests (and methods) overlap with those of paleoanthropologists. Archaeologists and paleoanthropologists are equally interested in finding clues to the emergence and evolution of human culture among prehistoric populations. Archaeological anthropologists try to reconstruct patterns of cultural behavior and lifestyles in archaeological populations as well. For example, experimental archaeology, a branch of archaeological anthropology, attempts to replicate past cultural processes to make sense of how archaeological deposits have come into being. This replication comprises all of past human activity, ranging from stone tool techniques of the early humans such as flint knapping and atlatl usage, and past agricultural techniques, to construction of past settlements. Ethnoarchaeology, another branch of archaeological anthropology, has become a logical extension to experimental archaeological research. It examines living cultures to verify what material evidences of their cultural activity look like.

Meanwhile, applied anthropology attempts to use the existing cultural knowledge to resolve contemporary human predicaments, and to fashion and accomplish related policy objectives. Its involvement in many settings of human thought and activity, ranging from administrative apparatus, business entrepreneurship, law enforcement, the field of medicine, public health, charity, and social service, to international development is a clear testimony to applied anthropology's concentration on culture.

It is within the purview of cultural anthropology however, the notion of culture has been gaining much of its conceptual elaboration. Espoused and extolled by generations of anthropology professionals, ranging from the nineteenth-century British social anthropologist E. B. Tylor's "that complex whole" (Tylor 1871) to the twentieth-century American cultural anthropologist Clifford Geertz's "web of significance" (Geertz 1973), culture has been the core concept *of* and *for* cultural (or social and cultural) anthropology. In theoretical traditions of anthropology in continental Europe such as British structural functionalism and French structuralism, culture received a good deal of theoretical attention and prominence. In the United States, as American anthropological movements of cultural relativism, personality research, cultural ecology, cultural materialism, and interpretive anthropology bear evidence, cultural anthropology has been a discipline clinging religiously to culture.

## Chapter Summary

This chapter introduces culture, cultural anthropology's key concept, with which human condition may be distinguishable. It examines some of the salient characteristics of culture which can be recognizable universally and explains how culture unites all subfields of anthropology with its all-encompassing theme.

- Culture is the most significant aspect of humanity. It refers to hosts of beliefs and behaviors that human beings learn and share as members of a species accustomed to collective social life. The notion of culture is the central organizing construct of anthropology.

- Learned, shared, symbolic, patterned, dynamic, and adaptive nature is considered as culture's most salient features.

- Culture is learned; the complex social process with which culture is gradually learned and transmitted across generations is known as enculturation.

- Culture is shared; whereas every living culture changes incessantly, its shared nature keeps generating an extent of consistency, endurance, and predictability in cultural behavior, and mapping cultural boundaries for behavioral expectations. Neither cultural behavior, nor cultural sharing is fully harmonious or complete, however. This is due to the existence of diverse and segmental social divisions, which are also the sources of tension, discord, and change.

- Culture is symbolic; it is saturated with linguistic and nonlinguistic symbols, and that makes symbolic mode of thought and symbolic representations possible.

- Culture is patterned; it is, to a certain degree, a system in which its various parts are intermingled to form a unitary whole. Culture's interrelated nature generates a pattern. Anthropological endeavor has always been to sort, analyze, and interpret this recognizable consistency. However, there may always be certain dysfunctional, inconsistent, and disorderly parts within a culture causing discord, conflict, and change.

- Culture is dynamic; whereas certain core cultural beliefs and practices endure, culture is incessantly changing. The dynamic processes which are causing cultural change include diffusion, invention, and globalization: the transmission of distinct cultural traits in the form of objects, ideas, and behaviors from its original culture to another through migration, trade, intermarriage, warfare, or other means of contact and interaction is referred to as cultural diffusion. A specialized form of diffusion is known as acculturation or forced borrowing. Assimilation is the process by which individuals of foreign and minority origin become integrated with the standards of the dominant culture. The rise of qualitatively advanced and ideologically or technologically oriented cultural forms as a consequence of a synthesis taking place in between such existing features is identified as invention or innovation. The intense interconnectedness and movement, evident in the massive global flow of natural resources, trade goods, human labor, information, technology, and finances around the world is referred to as globalization.

• Culture is adaptive; in order to cope with environmental stresses, humans primarily rely on culture. It has been instrumental for humans to develop forms of knowledge and technology as a way of strategizing sustenance, as the measure of curing and preventing diseases, as a way of fulfilling sociopsychological needs, and as a mode of transmitting learned skills to succeeding generations. Human cultural traits have been mostly adaptive throughout. Nonetheless, there have been instances, in which some cultural traits have become adaptively neutral, dysfunctional, or even fully maladaptive.

• Human condition is distinguishable from the conditions of all other life forms. This is mainly due to the considerable extent to which humans depend on culture in their continuing struggle for success in survival and reproduction. By stressing the point that human species prevailed by being able to adapt to the changes brought forth by environmental fluctuations and instability, biological anthropologist Rick Potts characterizes versatility as a hallmark of human evolution. Biological anthropologist Terrance Deacon states that, humans are the only species capable of symbolic mode of thought and representation, and their capacity for culture is as old as humanity itself.

• Culture unites all subfields of anthropology with its all-encompassing theme: biological anthropology studies the coevolving relationship between human biology and culture. Linguistic anthropology focuses on language, the most striking cultural feature of human beings. Archaeological anthropology concentrates on material evidence of past human culture. Applied anthropology seeks to use the existing cultural knowledge to resolve current human problems. For cultural anthropology, culture has been its core concept.

# Theorizing Culture: Growth of Anthropological Theory

© Flystock/Shutterstock.com

Anthropology arose as an academic discipline when the economic, social, and political forces in the age of Industrial Revolution paved the way for the rise of modern Europe and shaped the structure of the modern world. As agriculture and manufacture were undergoing significant changes, landless peasants in the countryside and wage laborers in expanding and industrializing cities became profoundly manifest European phenomena. Under mercantilist capitalism, or the system developed to control natural resources, trade, and commerce around the globe, some European states were rapidly transforming into nation-states and colonial powers. The colonial experience gave rise to new power relations between the colonizing Western nations and their colonized subjects.

While sociologists were concerned with the internal dynamics in the industrial society of the Western world that modernity had brought to bear, it was the anthropologists who turned to study culture of the nonindustrial, non-Western, and colonized others (the natives). It was more than mere coincidence that the leading intellectual traditions of anthropology in continental Europe were developed in countries such as Britain, France, and across the Atlantic in the United States. Britain was the greatest colonial power on earth with the others existing in plenty as subjects of the empire. France was a colonial force in its own right with access to the others in many distant lands. The United States was a geopolitical entity where the others inhabited in Euro-American colonizers' midst or on the wild frontiers of its territories. As such, exploring the exotic others, and juxtaposing their radically different ways of being with that of the anthropologists' own became a central preoccupation of anthropology. It was for this endeavor that the concept of culture was found to be useful for the anthropologists.

## Social Darwinism

However, one of the main rationalizations of human diversity which had been in vogue in the Western world would effectively underplay the significance of culture. This line of thinking would refer to the supposed parallels between human morphological (pertaining to shape and appearance) differences and sociocultural differences. By basing on the writings of European observers during the previous three centuries, and the emerging scientific reasoning of evolution culminated in the publication of Charles Darwin's *On the Origin of Species* (1859), nineteenth-century social philosophers concluded that human sociocultural variation was discernible through its deterministic links to human physiological variation. In the evolutionary scheme of humans, the salience attributable to human culture and human agency in shaping the evolutionary process was secondary at best. Accordingly, a specific culture's quality of **enculturation** (the broad process through which a culture was learned individually or collectively by formal and informal means), and a specific people's capacity for **agency** (individual actions, both personal and collective, that

Charles Darwin.

made it possible for individuals to take some measure of control over their own lives) were prefashioned and constrained by the biological traits they shared as a group. This school of social thought was referred to as social Darwinism or *biological determinism* (also discussed in Chapter 2).

Once the evolutionary process of human biology is treated as the deterministic factor, it can be used to rationalize sociocultural exclusion and racism; it can be used to claim certain cultures as innately superior over the other cultures within the terms of competition and the survival of the fittest. On this point, the views of the Englishman Herbert Spencer (1820–1903), a main proponent of social Darwinism, helped to justify the policies of colonialism and the prejudices of racial hierarchy that were very much the norm throughout Europe in his day. Spencer Euro-centrically considered the elite European culture as the pinnacle of progress which could be used as a criterion to assess the growth of all human cultures. European ascendancy

© Morphart Creation/Shutterstock.com

and control over the rest of the world, Spencer maintained, was a natural and progressive consequence of human evolutionary process in its movement toward perfection.

## Unilineal Cultural Evolutionism

The late nineteenth-century anthropologists' attempt to explore the way of life of the indigenous people and the efforts to categorize local cultures within a hierarchically arranged, universal set of evolutionary scheme have to be understood within this context. In this scheme, different cultural status is aligned in a single line that moves from the most primitive to the most advanced or civilized. Hence, it is known as **unilineal cultural evolutionism.** While there were other important anthropologists who shared the same line of thinking such as J. G. Frazer, the author of the twelve-volume ethnological study entitled *The Golden Bough* (1922), E. B. Tylor (1832–1917), and L. H. Morgan (1818–1881) were regarded as the most salient contributors to the above evolutionary scheme of culture.

In documenting the vast range of diversity noticeable among human cultures, both Morgan and Tylor viewed culture as a holistic quality that unites humanity. In this sense, they shared *the psychic unity of humanity,* a notion already circulating among some of their contemporaries such as German anthropologist Adolf Bastian (1826–1905). What they meant by this was the common possibility and destiny shared by all humans as the members of the same species, regardless of differences which were negligible in comparison.

Writing in his most well-known volume *Primitive Culture* in 1871, Tylor defined, "Culture or civilization, taken in its broad, ethnographic sense, is that complex whole which includes knowledge, belief, art, morals, law, custom, and any other capabilities and habits acquired by man as a member of society" (Tylor 1871). In this oft-cited definition, by referring to culture as "that complex whole" Tylor recognized it as a universal quality of humanity that transcended human diversity. Moreover, by stating cultural traits were "acquired" by humans "as a member of society," he recognized that culture was gained through the processes of enculturation, and not through biological inheritance. Put in another way, Tylor acknowledged that some of the basic characteristics recognized as inherent features of being human were in fact the consequences of humans' social upbringing, cultural learning, and cultural sharing. Additionally, Tylor considered cultural phenomena of "knowledge, belief, art, morals, law, custom, and any other capabilities and habits" as material phenomena in the world which were perceptible by the senses (or the bodily faculties through which sensation was roused). Furthermore, Tylor conceptualized culture qualitatively equating it with *civilization*. Accordingly, humanity was consisted of societies that were equally capable of acquiring culture. However, each society gained it in different amounts in the process of ascending through the rungs of the cultural evolutionary ladder.

Tylor's concept of cultural survivals further supported his view of cultural holism. Cultural survivals, he contended, were cultural traits that had unexplainably survived the test of time and continued throughout despite losing their original societal functions. Tylor believed in the prudency in focusing on cultural survivals when reconstructing human evolutionary process.

American anthropologist Morgan saw cultural traits as patterned, orderly, and law like, a salient position he shared with Tylor. Elaborating on the observable patterns of kinship and their plausible connections to patterns of sustenance, Morgan maintained that the patterns of various cultural traits were linked.

Morgan also considered culture as a universal quality of humankind. Writing in 1877 in his *Ancient Society*, Morgan proposed a three-tiered, universal, and unilineal process of cultural evolution: savagery (with three substages related to technological features of fire, bow, and pottery), barbarism (with three substages related to animal domestication, agriculture, and metal work), and civilization. According to Morgan, these three stages of human growth have their parallels in human adaptive strategies, respectively: foraging, agriculture, and state formation as well as urbanization. His efforts to seek connections between the patterns of kinship and the patterns of adaptive strategies within a universal scheme of human evolution was further testimony to the point that Morgan's notion of culture was a holistic and systemic one (Morgan 1877).

Morgan, just like Tylor, was convinced that any understanding of culture should begin with its material foundations. He went to great lengths to explain how, in the process of human evolution, technological progress had been a driving force of cultural progress and change. Accordingly, Morgan saw cultural change noticeable in every domain of culture, as a reflection of technological progress. This materialist explanation was particularly appealing to Morgan's contemporary and influential political economist Karl Marx, as evidenced in the latter's posthumously published volume *The Origin of the Family, Private Property, and the State* (Marx 1884). Morgan's materialist analysis of culture also gained notable traction at the hands of some twentieth-century American anthropologists with materialist leanings, including cultural materialists such as Marvin Harris (1927–2001).

Conceptualizing culture in holistic terms, Morgan and Tylor aligned themselves with the presupposition that all humans as members of the same species were bonded in origin, fate, and potential. In their view, culture was a unitary concept that crosscut the steps of evolution; whereas evolution differentiated specific societies qualitatively, culture coalesced them holistically. To this extent, the late nineteenth-century evolutionary anthropologists such as Morgan and Tylor were distinguishable from social Darwinists of their day.

Nevertheless, in their unilineal evolutionary schemes of humanity, cultures were classified and hierarchically arranged as more primitive or more civilized; more primitive cultures could move through the stages of progress in the same sequence and eventually reach the Euro-American cultures representing the pinnacle of civilization, but their movement would be at a different rate. This made culture essentially a qualitative concept with which societies were classifiable according to the extent of "culture" they possessed. In effect, therefore, the late nineteenth-century evolutionary anthropologists such as Morgan and Tylor had been maintaining an implicit alliance with social Darwinists.

## Empiricism and Cultural Relativism

**The deductive approaches** to culture or the processes of developing particular cultural observations through general explanations, such as those proposed by evolutionists and diffusionists, came under heavy criticism from a German-born American anthropologist named Franz Boas (1858–1942), a founding figure of American anthropology. Trained originally as a physicist, a geographer, and a mathematician, Boas went to Baffin Island in Arctic Canada in 1883 to conduct geographical research. During this tour in which he was able to spend a year among the Inuit or the *Eskimo*, the native people of the island, he became convinced that, only by living with people whose cultures were different from one's own, and thereby, deepening appreciation of their cultural traits, one would truly become capable of understanding cultural differences. Later, after immigrating to the United States, he also carried out ethnographic field research among the Kwakiutl Indians, also known as the *Kwakwaka'wakw* Indians, in the Canadian Pacific. In 1896, when he assumed the position of anthropology professor at Columbia University, New York City, Boas made a conscious and consistent effort to place the fledgling discipline on firm empirical footing.

Boas advocated an **inductive approach** to cultural theorizing: gathering specific ethnographic data before arriving at generalizations. His vision of anthropology was one of methodological rigor and scientific accuracy based on empirical evidence. Boas believed that, comprehending the views of the native cultural actors (those who participated in the culture being studied) or **emic perspective** was quite essential for anthropologists, if they would grasp the complexity of cultural phenomena. He was convinced that the sorts of sweeping generalizations evidenced in evolutionary and diffusionist analyses of culture were due to their heavy reliance on anthropologists' own, observer-oriented views, known as **etic perspective.** As the mentor for the first generation of American anthropologists, Boas insisted on conducting detailed ethnographic fieldwork, an insistence to which his students such as Margaret Mead, Edward Sapir, Robert Lowie, Ruth Benedict, Alfred Kroeber,

Melville J. Herskovits, Paul Radin, Jules Henry, and Ruth Bunzel mostly adhered. Boas was also known for purposefully recruiting female students to the anthropology graduate program at Colombia University, and it showed his recognition that researching a specific culture would never be satisfactory unless the issues such as gender that limited the ethnographer's access to certain aspects of culture were addressed and dealt with.

The empiricist approach to researching culture based on in-depth ethnographic fieldwork was directly related to Franz Boas' other core belief: Each culture was a unique product of its own history; no culture was therefore, more advanced than the others or vice versa. Therefore, according to Boas, any assessment of a specific culture warranted only its own standards—no more, no less. This Boasian position of culture, known as **cultural relativism,** became one of the main tenets of anthropology, although critics chose to refer to it as *historical particularism* (also discussed in Chapter 1).

## Structural Functionalism

The classical French sociologist Emile Durkheim (1858–1917) is often referred to as the founder of structural functionalism. Nevertheless, this theoretical focus came to be considered a British school of anthropological thought, mainly due to the works of Bronislaw Malinowski and A. R. Radcliffe-Brown. In his book *Rules of Sociological Method*, Durkheim made the following observation, fundamental to all of his writings: *social facts* "consist of manners of acting, thinking, and feeling external to the individual, which are invested with a coercive power by virtue of which they exercise control over him" (Durkheim 1976 [1895]). Accordingly, the most salient traits of social facts were their externality and coercion; social facts were "states of collective mind" which were distinguishable from the forms these states took when manifested through the minds of individuals. In similar vein, social facts were obligatory and coercive, as manifested through the constraint they exercised on the individual both directly and indirectly. Durkheim's social facts were consisted of the most clearly delineable structural features of society such as population size and expansion, as well as those structural features which were not readily apparent or distinguishable such as currents of public opinion and interest. Society, Durkheim insisted further, was a category of its own—it was *sui generis* (unique).

The early twentieth-century British social anthropologists found Durkheim's above emphasis on social facts particularly appealing as it resonated through in their own studies of kinship systems, customs, morals, legal rules, political organizations, economic transactions, as well as religious beliefs and rituals among different cultures. They were skeptical over the evolutionary and diffusionist approaches to the study of social and cultural institutions that they perceived as speculative and historical. They also found Durkheim's theorization that society was a structural whole in which individuals were constituencies especially meaningful. Accordingly, Malinowski and Radcliffe-Brown were pushing for a theoretical shift. Their objective was to pursue a theoretical paradigm capable of expanding sociocultural inquiry beyond the purview of the evolutionary and the diffusionist paradigms while identifying sociocultural institutions as functional and integrated parts of a social system. It was as a result of their pursuit of the above objective,

**structural functionalism** came into being as a central theoretical construct of anthropology. It focused on the significance of social phenomena as they functioned to serve for the maintenance of a particular culture's systemic whole.

Whereas they devised its distinct versions, Malinowski and Radcliffe-Brown shared a couple of tenets, pivotally significant to structural functionalist school of thought in anthropology.

First, they both were convinced that all cultures were functionally cohesive wholes; cultures were composed of a bundle of distinct, yet functionally interrelated parts. The existence of different parts of a culture and their relationship, these structural functionalists believed, was explainable through the organic analogy. Just like a biological organism was able to live, reproduce, and function through its integrated system of parts and organs, a culture was able to retain its necessary processes through the collective interaction of its distinct parts. In this cultural organism, institutions such as kinship, religion, and political organization were functionally related as organs, just as individuals were analogous to the cells of that organism. As a corollary to this proposition, it followed that no cultural trait could ever have been evaluated or interpreted independently of the integrated whole in which it was embedded. It also went without saying as a second corollary that a change in one part of a culture would highly likely to have brought forth changes to the other parts of that systematic cultural whole simultaneously.

© Francky38/Shutterstock.com

Second, Malinowski and Radcliffe-Brown were ardent believers of in-depth studies of cultures based on intensive fieldwork; underlying this belief was the functionalist standpoint that the reality was to be found in the current manifestations and functions of the social phenomena. They rejected the earlier evolutionary and diffusionist approaches as privileged and speculative theorizing over the discovery of facts. Malinowski in particular, insisted on experiential engagement in fieldwork through immersion in the culture being studied. He pointed out that it was crucial for the ethnographer to empirically grasp the inconsistencies between what people say they do (i. e., norm) and what they actually do (i. e., action). Accordingly, Malinowski carried out his comprehensive ethnographic research among the Trobriand islanders in the Western Pacific (1915–1918). Likewise, Radcliffe-Brown conducted his fieldwork among the Andaman islanders in the Indian Ocean (1906–1908), and the aborigines in Western Australia (1910–1912).

There were important differences between the versions of structural functionalism advocated by Malinowski and Radcliffe-Brown, nevertheless. Although both held that myriad facets of culture have to be examined in regard to their present manifestations and functions, Malinowski differed from Radcliffe-Brown when he suggested that sociocultural institutions existed and functioned to satisfy *individual needs*. In his view, understanding various aspects of behavior in terms of individual motivations was crucial for an ethnographer since every feature in a culture performed a useful function to ensure the well-being of individuals. This was an overarching theme running through all of the topics of Malinowski's analytical grasp and strength, ranging from kinship, marriage, reciprocity, and magic, to myth.

According to Radcliffe-Brown, cultural functions existed and functioned to satisfy *societal needs*. Unlike Malinowski, Radcliffe-Brown focused primarily on social structure

© Nadiia_foto/Shutterstock.com

and the way social phenomena functioned to maintain social order. Inspired by the ideas of the French positivist philosopher Auguste Comte (1798–1857) and Emile Durkheim, he pointed out that *the social* constituted a discrete level of reality, distinguishable from those of biological forms as well as inorganic matter. Therefore, continued Radcliffe-Brown, the social phenomena had to be explained within a social level, and through a social matrix only. He proposed that individuals, the constituent units of the integrated societal whole, were there to perform roles, and thereby, to preserve the well-being and the continuity of social structure. Mere occupants of social roles, individuals were ephemeral, impertinent, and indeed, replaceable, Radcliffe-Brown stated.

Structural functionalism, dominant in American anthropological theory in the 1950s and 1960s, gradually lost its theoretical appeal and vigor toward the early 1970s. It was critiqued for being excessively classificatory or typological, circular, and antihistorical.

# French Structuralism

The theme of the *psychic unity of humanity* was reintroduced to anthropological discourse of culture by a French anthropologist named Claude Levi-Strauss (1908–2009) whose illustrious career spanned over a better part of the twentieth century. Drawing on the theories of structural linguists such as Ferdinand de Saussure and Roman Jakobson, and using data from his ethnographic research among Amazonian Indians, Levi-Strauss constructed a theory recognizing the mental structures that strengthened sociocultural behavior. He contended that human culture was fashioned by certain mental codes preprogrammed into human brain, and they concurrently made humans capable of classifying and understanding reality, mainly in terms of binary oppositions or pairs such as left-right, night-day, good-evil, nature-culture, male-female, young-old, hot-cold, and raw-cooked. Cultural differences arose as consequences of environmental and historical factors that altered the aforesaid inherent mental codes. Cultural variations, according to Levi-Strauss, were only superficial; whereas the content elements would differ from one culture to another, the structure of such elements would remain consistent since the structure of the mind was basically the same for all humans (Levi-Strauss 1963).

Levi-Strauss strove to demonstrate the link between culture and cognition mainly through his structural analyses of kinship and myth, recognized as pioneering studies on these topics. In his book *The Elementary Structures of Kinship* (Levi-Strauss 1969), Levi-Strauss argued that the elements of kinship, just like the phonemic elements in language, were the products of the unconscious, logical structure of the mind; therefore, these basic constituents of kinship were helpful to fathom the logical structures underlying the sociocultural relations of kin-ordered societies.

Likewise, in books such as *The Raw and the Cooked* (Levi-Strauss 1983) and *From Honey to Ashes* (Levi-Strauss 1973), Levi-Strauss explained how the structure of myth provided fundamental structure in comprehending cultural relations. He presented what he saw as the basic paradox in the study of myth in the following way: "If the content of myth is contingent (i. e., arbitrary), how are we to explain the fact that myths throughout the world are so similar?" By way of answering the above question, Levi-Strauss proposed that the similarity came from the universal rules governing mythical thought. These universals, he argued, were linked to the universal laws governing all spheres of human thought. By unbundling the fundamental constituent units of myth or *mythemes,* linked to each other as binary oppositions, it was possible to uncover the basic logical processes which were at the root of mythical thought universally, Levi-Strauss proposed. Accordingly, myths functioned in all cultures to "provide a logical model capable of overcoming a contradiction."

Levi-Strauss' structuralism has been criticized for its abstractionist approach to culture, oftentimes found to be unreceptive to empirical testing. Levi-Strauss has also been criticized for his primary focus on men as the principle actors in sociocultural affairs, particularly, in his structural study of kinship. However, some contemporary anthropologists continuously find Levi-Strauss' structural analyses, with which he explained cultural differences as variations in fundamental themes of universal human thought, intriguing and useful. In 2009, when he passed away at the age of almost 101, Claude Levi-Strauss was arguably one of the most celebrated anthropologists in the world.

## Neo-Evolutionism, Cultural Ecology, and Cultural Materialism

Leslie White (1900–1975), an American anthropologist trained under the Boasian tradition, undertook the task of upholding evolutionary approaches to humanity and culture once again. A unilineal evolutionist himself, White believed that cultural evolution was a general course of action embracing human culture in all its variety and profundity. Therefore, he attempted to create a theory explaining human history in its totality by stressing the process of cultural evolution as the central organizing construct of that theory. Writing in 1959 in his book *The Evolution of Culture,* White suggested that, "Culture evolves as the amount of energy harnessed per capita per year increases or as the efficiency of the means of putting energy to work is increased" (White 1959, 368–69). Accordingly, the driving force of evolution has been particular cultural systems' increasing capacity to harness energy or their advancing levels of technology, or both. Leslie White presented this *basic law of evolution* through the equation $C = ET$ where, $C$ was culture, $E$ was a measure of energy consumed, and $T$ was the measure of technological efficiency in regards to utilizing energy. This model of cultural evolution, dubbed by White as **neo-evolution,** rekindled anthropological interest in evolutionism in the 1960s.

By using the above criteria, Leslie White recast the main steps of cultural evolution proposed by nineteenth-century evolutionary anthropologists while distinguishing several salient instances at which decisive changes in human evolution occurred. Accordingly, the agricultural revolution of antiquity was a decisive juncture in human cultural evolution. Instead of totally depending on the energy of their own muscles as their ancestors did, these early human agriculturalists learned to utilize the energy of domesticated plants and animals. The fuel revolution at the beginning of the nineteenth century under which humans learned to capture energy from natural resources (such as coal, oil, and gas) to use for the steam engine and the internal combustion engine was another salient turning point in cultural evolution. The technological capability to harness nuclear energy obtained in the mid-twentieth century has been, according to White, an equally critical turning point in the evolutionary process.

The possibility of constructing a comprehensive cultural theory of entire human evolution was questioned by Julian Steward (1902–1972), an evolutionary thinker and a pioneer of ecological approaches in cultural anthropology. Steward characterized White's approach as *universal evolution,* citing that it was an analytical framework designed to pursue general rules universally applicable to culture. According to Steward, the above proposition was based on the erroneous assumption that the evolutionary process has been the same among cultures everywhere. Steward did not see cultural complexity evolving through time in a single way. Rather, adopting a more nuanced approach than White's theory, he assumed cultural evolution as a process potentially taking multiple paths simultaneously. Accordingly, the primary factors of evolution such as ecology and economics, as well as the secondary factors like political system, ideologies, and world views, tended to push the evolutionary process of a given culture in myriad directions concurrently. By emphasizing this factor, Steward called his own perspective as *multilinear evolution.* This analytical and explanatory focus, for which Steward was the main contributing anthropologist during his time, was also known as **cultural ecology.**

While focusing on the interaction between a given culture and its environment, Julian Steward also concentrated on the evolution of groups of cultures. He contended that cultures confronting similar sorts of environmental challenges have a higher probability of developing similar sorts of technological solutions. Successively, such adaptive measures paved the way for the growth of collateral sociopolitical institutions, Steward pointed out. It was for this reason he entertained the possibility of constructing theoretical frameworks, applicable to analyze pervasive cultural features in a specific area or region.

Rising into prominence as a cultural theory in the late 1960s, and prevailing throughout the 1970s and the 1980s, **cultural materialism** was a theoretical perspective embracing the evolutionary approaches to culture such as unilineal evolutionism, neo-evolutionism, and cultural ecology. It was also an attempt to situate such approaches within an expansive framework of materialist orientation in Marxian thought, simultaneously. According to Marvin Harris (1927–2001), its principal proponent, cultural materialism was a materialist approach to culture capable of accomplishing anthropology's primary task: offering causal explanations for diversity in thought and behavior found among the members of myriad human cultures around the world. Harris critiqued the anthropologists with idealistic views of culture for their efforts to understand what was going on in the head of the native cultural actors. According to Harris, this approach, known as emic perspective, was largely pointless in that the cultural practitioners were generally unaware of the adaptive reasons on which their actions were based. Instead, he proposed, anthropological inquiry of cultural phenomena ought to have been based on etic perspective, the view of the anthropological observer. Rather than resorting to subjective explanations of cultural behavior, Harris stressed further, anthropologists ought to have been pursuing objective explanations through the steps of scientific research methodology—formation of hypotheses, collection of empirical evidence, quantification, and testing theories. "Empirical science," wrote Harris, "is the foundation of the cultural materialist way of knowing" (Harris 1979, 29).

Cultural materialist perspective offered to explain cultural similarity, difference, and change through a three-tiered societal framework: infrastructure, structure, and superstructure. It recognized infrastructure or *material realities,* consisted of technological, economic, and reproductive (demographic) factors, for playing the primary role in fashioning and influencing the other two components of culture. Accordingly, the cultural significance of structure or *organizational aspects of culture,* which included kinship and political economy, as well as superstructure or *ideological and symbolic aspects of society* composed of religion, worldviews, and aesthetics was only secondary. Therefore, material constraints arising from universal human needs for sustenance, shelter, and procreation were much more important in understanding cultural behavior than mental constraints of organizational and ideological significance. Succinctly put, cultural materialists maintained that people's actions shaped their beliefs, not vice versa.

Marvin Harris illustrated the effectiveness of cultural materialist approach by explaining the widespread reluctance evident among the people of India to slaughter cattle and eat beef within the context of ecological conditions and farming practices in India (Harris 1966, 1974). An emic analysis based on native reasoning would have found the causes for unwillingness to kill cows and eat their meat in Hinduism, the religion of the majority community in India, in which, reverential references to cows were not rare. Besides, as a belief system based on the concept of omnipresence of the Divine, and the presence of a soul in all creatures, including in cattle, the act of killing, let along with the eating of the

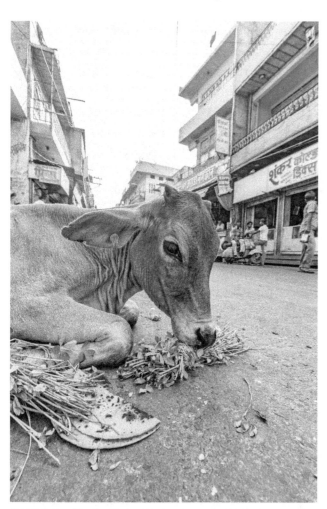

© travelview/Shutterstock.com

kill, would have been naturally accounted for as sin. However, an etic analysis would find root causes in rural India's economic needs and the corresponding agricultural practices. Cattle were the beasts of burden for Indian farmers who relied heavily on them for tilling the fields, for fertilizer, and even for transporting the produce to the market or the storehouse. Cow was further useful as the main source of dairy products. Furthermore, its refuse (cow dung) was a cheaply available source of fuel, and when mixed with clay and water, a thin coating used to make the floor of the wattle-and-daub houses smooth and less dusty. A sort of caretaker for Indian family, the cow was identified as an almost maternal figure. Hence, the affectionate term *go mata* ("bovine mother"). In brief, cattle were much more useful alive than dead. Marvin Harris thus effectively showed from this oftcited Indian example that, the actions of the cultural actors were driven by their material necessities. As he strove to demonstrate, cultural actors were neither

© Jeff Schultes/Shutterstock.com

aware that their beliefs were the consequences of their actions; nor did they aware of what adaptive reasons had in fact led to act in such ways.

Harris tried to reinforce the above point by analyzing a variety of other cultural beliefs and practices from his cultural materialistic perspective as well. For example, while focusing on the consumption of pork, which was remaining an abomination among over a billion of Muslims and Jews, Harris suggested that the root causes of this taboo stem not from the religious truths (i. e., Allah and Yahweh were heard to say that swine were unclean and unsuitable to consume or come into contact with) as conventional wisdom would have people believe. Rather, they have derived from the fact that raising pigs was ecologically maladaptive for the farming and pastoralist communities of the Middle East (Harris 1989, 35–60).

Marxian critics have largely dismissed cultural materialism as an instance of "vulgar materialism," based on idiosyncratic and superficial readings of Marx (Friedman 1974). Cultural materialist approach viewed the infrastructure–structure link as uni-directional. It was also clear on the point that this was not a link based on class conflict. Indeed, it assumed the position that upper and lower classes of society were equal beneficiaries of innovation and change. Cultural materialism was flatly dismissive of the role of ideology as well.

Louis Althusser

© Marusya Chaika/Shutterstock.com

By contrast, Marxism considered the nexus between infrastructure and structure as dialectically based. The dialectical approach of Marxism was founded on the premise that society was structured around contradictions, and they could be resolved only through fundamental social change. Karl Marx's dialectical materialist analysis of history, referred to as *historical materialism*, was centered on class conflict. Accordingly, in a class-based society, cultural change would only benefit the ruling class. Moreover, Marxism viewed material needs of the people and the resultant economic relations (or the *base* in Marxist terminology) as the factors that determined or conditioned noneconomic relations, social institutions, as well as prevalent ideas. However, Marx did recognize the salient role ideology played as a way of concealing the contradictions existing at the heart of a class-based society. Furthermore, by referring to class consciousness or the workers' (or *proletariat's*) awareness of their contradictory relationship with the capitalist class (or *bourgeoisie*), which was required to overthrow capitalism, Marx acknowledged the role of ideology for social change. This point was further elaborated by twentieth-century Marxist thinkers such as Antonio Gramsci (1891–1937) and Louis Althusser (1918–1990).

Cultural idealists and structuralists were equally unimpressed with the cultural materialist reliance on etic approach for cultural researching, which was in their view, incapable of grasping the thoughts and behavior of the members of a native society. Besides, according to cultural idealists, etic approach was full of ethnocentric biases. Postmodernists extended this criticism even further when they rejected positivist science as a reductionist approach inadequate for cultural learning. In their view, comprehending the details of cultural realities required nongeneralizing emphases such as polyvocality, reflexivity, and interpretation.

## Symbolic and Interpretive Anthropology

Developed in the 1960s as a weighty movement in anthropology against what its proponents regarded to be the sterile scientism of materialist and cognitive approaches to culture, **symbolic and interpretive anthropology** focused on symbols and related processes (such as myth and ritual). Its aim was to explore the way human beings ascribed meaning to such symbols and processes for giving their lives direction, order, and coherence. The most notable variants of this approach were evident in the works of Mary Douglas, David Schneider, Victor Turner, and Clifford Geertz.

Mary Douglas (1921–2007), a British social anthropologist influenced by Durkheim and the functionalist perspectives in anthropological theory, was interested in the nexus between culture and symbols. The forms of cultural symbolism, as Douglas implicated in her works, were universal; they also, as she stressed throughout, were reproducing and strengthening social orders concurrently. Douglas' most well-known volume entitled *Purity and Danger* (Douglas 1966) was a case in point. In this work on Jewish food consumption practices and related taboos, she pointed out the ways in which the taxonomy of pure (i. e., edible) and impure (i. e., inedible) animals in Jewish culture were closely linked to a symbolic system of boundary maintenance. The ideas on purity and pollution evident in the aforementioned food taboos, Douglas maintained, were reflective of a universal cultural feature—a figurative link between human body and society. Accordingly, the taboos in Jewish edible universe

© ChameleonsEye/Shutterstock.com

highlighting bodily vulnerabilities related to the ingestion of impure substances were symbolic means of strengthening vulnerable social order from harmful outside forces.

Well known for his pioneering studies on American kinship, David M. Schneider (1918–1995) identified culture as a system of symbols and meanings. Interested in the links between cultural symbols and observable events, he strove to explore how cultural symbols and meanings fashioned and governed societal rules. He reasoned that the cultural system informed and molded abstract norms, and they in turn, informed noticeable behavior in society. It is in this sense scholars have argued that Schneider, with some modification, still retained Levi-Strauss' original structuralist position of seeing culture as a set of relationships (Spencer 1996; Ortner 1981). Schneider applied his ideas on culture to his extensive studies of American kinship. In *American Kinship: A Cultural Account* (Schneider 1968), for example, he took a step in that direction, prompting researchers to examine kinship as a system of symbols and meaning, and not as a natural system founded primarily on biological linkage.

Victor Turner (1920–1983) was a British social anthropologist originally trained under the aegis of structural functionalist thought. However, he increasingly became frustrated in investigating the sets of underlying rules that gave shape and order to society. He was also discontented in inquiring on how people unthinkingly conformed to such rules, supposedly ensuring smooth functioning of society. Instead, Turner began to concentrate on symbols. As his focus gradually shifted from economics and demography to symbolism in social drama, ritual, pilgrimage, and theater, it became clear that Turner was not just interested in symbols themselves. Rather, his interest lied in seeking how symbols, as operators in the social process, instigated "social action" and exerted "determinable influences, inclining persons and groups to action" (Turner 1967, 36). Turner concentrated on the operational ability of symbols and symbolic action in moving social actors from various statuses, strengthening ties, creating social norms, and resolving contradiction. This focus helped him to identify symbols and symbolic action as salient means by which societies retained solidarity. Turner's intrigue on what symbols meant to particular groups of people as a resource of social action, and how symbols operated as active forces in social transformations, showed the unmistakable influence of Max Gluckman, his mentor at University of Manchester, who introduced him to conflict theory and political anthropology.

Rather than searching for generalized propositions or rules about human behavior, some symbolic anthropologists believed anthropologists ought to have been *interpreting* natives' reading of their experience, stories natives told themselves about themselves. This approach, sometimes referred to as interpretive anthropology, was set forth by anthropologist Clifford Geertz (1926–2006), its main proponent. Influenced by the ideas of the classical social theorist Max Weber, and sociologist Talcott Parsons (1902–1979) who advocated separation of culture from social structure, Geertz sought to hone and refine the concept of culture by concentrating on meanings embodied in symbols. He considered the symbols as vehicles of culture, because they expressed worldview, value orientation, and **ethos** or emotional communality that the members of a particular culture shared. Geertz wrote in his influential compilation of essays entitled *The Interpretations of Cultures* (Geertz 1973) the following: "Man is an animal suspended in webs of significance he himself has spun; I take culture to be those webs, and the analysis of it to be therefore not an experimental science in search of law but an interpretive one in search of meanings" (Geertz 1973, 4–5). Culture, in this sense, was a historically transmitted pattern of meanings, and the meanings were both the consequences and the causes of people's action; they were expressed in public symbolic forms such as word, ritual, and custom while making manifest that they were observable, readable, and analyzable like texts. Culture, Geertz maintained, was an ensemble of such meaningful texts that natives constantly have read or acted out.

These texts of symbolic meanings, Geertz continued, were multilayered documents owing to the fact that human experience was innately ambiguous, and that's why they had to be interpreted. The deciphering of a cultural text while placing primacy on the detailed, contextualized, and empirical description was what Geertz meant when he referred to **thick description.** He elaborated his thoughts in this regard in the essay entitled "Thick Description: Toward an Interpretive Theory of Culture" (Geertz 1973). Accordingly, ethnographers should focus on the layering of interpretations of all sorts, including ethnographer's interpretation, natives' interpretations, and reader's own interpretation. Geertz attempted to explain the multiple-layered nature of thick description by using a witty Indian anecdote:

> "There is an Indian story—at least I heard it as an Indian story—about an Englishman who, having been told that the world rested in turn on the back of a turtle, asked (perhaps he was an ethnographer; it is the way they behave), what did the turtle rest on? Another turtle. And another turtle? 'Ah, Sahib, after that it is turtles all the way down'" (Geertz 1973).

Geertz tried to further highlight the differences between the thin and thick description through an analogous comparison of a blink and a wink, an idea he borrowed from Gilbert Ryle (1900–1976), a British philosopher and phenomenologist: whereas physical movements involved in each were nearly identical, a wink, a voluntary and deliberate act, was quite capable of imparting distinctive meanings than a blink, a blandish, involuntary twitch. The blink and the sorts of winks coalesced to generate a stratified hierarchy of meanings. The task of the ethnographer, contended Geertz, was to decipher such hierarchies of cultural categories.

Geertz's treatment of culture as an ensemble of meaningful symbolic texts, provoked anthropologists to shift their focus from the functional aspects of culture to the ways symbols act as vehicles of culture. This was his single most important contribution to anthropological knowledge. He was among the handful of anthropological theorists and ethnographers who were frequently cited outside, as well as inside, the discipline. He was critiqued for being rhetorical, idiosyncratic, and unreceptive to empirical testing. Additionally, critics have cited his failure to focus on the construction of meaning and power from a historical and institutional perspective.

## Critical Perspectives

The anthropological notion of culture, which is claiming to be so central in explaining why people are what they are, and why they do what they do, has lost much of its message in translation (Ariyaratne 2012). For some time now, there has been a notable increase of calling for a re-evaluation on how the notion of culture has been used in anthropological discourse along the themes of the politics of representation, power and cultural otherness, as well as the links between space, identity, and the production of cultural difference. Three critical essays, influential and representative of the recent works devoted to interrogating the anthropological notion of culture are succinctly examined in this section.

In 1991, anthropologist Lila Abu-Lughod wrote a provocative piece to explain why "writing against culture" can be more prudent for anthropologists than writing for it. In this work, a devastating critique of the use and utility of the notion of culture, she maintained that the dominant paradigm of anthropology has always been, and will continuously be, the historically constructed distinction between self (the Western self) and other (the non-Western other); culture being chiefly instrumental in constructing and maintaining other, the aforementioned paradigm firmly rests on the concept of culture. The late nineteenth-century anthropological shift to culture, Abu-Lughod argued, was a strategic one primarily due to the political advantages over its predecessor, race: firstly, culture, often conceptualized as the life ways of specific groups that they learn and share through enculturation, and not from biological inheritance, is capable of retaining difference while removing it from the sphere of the natural and the innate; Secondly, the plural usage of culture (culture with lower case "c" with the possibility of a final "s") accommodates multiple differences, and this makes rigid hierarchical ordering with binary oppositions rather difficult. Nevertheless, continued Abu-Lughod, culture, just like race, enforces inequality. It is the tool with which the construction and maintenance of the other or the process of "othering" is done. This objective is accomplished in anthropological discourse through the overemphasis of coherence (Clifford 1988, 112), erasure of temporality, nurturance of discreteness (Wolf 1982), and retention of difference (Abu-Lughod 1991, 466–79).

Abu-Lughod viewed that within anthropology, the basic "issue of domination keep being skirted." Hence, she criticized the postmodern emphases on experimentation with ethnographic techniques, as became evident in dialogic or polyvocal ethnographic narratives. In these narratives, informants were often refigured as consultants and given voice. Abu-Lughod also critiqued the efforts of decolonization on the level of texts; such emphases, she believed, have retreated from the problematic of power—the power of anthropologist over anthropological subject and the basic configurations of global power on which anthropology is based.

As a way of writing against culture, Abu-Lughod proposed several strategies: focusing on the concepts of practice and discourse (instead of culture) was one of them because they work against the culture notion's presuppositions of boundedness. Another strategy would be to concentrate on connections and interconnections between the community being studied and the anthropologist, as well as the world to which the latter belongs. Yet one more strategy would be, according to Abu-Lughod, to experiment with what she called "narrative ethnographies of the particular." By closely concentrating on specific individuals and their changing relationships, one would unsettle "the most problematic connotations of culture: homogeneity, coherence, and timelessness" (Abu-Lughod 1991, 475–76).

Anthropologist Adam Kuper's work entitled *Culture: the Anthropologists' Account* (Kuper 2000) was an exploration of the historical roots of cultural theory with the stated aim of assessing the value of culture as an analytical concept. While briefly surveying German, French, and British intellectual traditions of culture and scrutinizing in detail the works of some of the main figures in postwar American cultural anthropology such as Clifford Geertz, David Schneider, and Marshall Sahlins, Kuper pointed out that the current anthropological usage of culture has a traceable and distinctively American genealogy. His critique of this American project of culture was primarily based on the premise that "it tends to draw attention away from what we have in common instead of encouraging us to communicate across national, ethnic, and religious boundaries, and to venture beyond them" (Kuper 2000, 247).

In Kuper's view, the problems associated with the concept of culture are fundamentally epistemological to the extent that they are insolvable by simply "tiptoeing around the notion" or by "refining the definitions" (Kuper 2000, x–xi). On this point, he was critical of the postmodern approaches, in vogue toward the 1970s and 1980s, for romanticizing culture, for failures of logic, and for having a "paralyzing effect on anthropology" (Kuper 2000, 220). Moreover, Kuper argued against the use of culture and multiculturalism in discussions of identity for assuming difference as the basis for distinct human collectivities and divisions such as gender, race, and ethnicity, and thereby, turning the notion of culture to a benign form of racism. He concluded that anthropologists ought to avoid the hyper-referential term of culture altogether. Instead, Kuper claimed, they should concentrate precisely on knowledge, belief, art, technology, tradition, or even ideology.

In 1992, anthropologists Akhil Gupta and James Ferguson coedited a volume in which they and the other contributors to the volume attempted to deal with the issues of space and place, along with some of the related themes such as location, displacement, community, and identity (Gupta and Ferguson 1992). What motivated them to focus on such issues, the coeditors pointed out, was the renewed interest in theorizing space toward the 1980s, evident in such poststructuralist and postmodernist concepts as panopticism (Foucault 1982), simulacra (Baudrillard 1995), deterritorialization (Kaplan 1987), postmodern hyperspace (Jameson 1984), borderlands (Anzaldua 1987; Rosaldo 2003), and marginality (Herzfeld 1997). Given the fact that anthropology has been traditionally observing an unproblematic link between identity and place, re-evaluation of the anthropological notion of culture, as well as the idea of cultural difference becomes imperative, Gupta and Ferguson maintained.

By uncritically assuming group identities (such as "tribe," "culture," and "people") and their spatial distribution as natural, ethnographers have been habitually unresponsive to the significant problems posed by such assumptions, Gupta and Ferguson pointed out. For instance, one such problem has been the issue of those who occupy grey spaces of territoriality such as migrant workers, nomads, transnational entrepreneurs, and professional elite. In much the same way, the unproblematic link between identity and place has made cultural differences within a locality unexplainable. Similarly, postcolonial hybrid cultures have been remaining unaccounted for. Moreover, the issue of comprehending social change and cultural transformation as situated within interconnected spaces has become crucial.

The critical issues of the sort, Gupta and Ferguson argued, cannot be addressed by textual strategies (such as polyvocal ethnographic texts in which the local voices are accommodated within the narrative, and collaboration with informants in ethnographic textual production) alone, although they can bring the politics of representation as a salient

© David Litman/Shutterstock.com

issue to the forefront. Rather, the aforementioned issues require a conceptual direction capable of taking us beyond the orthodox invocation of culture as a spatially localized phenomenon. This was why they proposed to focus on the transnational public spheres such as hybridity, the border lands, and public culture as alternative apparatus with which conventional notions of culture could be unsettled.

## Chapter Summary

This chapter situates the concept of culture on firm theoretical footing and reviews the growth of cultural anthropological theory. In so doing, it intends to assist students to get a sense of how the texts they are reading fit into a wider theoretical context of cultural anthropology.

- The notion of culture has been gaining much of its conceptual elaboration at the hands of cultural anthropologists.

- While applying the emerging scientific reasoning of evolution, social Darwinists concluded that human sociocultural variation was discernible through its deterministic links to human physiological variation.

- The late nineteenth-century evolutionary anthropologists viewed culture as a holistic quality that unites humanity. Nevertheless, in their unilineal evolutionary scheme, cultures were classified and hierarchically arranged as more primitive and more civilized.

- The empiricist and cultural relativist school of American anthropological thought insisted on methodological rigor and scientific accuracy stemming from emic perspective–oriented ethnographic data gathering. It also stressed the validity of cultural relativism, which was the notion that, any assessment of a culture warrants only its own standards.

- Structural functionalism concentrated on the salience of social phenomena as they functioned to ensure the structural continuity and the well-being of a specific culture's systemic whole.

- French structuralism was a theory recognizing the mental structure that strengthens sociocultural behavior universally. As its main proponents, Levi-Strauss strove to show the relationship between culture and cognition through his structural analyses of kinship and myth.

- According to neo-evolutionary theorists, the driving force of evolution had been a specific cultural system's growing ability to capture energy or their advancing levels of technology, or both.

- Assuming cultural evolution as a multilinear process, proponents of cultural ecology focused on the interaction between a culture and its environment.

- Cultural materialism was a theoretical construct embracing the evolutionary approaches to culture while trying to situate them within an expansive framework of Marxian materialist orientation concurrently.

- The ways with which human beings used symbols and related processes to draw life guidance, order, and coherence were the focus of symbolic anthropology. Interpretive anthropology conceptualized culture as a collection of meaningful texts that natives constantly have read or acted out; deciphering these multilayered, symbolic texts, according to interpretivists, was what ethnographers ought to have done.

- The use and the utility of culture as the core concept of anthropology faced increasing scrutiny along the themes of the politics of representation, power and cultural otherness, as well as the nexus between space, identity, and the production of cultural difference.

# CHAPTER 5

# Language: Encoding and Communicating about Experiential World

© Markus Mainka/Shutterstock.com

Human language is a pervasive and complex system of arbitrary vocal symbols involving combinatorial rules. It is with this system, human beings encode and communicate about their experiential world. More than anything else, it is the possession of language that differentiates humans from all other species.

Human propensity for language is biologically based. Whereas, humans basically being another ape, their expanded prefrontal cortex caused by anomalously large brain as well as their uniquely modified lungs, larynx, pharynx, glottis, vocal cords, mouth, lips, teeth, and nose, make them the only species who possess physical apparatus for spoken language. The lack of such structural changes has turned even their closest relatives among fellow primates such as chimpanzees and gorillas to creatures physically unequipped for speech.

Consequently, humans have become a new phylum (a major subdivision) of organisms in their intelligence ability.

## Human versus Nonhuman Communication

Still, other species do communicate by using a variety of methods, including body movement and motion, sound, and odor. For instance, a waggling dance of a honeybee inside the hive is to communicate to the other bees the direction, distance, and nature of its food source—it has kinetic, tactile, and chemical elements in it. Furthermore, some animals, such as cricket bugs, have auditory, but not vocal, methods of communication. In addition, recent researches on social interaction among nonhuman species have shown how various birds and social carnivores use a rich repertoire of vocal signals and gestures when structuring their extensive social groups.

The point is particularly true about social communication of primates. Based on their research findings, some primatologists and linguistic anthropologists in the last few decades have begun to question the long-held view that nonhuman primate communication behavior is limited to a set of instinctive reflexes or fixed patterns of action. In 1960s, researchers abandoned the doomed project of attempting to teach spoken language to apes and monkeys. Instead, they started to focus on the possibility of using American Sign Language (ASL) of the deaf to communicate chimpanzees, gorillas, and orangutans rose in home-like environments. This latter project was met with some modest, albeit significant success. Female chimpanzees named Washoe (Gardner and Gardner, and Van Cantfort, eds. 1989; Gordon 2004) and Lucy

© Hanna Podobrii/Shutterstock.com

(Carter 1982), a male chimpanzee named Nim Chimpsky (Hess 2008), as well as a gorilla named Koko (Patterson 1978) were among the apes on which these researches were conducted. Additionally, a chimpanzee named Lana was taught to use geometric figure symbols known as lexigrams to communicate (Rambaugh 1977). Furthermore, another female chimp named Sarah was taught to form simple sentences by using color plastic disks, and a bonobo named Kanzi was taught by the researchers to use lexigrams, geometric word symbols, and graphics (Gordon 2004). More to the point, the first ever long-term study of the language ability of an orangutan was conducted over the orangutan named Chantek (Miles 1993). Some of such study projects are still proceeding in earnest.

The findings of these researches suggest, in the absence of spoken language, nonhuman primates were still able to effectively use several design features of language such as cultural transmission, productivity, and displacement (discussed later) which up to this time, linguists thought that only humans were capable of using (Goodall 1986). However, critics argue that claims for language acquisition by monkeys and apes via either ASL or symbols are largely overstatements based on skimpy data (Terrace 1987; Pinker 2000).

Whereas nonhuman primates' communicative behavior is highly complex and sophisticated, it still remains true that human language is truly distinctive, and finding corresponding elements in animal communication that map onto the elements of human language is exceedingly difficult. The spoken and symbolic qualities of human language afford ample opportunity for humans to articulate and communicate an endless variety of meanings. By contrast, even the most complex instinctive sounds or *call systems* of nonhuman primates are restricted to a fixed number of isolated signals occurring in fixed sequences or in relatively unorganized combinations. Moreover, they are generally produced in response to specific environmental stimuli.

The aforementioned researches and the subsequent debates on them have been highlighting some of the long-standing questions on the origins, as well as the nature of human language and consciousness. What was later to become one of the most influential linguistic paradigms in this regard was originally proposed by MIT linguist Noam Chomsky (1975). Elaborating his notion of universal grammar (UG), Chomsky maintained that all humans are genetically endowed for language structure. Observing a human baby's acquisition of

language ability and a kitten's inability to gain possession of similar skills, Chomsky contended that humans are born with innate attributes for gaining language—they are equipped with a special language organ or the language acquisition device (LAD). Steven Pinker, an MIT colleague of Chomsky, recently articulated many of Chomsky's original insights and argued cogently that what allows human infants to acquire and reproduce language in their own is the existence of an "innate grammatical machinery of the brain." Language, Pinker contends, is a human instinct that

© orhan akkurt/Shutterstock.com

could have evolved into what it is today through the evolutionary actions of natural selection (Pinker 2000).

Biological researchers in England have pointed out the existence of a strong link between a muted gene identified as FOXP2 and human acquisition and utilization of language (Trivedi 2001; Dominguez and Rakic 2009). They seem to reinforce the notion that the linguistic abilities of human species, as well as the urge for speech evident in human behavior have a genetic basis.

Nevertheless, one of the most serious challenges to the notion that holds the existence of innate human language acquisition ability comes from a neurologist-cum-biological anthropologist serving at Harvard Medical School named Terrance Deacon (Also discussed in Chapter 3). Deacon is equally critical on the popular neuroscience positions that treat the brain as no more or less than a computer as well as the positions that reduce language simply into a mode of communication. Drawing from his research from neuroscience, and blending a knowledge of anthropology, linguistics, and philosophy, Deacon maintains that what differentiates *Homo sapiens* from all other species is their unique mode of thought which he dubs as *symbolic representation*. Language, according to Deacon, is only the outward manifestation of this novel mode of thinking. The symbolic mode of thought, writes Deacon, is the defining feature of language, and it is "an evolutionary anomaly." Even more importantly, it is the symbolic mode of thought that makes humans the *symbolic species*, the species that are capable of linking things that might only infrequently have a physical correlation. Deacon contends that, driven by human reproduction demands, human brain and human language have coevolved over millions of years (Deacon 1997).

# Nonverbal Forms of Communication

Communication, the process through which humans send and receive meaningful messages is hardly limited to spoken and/or written language. Humans also communicate with each other by using a wide variety of nonverbal forms. They range from haptics, artifacts, kinesics, vocalics, and chronemics to proxemics.

---

**TABLE 5.1   Nonverbal Forms of Communication**

Haptics (use of touch in communication)
Artifacts (appearance and adornment cues)
Kinesics Cues (forms of nonverbal communication based on body language)
Gestures (movements of the body-based communication)
Greetings (notable routines used in social encounters)
Sign Language (forms of nonverbal communication based on deliberate hand movements)
Vocalics (use of sound and silence in communication)
Chronemics and Proxemics (perception and uses of time and space)

---

Source: Gajaba Naraddage

In general, the meanings of nonverbal forms do not stem entirely from the actions themselves, just like the meanings of words do not necessarily flow from the specific sounds with which they are formed. Primatologists such as Alison Jolly have long suggested that human nonverbal communication behavior, also observable among monkeys and apes, has its roots in humans' primate heritage (Jolly 1972). Notwithstanding their biological basis, humans learn to use nonverbal codes of communication primarily through enculturation. Therefore, whereas some nonverbal cues may be conveying nearly universal meanings to the members of myriad cultures around the world, a plenty of others may be carrying specific cultural meanings decipherable and meaningful only to the members of particular cultures. As much as variation in the interpretation of nonverbal forms among different cultures is tremendously high, nonverbal behavior can cause misunderstanding, embarrassment, and frustration in intercultural encounters. Regardless, nonverbal behavior remains one of the most irreplaceable components of human communication.

## Haptics

**Haptics** refers to the study of the ways with which humans use touch in communication. Hugging, kissing, embracing, touching, tickling, slapping, punching, stroking, patting on the head or back, laying-on of hands, and shaking hands are among some of the most widely noticeable and intimately recognizable contact codes in interpersonal as well as intercultural communication. Every culture recurrently defines and decodes the repertoire of meanings and nuances attached to touching while addressing the questions such as: who can touch whom, what part(s) of the body, how frequently, and under what conditions. Inadvertence to such cultural meanings oftentimes leads to scandalous, if also hilarious, situations.

The following are just a few high-profile examples to the point reported by the international press recently: In April 2007, a nationwide furor began when Hollywood actor Richard Gere embraced Bollywood actress Shilpa Shetty, bent her back in an exaggerated kind of dance hold, and kissed her on the cheek and the neck at a televised fund-raising event for AIDS-awareness in New Delhi, India. Hindu nationalists reportedly have burned effigies of Gere in public while also denouncing Shetty for dishonoring her culture.

In the same vein, in March 2013, Mahmoud Ahmadinejad, President of Islamic Republic of Iran was criticized by the Iranian press for hugging the grieving mother of Venezuelan President Hugo Chavez as a gesture of consolation at Chavez's funeral. According to Iranian clerics who were reportedly outraged by the televised event, touching a woman who was not a close relative (a *nonmahram*) was forbidden under any circumstances, whether shaking hands or touching by the cheek and Ahmadinejad disrespected this Islamic (*sharia*) rule, and by so doing, dishonored his nation.

Likewise, in April 2013, Microsoft founder Bill Gates was slapped by the South Korean press for shaking hands with South Korea's President Ms. Park Geun-hye using one hand with the other tucked in the pant pocket. Gate's casual greeting gesture was denounced as rude, and grossly unmindful of Korean culture and its traditions.

Differences in touching behavior between various cultures frequently observable in public places have led some researchers to classify them as distinct characteristics between what they call *high-touch* (*contact*) and *low-touch* (*noncontact*) cultures (Hall 1966; Montagu 1978; Mehrabian 1981; Kottak 2008). Accordingly, cultures in the Middle East, South Asia, Eastern Europe, and Latin America are generally considered as high-touch cultures while those of northern Europe, North America, and East Asia are regarded as low-touch. However, critiques have pointed out the simplistic nature of the above dichotomy as it does not take into account the other salient factors, such as the links between communication and power (Leathers 1997, 126).

## Artifacts

In the context of nonverbal communication, **artifacts,** sometimes also referred to as *appearance and adornment cues*, are consisted of the whole host of accessories such as clothes, jewelry, shoes, handbags, scarves, hats, and sun glasses, as well as body modifications like piercing, hairstyles, tattoos, and odors. Metaphorically, body modifications are cultural inscriptions on the immensely rich and intricate text of communication, which is, the human body.

Religious dignitaries, political leaders, and pop-cultural icons around the world have been famous for their use of artifacts to convey public messages effectively. For example, when attending services, the pope wears a cassock made out of watered silk. His house-dress which is worn for daily and ordinary affairs has been a cassock with shoulder caps attached to it. All pontiffs of the modern era have also customarily worn the full regalia of the papacy for liturgical functions and formal occasions. Among them, the Triple Crown, the Ring of the Fisherman, the Papal Cross, and the Portable Throne have been the most prominent. The pontiffs also have oftentimes seen carrying papal insignia such as the image of two-crossed keys. The papal attire, regalia, and insignia have largely helped the pontiffs to inculcate an aura of solemnity and respectability for the papal office.

© thaagoon/Shutterstock.com

Mahatma Gandhi, the glasses wearing, shaven-headed, and brown-skinned man who fought for India's independence through nonviolence and passive resistance, conveyed two powerful messages through his dress, a loincloth worn by male practitioners of Hindu faith (*dhothi*). First, by dressing in an incompatible way to Anglo dressing habits Gandhi delivered the politically charged symbolic message: his nonconformity and resistance to the British Raj. Second, by choosing the *dhothi* as his dress he conveyed to the masses of India a populist symbolic message: his feeling of the people's pulse and admiration of their rustic way of life.

© Arthur Simoes/Shutterstock.com

Charlie Chaplin, best remembered for his work in the early days of the silent cinema, was well known for his use of accessories to express feelings and convey meanings. The attire of the famous Tramp character he introduced in 1914 was consisted of a bowler hat, a single-breasted black suit (often accompanied by a waistcoat), a white shirt with a wing collar, a black tie, and the cane, and that dress was essential to the Tramp's comedic performance, as well as to the satirically disguised social critique this vagrant character delivered.

The adoration and the use of fashion clothes, jewelry, scents, tattoos, hairdos, and stage props by more recent performing artists like Michael Jackson, Madonna, Britney Spears, and Lady Gaga have been instrumental for their fame to the same extent their singing and dancing skills have been contributing to their success. For instance, Jackson's meticulously crafted, stage costumes—the zipper-covered jacket, the military-inspired coats with their epaulets, crests, insignia, the glittery glove, and the fitting pants made of stretchy fabrics—were equally responsible for his rise to mega stardom, just as his singing skills and dance moves were pivotal for his success as a songster-cum-performer.

© Jaguar PS/Shutterstock.com

In a society known for stratification, what people wear, how people wear, and even what people carry may provide vital clues as to who they actually are; the above accessories and adornment cues become salient identity markers about ethnic and regional heritage, gender, age, and religious affiliation, in addition to socioeconomic status or class basis of the individuals. They help a person know about whom she/he is dealing with immediately, and based on that perception, to temper his/her level of formal and informal language and mode of interaction. This was what anthropologist Laura T. Gonzalez observed in her recent ethnographic excursion to Mumbai, an Indian metropolis. According to Gonzalez, by just focusing on the garments alone usually worn by Mumbai women, such as the sari, a long piece of colorful fabric elaborately draped around the body with one end draped over the head or over one shoulder, the *salwar kameez*, a long tunic worn over a pair of baggy trousers, or the scarves and face coverings such as the *hijab* and the *burka*, one can read so much about their lives, including history, beliefs, social roles, and cultural restrictions. Moreover, what is worn by men and children in Mumbai are equally important as identity markers, Gonzalez indicates (Gonzalez 2013).

However, recent ethnographies dealing with accessories of communication have also shown elements of strategic accommodation, nonconformity, and resistance. For instance, there are evidences as to the links between hegemonic relations and particular forms of gender resistance. On that point, exploring the puzzling adoption of veiling or head covering practices, considered as a traditional symbol of female subordination, by the lower middle class working women in contemporary Cairo, Egypt, anthropologist Arlene E. Macleod finds that veiling is a symbolic expression of such women's dilemma: working outside the home obviously brings material benefits, but it also creates an atmosphere in which a significant erosion of social status and traditional identity they would otherwise enjoy as home makers take place. Macleod contends that, within this ambivalent context, the new veiling has become a new style of political struggle involving elements of both acquiescence and resistance simultaneously. She characterizes it as an instance of "accommodating protest" (Macleod 1991).

Ethnographic studies on recently emerged youth subcultures in Tokyo, Japan, also indicate that, in the hand of cultural actors, accessories and adornment cues are neither merely conforming to existing social roles and cultural rules, nor are they simply following fashion trend. The Kogal subculture studied by linguistic anthropologist Laura Miller is a case in point. According to Miller, young Japanese women known as *Kogyaru* (young gals) who stomp on Tokyo's fashion centers such as Shibuya and Harajuku challenge dominant models of gendered behavior and language by fostering distinctly innovative cultural and linguistic behavior. By rebelling against the meek and quiet schoolgirl image of the typical Japanese girl, the Kogals wear a modified Japanese schoolgirl outfit with a shortened skirt, loose socks, and occasional platform shoes. Similarly, by getting super tan and bleaching their hair honey-brown or blonde, the Kogals attempt to appear in sharp contrast to the light skin tone and dark hair color of a typical Japanese person. The *Gonguro*, a subgroup of the Kogals, tries to appear even darker than the average Kogal tan. All different types of Kogals are also heavy users of sticker-pasted cell phones. In addition to the use of such accessories and adornment cues to make they appear scandalously different from the mainstream Japanese individuals, the Kogals draw from a variety of linguistic resources—English loanwords, slang, mathematical symbols, Cyrillic letters, and emoticons (emotional icons for messaging) or smileys—to make their language appear distinct from usual Japanese. In their ongoing struggle over female self-determination and autonomy, concludes Miller, the Kogal girls attempt to construct female-centered subcultural identities (Miller 2004, 225–47).

## Kinesics Cues

If artifacts are primarily identity markers, **kinesics cues** or the forms of nonverbal communication based on body language are primarily the markers of emotions and feelings that convey powerful meanings. The analytical study of body language signals, both intended and subconscious, is known as kinesics. As noted earlier, figuratively, human body is a text that can be read. When communicating verbal messages, people also constantly "read" the bodies of each other as they may provide vital clues to emotions, attitudes, and the state of the mind of the interlocutors. These kinesics cues may range from gestures, greetings, hand movements, arm movements, eye contacts, facial expressions, style of walking to the ways of standing and sitting. Certain body language signals are recognized almost universally. For instance, people know that fellow humans smile/laugh when they are happy and cry when they are sad regardless of their social, cultural, or geographical origin. Likewise, they read body language clues pertaining to emotions such as amusement, contempt, contentment, embarrassment, excitement, guilt, pride, relief, satisfaction, sensory pleasure, and shame, on most occasions, with a fair amount of accuracy. Humans convey and interpret such body language messages with relative ease, and in most cases, almost subconsciously.

However, kinesics cues may also impart complex and contextual messages that can be read and interpreted in multiple ways. As anthropologist Clifford Geertz once famously pointed out when referring to the many layers of an ethnographic narrative, whereas the acts of blinking and winking maybe almost identical as kinesics signals, the wink conveys an array of contextual meanings—ranging from a conspiratorial signal, and a coded message, to a mock message to someone by someone about an earlier blink by someone else—far richer than what the blink, the bland involuntary twitch, expresses (Geertz 1973).

© Roman Samborskyi/Shutterstock.com

In other words, signals of body language may deliver many and distinct messages in accordance with their linguistic context. For example, the kinesics signal of yawning can be an indication of sleepiness; yet, it may also be an instance of showing lack of interest over the matters being discussed, or even on the act of discussion itself; even more so, it may be signaling that a change of the topic is anticipated and desired.

## Gestures

In much the same way, different cultural actors act and react according to their culture-bound perceptions of and interpretations for various body language forms. This point which shows the way culture evolves with biology simultaneously can be further elaborated by focusing on **gestures** or the movements of the body (including movements of head, arms, hands, and face) with which myriad culture-specific meanings, including ideas, opinions, and emotions are expressed. Certain cultures have highly developed and intricate gesture systems, whose meanings are not immediately known to or deciphered by cultural outsiders. Hand and eye movements in Hindu and Buddhist traditions of iconography are a fine example to the point (Eck 1981; Schroeder 1990, 2008). Hand and eye movements in South and East Asian choreographic traditions (seen in dance-dramas such as *Bharatha Natyam*, *Kathak*, *Kathakali*, and *Manipuri* traditions in India, *Noh*, *Kabuki* theater and *Bunraku* puppet theater traditions in Japan, and Beijing Opera tradition in China) are also treatable as profound examples in this respect (Ghosh [1950] 2002; Brazell 1998; Wichmann 1990).

© jai7678/Shutterstock.com

# Greetings

In addition to cultural specificity, there are other salient factors influencing body language. For example, **greetings,** one of the first and notable routines humans everywhere perform in social encounters by combining speech and nonverbal communication features such as gestures, tend to convey meanings which are situationally dependent. While meaning variation is frequently caused by cultural particularity, it is also due to contextual factors such as the degree of formality or informality, and social factors such as gender, class, age, race, and ethnicity.

While certain kinesics signals happen on a conscious level, some others occur almost entirely on a subconscious level. For instance, human gestures such as head or ear scratching, eye rubbing, chin resting, lip touching, nose itching, arms crossing, and finger locking are mostly unintentional bodily clues that nevertheless convey meaningful contextual messages to interlocutors.

© Ochivis Pictures/Shutterstock.com

## Sign Language

Unlike such subconscious body language cues, **sign language,** the form of nonverbal communication primarily based on deliberate hand movements, has to be learned. Many varieties of sign language are in existence in the world today, including American, British,

Japanese, and Russian sign languages. For deaf and mute people, its main users, sign language is the primary means for communication. However, for some others like indigenous Australians, it is a reliable alternative to verbal communication. Indigenous Australian Sign Language is a different kettle of fish being a sign language used by people who are fully capable of communicating verbally. Indigenous Australians turn to sign language when verbal communication is undesirable in occasions such as hunting trips. They prefer to use sign language when speech is not socially sanctioned or appropriate as well. For example, on occasions of mourning by widows, and in ritualistic events considered as sacred, indigenous Australians communicate through their sign language (Kendon 1988).

© adriatricfoto/Shutterstock.com

## Vocalics

**Vocalics** refer to the uses of sound and silence in communication. **Sound** is a vocalics feature used by humans in combination of spoken language and kinesics cues or alone to express emotions, convey impressions, construct links, pass judgments, as well as to make others convinced or deceived. Human verbal communication is strikingly different from instinctive sounds or *call systems* of monkeys and apes. Still, when evolving as a species dependent on an intricate system of signs and symbols for communication, humans have retained a set of distinct sounds or calls with which some sort of physical and emotional state can be conveyed. This set includes laughing, sobbing, crying, screaming, groaning, and sighing. The contribution of sound to human communication is amply evident in the use of **paralanguage** or voice effects that accompany utterances. Paralanguage relies on *prosody* or voice qualities such as pitch, volume, tempo, and rhythm in speech, as well as vocalizations to modify or nuance meaning and express emotions. Linguists understand *"how"* it was said" is equally or even more significant than *"what* was said" because much besides the message's structure and content is associated with paralanguage.

Recent researchers have shown how people use sound to convey, among other meanings, seduction, (Farinelli in Guerrero and Hecht 2008) and vocal attractiveness (Semic in Guerrero and Hecht 2008).

Equally powerful feature of vocalics is **silence,** a form of nonverbal communication with its own specific cultural values and meanings. Linguistic anthropologist Keith Basso's classic study of Western Apache of Arizona reveals how Anglo-Americans have oftentimes misread silence, a preeminent feature present in many Native American cultures as deficiency or absence of intelligence, emotion, and estimableness. Basso contrasts such Anglo-American misinterpretations of Apache silence with equally caricaturized portrayals of Anglo-Americans *by* Western Apache *for* Western Apache. Accordingly, "the Whiteman" is recurrently presented in Apache households as a "loud-talking, overbearing, self-righteous, and unswervingly presumptuous bumbler" (Basso 1972, 45–47, 61).

Silence and its association with power in the context of the U. S. courtrooms is a subject studied by linguistic anthropologist Robin Lakoff (1990). She observes that the lawyers, some of the notable and frequent speakers in courtrooms, hold considerably less power than the judges. Furthermore, the judges who prefer to speak occasionally assume less power than the jurors who remain silent throughout the court proceedings. "Talking power" in this sense is present in silence, Lakoff points out (Lakoff 1990).

## Chronemics and Proxemics

**Chronemics** and **proxemics** refer to the perception and uses of time and space by humans as species accustomed to learned behavior. These are equally significant nonverbal communication forms across cultures. Writing in 1959 in his work entitled *Silent Language*, linguistic anthropologist Edward T. Hall stressed time and space as two of the most pivotal elements in intercultural communication. According to Hall, "time talks" just as "space speaks" (Hall 2013 [1959]).

Edward Hall classified cultures either as *monochronic* or *polychronic* based on their perception and uses of time while stressing the impact that can have on communication. According to Hall, monochronic cultures such as the United States, Canada, and the countries of Northern Europe, tend to perceive time as something tangible and orderly; hence, time can be scheduled, segmented, arranged, and managed. By contrast, polychronic cultures existing in countries of Sub-Saharan Africa, the Middle East, Indian subcontinent, and Latin America, tend to treat time as fluid, process-based, and deeply embedded in tradition and relationships.

By focusing on the way people of different cultural backgrounds define and organize social space through their own conceptual models, Edward Hall also identified four

© Sergey Nivens/Shutterstock.com

proxemically relevant categories of social spaces. Accordingly, *intimate* space may occupy one to twelve inches. *Personal* space individuals' use for casual purposes has a distance of one-and a half to four feet. What may be called *social* space contains four to twelve feet. Finally, *public* space may begin from a distance of twelve feet and extend beyond.

Whereas Edward Hall's study is currently recognized as a cornerstone research in the sphere of interpersonal, intercultural, and nonverbal communication, it does not address adequately the issues stemming from intracultural variability, gender, race, as well as power relations.

# Design Features of Language

American anthropological linguist Charles F. Hockett identified a number of *design features* existing in all human languages. Whereas some characteristics of human communication have been observable among nonhuman primates in their rudimentary capacity, there have been some design features that, according to Hockett, made human language distinguishable from all other forms of animal communication (Hockett 1963).

## Cultural Transmission through Learning

**Cultural transmission through learning** rather than through experience alone is one of such design features that makes human communication distinctive. Although the ability to acquire language is biological, languages are not passed from one generation to the next genetically. They are transmitted through the broad process of learning and sharing known as *enculturation* (discussed in Chapter 3). Adult members of specific linguistic communities advise and instruct the young by using their stored-up life recollections and encounters. Children gain most of their cultural knowledge and skills through listening to adults and sharing them with peers. In the process, they accustom themselves to their parents' life ways while becoming native to the language of their parents simultaneously. In other words, language learning occurs in social and cultural groups, not in the process of passing genetic traits. The language instinct of children to acquire the language of the specific groups into which they are enculturated is a universally recognizable phenomenon. Therefore, infants born to parents speaking one language and rose under the guidance of foster parents speaking another do not show any predisposition for the language of their biological parents.

© Paya Mona/Shutterstock.com

The centrality of enculturation in language learning is directly related to the fact that language is an intricate system of symbols and language-based communication (imparting and interchange of thoughts, opinions, or information by speech, writing, or signs) is a symbolic act. The words exist as symbols signifying things, actions, and ideas, since specific linguistic communities agree that they do. Therefore, the transmission of language conventions through enculturation, for the most part, is imperative for human communication.

## Arbitrariness

Symbolic nature of human language is also linked to another salient design feature: **arbitrariness.** It highlights that there is no intrinsic relationship between the sounds associated with the word and the physical object, action, or idea that the word signifies. The semantic link between the word and what it refers to is not iconic. Even the words treated as mimicries of specific noises such as splash, bang, boom, screech, buzz, rattle, meow, and bow-wow are not more than stylistic approximations of their original noises. In every language, linguistic symbols and what they represent maintain an arbitrary, yet culturally agreed on association. That is why languages around the globe have a variety of linguistic symbols to signify the same thing. For example, there is no reason as to why a large, grass-eating, four-legged, domesticated, and milk-giving bovine creature should be associated with *cow* in English, *vaca* in Spanish, *baqarah* in Arabic, *ushi* in Japanese or *gai* in Hindi. However, this arbitrary symbolic association makes perfect sense to each of the relevant linguistic community.

## Duality of Patterning

**Duality of patterning** is another attribute unique to human language. It refers to the fact that language has the capability of producing and transmitting an infinite number of units of meaning by combining a finite number of meaningless sound units in specific orders. Charles Hockett observed that language was patterned on two distinct levels: sound and meaning. A small number of "minimum meaningless but message-differentiating" sound units known as phonemes are strung together in various combinations to generate an endless variety of "minimum semantically functional" elements (Hockett 1963, 9) known as morphemes (discussed in the next section). They also proceed to form larger meaningful units such as words, phrases, sentences, and discourses. Communication systems of other species which are made up of strings of individual signals do not show any significant duality. Contemporary linguists recognize that human language in fact has multilevel patterning (Wallman 1992).

## Openness

Likewise, language makes it possible to blend, analogize with, and transform previous linguistic messages to generate inexhaustible amount of novel and creative expressions which are meaningful and comprehensible to the other speakers of the same language. The members of any given linguistic community are capable of creating new linguistic messages and understanding messages created by other members with remarkable ease and comfort, in addition to making sense of the same thing in multiple perspectives. This design feature, known as **openness,** was stressed by linguist Noam Chomsky as well.

## Semanticity

**Semanticity,** another distinctive design feature, refers to associative links between linguistic signals and features in the physical and sociocultural world of a linguistic community. Linguistic descriptions, although somewhat arbitrary and selective, have denotations, nevertheless. These denotations elicit explicit or primary meanings of reality for speakers of a language, which they, in turn, use to signify and comprehend aspects and processes of their world. For instance, the term "wind" denotes air in natural motion, and this associative link is commonly shared by speakers of English.

## Displacement

Unlike nonhuman forms of communication, human language makes known about things, people, or beings that are not physically present and events that are not happening at the moments of interactive engagement. In addition, it can refer to people, beings, events, and issues existing only in the figments of human imagination. As the symbolic process that underlies language allows humans to store and transmit information, their linguistic messages are capable of transcending or displacing spatial and temporal realms in communicative behavior. This characteristic is referred to as **displacement.** Probably language emerged to fulfill human ancestors' necessity as social hunter-gatherers to contemplate retrospectively and to use past recollections as guidance in strategizing present activities and future plans. Displacement became an indispensable language feature in accomplishing the above tasks.

## Prevarication

Language also allows people to make statements that deviate from or pervert truths. Known as **prevarication,** this design feature provides the means to equivocal utterances ranging from trivial lies, intentionally vague and ambiguous statements to deliberate fabrications. It indicates the ability to see events from the perspective of the other person and the skills to negate that perception by knowingly misrepresenting reality. Contrary to overwhelming evidence existing on equivocal utterances in human language, prevarication seems to be rare among the communication systems of other species. However, recent studies have revealed that

© icedmocha/Shutterstock.com

© irawlinson/Shutterstock.com

nonhuman primates possess rudimentary capacity for lying (Fouts 1997; Miles 1993). Hockett indicated that prevarication was rested on several other design features, namely semanticity, displacement, and openness: semanticity made a linguistic message meaningful and valid; displacement made the immediate context of the linguistic message insignificant, so a lie became a possibility; openness made meaningless messages feasible (Hockett 1963, 10).

Prevarication makes it possible for humans to exchange syntactically sound but semantically nonsensical linguistic messages (Chomsky 1957, 15). Chomsky famously illustrated this point by composing the sentence "Colorless green ideas sleep furiously." This statement, although grammatically correct, makes no sense semantically: by not being objects, "ideas" cannot be "green"; "green" things cannot be "colorless"; "ideas" are inanimate subjects so they cannot "sleep"; no one can "sleep" "furiously," either.

American linguist William D. Lutz, in a paper entitled *Language, Appearance, and Reality* (1987) cited examples for the pervasive use of language to deliberately mislead others in the domains of business, politics, and military. According to Lutz, this practice, known as **doublespeak,** was ranging from euphemism, jargon, gobbledygook or bureaucratese, to inflated language: euphemistic utterances was used to avoid distasteful reality, to mislead, and to deceive linguistic audience; jargon was used to make certain that people outside the group did not understand what was communicated; gobbledygook was to overwhelm the audience with words; and inflated language was designed to misrepresent reality.

In recent decades, some researchers (anthropological linguists, gerontologists, psychologists, and epidemiologists) were also focusing on the form of speech in English

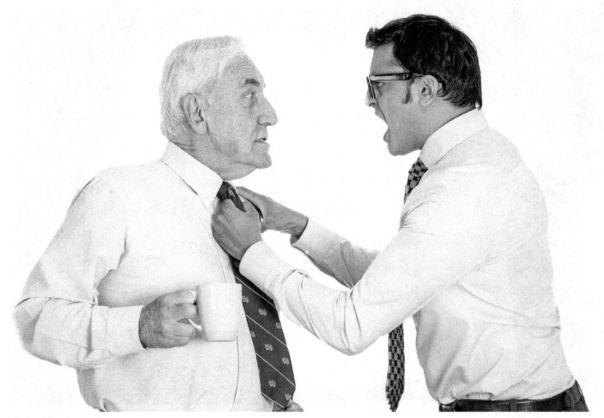

language known as **elderspeak.** These researchers found that elderspeak often used by medical professionals and caregivers when talking to their elderly patients was graceful and supportive at first glance. However, it was a form of English speech deeply reflective of society's negative attitudes toward the elderly and aging. Indeed, elderspeak was seen by most of the older people as a demeaning, patronizing, and condescending practice. Notwithstanding its well intentions, elderspeak has contributed to the proliferation of negative images of aging (Ferraro and Andretta 2012, 121; Kemper and Harden 1999; Levy 2002).

# Structural Elements of Language

According to *Ethnologue,* a comprehensive online database of language resources, even after several centuries of steady decline during the course of the modern era, there still exists roughly over 6, 900 spoken languages in the world (Lewis 2009). Distinct in linguistic characteristics and rich in cultural resources, many of these languages are mutually unintelligible. As such, they have become living proofs to the vast range and repertoire of human linguistic and cultural diversity. Despite enormous differences however, all languages commonly hold a logical structure, a specific arrangement that keeps its constituents connected. **Structural linguistics,** sometimes referred to as *descriptive linguistics,* focuses on unraveling the structural elements of language and the ways with which they make language functional. Structural linguistics studies the structure of language while paying special attention to four interrelated areas of analysis: phonology, morphology, syntax, and semantics.

The first initiative in studying a particular language begins with the isolation and description of its distinctive speech sounds, known as the phonetic inventory. As already mentioned, humans are the only living species physically equipped to talk. Consequently, they have the ability to produce and hear an inordinately high number of distinctive speech sounds. However, no living language has the entire range of sounds that the human vocal apparatus can produce. Instead, every language has a restricted series of speech sounds that it organizes according to combinatory rules to convey meanings.

## Phonology

**Phonology** is the area in linguistics that studies speech sound systems in languages, including phonetics and phonemics. *Phonetics* deals with the ways with which speech sounds are produced, combined, and represented by written symbols in general. *Phonemics* concentrates solely on phonemes of a language. **Phoneme** is a minimal, meaningless, and distinctive unit of speech sound—a sound contrast—that differentiates meaning in a specific spoken language. The number of phonemes in specific languages varies from about fifteen to one hundred and fifty. English has about forty to forty-six phonemes, depending on the way they are counted; these numbers include twenty-four consonants, nine vowels, and three semi vowels. Note that correspondence of phonemes and the twenty-six letters in English alphabet is not consistent. This inconsistency is caused by a number of reasons, and the following are some of them: firstly, different spellings are occasionally used to construct certain words giving many distinctive sounds—for example, in the words *apple, want, woman,* and *father* the letter *a* is pronounced differently; secondly, certain sounds like long *e* can be spelled in many ways as shown in the words of *meet* and *meat;* thirdly, in certain cases, two letters together produce just one sound as seen in the words *pneumonia,* **physics,** and **character;** fourthly, in some words such as *autumn, lamb,* and *island,* certain letters are not pronounced; fifthly, sometimes, the words that have same spelling are pronounced differently as the pronunciation of the verb *read* in present and past tense. Linguists get the help of International Phonetic Alphabet (IPA), a standardized alphabetic system of phonetic notation, in order to resolve problems stemming from such inconsistencies, as well as to accurately pronounce all of the peculiar and identifiable sounds in a particular language.

The isolation and description of phonemes is usually done by conducting a *minimal pair* test. Two words that differ from each other in just one minimal distinguishable sound and convey different meanings are considered as a minimal pair. For example, in the minimal pair *pin* and *pen,* meanings are different because /*i*/ is a different sound unit from the sound unit of /*e*/. Both of these minimal distinctive sound contrasts are, therefore, phonemes. Similarly, in the minimal pair *pit* and *bit,* the contrast between the sounds /*p*/ and /*b*/ distinguishes the two English words. Consequently, /*p*/ and /*b*/ sounds are phonemes. Note in both of the highlighted instances the minimal distinctive sound units (/*i*/ and /*e*/, and /*p*/ and /*b*/) do not carry meanings by themselves. Yet they are capable of indicating a difference in meaning. These are the rules observed in English for grouping sounds into phonemes. Accordingly, they are applicable to any minimal pair as shown in the following examples:

/*l*/o/t/ and /*n*/o/t/

/*t*/i/p/ and /*d*/i/p/

/b/*a*/t/ and /b/*e*/t/

/l/*i*/t/ and /l/*e*/t/

/t/a/*p*/ and /t/a/*b*/

Different languages observe different rules when categorizing sounds into phonemes.

## Morphology

**Morphology** is the study of the forms in which sounds combine to form **morphemes,** the smallest units of sounds that carry meanings. Although morphemes are often thought of as words, they do not necessarily have to be words. There are certain words in which one finds only a single morpheme, as in the word *cat.* Yet, there are many other words in which one observes the existence of two or more morphemes, as in the words of *arts* (/art/s/) and *artists* (/art/ist/s/). The thought that the morphemes are equivalent to syllables is also incorrect. On the one hand, many single morpheme words contain two or more syllables. The words like *nanny, apple,* and *banana* fit to this category. On the other, single syllable words have two or more morphemes as in the words of /run/s/, /bark/ed/, and *cat*/s/.

Every morpheme must be either a base or an affix. A *base* is a morpheme from which a word gains its primary meaning. For example, the morpheme *cat,* which gives the meaning of a specific animal, is the base morpheme of the word *cats*. A base is a **free morpheme**—a morpheme that can operate independently. It can make a word without the help of another morpheme. Accordingly, *cat* is a free morpheme. An *affix* is a morpheme that can come either at the beginning (*prefix*) or the ending (*suffix*) of a base morpheme. Unless attached to base morpheme, affix morphemes do not generate any meaning. It is for this reason an affix is referred to as a **bound morpheme.** The point is highlighted in the following example, the word *inactivity*:

*in* ("not"; a prefix; a bound morpheme)

*act* (a verb; "to do"; a base; a free morpheme)

*ive* (turning a verb into an adjective; suffix; a bound morpheme)

*ity* ("the state of being"; turning an adjective into a noun; suffix; a bound morpheme)

As this example demonstrates, the word *inactivity* (/in/act/ive/ity/) is a combination of a prefix (*in*), a base (*act*), and two suffixes (*ive* and *ity*). The base in this word is *act*. It is a morpheme capable of standing alone as a word. Hence, it is a free morpheme. By contrast, the affix morphemes of the word (*in*, *ive*, and *ity*) are incapable of generating meanings without their attachment to the base. Hence, they are bound morphemes.

## Syntax

As noted above in adequate detail, the study of phonological and morphological rules helps to understand how distinctive, meaningless, and minimal speech sound units are identifiable as phonemes; it also assists to learn how phonemes are strung together to form morphemes that give the words meanings. Comprehending these basic building blocks of a language is vital, whereas unraveling a language also requires making sense of the way morphemes are arranged into phrases and sentences to convey linguistic messages. Although they differ in form, all languages have rules by which words are structured to make phrases and sentences meaningful. These rules are referred to as **syntax.**

Some languages have sentence structure in which nouns precede verbs, and verbs precede object; in other languages the verb precede nouns. Still other languages observe the syntax rule that nouns and objects come before verbs. In English, for example, verbs are placed after nouns; adjectives generally appear before nouns as well. Consequently, English speakers know at once that Noam Chomsky's oft-cited statement "Colorless green ideas sleep furiously" is syntactically correct, although it sounds nonsensical. According to Chomsky, linguistic analysis should begin with syntax since, regardless of differences, all languages commonly hold the abstract rules governing the word order and actual syntax of any particular language, Chomsky maintains, stems from the aforementioned basic generic structure, which he dubbed as *UG* (discussed earlier).

## Semantics

Linguists such as Chomsky have been equally mindful of the way grammatical rules in every language deal with meaning. Known in linguistics as **semantics,** the study of meaning concentrates on the nexus of signifiers (words, phrases, signs, and symbols) and what they denote for most speakers of a language. Semanticists believe that once the meaning components of the words are specified, the way they behave in a sentence can be verifiable. Accordingly, kinds of verbs need particular kinds of subjects; for instance, an animate subject always cohabitates in a sentence with an animate verb. Motivated by this line of thought, and guided by Chomsky's model of UG, some linguists have attempted to isolate some contrasting units of meaning that they considered as universally recognizable. For example, linguists have identified that the following were among the contrasting meaning units of nouns: "animate" versus "inanimate," "human" versus "nonhuman," "countable" versus "uncountable," "male" versus "female," "adult" versus "non adult," and so on. They have dubbed these overlapping units of meaning contrasts as *universal semantics.*

The meaning of words, phrases, and sentences in specific cultural contexts is the focus of **ethnosemantics.**

# Language and History

**Historical linguistics** focuses on longer-term change in languages. Its analytical approach is both diachronic and comparative, as it may concentrate on studying incessantly changing language between successive points in time. Hence, its analysis is mostly **diachronic.** It may focus on investigating earlier and later forms of a single language to glean how change has occurred in that language, or a group of languages to understand their historical relationship. Comparison of earlier and later forms allows historical linguists to *reconstruct* how languages change over time. Hence, its analysis is also **comparative.**

# Language Family

Languages are sorted into possible groups by comparing sounds, vocabularies, and syntax of contemporary languages. Such methodical comparisons help historical linguists to reconstruct the process of change and to identify a common ancestral form or a **protolanguage** from which the compared group of languages have descended. Languages that have been changing divergently but have descended from the same protolanguage (*parent language*), are known as daughter languages. Hence, they are considered as the members of a **language family.** The use of family analogy for languages is as old as the study of historical linguistics. It began in earnest in the late eighteenth century with the English grammarian Sir William Jones' (1746–1794) suggestion that classical Greek and Latin might have descended from the same parent language from which Sanskrit, a classical Indian language, has diverged. All of the three daughter languages must have had a proto *Indo-European* ancestor, Jones pointed out. Since then, historical linguists have made significant progress in identifying the links among various languages. The larger Indo-European language family, under which several hundred related languages are classified, is consisted of the following subgroups: Albanian, Armenian, Baltic, Celtic, Germanic, Greek, Indo-Iranian, Italic, and Slavic (Lewis et al. 2013). Accordingly, the Germanic subgroup is the parent or mother language of English, Dutch, German, Flemish, Danish, Swedish, Norwegian, and Icelandic. All these Germanic daughter languages are, therefore, sister languages of each other.

The way people speak a language being one of the most noticeable features of any spoken language, historical linguists have been seeking to examine how **speech sounds** or the phonology of a language changes over time. For example, a massive shift that has taken place in vowel pronunciation during the fifteenth to eighteenth centuries in the English language, and its long-term implications have been studied. This process in which the long vowels gradually shifted upward is known as the **Great Vowel Shift** (GVS) (Dobson 1968; Baugh and Cable 1983).

In their effort to understand how languages change through time, historical linguists also look at **vocabulary,** another most conspicuous aspect of language. In this regard, one method takes the form of studying words for objects or ideas that are frequently used by many individuals across many contexts. These are also the words for which every language can be expected to have words for. Known as **core vocabulary,** this list of about 500 words consists of primary nouns (such as basic numerals, basic color taxonomy, and words for common anatomical features), pronouns, common adjectives, and primary verbs. Core vocabulary is helpful in identifying historical relationship among languages, determining the possible timeline in which they have diverged, and giving insights for reconstructing features of the parent language.

## Cognates

**Cognates** are the words in different languages identifiable as terms derived from the same word in their ancestral language. The literal meaning of cognates is "of the same stock," related, or kindred. Focusing on cognates is useful in identifying possible links and common features in between languages. The point can be illustrated by examining the English word "mother" and some of its equivalents in the *Indo-European Language Family*:

**Germanic**:
    **Germanic West:**
        English—"mother"
        Dutch—"moeder"
        German—"mutter"
    **Germanic North:**
        Icelandic—"modir"
        Danish—"moder" or "mor"
        Norwegian—"mor"
        Swedish—"mor"
**Balto-Slavic:**
    Lithuanian—"motina"
    Latvian—"mate"
    **Old Church Slavonic:**
        Russian—"mat" or "mama"
        Ukrainian—"maty"
        Polish—"matka"
        Czech/Slovak—"matka"

**Latin:**

>   Latin—"mater"
>   French—"mere"
>   Spanish—"madre"
>   Italian—"madre"
>   Portuguese—"mae"

**Celtic:**

>   Gaelic—"mathair"
>   Welsh—"mam"

**Classical Greek:**

>   Modern Greek—"mitera"

Albanian—"meme"

Armenian—"mayr"

**Indo-Iranian**

>   **Iranian**
>
>   >   Persian—"madar"
>   >   Kurdish—"mak"

**Sanskrit**

>   Sanskrit—"matr"
>   Hindi—"mata"
>   Panjabi—"maa"
>   Bengali—"maa"
>   Sinhala—"mava" or "amma"

## Loanwords

Historical linguists who study the process of language change and historical links in between languages have also been attentive to **loanwords,** the words "borrowed" or adopted by the speakers of one language from a different or source language. Borrowing, a result of cultural contact between two language communities is often an asymmetrical process. Adoption of loanwords does not always go in both directions as in the actual process of lending. For instance, when Germanic tribes were maintaining trading relationships with the Romans during the early centuries A.D., they were borrowing numerous loanwords from Latin, but only a handful of Germanic words were passed onto Latin in return.

The English language has been borrowing words from a variety of other languages just as many languages around the world have been incorporating English loanwords to their own lexicon. The point becomes conspicuously evident even when looking at some of the oft-used, food-related loanwords borrowed by English speakers from various source languages: "beef," "mutton," "pork," "salmon," and "veal" were adopted from French; "marijuana," "taco," and "tortilla" were adopted from Spanish, and "broccoli" and "macaroni" from Italian; "booze," "brandy" (wine), "cookie," and "waffle" have Dutch and Flemish origins; "noodle," "hamburger," "bundt" (cake) and "spritz" (cookies) have originated from German; "punch" (drink) was borrowed from Hindi, as well as "curry," and "mango" were adopted from Dravidian; "banana" (via Portuguese) and "yam" came

| TABLE 5.2 Some Food-Related English Loanwords | |
|---|---|
| **Source** | **Loanwords** |
| French | beef, mutton, pork, salmon, veal |
| Spanish | marijuana, taco, tortilla |
| Italian | broccoli, macaroni |
| Dutch/Flemish | booze, brandy, cookie, waffle |
| German | noodle, hamburger, bundt, spritz |
| Hindi | punch |
| Dravidian | curry, mango |
| Portuguese | banana |
| Chinese | tea |
| Japanese | soy, sushi |

Source: Gajaba Naraddage

from African languages; last but not least, English speakers adopted "tea" from Chinese while also borrowing "soy" and "sushi" from Japanese.

**Syntax** or grammatical structure of a language is also useful in comprehending the process of language change. For example, a comparison of old English with contemporary English is helpful to realize how word order has gradually become significant within sentences. In old English, just like in Latin, the ending of nouns showed whether they were subjects or objects. This factor made word order in old English relatively insignificant. Accordingly, "when he the king visited" would have been grammatically acceptable and conveyed the same message, just as "when he visited the king" would. Over many centuries of syntax, change has literally erased the above structural feature and that has made word order within a sentence pivotally relevant in contemporary English.

## Pidgin, Creole, and Lingua Franca

Manifold ways of culture contact in between speech communities such as trade, intermarriage, and warfare cause processes of language change paving the way for pidgin, lingua franca, and creole.

Commonly developed and employed as a means of communication between two or more groups of people (often trading partners) who do not have a language in common, **pidgin** is an elemental language with starkly simple syntactic

© Joanna K Drakos/Shutterstock.com

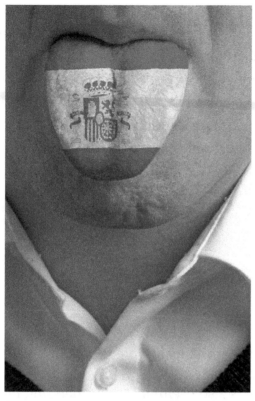

© vepar5/Shutterstock.com          © pjhpix/Shutterstock.com

rules and a limited lexicon. It may be constructed from phonetic and semantic elements, as well as from kinesics cues gleaned from a variety of other languages and cultures for the practical purpose of enabling different parties, who speak totally dissimilar languages to communicate with each other.

A pidginized language may become a **creole** language when it is nativized by offspring of pidgin users as their primary language. Although originated from a pidgin and its features drawn mainly from parent languages, a creole is a full-fledged and stable language with its own phonetic, semantic, and grammatical features.

**Lingua franca** is a common language used by various speech communities to communicate with each other. Unlike *vernacular languages* limited to their own speech communities, a lingua franca is a *vehicular* or *bridge language* that can penetrate the boundaries of myriad speech communities as a unifying second or third language to all of them. For example, English is the vernacular language in England, but it is one of the two vehicular languages or lingua francas in the Philippines. Filipino, the other lingua franca there, is used mostly to communicate across the country's linguistic groups. Likewise, India, a country with multiple vernacular languages, is known for using Hindi and English as bridge languages.

## Language and Culture

Linguist Noam Chomsky's contention that all humans are born with innate language acquisition abilities served as a significant reassurance for those linguists who primarily concentrated on linguistic code. Chomsky's influence in linguistics can be comparable to that of the early twentieth-century Swiss linguist Ferdinand de Saussure (1857–1913). Saussure distinguished *synchronic* linguistics (the study of language at a specific point in time) from *diachronic* approaches to language (the study of the history or evolution of language through reconstruction), known as *philological studies* at the time (Saussure [1916] 1966). As a consequence, scholars working on synchronic language studies came to be known as linguists. Saussure also differentiated between *langue*, the formal, grammatical system of language, and *parole*, actual speech. Langue, Saussure maintained, is a system of phonic elements whose links are governed by determinate rules. Much of linguistics since Saussure's time has been oriented to the finding and analysis of those rules. For example, following Saussure's lead, anthropologist Claude Levi-Strauss strove to demonstrate the links between the phonic elements of language, the elements of other cultural features such as kinship and myth, and the unconscious, logical structure of the mind (discussed in Chapter 4). Likewise, French scholar Roland Barthes (1915–1980) sought to extend Saussure's pioneering ideas on *semiotics* or the study of the "life of signs within society" (Saussure [1916] 1966) to every sphere of social life (Barthes 1968).

Chomsky's influence was equally phenomenal. His original insights on UG or meta-grammar into which all human languages fit and seen in the instance of children's acquisition of native language features in so little time and little effort, were championed by many of his followers. For example, Steven Pinker recently argued that human language instincts could have gradually evolved through the action of natural selection (discussed earlier). However, the far-reaching implication of Chomsky's position was that children require only learning certain parochial features of their native languages, and even much less learning of the native cultural features. Accordingly, linguists who focused solely on language structure began to treat culture's role in acquiring language during the process of human growth as secondary and less salient.

## The Sapir–Whorf Hypothesis

However, such stances also energized those linguists and linguistic anthropologists who remained convinced that language is a primary window through which a fuller view of culture can be gained. As early as in 1911, American anthropologist Franz Boas acknowledged the close link between language and culture when he pointed out that "a thorough insight into ethnology cannot be gained without a practical knowledge of the language," and when he mentioned that "the peculiar characteristics of language are clearly reflected in the views and customs of the peoples of the world" (Boas 1911, 73). Linguistic anthropologist Edward Sapir (1884–1939), one of Boas' students, espoused his mentor's position that each language has to be analyzed in terms of its own culture. Contrary to conventional view, contended Sapir, particular languages are not merely a medium of communication; rather, they are distinct structures that affect human experience through fashioning and guiding perception of experience. Writing in 1929, Sapir argued: "the worlds in which different societies live are distinct worlds, not merely the same world with different labels attached— We see and hear and otherwise experience very largely as we do because the language habits of our community predispose certain choices of interpretation" (Sapir 1929, 207). Accordingly, specific languages constitute distinct *thought worlds* that different speech communities inhabit. Whereas the people of the United States and Great Britain share the common language of English, pointed out Sapir, they do not share the same thought world as the geographical, political, and economic "determinants of the culture" are no longer the same (Sapir 1921, 214).

Sapir's own student linguistic anthropologist Benjamin L. Whorf (1897–1941) also saw language as a frame of reference that makes the worldview of a specific group of people orderly and unique. "The picture of the universe," wrote Whorf, "shifts from tongue to tongue" (cited in Hoebel 1958, 571). They both believed, by influencing the way people think and behave, language effectively shapes culture. This linguistic model which came to be known as the **Sapir–Whorf Hypothesis** or *the Whorfian Hypothesis* has been much discussed and debated. Its strong version, known as *linguistic determinism,* has been critiqued for its insistence on language's deterministic role in fashioning patterns of thought and behavior (Salzmann 2001). Its more benign version however, referred to as *linguistic relativity,* which argues for a mere influencing of linguistic choices and accompanying worldviews, has seen a recent resurgence in academic discourse.

According to the above early proponents (and the subsequent followers) of the hypothesis, the nexus of language and thought exists at the level of vocabulary, as well as grammar. Sapir pointed out that the way languages categorize or codify the experience of their speakers reflects the necessities, interests, concerns, and preoccupations of the community they

© Unai Huizi/Shutterstock.com

serve. Moreover, lexical encoding of experience serves as a guide to make the speakers more impressionable for the named features of their physical and social world. This is due to the fact, reasoned Sapir, that "objects or forces in the physical environment become labeled in language only if they have cultural significance" (Bonvillain 2003, 47).

As demonstrable proof for this thesis, Sapir presented his own English translations for an extensive list of environmental lexicalizations in the Paiute language, a language spoken by the Native American people bearing the same name and living in the semi-desert regions of the American Southwest. The list contains the terms for "divide, ledge, sand flat, semicircular valley, circular valley or hollow, spot of level ground in mountains surrounded by ridges, plain valley surrounded by mountain, plain, dessert, knoll, plateau, canyon without water, canyon with creek, wash or gutter, gulch, slope of mountain or canyon wall receiving sunlight, shaded slope of mountain or canyon wall, and rolling country intersected by several small hill ridges" (Sapir 1949 [1912], 91). The discrimination of characteristic features and qualities of their environment with distinct terms and details demonstrates how central and relevant such topographical elements have been for the Paiute people's daily existence, contended Sapir.

To support his contention, Sapir also referred to a plethora of words used for different varieties of snow by the Inuit in the Canadian Arctic. By contrast, the Aztecs in tropical Mexico, he added, use the same term for cold, ice, and, snow as such environmental features

© Alexandros Moridis/Shutterstock.com

have only a minimal bearing on the day-to-day routines of Aztec life. These lexical instances testify to the fact that, maintained Sapir, "people name details when their survival depends directly on their environment" (Bonvillain 2003, 48).

Furthering his mentor's position, Benjamin L. Whorf maintained that the grammatical structure of a language tends to condition the ways in which the speakers of that language think. Therefore, the grammatical structure of distinct languages leads the speakers of those languages to view the world diversely. On the basis of his research and fieldwork on Native American languages such as Hopi and Kwakiutl, Whorf suggested, a specific group of people's perceptions of time and promptness may be conditioned by the sorts of verbal tenses in their language. The absence of past and future tenses in Hopi language, according to Whorf's analysis, makes the Hopi speakers conceptualize time either as a state of becoming or as something happening now. The experiences described in Hopi, therefore, retain the fluidity of passing experience. By contrast, English grammatical structure divides time into past, present, and future while enabling average English speakers to perceive time in terms of discrete units. The experiences described in English, therefore, capture the sense of time manageability. Whorf concluded that the difference between an average Hopi speaker and an average English speaker regarding time conceptualization is correlated with grammatical differences between the languages.

## Language, Society, and Power

The Sapir–Whorf Hypothesis has shown the primacy of language in linking the "universe of thoughts" (Duranti 1997, 49) of various linguistic communities and concomitant cultures. Yet, many linguistic anthropologists believe that language is not an autonomously constructed system of lexical categories and grammatical rules. Rather, according to them, it is a set of practices whose features are very much shaped by various sociopolitical processes that linguists concentrating on linguistic code alone have conveniently ignored; this set of practices consisting specific ways of communication, address, reference forms, taxonomies, lexicalizations, and metaphorical expressions, reveals the links between language and power. As anthropologist Pierre Bourdieu characterized, language exists as a *linguistic habitus* (linguistic dispositions people gain in the routine course of everyday life) (Bourdieu 1982, 31; cited in Duranti 1997, 45). It is this domain that has been intriguing most linguistic anthropologists referred to as sociolinguists.

In the twentieth century, Swiss structural linguist Ferdinand de Saussure, French anthropologist Claude Levi-Strauss, American linguist Noam Chomsky, French semiotician Roland Barthes, and the likes pioneered the nexus of language and cognition placing linguistics at the center of academic discussion. It stimulated research in a number of areas paving the way for a "linguistic turn" (Lash 1991) in social sciences. In quite similar fashion, toward the latter part of the twentieth century, social sciences in general and anthropology in particular took a distinct performative turn. This was mainly due to the collaborative works by the likes of John J. Gumperz (1922–2013), Dell Hymes (1927–2009), and William Labov (1927–) on the links between language and social context, also due to the writings of Russian literary critic and scholar Mikhail Bakhtin (1895–1975), particularly on discourse. Consequentially, when linguistic anthropologists began to focus on linguistic usage, as well as evaluations of linguistic usage within the context of language and power relations, the earlier debate about language shapes culture and vice versa appeared increasingly frivolous.

## Linguistic Variation and Social Stratification

The investigative focus of **sociolinguistics** has been the mutual links between social and linguistic variation, as well as between social settings and linguistic registers. According to sociolinguists, social stratification and linguistic variation noticeable in differences like class, gender, ethnicity, race, religion, occupation, and age, correlate with variety in language use among speakers. Linguistic variation may come to pass in pronunciation, lexicalization, and grammatical preferences; it is most commonly present in linguistic forms such as regional and social *dialects.*

## Linguistic Registers

Sociolinguists are also keen to explore the "situation-specific use" (Hymes 1973) of language or *linguistic registers.* These registers, known for their specific vocabularies (Trudgill 1983, 11), are associated with specific social settings. For instance, the linguistic register used in the domains of medicine, law, or entrepreneurship may markedly differ from each other, just as they can differ from the registers associated with religious worship or intimacy. By the early 1960s, linguistic anthropologists have already begun to study some of these themes.

Hymes' contribution was salient in this regard. He ethnographically researched on how concrete groups of individuals who verbally communicate with each other on regular basis use language. Hymes referred to such groups as *speech communities.* Hymes was able to demonstrate the fact that by investigating speech communities—instead of concentrating on one version of a single language in use—linguists can uncover multiple variants or forms of the same language used by its speakers in various contexts. Hymes' was an effective critique of *linguistic competence,* the influential linguistic model presented by Chomsky. Linguistic competence is the knowledge of grammatical rules (grammaticality) required for decoding and producing language. This knowledge of linguistic code, according to Chomsky, is tacitly shared by all fluent speakers of a specific language. Instead of merely focusing on linguistic competence, linguistic inquiry should be based on *communicative competence* or the knowledge required for the speakers to use the code in manifold social and cultural contexts, proposed Hymes.

## Dialects and the Privileged Dialect

Hymes was ably assisted by, among others, Gumperz. His conceptualization of variants of language or dialects in terms of differential power between speech communities helped to pioneer the mutual links between linguistic variation and social stratification. As Gumperz defined along this line of thought, the speech community is "any human aggregate characterized by regular and frequent interaction by means of a shared body of verbal signs and set off from similar aggregates by significant differences in language usage" (Dil 1971, 114). Therefore, what is known as the "clean-slate, no-accent, and straight-from-the-dictionary" form of any given language is only the dialect of the powerful. Gumperz aptly dubbed it as the "privileged dialect." When people in speech communities become equally comfortable in using two variants of the same language, it is known as *diglossia*. In such instances, maintained Gumperz, it is the privileged dialect which is always treated as the "standard" version of the given language over the less privileged and stigmatized native dialect.

The reciprocal relationship between language variation and social stratification has been explored by linguist William Labov as well. In 1963, Labov pointed out that a sound change in speech may in fact be related to the social motivation of the speakers (Labov 1963, 273–309). He has been known for his pioneering research on social dialectology. Labov's works on the linguistic features in African American Vernacular English (AAVE) have been particularly influential (Labov 1966 1972).

# Heteroglossia

Originally published in Russian in the 1920s and 30s, the breadth of work with which Bhaktin has dealt including philosophy, literary criticism, and language, was introduced to English readers posthumously in the 1970s. His studies experienced a surge of scholarly attention in the late 1980s. The surge occurred within the context of the postmodernist critique leveled against what the postmodernists perceived as the monologic and authoritarian character of modernist art and culture. His concept of *heteroglossia* or the coexistence of diverse voices, which he spelled out in the essay entitled "Discourse in the Novel," is pivotal to understand his philosophy of language, and indeed, all thought.

Heteroglossia refers to *dialogic* as well as *extralinguistic* qualities of language. Language is essentially dialogic: every utterance of everyone always exists in response to all utterances that have ever been done in the past and that will be made in anticipation in the future. In this sense, saying something is to "appropriate the words of others and populate them with one's own intention" (Bakhtin 1981). As a result, language is indispensably relational, and engaged in an unending process of rearticulations of the world. Language is also extralinguistic: in every living utterance, qualities such as perspective, evaluation, and ideological positioning are inextricably bound to the similar qualities existed in utterances ever made previously in response, and to the similar qualities that shall exist in anticipation in all future utterances. Consequentially, language is incapable of being escaped from neutrality in that, the ideas contain in every word exist essentially as a part of their contextual blending. Bakhtin's ideas in this regard are worthy of quoting *in extensor*: "Thus at any given moment of its historical existence, language is heteroglot from top to bottom: It represents the co-existence of socio-ideological contradictions between the present and the past, between different socio-ideological groups in the present, between tendencies, schools, circles and so forth, all given a bodily form. These 'languages' of heteroglossia intersect each other in a variety of ways, forming new socially typifying 'languages'" (Bakhtin 1981, 291).

# Discourse

Bhaktin's deep apprehensions on dialogic and extralinguistic qualities of language mark a significant shift from perspectives on the nature of language and knowledge by main linguists such as Saussure and Chomsky. His ideas have been particularly stimulant for sociolinguists interested in **discourse** or a stretch of utterance in which diverse voices, styles, and worldviews intermingled to form a complex unity. Sociolinguists who proceed to adopt the approach of Critical Discourse Analysis (CDA) and examine how discourse reflects, reproduces, or resists power and inequality draw heavily from Bakhtin's views.

© nuvolanevicata/Shutterstock.com

# Chapter Summary

This chapter concentrates on language, with which humans encode and communicate about their experiential world. The chapter reviews linguistic researches that recognize language as a mode of thinking and expression unique to humans as a symbolic species. It also introduces linguistic anthropology's subdisciplines, focusing on each field's scope, core themes, and methods of investigation.

• Human language is an extensive and intricate system of arbitrary vocal symbols and combinatorial rules with which humans articulate and express their experiential world.

• Only human species are physically equipped for speech. Other species communicate by employing a number of methods including body movement and motion, sound, and odor. Recent researches on nonhuman primates have shown that they have a rudimentary capacity for language.

• Linguist Noam Chomsky and others (Steven Pinker) maintain that humans are born with innate attributes for language acquisition. According to biological anthropologist Terrance Deacon, symbolic representation, the novel mode of thinking unique to human species, is due to coevolution of human brain and language over millions of years.

• Humans also communicate by using various nonverbal forms. They range from haptics, artifacts, kinesics, vocalics, and chronemics to proxemics.

• Cultural transmission through learning, arbitrariness, duality of patterning, openness, semanticity, displacement, and prevarication are some of the design features of language.

• The structural elements of language are consisted of phonology, morphology, syntax, and semantics.

- The analytical approach of historical linguistics is both diachronic and comparative. Contemporary languages are classified by comparing phonetic elements, lexicons, and grammatical structures. Processes of language change born by culture contact generate pidgin, lingua franca, and creole.

- According to the linguistic model known as the Sapir–Whorf Hypothesis, the links between language and thought exist at the level of vocabulary and grammar; hence, by influencing people's thought and behavior language shapes culture.

- Sociolinguists explore the correlations between social and linguistic variation while also investigating the mutual links between social settings and linguistic registers.

# Anthropology of Art: Exploring Cultural Manifestations of Symbolic Creativity

© ChameleonsEye/Shutterstock.com

Although they are no different from other biological organisms in their pursuits to accomplish basic needs for survival, humans are peculiar creatures among other animal species. This is evident even from the simple fact that none of the human groups known to anthropologists spend all its time and energies in the practical concerns of daily living such as putting food on their mouths and having roofs over their heads.

Upon securing such needs of bodily existence, people in all societies spend ample time in the affective realm of expressive culture by leaving off practical matters and embarking on what gives means to live as human beings.

For instance, the native people of Northwestern California carve kitchen utensils such as spoons from wood, animal bones, and antlers while also embellishing them with designs which are visually pleasurable, but functionally immaterial (Jacknis 1995). Indeed, many foragers around the world are known for having spare time to spend extensively on activities such as the decoration of their utilitarian items, although they use up relatively less time on the daily routines of sustenance such as hunting, gathering, and (as in some instances) fishing. The items such as decorated ostrich eggshell canteens used by the San in the Kalahari Desert, Africa, boomerangs of the Australian aborigines, and harpoons and needle-cases of the Inuit in the Canadian Arctic testify to this fact. Similarly, Yoruba people in Nigeria, West Africa, decorate and carve elite paraphernalia such as royal stools, beaded crowns, umbrellas, whisks, scepters, gowns, and slippers enhancing their beauty, but adding no extra functional capability to such garments and personal gear in doing so (Anderson 2004). In much the same way, Kwakiutl or Kwa Kwaka' Wakw people of the Pacific Northwest build their multifamily dwelling houses by using long, flat pieces of cedar timber; they also paint them with designs by symbolically representing real and supernatural beings albeit such embellishments are not needed for the basic activity these houses are for—dwelling (Holm and Reid 1975).

© Jerrold James Griffith/Shutterstock.com

It may be difficult to figure where purely practical concerns leave off paving the way for cultural expressions to set in. However, conspicuous examples of the sort ascertainable from various cultures of the world testify to the fact that artistic expression is one of the most distinguishable features of being human.

# The Biological Roots of Art

As every culture involve in the creation and appreciation of art to a varying degree, anthropologists broadly agree on the point that art is a human universal. However, anthropological analyses of art may significantly vary from each other in terms of theoretical orientations and analytic frameworks, and deal with the themes as diverse as art's biological origins and formal qualities.

Anthropologist Alexander Alland adopts an evolutionary approach to art, an approach favored by several other scholars (Alland 1977; Dissanayake 1995). In Alland's judgment, the biological roots of art that extend back to human species' animal ancestors should be explored if one is to understand the elements that unite art in all societies. During evolutionary adaptation, humans have acquired certain physical and neurological features which proved to be quite useful in producing and appreciating art. For instance, the freeing of the forelimbs through habitual bipedalism and erect posture has helped the human hand to develop into a highly specialized organ capable of handling matter delicately. While the prehensile (grasping) hand's precision grip and manual dexterity enabled humans to produce fine detail required for painting and sculpture, well-tuned eye–hand coordination made forming intricate visual patterns possible. Indeed, visual acuity and depth perception achieved through three-dimensional (or stereoscopic) color vision, as well as the functioning of the hand on the basis of instructions formed from visual patterns have major implications for the sorts of art humans create (Alland 1977, 21–22).

Alland explains the uniqueness of artistic behavior by referring to *game*, which is restrained by a set of rules; game is, therefore, "structured playing." Game is distinguishable from *free play* as the latter can be referred to as "any activity that is not directly involved in survival" (Alland 1977, 25). Indeed, certain human behavioral traits such as free play and exploratory behavior, response to form and the recognition of preference for certain forms over others, and fine-grained perceptual discrimination paired with a sizable holding ability of memory are found among many animals of the mammalian order in general and primates in particular. The exploratory behavior allows an organism to familiarize with its surroundings through mapping and coding, just as free play provides a salient experiential opportunity for learning, self-remuneration, and life enhancement. According to Alland, the pivotal biological property that makes art possible in the human species is game, which is, as noted earlier, playing that embraces structured rules. Rules of the art game assume *form.* Alland maintains that formal rules are shown in the final art product itself. For example, they are frozen in sound and visual space involving all the fine art products, including visual art, music, literature, dance, theater, film, and the mixed media. These formal rules must be understood as culturally appropriate restrictions with which temporal and spatial components of the art work may be framed.

Alland insists that playing with form is central to art. Poetry, for instance, is a game that suppositionally comprises a set of guiding principles with which poetic creativity may be achieved. Poetry and all sorts of literature are to be considered more than just language in that they are types of "communication games" that exhaust language (Alland 1977, 27). Alland defines aesthetic as "appreciative of, or responsive to, form in art or nature" (Alland 1977, xii). Aesthetic response, considered to be one of the basic emotions in the human species, is either a positive or negative reaction toward an art product. It is an audience's response to form.

According to Alland, artistic behavior added a novel aspect for free play and exploratory behavior by making humans more attuned to form, functioning as an incentive for perceptual differentiation, assisting in the ordering of conceptual material, and forming information into structures. Artistic behavior becomes feasible only with the presence of, what Alland called *transformation-representation*. Therefore, art is definable as play with form which brings into existence some aesthetically successful transformation-representation. Seeing in this light, any work of art is a representation of something by something else, and it entails transformation of one sort or another. The "trick in art," writes Alland, is that human perceptions and emotions are "represented as transformations" (Alland 1977, 36). Main stratagem upon which all art is constructed is transformation. In visual arts, transformation occurs in the skillful arrangement of spatial elements and color of the art work, as well as in time compression. A painting, in this sense, is a representation made through transformation of ideas and/or reality on a two-dimensional surface with paints. In much the same way, a poem is a metaphoric transformation of experience into concentrated and tightened language to represent a novel experience.

The seductive characteristic is the essence of art, and that aspect is truly biological in its origin, Alland maintains. Functionally, art may be varied a great deal as differences take place both cross-culturally and historically. "What unites art in all societies," writes Alland, is "its game-like character in which symbolic transformation of formal elements provides the major stimulus for creativity" (Alland 1977, 20).

Whereas art may be fundamental to being human, in all known societies, it is shown in aesthetic experience, argues anthropologist Jacques Maquet: "Yes, many societies—all known societies, I dare say—recognize and actualize the human potentiality for aesthetic perception and appreciation" (Maquet 1986). Aesthetic experience is a fundamental mode of human consciousness—it, therefore, is a species-specific process. By focusing exclusively on visual art and emphasizing the formalist approach to art (discussed later) Maquet points out that, while the human component is more basic, it is through the cultural component, which is the realm of variety and multiplicity, "visual commerce" is established. Moreover, according to Maquet, as creation and appreciation of art are mental processes, inquiring into them through a wide range of cultural contexts assists one to understand the intricate links between the cultural, universal, and singular levels of aesthetic experience. The most promising heuristic mechanism to make sense of aesthetic dimension is the cross-cultural approach, he argues further (Maquet 1986).

Expressive culture is the domain in which human beings ensure their present and future well-being through joyous and passionate engagement with life, attach a symbolic value for the enhancement of life, and thereby make living worthwhile. Artistic activity makes a very important contribution in this regard as a vital part of expressive culture. Art comprises a vast array of forms and modes with which humans express themselves creatively and convey their creativity to the fellow members of their own species. Taking these factors into consideration, anthropologists seek to understand art in broad terms while contesting commonplace notions such as the difference between universal aesthetics and cultural aesthetics, and the supposed qualitative superiority of Western art over the so-called primitive art.

## Defining Art

Whereas people around the world recognize, appreciate, and create art, there is no universally accepted definition of art. As various scholars of art have long attempted unsuccessfully, arriving at an explicit and precise definition of art has been one of the thorniest matters around. It being the case, classifying and describing art in terms of its stylistic features or else, investigating it as a supplement to more tangible activities such as art's economic functions or the process of artistic training has been the approach customarily adopted by most studies of art. In contrast, a significantly less attention has been paid to the issue of aesthetics, which is what at the core of art. According to an "open" definition adopted by a comparative anthropological study of art and aesthetics, art "embodies culturally significant meaning that is encoded with uncommon skill in a traditional style and sensuous medium" (Anderson 2004, 321). This definition stresses several salient points: Art conveys cultural meanings of considerable significance; as various sensory modes serve as the basis of art, art works and artistic activities have some type of sensuous appeal; art reflects special skills with which it is produced.

According to the aforesaid definition, specific cultures may differ from each other when defining what is and what is not significant. Similarly, cultures may vary as to the extent of openness that the art works ought to maintain when the meaning is made manifest. Despite such differences, every known human culture invests art with culturally significant meaning. Art works are not merely about their own stylistic conventions and the delight stimulated by a sensuous medium. Everywhere, art works are also about some subject in the sociocultural matrix of which they are a necessary component. Often, art conveys several culturally significant meanings concurrently in a way that transcends ordinary modes of discourse and strengthens each other's messages (Anderson 2004, 277–303).

The above definition also indicates that the sensory modes of art are based on either fully and clearly expressed or tacitly understood guidelines set forth by specific cultures. The Western art traditions, for instance, have certainly preferred the visual and auditory senses as most appropriate for activities of art. Similarly, the artistic conventions in early India focused on poetry, music, and architecture as genuine art. They also relegated the visual arts and dance as art media of secondary importance even though Bharata Muni authored his seminal theoretical treatise on ancient Indian dramaturgy and histrionics named *Natyasastra* (literally, "dramaturgy") sometime in between the first-century B.C.E.

© J. Henning Buchholz/Shutterstock.com

and the third-century C.E. Additionally, early Indian art traditions did not heed to the artistic potential of the senses such as smell, touch, and taste. Nevertheless, ethnographic evidence suggest that other sensory modes were among the guidelines for art observed by certain cultures. Japanese sumo wrestling, for example, heightens the kinesthetic and tactile sensations to the level of art, both for the performers and the spectators.

Likewise, Japanese tea ceremony in which unsweetened tea is served amidst the aroma of incense is intended for lifting the participants' senses of taste and smell.

In much the same way, artistic activities such as the Arabian fualah get-together in which Arab women entertain their morning and afternoon female guests with sweet meats while letting them inhale dense fumes of scented incense aim to enhance the gustatory and olfactory senses of the participating women (Anderson 2004, 312–14).

Furthermore, the definition acknowledges that the skills with which art is produced are highly developed skills, recognized as exceptional capabilities of the artists by the members of all sorts of societies. For example, in foraging societies such as the San society in the Kalahari Desert, Africa, where labor specialization is minimal, singular talents of San musicians are readily recognized (Marshall 1976, 363; Schostak 1981, 321). Similarly, whereas Australian aborigines generally consider everyone in their society as a potential artist, they always distinguish those few with special artistic skills from the ordinary folks (Mountford 1961, 7). The above trait of art is commonly found in horticultural and pastoralist societies too. The Yoruba in Nigeria, for example, believe that the standards of excellence required

© Dmytro Zinkevych/Shutterstock.com

for wood carving and performing arts activities such as drumming can be met only by those who acquire artistic sensitivity through continuous effort and dedication (Abiodun 1987, 270). Likewise, although all Sepik men practice wood carving, only the carvers who demonstrate extraordinary skills are permitted to carve masks and similar objects of ritualistic significance. According to an instance analogous to the ones cited above, from nearly all Navajos who practice artistic creation in some form, only those who demonstrate unparalleled skills are singled out and rewarded by the Navajo (Witherspoon 1975, 152). Recognition and rewarding of individual artists for exceptional talent and skills has been a commonplace occurrence in Western societies as well (Anderson 2004, 318–19).

In every society, regardless of the degree of complexity existing in the division of labor, the artist's special skills are regarded as the skills pertaining to the mind rather than the hands. For example, in small-scale, foraging and horticultural societies where technical skills of the individual artists may be no greater than that of others, the artist's conceptual skills are conspicuously noticeable. In much the same way, in industrial societies of the West, where occupational specialty is highly pronounced, individual artists' cognitive abilities are acknowledged as extraordinary.

The special conceptual skills associated with art may be present among some nonartists as well. Clearly distinguishable from ordinary folks due to their highly developed artistic sensibilities, such art appreciators or aesthetes may be considered connoisseurs. Robert Thompson describes the instances of genuine connoisseurship among some Yoruba

© Art Amori/Shutterstock.com

who displayed a far greater skill in evaluating Yoruba art than the others (Thompson 1973, 23). The classical Indian aesthetic theory of *rasa* (literally, "taste" or "essence") also acknowledges the special ability of the connoisseur or the *rasika* in appreciating art. When the poet and the connoisseur are on the same "wave length," maintained the pre-eminent *rasa* theorist Anandavardhana (820–890 C. E.), the *rasika* understands the resonant field of emotions that the poet creates (Anandavardhana; Abhinavagupta; Ingalls et. al. 1990).

## Aesthetics and Cultural Aesthetics

**Aesthetics** refers to both theories about nature and value in art, and sensations associated with beauty. What is usually considered as universal aesthetics, anthropologists believe, is the accumulated corpus of ideas and standards developed in the West regarding the basic nature and value of art. Hence, it is a Western-centric notion.

According to the analysis of anthropologist Richard Anderson, four major aesthetic theoretical paradigms have developed in Western art: mimetic, instrumental, emotionalist, and formalist (Anderson 2004, 234–50). The *mimetic* theoretical paradigm places great importance to art's capacity to imitate the world either literally or else apprehending it in idealized form or symbolic means. *Instrumental* theories of aesthetics are based on the belief that art should be instrumental in transforming the world with the aim of making it a better place for human existence socially, politically, morally, and spiritually. Focusing on the innermost process of artistic expression that pressurizes the artist to let out potent personal thoughts, emotions, and perceptions, as well as on the cathartic release of the percipients' or the audience members' feelings, the *emotionalist* paradigm views art as an embodiment and expression of emotions. The *formalist* theory insists that aesthetic satisfaction is the only purpose for which art exists, and the social, cultural, and representational messages are mere distractions from that higher purpose. The formalist theory, therefore, concentrates on the formal qualities of art such as color, composition, sound, words, and movement, together with the artist's mastery of the medium.

## Cultural Aesthetics

However, the existence of various culturally specific notions associated with art or **cultural aesthetics** offered a solid ground for anthropologists to conclude that the "Western world does not have a monopoly on wisdom and insight regarding art" (Anderson 2004, 2). Culturally varied concepts of art help anthropologists to understand aesthetics as socially accepted ideas of quality (Thompson 1971). For instance, traditional Yoruba human figurines carved out of wood may not appear fully realistic or abstract, yet in terms of lineal and formic precision, symmetrical portraiture, and a glossy surface with which a play of light and shadows is generated, they are fully in line with native aesthetics of Yoruba people in the coastal region of West Africa. The aesthetic rules followed by Yoruba wood carvers are in accordance with the long-standing beliefs and consistent behaviors of Yoruba society in relation to artistic creativity and perception.

© PACO COMO/Shutterstock.com

# The Anthropological Perspective of Art

Whereas the anthropological perspective of art is often imbricated with the disciplines such as aesthetics, art history, art conservation, and studies of material culture, it is distinguishable due to its focus on studying art objects, forms, and artistic conventions in relation to their sociocultural context. In as much as art historians or art curators might be interested in the works and biography of an artist, anthropologists are keener to be aware of the matters such as the artist's status and role within the society at large. So, anthropologists not only conduct ethnographic research on a vast array of art products, but also the people who make them, the reasons, and the processes of making art, and the meanings that art objects convey to cultures.

Ethnographic data gathering, the emic approach, and the cross-cultural scope are among the main features of the anthropological perspective of art.

## Ethnographic Data Gathering

Anthropological perspective of art is primarily based on **ethnographic data gathering,** the investigative strategy centered on enduring personal observation and social participation (See Chapter 2). It is the vital entry point for the comparative study of art and aesthetics. Therein lays another salient feature to which anthropologists who study art adhered: Aesthetics is not a theory of beauty in its entirety. Whereas natural phenomena such as setting sun, blossoming flowers, and moon-lit nights may move feelings having likeness to those generated by art, the primary concern of anthropologists is the art, which are produced by the association of the human mind and body. A great deal of aesthetic diversity exists in every human society as individuals tend to hold different levels of thoughts on art, just as they hold different opinions on what is and what is not art. Regardless of such qualitative and quantitative differences however, anthropologists are primarily interested in the sets of beliefs and behaviors consistently shared by the members of society. In the same vein, they mostly pay attention to the aesthetic values held by a large segment of a population for a considerable period (Anderson 2004, 5).

## Emic Approach

Ethnography makes the *emic* **approach** to art possible. This is the research strategy with which ethnographers use the cultural concepts and categories that are relevant and meaningful to the culture under investigation. In contrast, the *etic* approach is the research strategy that stresses the cultural concepts and categories stemming from the ethnographer's own perspective and culture. The kinds of information conveyed in a statement such as "masks are carved out of wood from two species of trees" make it an etic statement since the given information can be verifiable by consulting a botanist. However, a statement like "native critics generally feel that masks carved from one type of wood are more desirable than those carved from the other" becomes an emic statement. To make a statement of the sorts, a native cultural consultant must evaluate it (Anderson 2004, 3). The emphasis on the emic approach provides opportunities to glean the meanings pertaining to artistic activity in the context of the native conceptual system as emic aesthetics exists only in the mind of native art connoisseurs.

## Cross-cultural Scope

Anthropologists are of the view that a prudent means to an in-depth understanding of any human endeavor requires investigating it in other human cultures. Anthropology's **cross-cultural scope,** they believe, potentially helps to ferret out the components that are shared and pan-human, as well as those that are not shared and culture-specific.

Anthropologists strive to study diversity in art and aesthetic systems existing in the world as it sheds light upon the ways in which different cultures attribute different values to art objects, and prefer certain art forms over the others, according to the culturally specific notions they hold on what constitutes aesthetics and artistic consummation.

Moreover, the cross-cultural learning of art and aesthetic systems allows anthropologists to tap into the vast and diverse reserve of human thought associated with art otherwise known only for native connoisseurs. The application of cross-cultural perspective to the study of art has indeed helped anthropologists to learn about aesthetics and art traditions developed outside the main currents of Western aesthetics (such as the theory of transcendental enjoyment or *rasa* ["aesthetic savor"] in early India) which have received scant attention from scholars until recently.

Furthermore, the cross-cultural study paves the way for anthropologists to move beyond the treatment of the arts in other societies as mere curiosities by offering resources to apprehend the metaphysical, cultural, and emotional meanings that they impart.

In addition, anthropologists maintain that the intellectual stimuli one receives from the cross-cultural understanding of aesthetics help immensely to examine one's own aesthetic philosophies, as well as the natural, social, and cultural worlds one is accustomed to in new perspectives. For instance, the new directions in Western art styles can be largely attributed to Western artists' positive exposure to the art and aesthetic systems in Africa and elsewhere in the early twentieth-century (Anderson 2004).

The supposed dissimilarity between universal and cultural aesthetics is imbricated with the distinction between Western art and what came to be known as primitive art. Recent anthropological studies on art stress the necessity to move beyond such problematic distinctions (Marcus and Myers 1995; Morphy and Perkins 2006). Traditional anthropology of art has been grown under the purview of the tenets and practices of Western art traditions. They have known for appropriating non-Western people's art (and cultures) as primitive, and hence, low in quality by Western standards.

# Primitive Art

Anthropologist Shelly Errington argues that the category of "primitive art" was invented in the nineteenth and twentieth centuries. Accordingly, understanding this invention requires a shift in focus from the notion of primitivism (which was unmasked by cultural critics as a Western ideological construct) to art itself.

## Art by Intention

Errington distinguishes between what she calls art by intention and art by appropriation. Accordingly, **art by intention** refers to objects which were made to be art by their original creators. Such objects were created "in contexts that had a concept of art approximating what we now hold" (Errington 1998). Artistic intention of the objects which were made to be art is unambiguous and recognizable. For example, visual art objects are created for a single purpose: to be looked at. So, paintings are hung on the walls of art galleries, murals are applied on walls, ceilings, or other large permanent surfaces, and sculptures are erected in gardens for viewing. Anthropologist Jacques Maquet coins such art objects as *art by destination* (Maquet 1986) as they are destined to be beheld.

## Art by Appropriation

Jacques Maquest terms the objects that became art at a later stage of their existence as *art by metamorphosis.* This distinction was originally made by the French art theorist Andre Malraux who contended that art transcends time through a process of metamorphosis (Malraux 1949; Allan 2013). Errington believes that Malraux's and Maquet's categorization does not adequately emphasize the legitimizing processes that, in effect, pronounced the objects (which were originally considered as other things) to be art.

To that end, Errington prefers to use the term art by appropriation. As she sees it, **art by appropriation** pertains to the host of objects that grew to be art because they were held as such at certain historical moments by certain people and institutions. The cluster of individuals and institutions concerned with defining and maintaining art may include art collectors, art patrons, art dealers, art fairs, art museums, art schools, and art galleries. Accordingly, the artifacts which were originally unrelated to art in terms of functionality, usage, and the context of production, such as ceremonial clubs, ancestral effigies, door lintels, and kava bowls became art in museums and art galleries.

## Art World

The individuals and the institutions involved in the processes of transforming diverse objects into art are known as the constituents of an **art world.** The network of people in an art world participated collectively in every aspect of art activity, including production, preservation, presentation, promotion, chronicling, criticism, commission, and selling. The participants utilize their knowledge on conventional means of getting things done collectively, and it is through this process artistic ideas become works of art (Becker [1982] 2008). The process includes all of the effort and concentration on producing the artistic idea, its execution (conversion of the idea into a physical form, such as a book, a film, a painting, a sculpture, a song, or a dance), manufacture and distribution of the required materials and equipment, all sorts of supportive activities (ranging from technical support to relieving art producers from routine household chores, so artists can produce art), as well as the creation and maintenance of the rationale (according to which all these related activities become meaningful and worthwhile).

An art world is a "loose network of overlapping subcultures held together by a belief in art," and it clusters around the opulent "art capitals" in the world, such as New York, Los Angeles, Berlin, Beijing, Brussels, Hong Kong, Tokyo, Rome, and Paris (Thornton 2008, 2014). While an art world may pervade across the globe, considering it to be a singular, monolithic entity functioning through an equally singularized art market is rather misleading. This is in view of the fact that multiple, overlapping, and crisscrossing art worlds can coexist in the globalized world (Cate 2003). However, the Western art worlds in the modern era have been consistent in their practices of defining and maintaining, or as Errington has put, "legitimizing" art (Errington 1998; Marcus and Myers 1995; Karp and Lavine 1991).

## Art and Globalization

Throughout human history, art forms and traditions have been always dynamic and receptive to change. Long before globalization became a part of public and academic discourse, new art forms and art institutions had been diffusing into local cultures around the world. Ever since the European colonial powers created the conditions for a fully integrated global economy and extensive cultural ties roughly five-hundred years ago, art forms and traditions have been sustaining notable changes globally.

## Deterritorialization of Art

However, the accelerated pace of cultural diffusion and the magnitude of change in the twenty-first century have been such that some social scientists observe the possibility that many traditions of indigenous art may be obliterated or globalized out of existence. As anthropologist Renato Rosaldo puts it, "cultural artifacts flow between unlikely places" to an extent that literally "nothing is sacred, permanent, or sealed off" any more (Jenkins 2001, 89). In many local contexts, the incorporation of native people into global networks has profoundly impinged upon the production of artworks by removing or weakening the connections between the artworks, the cultures, and the localities in which they are produced. It is this process of severing cultural practices from their places of origin and populations what French scholars Deleuze and Guattari referred to as **deterritorialization** (Deleuze and Guattari 1972). By spawning people's closer involvement with the art objects, forms and traditions alien to them, deterritorialization precipitates closeness in distance while widening the gap with what is physically close to them concurrently. In this sense, it must be understood as a process through which a proliferation of translocalized cultural experiences takes place (Hernandez 2002). The transcendence of cultural artifacts from their exclusive spatial and cultural boundaries effectively transforms them into products now accessible to the global market. Stated differently, deterritorialization paves the way for the *massification* of art. Without question, in the context of globalization, mass production and consumption of art activities, art products, and mass media productions have increased in an accelerated pace. Writing in 1936, German Marxist literary critic Walter Benjamin observed this massification of art and contended that mechanical reproducibility in the modern era had substituted a plurality of copies for a work of art which, in his view, was authentic and original. While referring to the idea of the "aura" of the art work and its absence in a reproduction, Benjamin wrote: "even the most perfect reproduction of art is lacking in one element: its presence in time and space, its unique existence at the place where it happens to be" (Benjamin 1968 [1936], 214–18).

The deterritorialization is considered a key feature of globalization. In general, it is intensified by the processes of mediatization, migration, and commodification which distinguish globalized modernity. Particularly, the midiatization or the global dissemination of mass media (such as the newspapers, magazines, the Internet, television, film, radio, and photography) which shape and frame the communicational processes, discourses, as well as the society in which that communication takes place (Lilleker 2008) has hastened the process of deterritorialization. This is easily recognizable through the examples such as the globally popular virtual sites of Facebook, Myspace, Twitter, Instagram, Bing, Pinterest, and the like, Hollywood-based feature film industry, the globally broadcast cable television networks, and the influence of such media outlets in shaping popular psyche around the world. As Arjun Appadurai, an anthropologist who studied cultural dimensions of globalization and public culture indicates (1990, 1996), the process of midiatization plays a pivotal role by making people able to expand and alter their imagination, which, in his view, has become a salient social practice in the globalized world. The work of imagination suggests the fusion of image, imaginary, and imagined community. According to Appadurai, it is through imagination augmented by the process of mediatization people gain access to and become familiar with remote cultural landscapes, cultural products, and cultural conditions alien to their own locality. The growth and modification of imagination and the resultant cultural distancing from the locality makes it extremely hard for a local entity to sustain and keep hold of its own cultural identity (Appadurai 1990).

## Reterritorialization of Art

Paradoxically, the deterritorialization of art permits the **reterritorialization** to transpire at a global level as well. This latter is the flip-side of the former. In the context of globalization of art, the reterritorialization has to be understood as the restructuring process in which territorial relocalizations of old art forms, institutions, and activities, as well as new art productions emphatic of locality and culture takes place. Accordingly, artists and craftsmen in many local contexts have begun to produce specific types of work symbolizing their cultural/ethnic identity and heritage. Destined for wider markets, such products have begun to be identified as **ethnic art.**

© ChameleonsEye/Shutterstock.com

## Sri Lanka's Kandyan Dance

Anthropologist Susan A. Reed's work on the dance in South Asian island nation of Sri Lanka is appropriate in this context. She focuses on Sri Lanka's state-supported Kandyan dance which has become an index of national identity and an emblem of the island's majority

Sinhalese ethnic group. Reed investigates the process of creating a national dance out of a local ritual performance known as the *kohomba kankariya* and the consequences of that transformation (Reed 2010). She does so while situating kandyan dance in relation to the cultural policies of the postcolonial state which have long-dominated dance, music, and other forms of art in Sri Lanka, and the changes brought forth by the process of globalization. Reed observes that the earlier village ritual performed by men of the hereditary drummer caste as an all-night ceremony has now transitioned to an edited and condensed version of stage event performed primarily for artistic and cultural purposes. Over the recent decades, the ritual has shed its caste and gender divisions while gradually expanding on to scores of performance occasions ranging from high schools, universities, folk art centers, dance schools, Buddhist temples and tourist hotels to a variety of international arenas. In 2000, the dance was designated by the state as a Sri Lankan masterpiece of Intangible Cultural Heritage for UNESCO (Reed 2010, 196). Succinctly stated, kandyan dance became a deterritorialized product of performing art and in the process, it has lost much of its ritualistic significance.

Despite the shift toward the visual and spectacular and the popularity it garnered both nationally and internationally as a result, *kohomba kankariya*'s efficacy as a benevolent ritual still reverberates among some segments of the ritual specialists, participants, and observers. According to Reed, some who voice their concern on the commodification of the traditional ritual attempt to revitalize it as an effectual ritualistic practice in the contemporary context.

© SamanWeeratunga/Shutterstock.com

Differently stated, to salvage kandyan dance from what is perceived as the onslaught of commercialization some movements are under way to reritualize it (Reed 2010).

A similar situation is described by anthropologist R. Anderson Sutton in an account on local music and dance traditions among the Makassarese people of South Sulawesi, Indonesia (Sutton 2002). Sutton examines how, undeterred by the cultural pressures stemming from Indonesian state policies of music and dance, as well as from the global forces of art commodification, Makassarese performers seek to capacitate local music and dance performance through "calling back the spirit" or reritualization.

## Bollywood Film Industry

India's film industry offers a compelling pop culture example for the deterritorialization and reterritorialization of art. For decades, the Hollywood-based, big-budget feature films have been attracting a sizable chunk of movie-goers globally. Their continuing popularity in far-flung places indicates how such highly mediatized Western art products have penetrated through spatial boundaries while making inroads into specific cultures. In India, a country with a potential audience of a billion people, one finds a formidable local competitor to Hollywood films. These feature films, the products of Mumbai-based Indian film industry known as Bollywood and its cousins in the South Indian film industry, have been popular not only among the home audience, but also among the sizable Indian diaspora existing around the world, including in the United States. In addition, they find receptive audiences in the Middle East, the Mediterranean, Southern and Eastern Africa, the Far East, and the Caribbean. Hindi-speaking Bollywood movies have been dubbed into many other languages ranging from Russian and Mandarin Chinese to French, as well.

The Indian obsession of Bollywood movies has been phenomenal, because Indians are "born of them," says Suketu Mehta while writing a feature column for *The New York Times* (Mehta 2004). According to him, the success of Bollywood movies at the box office and in the struggle for the hearts and minds of Indian movie-goers lies on the sorts of stories they tell and how they tell them. All Bollywood movies tell stories which are precynical, unambiguous, melodramatic, stereotypic, and in the Indian context, progressive. The themes they carry in their stories such as immaculate love triumphing over all social divisions and evils, unhindered faith, unreserved patriotism, and the nobility of motherhood can tap into Indian sentiments as they resonate with the unambiguous messages stemming from India's narrative traditions and literature of long standing such as *Ramayana* and *Mahabharata*. Moreover, every Bollywood film is a musical—each film has, on the average, between five to fourteen songs and related dances. Song is being more forceful than dialogue, "emotion is communicated through song" (Mehta 2004). The use of song and dance for storytelling and for conveying emotion echoes India's rich tradition of dance-drama seen in classical *Bharatanatyam* and the like.

Although the global appeal of Bollywood films is real, it is also in most part segmental. Even if many Bollywood box office hits are big-budget productions, they lack special effects and the futuristic elements such as interplanetary spaceships and warfare. Most Americans may find the plots of Bollywood films to be thin, nonedgy, stereotypic, melodramatic, and even illogical. Although music-and-dance-friendly, Western audiences

© testing/Shutterstock.com

may not always find Bollywood heroines as permissive and flirtatious as their Hollywood counterparts. Similarly, Bollywood male protagonists may appear to male audiences in the West as nontechno savvy, unexciting individuals with laid-back life styles. Yet for the home audience, Bollywood films are locally born global art products that can be devoured in no time; for the children of global Indian diaspora several generations removed from home, they construct a "simulated India-world" away from India (Mehta 2004).

The programs' producers for Indian Television networks must have taken a page from the book of Indian cinema. They often adopt popular Western sitcoms, soap operas, and the like, and when they do, always make certain to localize such programs. The TV programs like *Indian Idol* (produced following its American counterpart *American Idol*) attract such large audiences regularly because what they convey resonate with local cultural experiences (Sengupta 2006). Modernities are mediated in globalized India, says anthropologist Purnima Mankekar while referring to Indian TV serials and commercials which depict women as modern and traditional concurrently (Mankekar 1991, 91, 2010, 421–35). In such mediated portrayals, Indian women use modern appliances to run their homes while fulfilling the role of dutiful housewife and nurturing mother simultaneously.

## Californication

The song entitled *Californication,* sung by the U.S. rock band The Red Hot Chili Peppers, is a fine pop culture example that attempts to capture the process of deterritorialization and reterritorialization as a perpetual part of the evolving global culture. In this song, California is presented metaphorically as a place where the mediated fantasies of globalized modernity thrive. Accordingly, a trend that is taken up in California will probably be upheld everywhere in the global community as they will generate translocal cultural experiences. The same tidal waves which destroy local culture and space during deterritorialization open vistas for reterritorialization to flourish, the last lines of the song renders.

The ways with which deterritorialization leads to translocalized cultural experiences and reterritorialization brings about territorialized cultural experiences in globalized modernity are certainly intriguing to observe. Nonetheless, some anthropologists have indicated the need to move beyond merely acknowledging the impact of the processes and focus on how the distance between people's imagined places and the actual localities reflect and strengthen the global contours of power and privilege.

## Urban Youths in Kathmandu, Nepal

Adopting this line of sight, anthropologist Mark Liechty explores how urban youths in Kathmandu, Nepal partake in what is turning into a globalized, cosmopolitan youth culture that they have gleaned from films, magazines, books, and travelers' narratives. For these Nepali youth, the bustling, cosmopolitan streets in Kathmandu's tourist district known as Thamel open the window through which to slip briefly into "the imagined pleasure of modernity" (Liechty 2010, 40). These young punks coming from middle-class backgrounds believe that the studied presentations of the tough-guy persona, striking postures, intricate dance movements, fashioned bodies, and fashionable clothing loosely adopted from English action films, Kung Fu movies, and the media images would take them there. Per Liechty, whereas their bodies navigate the streets of Thamel, the mind seems to be roaming in that shadow universe of foreign "modernity," filled with gangs, all-night bars, video games, drugs, and transnational sexual fantasies. In the meantime, hundreds, and thousands of people from around the globe visit Kathmandu every year, each carrying with them mediated memories of the mysterious and exotic land which they know only through films, magazines, tourist brochures, coffee-table books, and travelers' memoirs. "In places like Thamel," says Liechty, "first and third worlds ('modernity' and 'tradition') implode into one another; both tourists and locals come to Thamel to find the 'others' they imagine." More revealingly, only the Western tourists who nostalgically look for the exotic other in the periphery "may actually indulge their fantasies *in* the other's space." And, this reality discloses and strengthens the existing global structures of power which firmly situates Nepali youth in a persistent state of self-peripheralization. Hence, they are *"out here* in Kathmandu" (Liechty 2010, 48) (emphasis added).

## Art, Power, and Resistance

The links of art to social contexts and socially critical implications of art are hardly uncertain. The interlacement of art with the core power systems such as economics, politics, class, race, and gender confirms that the elite and the privileged classes often appropriate art forms of the underprivileged groups for the well-being of their own. Similarly, marginalized groups also use art forms as a way of expressing resistance, and a way of opening space for alternative vision of reality.

As the following instance indicates, art may become a powerful source of memory and future way of knowing, as well as a venue with which the demands for social justice and democracy may be advanced.

## Marcelo Brodsky's Buena Memoria ("Good Memory")

The Mothers of the Plaza de Mayo was an association formed by Argentine mothers whose children were "disappeared" during the state terrorism of the military dictatorship, between 1976 and 1983. In 1977, the group began to organize silent weekly protests at the Plaza de Mayo in Buenos Aires, in front of the Casa Rosado presidential palace. They were the acts of public defiance taken in the face of the state terrorism intended for silencing voices of dissent.

One of the most effective ways through which this protest movement sustained its momentum was its innovative use of photographic images as a way of preserving social memory. The images came from a photographic text entitled Buena Memoria ("Good Memory"), created by the Argentine artist Marcelo Brodsky (b. 1954). It contained photographs from family albums, videos, and personal and literary documents. The work looked deceptively simple, yet deeply touchy, as it was primarily a visual memorial for the victims of state terrorism in Argentina in the 1970s and the 1980s (Schube 2003). For example, one of the central images of the work was a graduation photograph of the class of 1967 at the *Colegio National* in Buenos Aires, and it (and the photographs of similar sort) helped Brodsky to reconstruct the biographies of his friends and his own brother Ruben who went on missing during that time of terror. The counternarratives produced by these visual images surely invigorated the process of resisting the state's efforts to wipe off the histories of repression and violence in Argentina. Moreover, they were immensely useful in legitimizing the calls for social justice and democracy (Tandeciarz in Emmanuel 2006).

The examples of political theater given below highlight how artistic performances come to be an important venue for political critique and resistance.

## Augusto Boal's Theater of the Oppressed

A set of interactive and politically expressive theatrical forms and techniques created by a Brazilian theater practitioner named Augusto Boal (1931–2009) began to energize the theater world in the early 1970s. Taking cues from the Brazilian educator and philosopher Paulo Freire's work *The Pedagogy of the Oppressed* (Freire [1970] 2000), Boal introduced these theatrical forms under the rubric of the **Theater of the Oppressed.**

The Theater of the Oppressed was distinctive at least in two interdependent aspects: First, following the ideas of the German playwright and drama theorist Bertolt Brecht (1898–1956), it stressed the theater's role of social engagement and the use of drama as a social, as well as an ideological forum to bring about change. Boal insisted that the theater ought to be "a rehearsal for the revolution" (Boal 1979). The production of the Theater of the Oppressed often highlighted the theme of social injustice while providing a venue through which disenfranchised voices could be heard.

Second, in the Theater of the Oppressed, the emphasis on the partnership between the spectator and the actor is intriguingly evident. The audience come to be active participants in altering the reality in which they are living. Therefore, the audience members become spectators and actors simultaneously: they turn into "spect-actors." The message of using theater as a venue for social and political change, which Boal passionately delivered through his theater workshops, resonated with politically and artistically motivated adherents in South America (especially, in Brazil, Peru, Argentina, and Ecuador), North America (in the United States) and Europe (particularly in France). By the time of his death in 2009, the Theater of the Oppressed had widen into an international theater movement with participants in dozens of countries around the world (Weber 2009).

## Street Theater

Performed in outdoor public places (such as car parks, bus or railway stations, shopping centers, and street corners) without elaborate costumes and props, amplified sound, or even a specific paying audience, **street theater** is a theatrical form adopted by the actors ranging from buskers (street performers who perform for gratuities such as food, drink, or little money) to theater practitioners who, either want to experiment with performance spaces, or to promote a cause of sociopolitical significance.

© Maljalen/Shutterstock.com

The legacy of street theater may be traced back to folk theater traditions, which have continued for a long time. The current street theater traditions in the West, for example, can be traced back at least to the medieval carnival, a season or festival of merrymaking before Lent during the Christian era (and the pre-Christian rites related to the coming of spring and the rebirth of nature), and *commedia dell'arte* ("comedy of craft"), an improvisational theater form that originated in Italy in the sixteenth century, and gradually developed into various configurations in the subsequent centuries throughout Europe.

The legacy it inherited from its predecessors as a permissive space for mocking and contesting authority, hierarchy, and dogma made street theater an attractive venue for socially and politically motivated theater practitioners around the world.

In 1965, for example, a group of U.S. theater practitioners known as *San Francisco Mime Troupe* (SFMT) began to present politically and socially significant issues through their performances on the wayside and open theater locations such as public parks. Inspired by the writings of the Argentine-born–Cuban revolutionary Che Ernesto Guevara (1928–1967), the group dubbed their theater form as **Guerilla Theater** (guerilla denotes the "little war" in Spanish), pledged for revolutionary sociopolitical change. The presentations of the guerilla theater were distinctive in several ways: At the outset, these were spontaneous and unpredictable theatrical acts performed in improbable public locations for unwitting audiences; Moreover, these outdoor theatrical events were protest-oriented and satirical performances containing elements of profanity, nudity, and other carnivalesque techniques (discussed later). Until 1970, the outdoor shows of the guerilla theater were commedia del'arte-type satires adopted from classical plays to anachronize and satirize the evils of the present-day; Similarly, the guerilla theater shows contained some features of the agit-prop (agitation-propaganda) theater devoted to promote Marxist political propaganda in the 1930s, as well as some characteristics adopted from Dada movement of the European avant-garde artists in the early twentieth century; What is more, they often involved the themes highlighted by the radical social movements in the turbulent decades of the sixties and the seventies, such as the Vietnam war, the woes of capitalism, and racial and gender inequality. The guerilla theater's leftist radicalism became amply evident in 1967 when the SFMT with its play satirizing the Vietnam war (L'AMA MILITAIRE) got down to perform for the audiences across the midwestern college campuses, the same audiences targeted by the recruiters of the DOW chemical company, the makers of napalm (a flammable liquid infamously used in the Vietnam war).

South Asia offers another fine example for using street theater to combine performance with resistance.

Street theater in India, sometimes known as *Thirst Theater*, has inherited an enduring and rich tradition of folk play. However, in its modern form, street theater became popular only in the 1940s with the emergence of the Indian People's Theater Association (IPTA), India's first movement for organized political theater. Street theater as the left-wing political activism has even more recent history as its pioneer theater movement, known as the People's Theater Front (*Jana Natya Manch*) or *Janam* ("Birth"), came into being only in 1973. It was formed by a New Delhi-based group of radical theater amateurs, led by a communist playwright and director named Safdar Hashmi (1954–1989). His murder during a show on

© reddees/Shutterstock.com

the outskirts of Delhi in 1989 was a watershed in India's street theater as thousands of politically conscious theater practitioners took to the street with dramatic performances as a direct response to the killing. Today, Hashmi's birthday, 12th of April, is celebrated across India as the National Street Theater Day. Likewise, many groups of theater practitioners across India today take up street drama as an effective way, with which sociopolitical predicaments in current Indian society can be meaningfully addressed.

The themes of Indian street theater range from more general topics such as the evils of capitalism and globalization, to more locally significant issues such as communal disharmony, caste-related repression, the burden of dowry, as well as rape and violence against women. Indian street theater practitioners have also been keen to act out certain local events of the recent past to highlight the issues of sociopolitical significance. The 1984 death of thousands of people after a toxic gas leak from the Union Carbide's pesticide plant in Bhopal, and the 2012 Delhi gang rape of a girl known to the public only as "fearless girl" (*nirbhaya*) are a pair of such instances (Das and Raab 2012; Liu 2016).

One of the pioneer groups of theater practitioners to use modern street theater in Nepal to expose the repressive character of the political system has been a theater group called *Swarnam* ("Representing Everyone"). It was founded in 1982 by Ashesh Malla (b. 1954), a playwright and radical political activist, with the support of like-minded undergraduates at Tribhuwan University, located in Nepal's capital Kathmandu. In 1981, when his play "Hands Raised in Protest" (*Murdabadma Utheka Haathharu*) was prohibited by the Nepali authorities after only three performances, Malla and his theater group decided to take their critic of the repressive political system to the people through the medium of street theater. Today, Ashesh Malla is regarded as the founder of Nepali street theater, known to locals as *sadak naatak* (Liu 2016).

In Sri Lanka, too, modern street theater is in the space of satire generated by the island's long tradition of folk and ritual performances. The comic interludes in the healing rituals known as *thovil,* as well as the satirical performances of entertainment in the folk dance form called *sokari* and dance drama referred to as *kolam* are important in carving the above space of satire (Sarachchandra 1953; Obeyesekere 1999). Although it permitted occasional parody of the political elite (especially, in *kolam*), it was primarily a space limited for amusement, and not for political disruption.

Modern political street theater in Sri Lanka truly began in 1974 when Gamini Haththotuwegama (1938–2009), a radical theater practitioner (and an unorthodox university don), commenced performances while traveling across the country with his young and energetic group of actors, equally committed to street theater. Taking politicized ("critically ideologically conscious") theater (Haththotuwegama in Dharmasiri 2012, 228) to a wider section of the spectators (such as the peasants in the remote villages, dwellers in urban slums, workers in the factories, and passersby on the street), often unfrequented by theater practitioners who confined to traditional enclosed proscenium theater halls in cities was one of the group's stated goals. In that endeavor, Haththotuwegama "transcreated" (nativized original texts so they may be able to go through linguistic and cultural transformation to suit new sociopolitical, and cultural settings) some works of the well-known dramatists such as Shakespeare and Brecht. Additionally, he and his troupe of "open street drama" (*Vivurtha Veedi Natya*) presented their open dramas (with or without prepared scripts), spontaneously created theatrical events to suit the occasion, and presented mimic performances. Their performances often parodied and criticized the capitalist and consumerist ethos that has encroached into everyday living, repressive governance, and communal disharmony (Dharmasiri 2012).

## Mikhail Bakhtin's Notion of Carnivalesque

A term coined by the Russian literary critic Mikhail Bakhtin (1895–1975), **carnivalesque** or folk humor refers to a speech genre that transpires across an array of cultural sites, especially in carnival itself. Bakhtin believed that, as a literary mode, carnivalesque is capable of subverting and liberating the assumptions of the dominant style or atmosphere (Bakhtin 1984; Storey 2012). He hypothesized that the experiences of lived immediacy and joy constructed through collective festivity can offset anxiety caused by hierarchical structure and all forms of conventionality and inequality. Therefore, the metaphor of carnival should be applied to the structure of narratives using what Bakhtin calls *dialogism.* The creation of a situation, in which diverse voices can be heard and interact is what he means by dialogism. The act of carnivalization, Bakhtin believes, inverts convention, enables dialogue (hence, gets rid of authoritarian voice or monologue), and celebrates a grotesque cannon of the body.

In his work, *Rabelais and His World* (1965) and *Problems of Dostoevsky's Poetics* (1929), Bakhtin identifies carnival as central to his discussion of carnivalesque. Accordingly, carnival is a sort of syncretic and ritualized pageantry, in which the display of excess and grotesqueness becomes distinctive. Its most defining feature is the celebration of life in a joyful and exuberant way. Carnival inhabits on the marginal space between art and life in that it is an alternative way of living molded according to a pattern of play. Carnival may be characterized as a performance, but it is a performance, in which no boundary between performers and spectators could be clearly demarcated. Carnival provides a possibility to offer new perspectives and a new order of things.

Bakhtin identifies the following categories as crucial in generating "carnivalistic sense of the world": free and familiar interaction between people, misalliance, eccentric behavior, and sacrilege (Bakhtin 1984; Storey 2012).

Accordingly, the carnival creates an atmosphere, in which generally separated people may be able to get together and express themselves freely. Highlighting universal participation in the medieval carnival, as well as "free," "frank," "absolutely gay," and "fearless talk" existed among its participants, Bakhtin maintains that the potency of carnival was to be found in the nonseparation of the participants from the spectators. Moreover, it was a cultural form confined in time, not in space. It penetrated private spaces such as the household, just as it prevailed upon in public spheres such as the town square. Yet, he continues, the participants of the medieval carnival always treated the town square and streets that approximated it as the carnival's central location, where every participant was entitled and able to share the sense of belonging.

© Pisu80/Shutterstock.com

Similarly, the character and atmosphere of the carnival makes it possible to link discrete and opposing categories, such as high and low, old and new, and sacred and profane.

Moreover, it is a space receptive to behavior revealing the hidden facets of human nature, the facets usually barred from other venues.

What is more, the carnival is a site of blasphemy, peccability, and profanity, where parody of things (which are usually considered sacred) is permitted.

Bakhtin maintains that the above categories do not stem from abstract concepts such as freedom, equality, and solidarity. Rather, they are to be perceived as lived experiences of the world displayed in sensual forms of ritualistic acts that are played out as if they were pertained to life itself (Bakhtin 1984; Storey 2012).

In contemporary world, carnivalesque remains a prospective counterpower in everyday affairs of ordinary life and activism although it is considerably restricted in its potential by the authoritarian constructions of spaces of monologue (Robinson 2009).

## Occupy Wall Street and Carnivalization of Art

Occupy Wall Street (OWS) was the name given to a protest movement that eventuated on September 17, 2011, near New York City's Wall Street financial district, igniting global public imagination and spawning similar resistant movements throughout the United States and around the world. The leaderless movement that retained its momentum

© Daryl L /Shutterstock.com

throughout the fall of that year and a part of the spring that followed, was consisted of loosely knit groups with diverse persuasions and interests, such as antiglobalization, anticonsumerism, anticorporatization, and antiausterity advocacy (Sledge 2011; Farrell 2011). The common opposition to wealth inequality, political corruption, and corporate influence on government played a central role in galvanizing camaraderie among the protestors.

Intriguingly however, street art also contributed significantly in generating creative energy. On that count, the populist grassroots movement was replete with instances of occupation, civil disobedience, picketing, demonstrations, and internet activism, but it was also filled with art inspired by the movement's message of nonconformity and resistance. The art activities included poster advertising, site-specific performances, and pop-up exhibitions. Additionally, the movement's ad hoc Committee for Arts and Culture also highlighted spoken word performances and poetry reading events in its prime venue, Manhattan's Zuccotti Park. In the process, art emerged as a main vehicle for expressing the OWS movement.

According to anthropologist David R. Graeber's reflective analysis, the movement turned into an anarchist project in the most fundamental way as it gradually gathered pace (Graeber 2011). He cites the following reasons to justify his characterization: lack of

© Glynnis Jones/Shutterstock.com

recognition of the existing political institutions and the legal structure, and their embracement of nonhierarchical consensus decision-making and prefigurative politics. The way OWS protestors contributed to that anarchist project through resistance-oriented art activities was intriguing.

The original protest was initiated by a provocative poster, advertised by the Canadian anticonsumerist and pro-environmentalist magazine *Adbusters* in its July 2011 issue. The poster carried an image featuring a ballerina atop Wall Street's giant bronze statue of the charging bull, a symbol of hawkish financial optimism and growth. The ballerina was seen perching elegantly on one leg on the bull, turning out and extending the other leg behind her supple body, and stretching her arms serenely against the grey skies. In contrast to the bull's muscular mass, the ballerina was lithe in stature. Moreover, her serenity was strikingly different from belligerent aggression of the bull and the riot police whose emergence from the foggy background with helmets and gas masks was visible. In this act of carnivalization of art, the poster designer could turn an icon of the U.S. financial capital into an ironic image.

The symbolism of the poster set the tone of the protest movement, which proved to be capable of "igniting something powerful in the public imagination that has held fast" (Beeston 2011). Consequently, the bearers of Guy Fawkes masks began to show up in the protest venues stylistically rendering the best-known members of the Gunpowder Plot (who attempted to blow up the House of the Lords in London in 1605). Their presence indubitably showed the growing sentiments of antiestablishment among the protestors and their sympathizers.

*Ocularpation: Wall Street* was the site-specific work of performance art devised by artist Zefrey Throwell to "dress down" and expose the reality of workings on the famous financial artery of the United States and the economy (www.zefrey.com 2011). Fifty men and women, the members of an organization called the Young Naturalists and Nudists of New York City, participated in this performance which took place in the precincts of Wall Street on August 1, 2011. "It was an early Monday morning like any other on Wall Street," writes Melena Ryzik, an Art and Design columnist for *The New York Times*, describing the above act of performance (Ryzik 2011). It did not take too long to turn it like no other, however. Seconds before the clock struck seven, Throwell's ladies and gents, clad in gray suits and navy dresses, appeared along Wall Street while chatting into their headsets or cellphones. Suddenly, some of them started to loosen their ties, unbutton blue shirts, take off pants, and lift skirts flashing bare naked bodies. Then they began to mimic the typical Wall Street workweek in nonchalant detail: stock trading, street sweeping, newspaper reading, coffee-fetching, hot-dog vending, dog-walking, and prostituting! The nude actors were arrested immediately by the police officers stationed near the New York Stock Exchange and given summons for disorderly conduct, before being released eventually. The rest of the actors of the orchestration, including Zefrey Throwell who took part by playing the role of the naked hot-dog vender, were busy in getting their arrested colleagues back to the fold and explaining the project's purpose to the pedestrians who seemed visibly stunned to glimpse the sudden expanse of flesh. The sassy display lasted for nearly five minutes.

## Chapter Summary

This chapter proceeds to explore another very distinctive aspect of being human: artistic expression and appreciation or symbolic creativity seen across cultures. The chapter deals with art's biological origins and formal qualities, as well as the salient aspects of the anthropological perspective of art. It also explores the themes of art and power, art and media, and art and globalization.

- Artistic expression is one of the most distinctive aspects of being human. Whereas most anthropologists hold the view that art is a human universal, they often differ from each other in terms of their theoretical orientations, analytic frameworks, and the themes that they incline to elaborate.

- Anthropologist Alexander Alland focuses on the biological roots of art that extends back to the animal ancestors of human species. He maintains that the seductive aspect, which is the essence of art, is truly biological in its origin. Alland argues further, art may be varied vastly as functional differences take place both cross-culturally and historically, yet what makes art a human universal is its game-like character in which symbolic transformation of formal elements becomes a main enticement for artistic creativity. Accordingly, art is definable as play with form which brings into existence some aesthetically successful transformation-representation.

- The cross-cultural perspective assists anthropologists to ferret out the art forms, modes, and aesthetics that are shared and panhuman, as well as those art traditions that are not shared everywhere and considered culture specific. Recent anthropological studies on art have been emphasizing the need to move beyond the traditional dichotomy of Western and non-Western art and to adopt a critical ethnographic approach on the practices and processes that drives the Western art world.

- The array of artifacts which were made to be art by their original creators is referred to as art by intention. Similarly, the host of artifacts primarily made for purposes other than art by their original creators yet developed to be art later is known as art by appropriation.

- The anthropological perspective to art lays stress on the emic approach or the research strategy with which ethnographers may be able to use the cultural concepts and categories which are relevant and meaningful to the culture under investigation. The emic approach provides opportunities to explore the meanings pertaining to artistic activity in the context of the local conceptual system as emic aesthetics exists only in the minds of native art connoisseurs. What makes the emic approach possible is the anthropological fieldwork method of ethnography, as it is based on enduring personal observation and social participation.

- Despite the qualitative and quantitative differences on art, the primary anthropological concern has been the exploration of the sets of beliefs and behaviors consistently shared by the members of society. In much the same way, anthropology of art focuses on the aesthetic values held by a large segment of a specific group of people for a considerable period.

- Long before globalization became a part of public and academic discourse, new art forms and art institutions had been diffusing into local cultures across the globe. However, the accelerated pace of cultural diffusion and the magnitude of change in the twenty-first century has been unprecedented. In the context of globalization of art, a notable severance of cultural practices from their places of origin and people, as well as a simultaneous spawning of people's closer involvement with art objects, forms, and traditions alien to them have been observable. The above process, which is known as the deterritorialization of art, has been permitting the reterritorialization to transpire at a global level as well. This latter, the flipside of the former is the restructuring process in which territorial relocalizations of old art forms, institutions, and activities, as well as new art productions emphatic of locality and culture takes place. As a result, the deterritorialization and reterritorialization of art bring forth translocalized and territorialized cultural experiences in globalized modernity.

- The Theater of the Oppressed was a set of interactive and politically expressive theatrical forms and techniques created by the Brazilian theater practitioner Augusto Boal in the early 1970s.

- Guerilla Theater was a theater form adopted in 1965 by a group of U.S. theater practitioners known as *San Francisco Mime Troupe* (SFMT) to present politically and socially significant issues on the wayside and open theater locations such as public parks.

- Street theater is a theatrical form, with which either politically charged or experiment-oriented dramatic performances are presented (by the actors ranging from buskers and theatrical practitioners) in outdoor public places without elaborate costumes and props, amplified sound, or a specific paying audience.

- South Asia offers another fine example for using street theater to combine performance with resistance. Street theater in India is a front for the left-wing political activism. Likewise, modern street theater in Nepal is meant to expose the repressive character of the political system. By the same token, Sri Lankan street theater often parodies and criticizes the capitalist and consumerist ethos that has encroached into everyday living, repressive governance, and communal disharmony.

- A term coined by the Russian literary critic Mikhail Bakhtin (1895–1975), carnivalesque or folk humor refers to a speech genre that transpires across an array of cultural sites, especially in carnival itself. The act of carnivalization, Bakhtin believes, inverts convention, enables dialogue (hence, gets rid of authoritarian voice or monologue), and celebrates a grotesque cannon of the body.

- Occupy Wall Street (OWS), the protest movement that eventuated on September 17, 2011, near New York City's Wall Street financial district, could ignite global public imagination and spawn similar resistant movements throughout the United States and around the world. Intriguingly, street art also contributed significantly in generating creative energy. The way OWS protestors contributed to that anarchist project (Graeber 2011) through resistance-oriented art activities was characterizable as an instance of carnivalization of art.

# Kinship, Descent, and Marriage: Comprehending Relatedness

© Marino A/Shutterstock.com

**K**inship is the system of meaning and power that cultures construct based on biology, marriage, and choice to ascertain relatedness, mutuality, rights, and obligations. As a species accustomed to collective social life, human beings bring groups into existence through a variety of other means such as education, profession, religious origin, linguistic link, and political association. Even so, the power of kinship arteries to supply and protect group resources, endure group reproductive success, and influence group-affiliated sociopolitical and economic systems remains incomparably high.

The study of kinship opens a vista for anthropologists to delve into the everyday affairs of closely knit kin groups, such as family, which are deep in engagement and rich in intimacy.

In like manner, it provides an avenue to explore many of the emotionally laden and ritualistically elaborate life events occurring on special occasions, such as wedding ceremonies, birthday parties, holiday celebrations, family get-togethers, and bereavement gatherings.

As the everyday activities and specific events in family are usually interlaced with what is taking place outside of the household, individual's home enculturation fashions their interactions within the large society considerably. Put another way, how individuals treat one another, behave in group roles, and steer through age, gender, sexuality, race, ethnicity, and other such social divisions often mirror how they navigate the affairs within their own family. By the same token, discussion and debate within the large culture over cultural norms, values, and worldviews may reflect and shape the dynamics within family and other kin groups. Consequently, kinship also becomes a space in which the meanings of kinship categories are constantly negotiated, contested, and resisted.

## Diagramming the Universe of Kin

There are several ways with which kinship links can be shown on paper. Genealogical charts are sometimes drawn literally as trees, beginning with a salient founder, known as apical ancestor or progenitor, and then branching up to show the ancestry, descent, and relationships of all members of a family. These diagrams are known as *family trees* or *genealogical trees.*

Sometimes, kinship diagrams are also depicted in the form of a chandelier with hanging branches representing a number of kin. On certain other occasions, the stress is laid on a designated individual known as Ego as well. Accordingly, Ego is placed in the center of the diagram and all other relatives (e. g., parents and grandparents) are shown radiating out in expanding concentric circles or spheres. The purpose of all these diagramming methods is to present kin ties schematically while maximizing simplicity and minimizing complexity.

Anthropologists would draw a *kinship diagram* or a streamlined visual schema to present data on kinship links of Ego. A kinship diagram/chart is a schematic representation of all of Ego's relatives, as recollected by Ego. Identifying Ego, considered as the point of reference, is salient since information on kin connections, terminology, and role obligations must be gleaned according to Ego's location within the diagram.

Mapping all the relatives in a kinship diagram requires the use of symbols, letter symbols, and compound strings. Kin relationships such as a relative's gender identity, a deceased relative, an adopted relative, marriage, cohabitation, separation, parentage, and siblings are shown through a host of standard symbols. For example, the phallic triangle is used to show a male relative, a circle for a female, and a square for a transgendered individual or kin whose information on gender identity is not available. Similarly, either equal sign or bracket under two individuals (shown in the kinship diagram) is used to symbolize marriage. Likewise, a vertical line is used to represent descent or parentage, and a horizontal line or a bracket over two individuals to symbolize sibling relationship (See FIGURE 7.1).

Certain relatives such as mother, father, sister, brother, daughter, son, wife, and husband are represented through the first (upper case) letter of the kin link: mother (M), father (F), sister (Z), brother (B), daughter (D), son (S), husband (H), and wife (W). As an extension of this method of abbreviations, compound strings are used to show certain relatives in

## FIGURE 7.1   Symbols Used in Kinship Diagrams

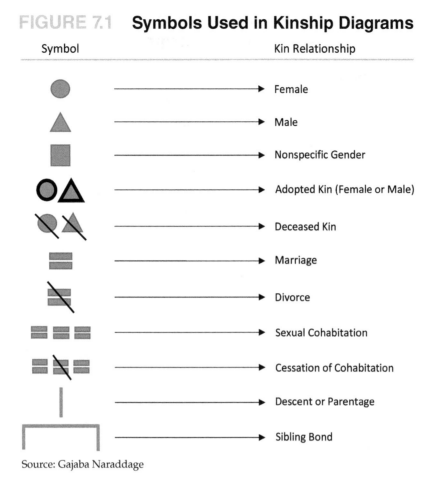

| Symbol | Kin Relationship |
| --- | --- |
| ● | Female |
| ▲ | Male |
| ■ | Nonspecific Gender |
| ◯△ | Adopted Kin (Female or Male) |
| ◑△ | Deceased Kin |
| ▬ | Marriage |
| ▬ | Divorce |
| ▬▬▬ | Sexual Cohabitation |
| ▬▬▬ | Cessation of Cohabitation |
| │ | Descent or Parentage |
| └─┘ | Sibling Bond |

Source: Gajaba Naraddage

a kinship diagram: mother's sister (MZ), mother's sister's daughter (MZD), mother's sister's son (MZS), father's brother (FB), father's brother's daughter (FBD), father's brother's son (FBS), grandfather (GF), and grandmother (GM).

The approach is the most commonly used method by anthropologists when naming relatives in kinship diagram. However, some anthropologists prefer to use another method of abbreviations. According to that method, the first two letters of the kin term (with the capitalized first letter) are used. For instance, mother is indicated Mo, father is Fa, daughter is Da, son is Sa, sister is Si, brother is Br. The same rule is observed for consanguineal kin. Accordingly, father's sister's daughter becomes FaSiDa, just as mother's brother's son becomes MaBrSo. Affinal kin are written in the same way as well. So, brother-in-law becomes WiBr. The same kin link is also designated either as HuWiBr (if Ego is a female) or as WiHuBr (if Ego is a male) (See FIGURE 7.2).

## Searching for Kin-Naming Patterns

Anthropologists find that by collecting kinship data for the people being studied and linking them into local genealogy they can get the hang of who people are and how they relate to one another. Anthropologists also know that they may be able to get a better grip of how people deal with social, economic, and political affairs by examining a society's kinship relations. Even more so, they understand that the study of kinship is pivotal to making

**FIGURE 7.2    Letter Symbols and Compound Strings Used in Kinship Diagrams**

| Letter Symbol | Kin Term |
| --- | --- |
| M | Mother |
| F | Father |
| S | Son |
| D | Daughter |
| B | Brother |
| Z | Sister |
| H | Husband |
| W | Wife |

| Compound String | Kin Term |
| --- | --- |
| MZ | Mother's Sister |
| MZD | Mother's Sister's Daughter |
| MZS | Mother's Sister's Son |
| FB | Father's Brother |
| FBD | Father's Brother's Daughter |
| FBS | Father's Brother's Son |
| GF | Grand Father |
| GM | Grand Mother |

Source: Gajaba Naraddage

sense of how culture works, since kin ties extend well beyond the bounds of immediate family and deep into all aspects of cultural life. Indeed, kinship and its relevance to human social life has been one of the main premises anthropologists have generally agreed on ever since it was brought to attention by early anthropologists such as Lewis Henry Morgan.

## Kin Term

A **kin term** is a word used in a language to primarily classify a relative. For instance, kin term "father" informs about the relative's gender, as well as the nature of relationship through which the father may be distinguishable from other male relatives such as the uncle, the brother, and the son. However, the father may be a reference to the genitor (biological father), the pater (social father), the adoptive father, the stepfather, the godfather, or even Holy Father. In like manner, kin term "mother" informs about the relative's gender and the nature of relationship through which the mother may be distinguishable from other female relatives such as the aunt, the sister, and the daughter. However, the mother may be a reference to the genitrix or genitress (biological mother), the mater (social mother), the adoptive mother, the stepmother, the godmother, or even Holy Mother. What these examples illustrate is the fact that kin terms usually lump together multiple genealogical relationships or kin types.

All human societies share a basic set of principles for social organization. Anthropologists observed only six distinct kinship terminological systems in the world, despite the existence of vast geographical and cultural variation. In all of them, the variation is based on the categorization of Ego's siblings and cousins. Early anthropologists named each of these six systems after a core group in which the pattern was present. They are as follows: *Eskimo, Hawaiian, Sudanese, Crow, Omaha,* and *Iroquois.*

## Eskimo System

The Eskimo system of kinship terminology specifically identifies the kin within the nuclear household by focusing on gender and generation: mother, father, sister, brother. These terms of reference are not used for any other relatives. All other types of relatives are grouped together into several large categories. Paternal siblings are distinguished from parents and treated separately in accordance with their gender as aunts and uncles. The same kin terms may be used to identify the spouses of the aunts and uncles as well. All relatives of Ego's generation are lumped together and referred to as cousins. The features make it amply clear that the Eskimo kin-naming system lays stress on the nuclear family.

The Eskimo system does not distinguish the relatives on the mother's side from those on the father's side either. Thus, the same kin terms of reference are used for all aunts, uncles, and cousins, regardless of the side of the family to which they belong. By favoring kin within the nuclear family over more distant relatives, the Eskimo system of kinship terminology demonstrates that it is based on the principle of bilateral descent (discussed later).

The Eskimo kin-naming pattern is mostly found among the people of simplistic and small-scale societies, such as the Inuit (Eskimo) foragers in the Canadian and Alaskan Arctic, as well as among the people of complex, industrial societies, such as the urbanites in North America and Europe. What this occurrence shows is the fact that, despite vast sociocultural differences, both foraging and industrial societies tend to prefer mostly independent nuclear families over other family types.

## Hawaiian System

The Hawaiian system is a simple classificatory system in which all relatives of the same generation and gender are identified by the same kin term. Thus, Ego refers to all female kin in his or her parent's generation (mother and mother's sisters) as "mother," while also referring all male relatives (father and father's brothers) as "father." In like manner, Ego identifies all female relatives in Ego's own generation (sisters and female cousins) as "sisters," while recognizing all male kin (brothers and male cousins) as "brothers." As a result, the Hawaiian kin-naming system has only four distinct terms of reference: mother, father, sister, and brother. As all of Ego's cousins are identified as brothers and sisters, marriage of cousins is generally discouraged. Equally salient, this kin-naming system is generally associated with the principle of ambilineal descent.

The least distinction among kin in the Hawaiian kin-naming pattern strongly suggests that it lays stress on the extended family while de-emphasizing the nuclear family. Widely seen in the islands of Polynesia, the Hawaiian kinship terminology is a system used by about a third of the world's small-scale societies.

## Sudanese System

The Sudanese system separately identifies almost each one of Ego's relatives in accordance with their genealogical distance from Ego and the side of the family, as well as their gender. There may be eight distinct terms of reference for cousins, all of whom are distinguished from Ego's siblings (sisters and brothers). The intense efforts evidently made to differentiate relatives from each other strongly suggest that the society seems to have a higher tendency to distinguish individuals based on social divisions such as class status, professional accomplishments, and political capital. Indeed, the Sudanese system is mostly found in societies with patrilineal descent and a substantial degree of social complexity.

The Iroquois, Crow, and Omaha systems of kinship terminology trace kinship either from father's side (patrilineal descent) or mother's side (matrilineal descent). Hence, they are kinship-naming systems sticking to unilineal descent, meaning kinship is traced from one side only.

## Iroquois System

In the Iroquois system, for example, the father and the father's brother are identified by the single kin term "father," just as the mother and the mother's sister are referred to as "mother." However, the father's sister and the mother's brother are identified by separate terms. The "merging" evident here is associated with shared membership in unilineages. The Iroquois kinship terminology may be operating either in patrilineal or matrilineal systems. The system gives different terms of reference for kin on Ego's mother's side and father's side, distinguishing between cross and parallel cousins. There exists a preference for marriage to cross cousins in societies that use the Iroquois system.

## Crow System

A kin-naming system of matrilineal descent, the Crow kinship lumps relatives together based on descent and gender. Ego's siblings and parallel cousins of the same gender are identified by the same term of reference. Mother and mother's sisters are referred to by the same kin term as well. The relatives in the matrilineage of Ego's father are grouped together across generations. This feature indicates that the father's side of the family is relatively insignificant.

## Omaha System

A patrilineal system, the Omaha kin-naming pattern is almost a mirror image of the Crow system. Ego's siblings and parallel cousins of the same gender are identified by the same term of reference. Father and father's brothers are referred to by the same kin term as well. The relatives in the patrilineage of Ego's mother are grouped together across generations. This feature shows that the mother's side of the family is relatively insignificant.

Any attempt of scaling these kinship terminological systems from the least complex to the most complex is meaningless as anthropologists find them to be meaningful and orderly. For instance, for an outside observer, the Sudanese kinship terminology may appear as an extremely complex system which is almost unfathomable. However, the consistent application of its principles by the people who are accustomed to it shows for certain that the system is internally logical and coherent.

# Distinguishing Relatives

Anthropologists have identified several yardsticks with which diverse groups of people across the globe sort relatives into distinct categories. Accordingly, a society's preference to group certain kin together while separating others may hinge on different combinations of the following principles: Generation, Gender, Lineality versus Collaterality, Consanguinity versus Affinity, Relative Age, Bifurcation, and Gender of the Linking Kin.

## Generation

A common yardstick used to distinguish relatives in many kinship systems is the generation to which the relatives belong. Ego's first-attending generation is consisted of, for example, Ego's mother, father, and their siblings. Moreover, grandmothers and grandfathers are to be found two generations above Ego. Furthermore, Ego's first descending generation is usually made up of Ego's sons, daughters, nieces, and nephews, while Ego's own generation is comprised of Ego's siblings and cousins.

## Gender

Certain kin are grouped together on the basis of common gender. For instance, mother, mother's sister, grandmother, sister, daughter, and granddaughter are always females, just as father, father's brother, grandfather, brother, son, and grandson are males. In English system prevalent in the United States, cousins are not differentiated on account of individual's gender, yet distinguishing aunt and uncle involves gender and generation.

## Lineality versus Collaterality

Ego's direct ancestors and descendants such as father, grandfather, sons, and grandsons or lineal kin are distinguished from indirect ancestors such as parents' siblings, siblings, and their descendants or collateral relatives. In this sense, **lineality** refers to relatives connected to Ego through a lineal relative (See FIGURE 7.3).

   If lineal kin are to be the main trunk that connects an Ego to his or her ancestry and progeny, collateral relatives may be pictured as the side branches off that main trunk (See FIGURE 7.4).

## Consanguinity versus Affinity

In certain systems of kinship, kin links based on descent or **consanguinity** (Latin roots: *con,* meaning *with,* and *sanguineus,* meaning *blood*) are distinguished from those based on marriage or **affinity** (Latin roots: *affinis,* meaning related to, and *ity,* suffix is used to make it an abstract noun). Therefore, a distinction is made between the people who are related by blood (consanguines or consanguineal kin) and by marriage (affinals or affinal kin). The kinship system used in the United States differentiates Ego's sons from sons-in-law, daughters from daughters-in-law, and sisters from sisters-in-law. However, this rule does not seem

## FIGURE 7.3   **Lineal Kin**

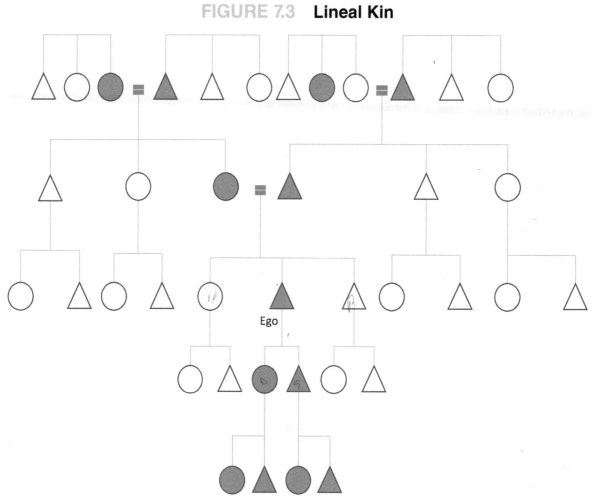

Source: Gajaba Naraddage

consistently applied in Ego's parent's generation. For example, both the blood relative mother's brother and the affinal kin mother's sister's husband are recognized by the same kin term: uncle. In matrilineal societies, the mother's sister is considered lineal kin. However, the father's sister is treated as an affine.

## Relative Age

The use of relative age as a salient criterion in distinguishing relatives is evident in some kinship systems. Accordingly, relatives of the same grouping may be differentiated on account of being older or younger than Ego.

## Bifurcation

Certain kinship systems make use of the distinction of bifurcation when referring to relatives on Ego's mother's side and father's side. In such systems, for example, different kin terms are utilized to recognize Ego's mother's brother and father's brother. No such distinction is evident in the system used in the United States. For instance, Ego's grandparents, aunts, uncles, and cousins are referred to by using the same kin terms regardless of the side of the family to which they belong.

**FIGURE 7.4    Collateral Kin**

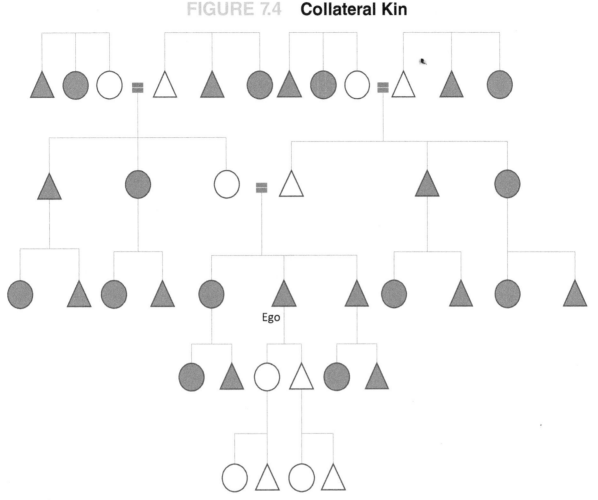

Source: Gajaba Naraddage

## Gender of the Linking Kin

The connecting relative's gender becomes salient in separating different sorts of kin in some kinship systems. By way of illustration, Ego's relatedness to the *cousins* does not hinge on the gender identity of Ego or the cousins, but on the gender of their parents (linking kin). According to this principle, mother's brother's children and father's sister's children are identified as **cross cousins.** Consequently, the above cousins are distinguishable from mother's sister's children and father's brother's children, known as **parallel cousins.**

## Constructing Groups of Kin: Descent

Cultures employ several ways to organize kin-based social groups. One salient way of kin-ordered social group formation has been the rules of descent, which stipulate the type of relationships from one generation to another. The membership of a descent group is essentially based on consanguinity or "blood" relationship. Ego's mother, father, parent's siblings, brothers, sisters, grandparents, and grandchildren are usually considered as the members of a descent groups. The spousal partners of parents' siblings are excluded for being affinal relatives. Typically, a **descent group** is comprised of an assemblage of kin who consider themselves as lineal descendants of a progenitor (founding, apical, or common ancestor) or progenitress (founding, apical, or common ancestress) stretching back over two generations. The imagining of their common progeny through a chain of parent–child connections, as well as the rights, responsibilities, and restrictions associated with that imagining function as a sociocultural adhesive to stick the descent group together.

## Unilineal Descent

In order to avoid situations in which different descent groups' membership loyalties lapping over each other, societies structured on the basis of kinship take diligent steps to sharply define and thereby restrict descent group membership. One of the most common ways of specifying descent affiliation is known as **unilineal descent.** Under unilineal descent rules, claims for descent group membership are validated by establishing a direct line from a progenitor or progenitress (progenitrix) exclusively through Ego's male or female ancestors, but not both. As the membership of either the mother's or the father's descent group is automatically ascribed to everyone at birth, confusion over where to look for someone's primary group allegiance does not arise.

## Matrilineal Descent

Tracing genealogical link exclusively through females from a progenitress is known as **matrilineal descent.** It is sometimes referred to as *uterine descent* also. A matrilineal descent group is consisted of a female Ego, her mother, the mother's mother, the mother's siblings, the mother's sister's children, the siblings, the sister's children, Ego's own children, and the children of her daughters. While every male kin automatically become a member of his mother's descent group, his own children become members of his wife's descent group, not his (See FIGURE 7.5).

## Patrilineal Descent

Establishing kin connection exclusively through males from a progenitor is known as **patrilineal descent.** It is sometimes referred to as *agnetic descent* also. Patrilineal descent is comprised of a male Ego, his father, the father's siblings, the father's brother's children, the siblings, the brother's children, Ego's own children, and the children of his sons. While every female relative automatically becomes a member of his father's descent group, her own children become members of her husband's descent group, not her (See FIGURE 7.6).

Matrilineal and patrilineal descent patterns are virtually mirror images of each other. Just as a woman cannot pass on descent to her own children within the patrilineal system, a man cannot transmit descent to his offspring within the matrilineal system.

### Lineage and Clan

Anthropologists have identified two main forms of unilineal descent groups: lineage and clan. **Lineage** is a unilineal kin-ordered group whose members can clearly demonstrate their common progeny, tracing genealogical links through several generations to a progenitor. Hence, lineage may be characterized as a form of *demonstrated descent.*

**FIGURE 7.5**  **Matrilineal Descent**

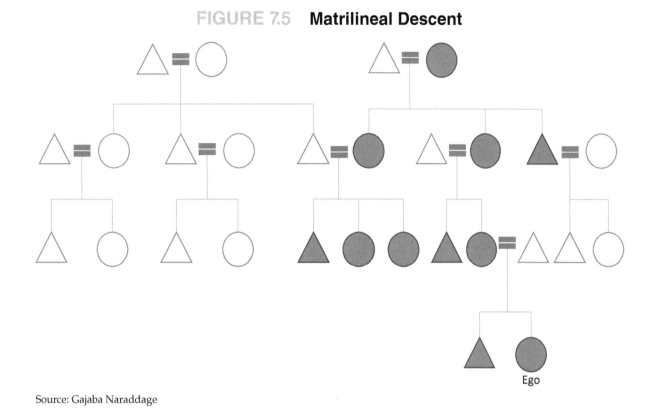

Source: Gajaba Naraddage

**Clan** is an extended unilineal kinship group whose members believe them to be descended from a progenitor even though they may not be able to demonstrate their common progeny through known kin. Hence, clan is conceivable as a form of *stipulated descent.* Clans may be either *matriclans* or *patriclans.* In matriclans, newborns are recruited as new group members from women of their group, whereas in patriclans, newborns are recruited as new group members from men of their group.

## Cognatic Descent

Reckoning genealogical links without unilineal restrictions is known as **cognatic descent.** In this way, descent may be traced through both the mother's and father's ancestors. The relatives reckoned through this system of descent are referred to as cognates, meaning kin by birth, or of ambilineal, parallel, and bilateral.

### Bilateral Decent

The most common and the best known of cognatic descent system is **bilateral descent.** It is found among most people of European ancestry in North America, in many European societies, as well as among many people in the world who practice foraging for sustenance. Under bilateral descent, an Ego may be able to recognize all consanguineal kin traced through both the mother's side, and the father's side of the family. This descent rule relates an Ego to virtually all his or her lineal kin, such as parents, all four grandparents, all eight great grandparents, and all third and fourth cousins (See FIGURE 7.7).

## FIGURE 7.6    Patrilineal Descent

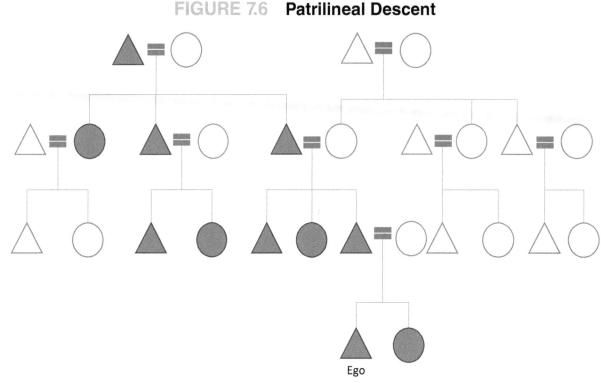

Source: Gajaba Naraddage

## Kindred

The **kindred** is a network of relatives, traceable through bilateral descent, and linked to Ego and Ego's siblings. In kindred, Ego and Ego's siblings share precisely the same group of kin, such as parents, grandparents, aunts, uncles, and cousins. Aside from siblings, everyone else has a different set of relatives. For example, Ego and Ego's brothers and sisters have the same members of their nuclear family and the same consanguineal kin of extended family. However, Ego's father will count Ego, Ego's brother, and Ego's sister as members of his bilateral descent group, yet he will not consider his wife (Ego's mother) as part of his kindred as she and all her consanguineal relatives are linked to Ego's father through affinity. Alternatively put, Ego's kindred group members do not share quite the same group of kin unless they are related to Ego as siblings.

As the kindred is organized laterally (relating to the "side") rather than lineally (relating to the "line"), Ego becomes the central figure from whom the extent of each kin link is calculated. This means that the kindred is incapable of functioning as a group without the presence of Ego. Usually, the expiry of Ego heralds the end of the kindred formed around that Ego as well. The lack of self-continuance indicates that the kindred is not a genuine descent group, but an ego-centered network of bilateral kin.

Unlike unilineal descent groups (such as matrilineage and patrilineage) based on extended family and lineage, the kindred are formed by concentrating on Ego's nuclear family. Its ego-centeredness and focus on nuclear family makes the kindred a good candidate for social grouping in industrial societies in North America and Europe. In the United States,

FIGURE 7.7 **Bilateral Descent**

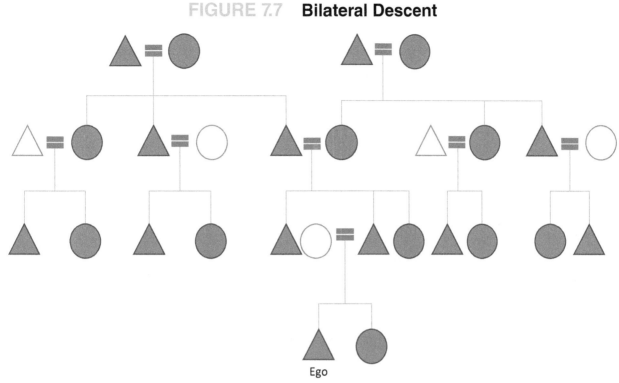

Ego

Source: Gajaba Naraddage

for example, most individuals of European descent can recognize the members of their kindred, a network of blood relatives on both mother's and father's side of the family. Although simply known as relatives, such kin are invited for important occasions such as family weddings, reunions, and bereavement gatherings. "Kissing cousins" or the relatives with whom Ego is in close enough terms to invite for special occasions and to greet with a kiss are a fine example to the members of an Ego's kindred.

# Constructing Groups of Kin: Marriage

A pervasive feature of human kinship and social organization, marriage often assumes a pivotal role in forming a family, the basic structural unit of society. Equally significant, the members of a family reciprocally serve to fulfill a variety of individual and group obligations ranging from biological and economic to cultural, and thereby, making the functioning of society possible. It is for this reason a discussion of marriage and family becomes indispensable for the study of relatedness, and its individual and group concerns.

## What Is Marriage?

**Marriage** is generally referred to as a socially binding, culturally sanctioned, status transforming, enduring, sexual, companionate, and frequently procreative union between two or more individuals that establishes a set of reciprocal rights and obligations between the married partners, their offspring, and their kin groups. Some form of marriage or marriage-like relationship exists almost everywhere among humans. Prototypically, marital relationship may involve two adults of the opposite sex—a man and a woman. It stresses the procreative aspect of marriage, as well as the necessity to regulate sexual access between males and females stemming from the fact that in every society males and females are potentially and continuously receptive for sexual activity. Despite the fact that marriage is a customary practice in almost all societies, people in many societies are at variance in deciding how one marries, whom one marries, how many individuals a person can be married concurrently, what rights one shares with married partners (including the degree of sexual access one may have toward the partners), and what obligations one ought to fulfill as a married partner.

## Marriage as a Rite of Passage

Notwithstanding this enormous cultural diversity, in every society, marriage is considered a salient rite of passage. For certain, it is an occasion that transforms the social status of the participants from single individuals to married partners. However, marital union is a status-changing event not only for the individuals who are most directly involved, but also for their families and the communities they interact with. It is an instance in which the social status of the married partners' kin changes from unrelated, independent families to affinal relatives. Likewise, marriage is an incidence that transforms the social status of involving communities from independent social units to group alliances. The change of social status is often accompanied by the adoption of new social roles, and the rights and the responsibilities associated with such new roles.

## Love Marriage

The marriage based on romantic love or **love marriage** places individual's emotional interests and desires above the interests of the group. The marriage between two individuals who are in love is often considered as an ideal marriage practice originated in the West and disseminated throughout the globe afterward. Nevertheless, as Jankowiak and Fisher point out, romantic love leading to the union of two like-minded persons is an element noticeable in almost any culture (Jankowiak and Fischer 1992, 153). The marriage is the crucial rites of passage that transform a bachelor into a husband and a bachelorette into a wife. In love marriage, it is the rituals of courtship that facilitate this transformation since the two involving individuals begin to assess each other's attraction and compatibility within the course of these rituals. During the nineteenth century, the love-related activities in Western societies such as church fairs, picnics, and group dances were both private romantic moments and familial social events simultaneously. Subsequently however, such practices were gradually replaced by a host of privatized rituals of dating, lovemaking, and marriage. In her study of American love in the twentieth century, Eva Illouz reveals how these new rituals ranging from giving private and personal gifts (e.g., giving a dozen of red roses), and having intimate dinners, to traveling for romantic escapades, have transformed the experience of romantic love into an exclusively privatized space of lovemaking within the context of consumer capitalism (Illouz 1997; Hirsch and Wardlow 2006).

© Shashank Agarwal/Shutterstock.com

The choices individuals make in marriage tend to be influenced or limited by factors such as the well-being of the marital partners and their offspring, as well as the endurance of family alliances established through marriage.

## Arranged Marriage

Marital affairs may take the form of **arranged marriage** sometimes. Anthropologist Serena Nanda indicates that arranged marriage remains as a viable and widespread practice among the city-dwellers and the country folks alike in rapidly transforming modern India, as well as among Indian diaspora around the world, just as it had existed in the past among the people of traditional India (Nanda 1992, 34–45).

In a somewhat rare practice, the act of promise or agreement that two individuals will be married in the future is reached for the marital partners by their parents, guardians, or kin groups very early on. Henceforth, the intended partners in marriage are treated as *betrothed* or *engaged* to each other.

According to the more common custom however, the process of seeking suitable spousal partners for the bachelors and bachelorettes is commenced when they reach the appropriate age for marriage. Usually, seeking a match for the sons and marrying off the daughters require a great deal of scrutiny and time as matters such as physical attractiveness, perceived compatibility, education, occupation, and the character of the bride and the groom, as well as caste endogamy, family status, wealth, dowry, and potential business alliances are taken into consideration (Mines and Lamb 2010, 10).

As anthropologist Applebaum finds its frequent occurrence in contemporary Japanese society, arranged marriage does exist in industrial societies as well (Applebaum 1995).

© Lucky Business/Shutterstock.com

The increasing global popularity of virtual dating sites, mail-order-brides, and online matrimonial advertisements shows how the Internet has emerged in recent years as a venue for arranging or facilitating the processes of spousal selection.

## Rules Concerning Sexual Relations and Marriage

Every society has some form of rules with which mating relations and marital practices are regulated. The rules governing sexual relations, to follow anthropologist Robin Fox (1983), are distinguishable from the rules systematizing marital practices. Marriage is established and sanctioned by the rules that forbid marrying certain kin, dictate number of spouses one can have, allow for dissolving marriage and remarrying, specify the sorts of exchanges and rituals to sanction marriage, and verify marital rights and responsibilities. As the marital

© Tricky_Shark/Shutterstock.com

relationship implies the right for sexual access, banning marriage to certain types of kin and prohibitions against having sexual contact with certain categories of relatives coincide with each other.

## Incest Taboo

Among the most ubiquitous and basic rules that pertain to regulation of sexual encounters is the **incest taboo.** It is the categorical prohibition against having sex with each other by close relatives or primary kin. The most universally observed form of incest taboo entails forbidding sex between the members of nuclear family—between mother and son, father and daughter, and brothers and sisters. The instances in which the members of the royal families among the ancient Incas, Egyptians, and Hawaiians could mate with and marry their siblings were the rare, albeit notable, exceptions to this rule. The mating restrictions between close relatives almost always extend beyond the nuclear family to other close relatives such as parents' siblings, siblings' children, grandparents, and grandchildren.

However, in terms of the range and the type of sexual prohibitions, significant cultural variations do exist. For example, in societies such as the United States in which kinship relations are structured in accordance with the *bilateral descent* (that is, the Ego's mother's and father's relatives are treated on equal grounds simultaneously), all of Ego's half-siblings are considered incestuous. Bilateral nature of American kinship system is further reflected in the kin term *cousin* that does not distinguish between cross and parallel cousins. In some states in the United States, getting married to and having sexual contact with first cousins is forbidden by law. While referring to these forbidden relatives, anthropologist Martin Ottenheimer points out how a pre-Darwinian model based on biological origins of social evolution gained popularity after the mid-1800 in the United States when evolutionary models of human behavior were patronized by the world of fashion (Ottenheimer 1996).

In societies in which kin links are systematized in terms of the *unilineal descent* (that is, the Ego's descent traced through a single line, either the mother's or the father's), such as the Lekhers, the matrilineal inhabitants of Mizo Hills in the border region of India and Myanmar, mating with (or getting married to) maternal half siblings is fully acceptable. Moreover, distinguishing cross and parallel cousins as separate categories of kin is essential to unilineal systems. Therefore, having sex with (and getting married to) cross cousins is not

incestuous for the Yanomamo in the Amazon yet mating with parallel cousins is incestuous and strictly forbidden.

Sanctions for the incest taboo transgressions indicate the existence of an equally noticeable cultural diversity. In some societies, when incestuous instances become known to the public they may be casually condemned as disgraceful acts and the public expression of disapproval is usually the end act in such situations. By contrast, in certain other societies where the incest taboo is entwined with religious and moral ideologies, taboo violations can be accounted for as far more serious transgressions that could sap harmfully into the society's moral fiber, and accordingly, the violators are severely penalized.

Regardless of such cultural variations, the incest taboo's cross-cultural existence has long been drawing anthropological attention. Among the explanations offered for its continued presence and possible origins, three theories are frequently cited. One of them refers to avoidance of inbreeding on the immediate family to ward off the perceived harmful effects, as well as to promotion of genetic variability. Another explanation, closely associated with anthropologist Bronislaw Malinowski (1927), relies on the premise that restrictions on mating with close relatives have long-prevented conflicts over sexual access, minimized role ambiguity, and enhanced functioning of the family as a viable economic and social unit in society. Still another theory, championed by anthropologist Claude Levi-Strauss, holds that the incest taboo has been functioning as an effective means for building and strengthening interfamily alliances which have been pivotal to reduce conflict, enhance cooperation, and strategize resource depletion.

## Exogamy

Closely associated with the incest taboo are the rules of **exogamy** or cultural prescriptions for marrying outside of a certain group. Usually, the group of relatives specified as kin one should not marry are the same categories of relatives forbidden by the rules of incest. In this sense, the incest taboo is essentially a rule that ensures the prevalence of nuclear family exogamy. The rules of exogamy nudge close-knit kin groups to look outside of their immediate circle for potential marital partners. Therefore, exogamy is considered "marrying out." This rule helps to reduce conflicts that can arise over sexual encounters among the members of the primary cooperating groups, and thereby to enhance family harmony. It also generates opportunities to form socioeconomic and political alliances mutually beneficial to all involving parties. Levi-Strauss in his influential work on kinship and marriage entitled *The Elementary Structures of Kinship* (1969) argued cogently that marriage basically involves a formation of exchange alliances between the kin-units of "wife givers" and "wife takers."

## Endogamy

**Endogamy**, by contrast, is the rule whereby individuals are supposed to find marital partners within the social groups to which they belong. Hence, endogamy is considered "marrying in." Endogamous marriage exists in varying forms in different societies and cultures around the world. They range from *lineage endogamy* and *village endogamy* to *class endogamy*. In addition, two main endogamous forms of cousin marriage exist.

One of them, known as *parallel cousin marriage,* is marriage between parallel cousins (either between children of one's mother and one's mother's sister or between children of one's father and one's father's brother). The term "parallel" is used here to stress that the linking siblings belong to the same gender. The marriage between parallel cousins is the preferred form of endogamy among myriad Muslim communities in North Africa and the Middle East.

The other main endogamous form of cousin marriage, referred to as *cross-cousin marriage,* is marriage between cross-cousins (either between children of one's mother and one's mother's brother or between children of one's father and one's father's sister). The term "cross" is used in this context to emphasize that the linking siblings belong to different genders. The marriage between cross-cousins is a preferred form of endogamy among Tamil Hindus in South India and Sinhalese Buddhists in neighboring Sri Lanka. However, cross-cousin marriage is not a dominant form of marriage in either of these societies.

Endogamous marriage assists to keep social, economic, political, and cultural distinctions of the groups unaffected. In stratified societies, endogamy also helps to preserve and strengthen the privileges of those in the higher echelons of society through consolidation of power and wealth.

© Arjan Ard Studio/Shutterstock.com

The way status considerations influence selection of marital partners is amply evident in the practices of hypergamy, hypogamy, and isogamy. *Hypergamy* or "marrying up" refers to marriage with a partner of higher status. Status-oriented spousal selection frequently focuses on factors such as class, caste, and education of the spouse, physical features such as skin complexion, body size, and height of the partner, as well as the related factors such as age. Accordingly, hypergamy has its subtypes such as *height hypergamy* (marriage into a partner taller than oneself) and *age hypergamy* (marriage into a partner older than oneself). The opposite practice of hypergamous marriage is *hypogamy* or "marrying down." It refers to marriage with a partner of lower status. *Isogamy* or "marrying equal" is marrying a person of equal status.

# Forms of Marriage

Depending on the number of partners who may be married, marriage can take varying forms. They reflect social and cultural diversity. Anthropologists have identified two distinct forms distinguishing between societies that allow more than one marital partner and those that refuse to do so.

## Monogamy

**Monogamy** is one of them, and it is the form of marriage whereby the union between a pair of individuals takes place. If the pair is heterosexual, it is a marital relationship between two

© CatherineLProd/Shutterstock.com

individuals of the opposite gender. Cross-culturally, heterosexual monogamy is the most commonly practiced and legally sanctioned form of monogamous marriage. Occasionally, the two partners may be of the same gender as well, and in that case, the pairing is essentially homosexual. In the contexts such as North America and Europe where divorce and remarrying have increasingly become common and acceptable, individuals tend to practice **serial monogamy,** a form of monogamy whereby people are permitted to remarry any number of partners successively.

## Polygamy

Whereas monogamy is the legally recognized form of marriage in many countries, it is not the most common of all marriage forms. As far as the number of societies and cultures in which it is permitted is concerned, **polygamy** or the form of marriage whereby the union between multiple partners is possible has most practitioners. Polygamy is sometimes called *plural marriage* also. Practitioners of polygamous marriage are most often found among traditional agriculturalists and pastoralists in various regions of Asia and much of sub-Saharan Africa. Even in such societies and cultures however, polygamy remains only as an ideal or preferred form while monogamy has an exceedingly high number of practitioners.

### Main Forms of Polygamy: Polygyny

Polygamy has two main forms: polygyny and polyandry. **Polygyny** is the marriage between a man and multiple women. As a recent study indicates, polygyny exists as the favored form of marriage in approximately 80 percent to 85 percent of cultures around the world (Lloyd 2005). According to anthropologist George Murdock's earlier data, about 75 percent of world's cultures favor polygyny over other marital forms (Murdock 1949, 28).

Depending on cultural preference, the participants of polygyny have adopted two main types of residence. According to one such type, the husband, the cowives, and their children choose to live together in one dwelling. Usually, this residence is a dormitory-style home containing several private or semiprivate rooms for each cowife and her children along with common recreational areas. According to the other residence pattern, the cowives and their children prefer to live in separate dwellings located near each other.

In a common variation of polygyny known as *sororal polygyny,* a man can marry multiple women who are sisters. Usually, the plural wives of sororal polygyny can extend the existing sibling bondage to reliable companionship in polygynous household. As sister-wives, they can get rid of jealousy and forming emotionally supportive and mutually beneficial ties more easily than the cowives who are not known or related to each other prior to polygynous partnership. In this sense, sororal polygyny helps to minimize potential conflicts that can arise from situations such as the common husband's favoritism extended to one wife and her children over the other wives and their children (See FIGURE 7.8).

© Everett Historical/Shutterstock.com

In a polygynous society, a man is often capable of increasing his family wealth through marriage. In societies where a family's labor supply is pivotal to its productivity, having plural wives–and consequentially having multiple children–make that family resourceful. Especially, having several male children helps a polygynous man to build salient marriage alliances with other lineages. In doing so, he can strengthen his own lineage, earn prestige, and elevate his social position as well.

As noted earlier, even in societies where polygyny is the favored form of marriage most people practice monogamy. The actual occurrence of polygyny is considerably inhibited by several factors, and most conspicuous among them is polgynyous marriage's close association with wealth and power. Ordinarily, getting married to many wives is a feat only the

© Gereeva Maria/Shutterstock.com

wealthiest men can afford as bride wealth payments and maintaining more than one household can be costly. Therefore, polygyny has become a privilege of the elite on numerous contexts and occasions. For instance, in the highly stratified African kingdom of Swaziland, the king customarily chooses a new bride after annual reed dance, a privileged practice to which ordinary Swazi men are not entitled. In Islamic societies, a man is permitted to have as many as four wives on the prerequisite that he can look after all equally well, both materially and emotionally. Under such circumstances, most ordinary men in Islamic societies prefer to practice monogamy, instead of polygyny.

The regular link between polygyny and power in societies that practice it is also related to the demographic problem of the sex ratio. The number of men and women being approximately equal in most human populations, excess women of reproductive age are required for a polygynous marriage system to function. This numerical discrepancy is oftentimes lessened by setting limits on the number of wives a man can have, postponing the age at which men can marry, and hastening the age at which women may marry. Consequentially, in polygynous societies, powerful and wealthy men marry multiple women. However, powerless and poor men marry at a later age, marry equally deprived women, engage in on affairs noncommittal to marriage, or stay unmarried although not by their own choosing.

Jealousy and dissention among cowives may threaten domestic restfulness in a polygynous household while impeding smooth functioning of the family. Polygynous men attempt to remedy or minimize this problem by establishing separate living quarters for each wife and her children, setting a hierarchical relationship among cowives along the line of seniority

© Everett Historical/Shutterstock.com

**FIGURE 7.8**   **Polygyny and Sororal Polygyny**

Polygyny

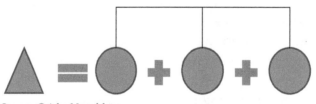

Sororal Polygyny

Source: Gajaba Naraddage

and age, and defining each wife's role accordingly. Perhaps, the sororal polygyny may have begun, among other reasons, as a way of regulating competition and alleviating friction among women in polygynous marital partnership.

Nevertheless, according to some studies based on sub-Saharan Africa, Southwestern Asia, and elsewhere, as among the growing "Christian polygamist" minority in the Rocky Mountain states of the United States, women's attitude toward polygyny in societies where it is practiced is not entirely negative (Shahd 2005; Kilbride 2006; Goodale 1971; Johnson 1996). Women in polygynous household seem to welcome the presence of a cowife as it provides them a useful partnership in sharing house chores and childcare, as well as a daily companionship. However, it is also evident that most young and educated women in these same societies tend to have unfavorable attitudes toward polygyny.

## Main Forms of Polygamy: Polyandry

The mirror image of polygyny is **polyandry.** It is the marriage between a woman and multiple men simultaneously.

A rare marital practice, polyandry is found occasionally in Polynesia, as among the Marquesas islanders, or in Canadian Arctic, as among the eastern Inuit. However, it is mostly known as a practice in the Himalayan states of Tibet, Nepal, and Bhutan, as well as in parts of India, as among the Toda of southern India.

*Fraternal polyandry* is a varying type of polyandry. It refers to a polyandrous marriage in which a woman can concurrently marry several men who are brothers. Tibetan polyandrous union mostly fits to this pattern as the marriage of brothers to a single woman is preferred by Tibetan polygamists. Whereas now it is almost extinct, fraternal polyandry has existed among the Sinhalese in the central highlands of Sri Lanka as well (Pieris 1956, 204–11). Known as "eating in one house" (*eka ge kema*), the practice was known to have existed as recently as in the first half of last century (Yalman 1967, 108–12; Leach 1955, 182–86).

Another variation of polygamy is known as *associated polyandry*. This polyandrous marriage usually begins as a monogamous relationship between husband and wife. A second man enters the relationship subsequently, and the cohusbands commence their polyandrous union with the joint wife thereafter (Yalman 1967, 108–12). The upcountry Sinhalese have practiced this form of polyandry also. In the Sinhalese case, the second relationship is often initiated by the wife (Pieris 1956). Associated polyandry has existed among wealthy Marquesas islanders in Polynesia, and in that case, recruitment of junior husbands to the polyandrous union was quite frequently done by the senior husband as a way of increasing the labor force of the family (Stephens 1963).

Anthropologists have suggested several reasons for the existence of polyandry. According to one such reason, polyandry may occur in societies where there are insufficiencies of women. A differential death rate in infancy alters the level of sex ratio at birth leaving an excess of males. It is suggested that the persistence of an uneven sex ratio conducive to polyandry in certain contexts, as in the case of the Toda of South India, might be attributable to female infanticide. However, when W. H. R. Rivers was conducting fieldwork among the Toda in the early twentieth century female infanticide was no longer practiced, yet there surely remained a fully organized system of polyandry (Rivers 1906). The ethnographic studies on societies where it is among the preferable marital types suggest that there are other salient correlates of polyandrous marriage.

© Aaron Amat/Shutterstock.com

According to another explanation, it is possible that the cultural preference for polyandrous union may have originated as a way of solidifying family resources such as land, property, and wealth, and thereby, as a mean for boosting family members' overall standard of living. Polyandry helps to minimize the fragmentation of ancestral property in places where land shortage is an acute problem. For instance, in Tibet, where arable land is limited, and inheritance is in the male line, brothers prefer to a contract a polyandrous union with a single woman rather than having a separate wife for each and having to split up the family land among multiple heirs. In this sense, polyandrous marriage is an effective system for keeping the paternal estate undivided and avoiding increased pressures on resources (Goldstein 1987).

It has also been suggested that in societies where men must be away from home for activities such as herding, trading, and military expeditions, polyandry makes certain that households will likely have at least one man at home to fulfill male domestic and economic tasks. The incessant supply of male labor by polyandrous brothers in Tibetan households is given as a fine example to this point (Silk 1997, 375–98). In the same vein, during the time of the Kandyan kingdom (from the sixteenth century to nineteenth century) in Sri Lanka, when upcountry Sinhalese men were required to be away from home for public service known as *rajakariya* ("service for the king") leaving their families unattended for several months, polyandrous brothers at home had tended to family farms and cared for the joint-wife and children. Indeed, it was mostly during this time fraternal polyandry had

**FIGURE 7.9** **Polyandry and Fraternal Polyandry**

Polyandry

Fraternal Polyandry

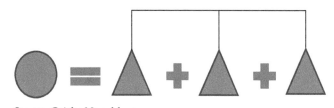

Source: Gajaba Naraddage

prevailed as a preeminent marital practice among the upcountry Sinhalese (Pieris 1956) (See FIGURE 7.9).

As shown from the foregoing discussion, marriage is not dependent on marital partners' selections and desires alone. Often, it involves a whole host of other considerations ranging from descent alliances to economic considerations. The point becomes further evident when examining how a couple usually take up residence somewhere after getting married.

# Postmarital Residence Patterns

In every society, a newly married couple may take up residence somewhere, and their choice oftentimes correlates to the types of kinship systems and reflects issues that are salient within each society such as ecological circumstances, economic concerns, and formation of political alliances. Anthropologists have identified five postmarital residence types to which most patterns of residence after marriage fall into.

## Neolocal Residence

In societies where **neolocal residence** is predominant, newlyweds set up an independent household in a location apart from either the husband's or wife's kin. This residence pattern which emphasizes the independence of the nuclear family tends to be found in societies in which kinship system is bilateral, and cultural traits of individualism are mostly favored over those of collectivity. Whereas neolocal residence is found in societies around the world, its most conspicuous presence is in industrial societies such as the United States, Canada, and most of Europe where individual mobility and nonfamily-centered economic activity are prominently present. According to anthropologist George Mudrock's *Ethnographic Atlas*, only about 5 percent of societies in the world observe neolocal residence (Murdock 1967) (See FIGURE 7.10).

FIGURE 7.10    **Neolocal Residence**

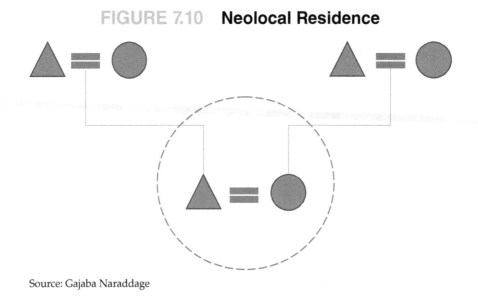

Source: Gajaba Naraddage

## Patrilocal Residence

**Patrilocal residence** is the married partners' customary living with or near the husband's father. This can mean anything of the following: residing in husband's father's own house; on the husband's father's own property; in the same village or neighborhood where husband's father lives. Sometimes, the term *virilocal residence* is also used to designate the above form of postmarital residential pattern with a slight variation. Virilocal residence is referred to indicate living with husband's father's relatives. Usually, patrilocal households are sizable extended families. In addition to new marital partners, they consist of the husband's father and mother, their sons, their sons' wives and children, as well as their daughters who are still living with them until they are given away in marriage. Married daughters reside with their husbands' kin. Patrilocal residence is strongly linked to patrilineal descent systems under which property inheritance takes place through the father and the other members of patrilineage. As 69 percent of residential households in societies fall into this category, patrilocal residence is clearly the most common postmarital residence pattern in the world (Murdock 1967) (See FIGURE 7.11).

FIGURE 7.11    **Patrilocal (Virilocal) Residence**

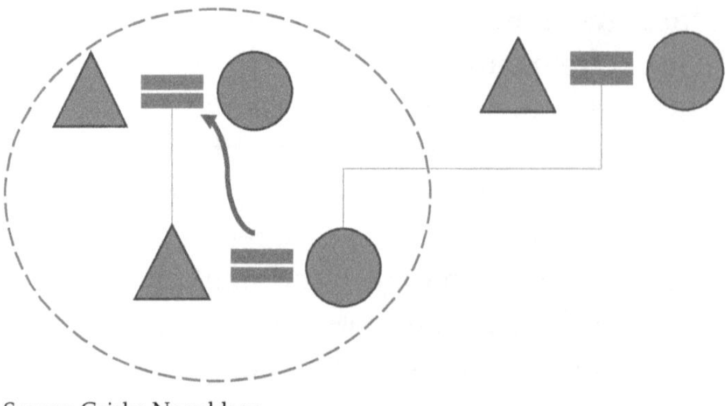

Source: Gajaba Naraddage

## Matrilocal Residence

**Matrilocal residence** is the new spouses' customary living with or near the wife's mother. This may take any of the following forms: residing in wife's mother's own house; living on the wife's mother's own property; living in the same village or neighborhood where wife's mother lives. Some anthropologists prefer to use the term *uxorilocal residence* to designate the above postmarital residential pattern with a minor variation. Uxorilocal residence is used to designate living with wife's mother's relatives. In addition to the pair of new marital partners, matrilocal households usually consist of wife's mother and father, their daughters, their daughters' husbands and children, as well as their unmarried sons. Married sons reside with their spouses' relatives. Matrilocal residence pattern is exclusively associated with matrilineal descent systems within which mother to daughter property transfer rule is observed. This residence pattern occurs in 13 percent of societies in the world (Murdock 1967) (See FIGURE 7.12).

**FIGURE 7.12 Matrilocal (Uxorilocal) Residence**

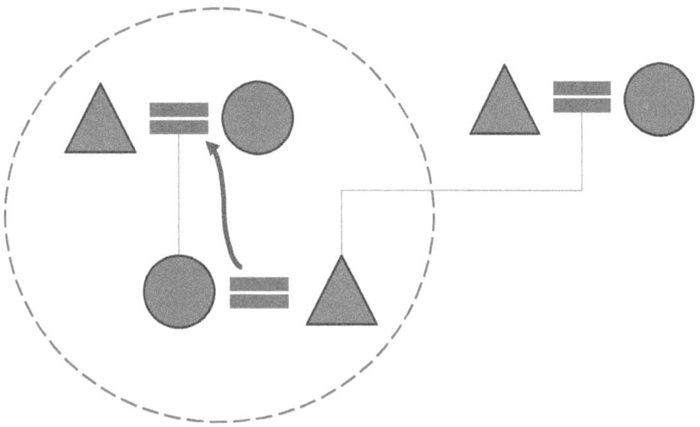

Source: Gajaba Naraddage

## Bilocal Residence

In **bilocal residence,** new partners in marriage live alternatively and flexibly with or near the husband's and wife's relatives, depending on the resources available. Found mostly in societies with bilateral kindred, this pattern of postmarital residence allows newlyweds to weigh factors such as resource availability or scarcity and the composition of households, before adjusting living arrangements accordingly. This pattern of residence, sometimes referred to as *ambilocal residence* (Latin term *ambi* means "both"), is observed in 9 percent of societies (Murdock 1967) (See FIGURE 7.13).

## Avunculocal Residence

Sometimes, the married partners in matrilineal societies live with the husband's mother's brother (maternal uncle). Building on the Latin term *avunculus,* meaning "mother's brother," this pattern of postmarital residence is dubbed by anthropologists as **avunculocal residence.**

FIGURE 7.13   **Bilocal (ambilocal) Residence**

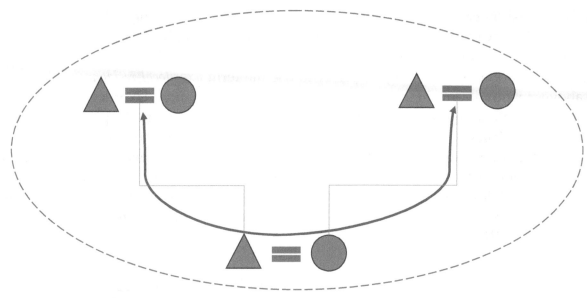

Source: Gajaba Naraddage

Unlike in matrilocal residence in which the newlyweds' place of domicile is primarily noted, in this residence pattern stress is laid on property inheritance, labor patterns, and social status that connect men in a system of matrilineal descent. According to the rules of matrilineal descent, a man's wealth and status cannot be transferable to his own son as his son is a member of his wife's group of kin, not his own. Therefore, a man transfers his wealth to his sister's son, a member of his own matrilineage. Conversely, a man gains wealth and status from his maternal uncle, a member of his own matrilineage, not from his own father. Avunculocal residence is the least practiced residence pattern after marriage with only 4 percent of societies in the world known for adopting it (Murdock 1967) (See FIGURE 7.14).

FIGURE 7.14   **Avunculocal Residence**

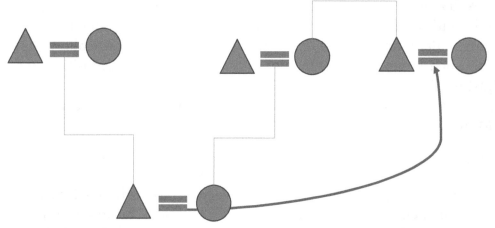

Source: Gajaba Naraddage

# Divorce and Widowhood

The levirate and the sororate, the customary forms of spousal selection found among certain foragers, farmers, and herders, are intended to fulfill the marriage contract and maintain the alliance between descent groups even after the death of one of the marital partners.

## Levirate

The **levirate** is the spousal preference rule in which a widow marries her deceased husband's brother. Practiced in a wide variety of societies in West and East Asia, India, Africa, and Oceania, it is closely linked with patrilineal societies in which a man, his sons, the sons' spouses, and their children, are usually the main constituents of family. In such societies where having male heirs is highly valued and appropriated, the levirate ensures the continuity of a man's lineage even after his death. For example, the ancient shepherded Jews have considered this spousal preference as an obligatory rule. By bearing and rearing sons fathered by deceased husband's brother in his name, a widow essentially continued the dead man's lineage (Old Testament/Deuteronomy 25: 5–10). In the same vein, the levirate serves as a mechanism to look after the interests of the widow as she essentially severs links with her original family when marrying a man. Furthermore, the levirate functions to endure the connections established between the two descent groups stressing the salience of marriage as an alliance between two groups rather than individual partners (See FIGURE 7.15).

If a man dies without a son, the continuity of his lineage becomes problematic. Anthropologist E. E. Evans-Pritchard long ago described the two solutions for this problem used by the Nuer cattle herders of East Africa (Evans-Pritchard 1951; O'Brien 1977). One of the ways with which the Nuer remedied the problem of lineage continuity without a hiatus was by creating a social father (pater) through the institution known as *female husband*. According to this custom, one of the deceased man's daughters can "marry" a woman and serve as the social father to the wife's children. These children are then considered as the children of her lineage. The actual biological father (genitor) of those children is literally insignificant to the Nuer since the sole purpose of the social father in this context is to establish the continuity of the deceased man's lineage. The female husband can also actually marry a man and have children by him, but they, according to the Nuer patrilineal rules, would always be counted in his lineage.

The Nuer people find another way to establish male lineage when confronting the sonless complication in a family. According to this solution, the continuity of the dead man's lineage is restored through a *ghost marriage*—by allowing male kin of the deceased person to marry the widow and let the woman bear sons in his name. These children are then treated as the members of the dead man's lineage since the man who marries the widow is considered the ghost of the deceased husband.

## Sororate

The **sororate** is the marriage preference rule in which a widower marries his deceased wife's sister. In the event of no unmarried sibling, the deceased wife's family is generally obliged to supply some equivalent kin as a substitute, and oftentimes, the daughter of the deceased wife's brother may become this substitute wife (See FIGURE 7.15).

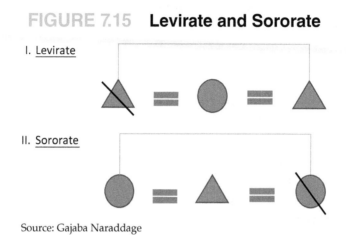

FIGURE 7.15 **Levirate and Sororate**

I. Levirate

II. Sororate

Source: Gajaba Naraddage

# Types of Family

Families are in two basic types, and they are the nuclear family and the extended family. These family types are formed through the conjugal or marital bond and the consanguineal relations, respectively. Additionally, there are family types established through individual choice.

## Nuclear Family

Usually composed of two generations of kin, the **nuclear family** is a kin unit consisting of a pair of parents accustomed to neolocal, monogamous living, and their unmarried children. It is a family centered around the conjugal (marital) link between the heterosexual spousal pair, their offspring, and their residence in an independent household located apart from the households of the spousal partners' kin.

By focusing on an individual's changing relationship to the nuclear family during that individual's life course, anthropologists differentiate the **family of orientation,** or the family in which one is born and grows up, and the **family of procreation,** or the family in which one becomes, or one is having the probability of becoming, a procreator (a parent). Accordingly, an individual's childhood family is the family of orientation, as the parental and sibling relationship may be pivotal to the individual during the time in which he or she develops from a child into an adult. In the family of procreation, as married individuals often do, the stress is laid on spousal partner and children. Either way, in most societies, nuclear family ties such as parental and sibling relations take priority over connections with other relatives (such as relations with affinal kin or nonblood relatives).

As its size is usually smaller, the nuclear family is structurally well-suited for increased mobility. For example, foraging nomads in the world habitually keep their family size in check by observing the spacing of births. Foraging mothers take a long period to nurse their kids so they can customarily maintain long interpregnancy intervals. As their society is

© Marzolino/Shutterstock.com

based on nuclear families, foraging nomads can move across vast terrains with relative ease in search of food, and it is strategically advantageous for them when surviving in conditions of scarcity.

Similarly, in modern industrial societies, nuclear families facilitate movement as people constantly pursue the goals of individual progress, independence, and economic success. Therefore, having a family with a multitude of dependent children or having wider kinship connections (with obligations to fulfill) are usually considered as stumbling blocks in accomplishing individual goals. Writing in 1968, anthropologist David M. Schneider observed that, the above view of nuclear family has become established as the standard family type with which other family types may be assessed (Schneider [1968] 1980).

The idealization of the nuclear family as the mainspring of the culture in the United States was mainly a twentieth-century ideological project, contend some anthropologists. They emphasize several interrelated points: the nuclear family did not exist in its idealized

form among the early Euro-American settlers, and it did not play a considerable role during the colonization of the North American land mass, or even after establishing the United States. The emergence of the idealized, twentieth-century nuclear family was a consequence of the industrialization in the nineteenth century. Furthermore, the nuclear family model was not a uniformed or universal one, and the practitioners who conformed to this idealized model were mainly the twentieth-century middle-class white Americans (Coontz 1992; Carsten 2004) (See FIGURE 7.16).

## Extended Family

The **extended family** is consisted of three or more generations of kin, such as the parents, the children, and the grandchildren. If the nuclear family clears the way for geographical mobility, the extended family smooths the path for geographical stability, as well as intergenerational continuity. While it is commonplace around the world, the extended family is the favored family type among sedentary family farmers and pastoralists as such groups constantly need more people to get agricultural and herding activities done. Usually, the rules of descent determine which children reside with their parents after marriage. Accordingly, in patrilineal societies where descent and inheritance are traced through male line, sons remain with their parents while daughters leave their natal homes to join husbands' families. Conversely, in matrilineal societies where descent and inheritance are traced through females,

FIGURE 7.16   **Nuclear Family**

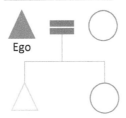

Source: Gajaba Naraddage

adult married sons oftentimes leave to join their wives' natal families but daughters (and their marital partners) reside with their parents.

© ESB Professional/Shutterstock.com

When sets of male siblings do not leave their parents and unmarried sisters at marriage but bring their spouses and dependent children to live with them in the same natal home, the **joint family,** which is a variation of extended family, occurs. Therefore, a typical joint family is made up of a married couple, unmarried daughters, their married sons, their sons' wives and children, and even grandsons' wives and great-grandchildren living in one household (Wadley in Mines and Lamb 2010, 14). In a joint family unit, the eldest male member is customarily considered the head of the family (See FIGURE 7.17).

FIGURE 7.17   **Extended Family**

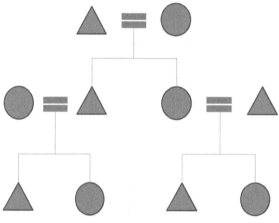

Source: Gajaba Naraddage

## Blended Family

When previously divorced individuals remarry and bring the children they have inherited from previous marital affairs into a new household, the **blended family** usually takes place. The emergence of the family types such as the blended family reflects the predicaments that the two-parent-based nuclear families must endure in the presence of, among other things, the high rates of divorce and remarriage (serial monogamy). Blended families typically involve an intricate network of relatives, including previously divorced spouses, their new marriage partners, children inherited from previous marriages, children from new marriage, as well as multiple sets of grandparents and similar kin (See FIGURE 7.18).

FIGURE 7.18   **Blended Family**

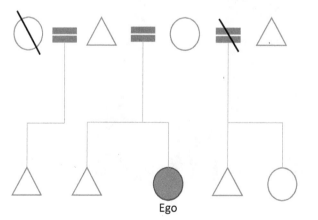

Source: Gajaba Naraddage

## Single-Parent Family

The **single-parent family** is a family with underage children headed by a parent who is widowed, separated, and not remarried, or by a parent who has never married.

In recent decades, American children living in households headed by a single parent has steadily risen. Even more noticeable, the single-parent family households headed by females have increased undeviatingly. During the 1960 to 2016 period, the percentage of children living with only their mother nearly tripled from 8 to 23 percent, according to the annual report on America's Families and Living Arrangements released by US Census Bureau on November 17, 2016. Studies have shown that most single-parent mothers have not been able to bring themselves and their families above the poverty threshold (Chandler 1989; Franklin 1992). The increase of poverty in households that are headed by women is often discussed in relation to the **feminization of poverty** (See FIGURE 7.19).

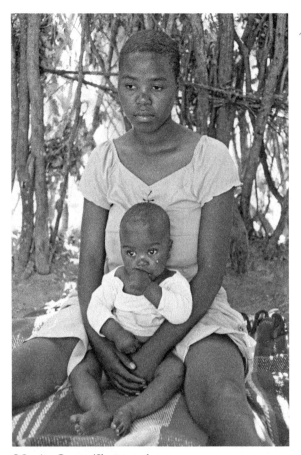

© Lucian Coman/Shutterstock.com

FIGURE 7.19 **Single-Parent Family**

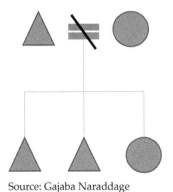

Source: Gajaba Naraddage

## Transnational Family

The English adjective *transnational* is generally dubbed as "extending or going beyond the national boundaries." Accordingly, the **transnational family** refers to sustained links of family members and networks of relatives across the borders of multiple nation-states. This family type is a fine example to the development of territorially delimited, geocultural family systems within the context of transnational migration. Transnational families tend to carry out family relations and functions *across* rather than *within* specific geopolitical spaces. As migration is not always unidirectional, and as it does not always facilitate permanent settlement in a country of destination, family members residing in two or more countries and having fluid relationships between them has become a common occurrence. As such, familyhood takes place across national borders, and family members must contend with multiple residences, identities, and loyalties. Furthermore, transnational families must grapple with inequality among their members, usually caused by differential access to resources, mobility, and lifestyles (Bryceson and Vuorela 2002, 3–7).

However, the consequences of spatially fractured relationships are considerably lessened by extensive social networks that transnational family members often manage to construct and maintain. As Fernando Herrera Lima argues, such social spaces that hold transnational families together may be stronger than the legal and physical forces that keep individual family members separate (Herrera Lima 2001, 89).

Recent research on the flow of female migrant labor to Europe from Latin America (Gutierrez Garza 2019), and to the Middle East from South Asia (Gamburd 2010) show how stricter migration control and disproportionately segregated migrant markets in affluent countries put limits on familyhood across borders on the one hand while also aiding to produce new and distinct family relationships on the other. For example, Latin American women migrate to Europe to become employees either in domestic service or in the sex/leisure industry. They favor marrying a European man to get legalize undocumented status in the host country (*matrimonio por residencia*). Sometimes, they choose to marry a man for a relationship characterizable as love (*por amor*) also.

© Cabeca de Marmore/Shutterstock.com

Both instances can lead to distinct transnational family relations, for which the country of origin could not necessarily be the prime reference any longer (Gutierrez Garza 2019) (See FIGURE 7.20).

FIGURE 7.20 **Transnational Family**

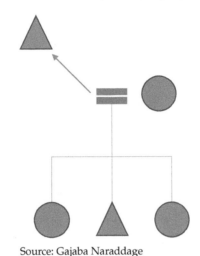

Source: Gajaba Naraddage

## Sexual Cohabitation or Living Together

Known as "living together" in colloquial parlance, **sexual cohabitation** takes place when two people of the opposite sex cohabitate sexually on a long-term basis and share economic, social, and other responsibilities of family (such as child-rearing) without getting married to each other. Among young adults in the United States (as well as in the other countries in the West), sexual cohabitation is increasingly becoming the first coresidential union. Sometimes called de facto marriage, it is increasingly considered as an apt substitute for conventional marriage.

In addition of using it as a way of trying out marriage to test the compatibility with their partners, and a path for enjoying sexual relationship while avoiding responsibility and commitment, there are several other important reasons for choosing to live together with a sexual partner. They include economic reasons such as reducing the high costs of living and housing through sharing, as well as social and emotional reasons such as finding conviviality and companionship (See FIGURE 7.21).

FIGURE 7.21 **Sexual Cohabitation (Living Together)**

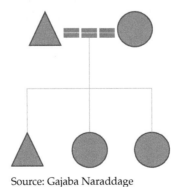

Source: Gajaba Naraddage

## Family of Same-Sex Partners

The **family of same-sex partners** or *same-sex family* occurs when two people of the same gender begin to share a lasting sexual relationship and cohabitation while also sharing legal, economic, social, and other responsibilities of the family (such as parenting children).

© andreonegin/Shutterstock.com

The family of same-sex partners is not the same as the Nuer practice of creating a social father (pater) through the institution known as *female husband* to protect a dead man's lineage continuity (see above in this chapter). The Nuer female husband does not maintain sexual partnership with the dead man's wife, although they share household and family responsibilities. However, a kin unit like the same-sex family did exist among some native American groups. It was not uncommon for many native American cultures of the Great Plains to maintain socially approved homosexual marital relationships even in the early decades of the twentieth century (See FIGURE 7.22).

## Constructing Groups of Kin: Kin by Choice

As mentioned earlier, in most societies, families are formed through marriage publicly acknowledging marital partners' commitment, as well as a new alliance between the groups

FIGURE 7.22 **Family of Same-sex Partners**

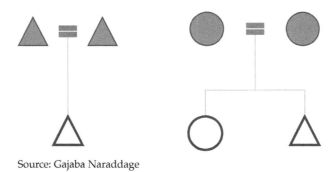

Source: Gajaba Naraddage

of affinal relatives. We learned further, families are also formed, recognized, and maintained through consanguineal kin or groups of kin related by blood.

However, families are also established through individual choice, especially in industrial countries. Increasingly, the **family by choice** is being practiced by individuals who moved away from his or her consanguine kin, as well as individuals who haven't committed to a marital relationship. Family by choice or chosen families may include adopted children, living companions, kin of each member of the household, dearly neighbors, coworkers, friends from childhood, high school or college, pets, and the likes.

© NeonShot/Shutterstock.com

The Lesbian, Gay, Bisexual, Transgender, and Queer (LGBTQ) community popularized the term by identifying with it (Weston 1991), before same-sex marital practices were legalized in the United States on June 26, 2015.

## Family and Kin in Global Perspective

The growingly notable presence of family by choice and other nontraditional family types is a clear indication that, there is much happening in today's globalized world while changing our perception of how family and kinship work. In addition to the consequences of the exceptionally high levels of mass migration and family dispersion throughout the world, the impact of the spread and commercialization of assisted reproductive technologies, such as intrauterine insemination (IUI), in vitro fertilization (IVF), surrogacy, cloning, and sperm and egg donation have significantly altered people's perceptions and experience of family and kinship in recent decades. Organ donation and transplantation has generated new conversance with what it means to be a relative as well.

For instance, the recent proliferation of DNA testing to determine donor siblings and donor parents has not only problematized the links between donor-conceived siblings and the connections between donor-parents and donor-conceived offspring but also the ideas of sibling relationship and parenthood (Harmon 2007, *The New York Times*). Likewise, the stories of women from the developing world who involve in a new cottage industry of gestating surrogate babies for would-be-parents in the developed world have complicated the very idea of parenthood further (Cohen 2009, *The Wall Street Journal*).

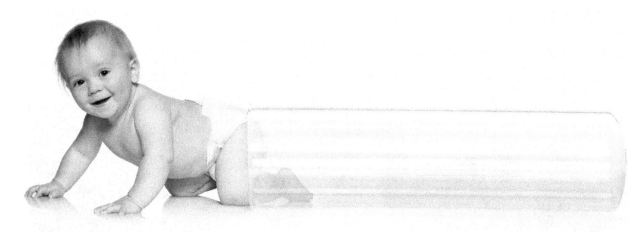

© Gladskikh Tatiana/Shutterstock.com

The family may be remaining a basic kin unit transgressing spatial and cultural boundaries. As sociologist Goran Therborn maintains, there is no empirical evidence for declaring postfamily society (Therborn 2004). Notwithstanding the family institution's remarkable ability to adapt and thrive, no one doubts that it has undergone profound changes in recent decades. The continuity and change in the institution of family shows that this theme warrants continuous anthropological discussion. Additionally, it indicates that alternative approaches to family, as well as to kinship are to be envisaged and accommodated (Carsten 2004).

# Chapter Summary

This chapter focuses on kinship, the system of meaning and power with which humans construct some of their most stable, reliable, enduring, and distinctive relationships. The chapter examines the various strategies people use to form kinship ties through descent, marriage, and family cross culturally, discussing the implications of kinship's changing expressions in the twenty-first century.

- All diagramming methods of kinship have a single-most important purpose: schematic depiction of kin ties with maximal simplicity and minimal complexity. A kinship diagram is a streamlined visual schema with which all of Ego's relatives, as recollected by Ego are represented. Mapping all the relatives in a kinship diagram entails the use of symbols, letter symbols, and compound strings.

- Oftentimes, marriage takes up a key role in forming a family, the basic structural element of society. It is definable as a socially binding, culturally sanctioned, status transforming, enduring, sexual, companionate, and frequently procreative union between two or more individuals that establishes a set of reciprocal rights and obligations between the married partners, their offspring, and their kin groups.

- Some form of rules exists in every society to regulate mating relations and marital practices. Despite cultural variations, the incest taboo or the categorical prohibition against having sex with each other by primary kin has become the most ubiquitous and basic rules with which sexual encounters are regulated. Closely linked with the incest taboo, the cultural rules of exogamy prod closely woven kin groups to look outside of their immediate circle for potential marital partners. The cultural prescriptions of endogamy, by contrast, allow individuals to find suitable marital partners within their own social groups. As shown in the practices such as hypergamy, hypogamy, and isogamy, the spousal selection may be influenced by status considerations as well.

- Contingent upon the number of spousal partners involved, variances in marriage forms do occur, and such variant forms reflect social and cultural diversity. Anthropologists have pinpointed two distinct forms distinguishing between societies that allow more than one spousal partner and those that refuse to do so: monogamy and polygamy.

- Monogamy is the form of marriage through which the union between a pair of individuals takes place. Serial monogamy is a differing form of monogamy prevalent in North America and Europe. It permits individuals to remarry any number of partners respectively.

- Polygamy, on the other hand, is the form of marriage with which the union between multiple partners becomes possible. Polygyny and Polyandry are the two main forms of polygamy.

When a man marries multiple women at the same time, it is referred to as polygyny. Sororal polygyny is a common variance of polygyny; in this variance, a man may marry two or more women who are sisters. In a society where polygyny is practiced, a man may increase family wealth, strengthen his lineage, earn prestige, and elevate social status through marriage. Polygyny's close association with wealth and power, as well as the demographic problem of the sex ratio contributive to polygyny in certain contexts are among the possible reasons for its existence as a main form of marriage.

- Likewise, when a woman marries multiple men simultaneously, it is known as polyandry. Fraternal polyandry is a variant form of polyandrous union. In this form, a woman may concurrently marry two or more men who are brothers. The possibility of strengthening family wealth through incessant supply of mail labor, and the existence of an uneven sex ratio conducive to polyandry in certain contexts are among the possible reasons for the existence of polyandrous marriage.

- Anthropologists have singled out the following types to which most patterns of residence after marriage fall into: neolocal residence, patrilocal residence, matrilocal residence, bilocal residence, and avunculocal residence. Setting up an independent household in a location apart from either the husband's or the wife's kin is referred to as neolocal residence; the married partners' customary living with or near the husband's father is known as patrilocal residence; the married partners' usual living with or near the wife's mother has a bearing on matrilocal residence; the new marital partners' alternative and flexible living with or near the husband's and the wife's kin is pertained to bilocal residence; the new spouses' living with or near the husband's maternal uncle applies to avunculocal residence.

- Families are formed through consanguineal and affinal kin. Increasingly however, families are also established through individual choice, especially in industrial countries.

- In addition to the consequences of mass migration and family dispersion throughout the world, the impact of the spread and commercialization of assisted reproductive technologies have significantly altered people's ideas and experience of family and kinship in recent decades.

# Subsistence: Strategizing Sustenance

© Senderistas/Shutterstock.com

The term *economics* originates from the Greek root words of *oikos* ("household") and *nomos* ("law" or "custom"). Therefore, economics is to be managing households, literally. As household is the fundamental economic unit in society, economics is meant to be managing a society's way of sustenance.

The economic sphere is comprised of production, exchange, and consumption. *Production* involves the extraction of resources, as well as the utility of labor and technology in the process of acquiring material goods and services. *Exchange* must do with the circulation of resources or the flow of goods and services between individuals. The satisfaction of individual needs through the depletion of subsistence resources (including production outcomes) is referred to as *consumption.* Taken together, these three elements constitute an **economic system.** An organized arrangement of production, exchange, and consumption is the economic system of a specific population. How goods and services are produced, consumed, and exchanged are linked in such a way that if one process changes, the others change as well.

Whereas the consumption is the key to human survival, it is the production that makes consumption possible. In this sense, the production is considered as the initial step of the economic process. In this process of producing the necessities of life, nature's raw materials are transformed into a form appropriate for human consumption. For instance, the wheat is not consumable unless it is harvested, unhusked, grinded, and transformed into flour suitable to make bread. Therefore, transforming the wheat into flour or bread involves the production process. Even the machinery used to plant the wheat and the infrastructure involved are essentially linked to that process.

# Mode of Production

A **mode of production** is a way of organizing production. Mode of production is the term used by Karl Marx to refer to a society's organization of economic production. Eric Wolf, an anthropologist with a Marxist bent, defines mode of production as "a set of social relations through which labor is deployed to wrest energy from nature by means of tools, skills, organization, and knowledge" (Wolf 1982, 75). In Marxian Thought, mode of production is a specific combination of two important factors: *productive forces* and the *relations of production.*

The productive forces are the **means of production,** such as technology, land, and capital (infrastructural and natural). They are the technological knowledge and the materials used in production. Marxist analysts do not consider labor as a means or factors of production although orthodox economists often do. For Marxists, labor is inalienable from the laboring individual(s); as a human activity, it can only be performed. Therefore, ownership of the result of human labor cannot be considered as a relationship between an individual and the products and services; rather, it is a relationship between two or more individuals about the products and services. Accordingly, the ownership rights can be particularized, so individuals may be able to alienate, consume, or reinvest the results of labor.

The **relations of production** are the totality of socioeconomic and technological relationships into which people should enter to sustain themselves and to engage in various production activities. They are the limited sets of socioeconomic and technological roles people find themselves in, that they must embrace for survival, as they participate in production. The relatively stable economic structure such relationships keep forming, in turn, corresponds to the division of labor that divides the participants in the production process into different groups or classes. Marx used these socioeconomic relationships to typify specific epochs of history. For example, Marx saw a slave master's relationship to his slave as a socioeconomic relationship distinguishable from a feudal lord's relationship to his serf who worked as an agricultural laborer in the fief or lord's estate. In like manner, Marx highlighted a capitalist's relationship to a wage worker, which is dissimilar to a feudal lord's relationship to his serf. In a Marxian analysis, the nature of the relationship that links classes to one another in a specific society is directly related to how production is carried out. The origins of class inequality, Marxian analysts maintain, is found in the production phase of economic life.

Marx identified several modes of production in human history, distinguishable from each other: slavery/ancient, kin-ordered, Asiatic, tributary, capitalist, socialist, and communist. Among them, anthropologists have found kin-ordered, tributary, and capitalist modes of production quite useful in understanding the political economy of a variety of recent and contemporary cultures in the world (Wolf 1982). The *kin-ordered production*, sometimes known as the domestic mode of production, is based on marriage, family, and other kin links between individuals. The kin-ordered production is based on use, not exchange. Therefore, production surpluses are usually shared and consumed, not stored. The kin-ordered production involves the division of labor based on age and gender. For instance, men usually hunt with their patrilineal kin while women gather food, work in the gardens, and tend to house chores with fellow women of the group. In the *tributary mode of production*, peasants or the primary producers pay tributes to rulers in the form of material goods or labor. As the owners of property, the ruling elites may be able to extract resources from the peasants and accumulate wealth through controlling the exchange systems and using force to keep peasants as subordinates. Often, tributary production takes place in societies where chiefdom exists as the primary political organization. In the *capitalist mode of production*, the members of the capitalist class or the bourgeoisie own the means of production. Moreover, the members of the working class or the proletariat must sell their labor to the capitalists to survive. The capitalists either retain possession of the surpluses of wealth as profit or reinvest in production to generate even more wealth.

A forerunner to the concept of mode of production was the mode of subsistence.

## Subsistence Strategies

The mode of subsistence was referred to by the capitalist economic theorist Adam Smith when he classified societies according to the way in which a society's members provided for their necessities (Montes and Schliesser 2006, 295). The early American anthropological theorist L. H. Morgan also used the phrase "the arts of subsistence" when he proposed a three-tiered, universal, and unilineal process of cultural evolution. Per Morgan's evolutionary scheme, every human society either had pass or would pass as it evolved from the bottom stage of savagery and the middle stage of barbarism to the top stage of civilization, eventually. Morgan went to considerable lengths to explain how technological advancement had played a pivotal role in cultural progress and change. The savages could climb up the rungs of evolutionary ladder due to innovative technological features such as learning to utilize fire, bows-and-arrows, and pottery. Likewise, the barbarians advanced due to plant and animal domestication, as well as metal work. In the same way, technological feats such as the growth of writing helped human societies to develop state systems and reach the heights of full-fledged civilization. Morgan pointed out that the stages of human growth or what he called "ethnical periods" had their parallels in the different arts of subsistence. These subsistence modes included "natural subsistence upon fruits and roots," "fish subsistence," "farinaceous subsistence of cultivation," "meat and milk subsistence," and "unlimited subsistence through field agriculture" (Morgan [1877] 1963).

Upon reading Morgan, his contemporary and influential political economists Karl Marx and Friedrich Engels were convinced that under ethnical periods Morgan was indeed referring to the *precapitalist modes of production*. What they meant by the above term was the methods of producing the necessities of life which had existed in the past before bowing out for the capitalist mode of production. (See Chapter 4 for a discussion of Morgan's Unilineal Cultural Evolutionism).

The pejorative terms such as savagery and barbarism are no longer in the standard analytic vocabulary of anthropology, just as the power-laden evolutionary schemes such as the one constructed by Morgan do not find much credence in contemporary anthropological discourse. Despite that, as they attempt to understand the ways with which various human societies extract resources for sustenance, anthropologists have been finding Morgan's systematic classificatory scheme and the depths it gained from a wide variety of ethnographic data collected by Morgan quite useful.

Morgan's emphasis on the correlation between specific advancements in technology and the specific modes of social organization attracted anthropological attention the most as evident in Yehudi Cohen's use of the term *adaptive strategies* to describe what members of a society do to sustain themselves (Cohen 1971). Taking a similar path to the one taken by Morgan, Cohen developed a classification of societies based on the mutual relationship between their economic systems and their social features. As economic typology corresponds to social typology, Cohen argued, societies with a similar adaptive strategy are more likely to have similar sociocultural features than not (Cohen 1974). For instance, there are explicit sociocultural parallels among societies that have foraging (or hunting and gathering) as the main food procurement strategy. Cohen's typology that recapitulated Morgan's original thoughts identified five basic types of subsistence (or adaptive) strategy: foraging, pastoralism, horticulture, intensive agriculture, and industrial agriculture. This categorization is now broadly accepted by anthropologists although they fully rebuff unilineal schemes of cultural progression.

## TABLE 8.1    Basic Types of Subsistence Strategy

Foraging (Hunting and Gathering)

Pastoralism (Nomadic Pastoralism and Transhumance)

Horticulture (Extensive Agriculture)

Intensive Agriculture (Sedentary Agriculture)

Industrial Agriculture (Agribusiness)

Source: Gajaba Naraddage

# Foraging

Among the peoples of the world who have adopted various subsistence strategies, foragers or hunter-gatherers are the only people who may be referred to as food collectors. Whereas all others produce food for living, foragers domesticate neither plants nor animal species except the dogs on occasion. Instead, foragers roam over vast stretches of land to collect what nature offers to them—a broad range of wild plant food, wild game animals, and fish—for subsistence. **Foraging** or *hunting and gathering*, therefore, is the mode of subsistence primarily based on hunting, fishing, and gathering a variety of wild foodstuffs.

Roughly twelve-thousand years ago, virtually all humans were foragers. Therefore, foraging is the oldest human strategy of food procurement. According to some researchers, human beings share the trait of foraging with nonhuman primates, as well as with many other animal species (Stephens and Krebs 1986). Even if this proposition offers some intriguing insights on the food strategies adopted by humans in response to the environment where they live, it also tends to reduce human behavior to biological processes. Moreover, it inclines to overlook how specific cultural practices may have fashioned subtleties of foraging behavior among the world's diverse groups of hunter-gatherers. For example, there are occasions in which foragers found to be manipulating wild plant food, and even cultivating, irrigating, pruning, and sowing seeds. Many foragers also practice periodic burning to encourage edible plant growth and to enhance browsing or grazing for game animals. Today, only a miniscule of the human population continuously practices foraging for living. Even those who are generally recognized as contemporary foragers practice a mixed subsistence. For example, the tropical foragers in South America practice gardening, in addition to foraging; likewise, the foragers in the Nordic region and Eurasia are engaged in reindeer herding. Similarly, hunter-gatherers in some parts of Africa, as well as in South and Southeast Asia, pursue trading on the side.

Foragers are a diverse group of peoples living in a broad range of conditions. Anthropologists have focused on the areas such as the links between foraging and the environment, the variations in types of food procurement, the degree of nomadism, gender and division of labor, postmarital residence, and the frequency of external and internal warfare. Such areas of focus have helped anthropologists to distinguish foraging groups, and thereby to get a nuanced understanding of them.

For example, some researchers have sought to typify foraging societies into three distinct sets, namely, pedestrian, equestrian, and aquatic. In this classification, foragers' way of movement or lack thereof is stressed. Accordingly, pedestrian foragers are the people who are accustomed to diversified hunting and gathering on foot. Similarly, equestrian foragers are the hunter-gatherers who concentrate mostly on hunting large mammals from horseback. Likewise, aquatic foragers are the hunter-gatherers who focus on fishing and hunting marine mammals while riding boats to do so.

Some anthropologists differentiate two starkly dissimilar types of foraging, and their emphasis is the relationship between the environmental contexts and foraging. These categories are the temperate-climate and circumpolar foraging. Temperate-climate foragers live and forage in warm, temperate areas, such as the southern Africa. They subsist on perishable wild food and game, live in casually constructed shelters, and migrate several times during a year. Today, most such foragers in southern Africa live in reservations. For the most part, they have given up foraging.

Circumpolar foragers live and forage in cold areas, such as the polar regions of North America, Europe, and Asia. They subsist on large marine and terrestrial animals, wear warm clothes and boots, use tools such as harpoons, nets, and knives, live in either igloos (dome-shaped houses, typically constructed from blocks of solid snow) or log houses, and use sleds pulled by dogs to haul water and other supplies. Today, most such foragers use modern tools for hunting and fishing, and dwell in durable houses with modern facilities.

While summarizing the historical trajectories of the world's foraging populations in very broad strokes, anthropologists Richard B. Lee and Richard Daly distinguish several categories of foragers as well (2004). Accordingly, at one end of a continuum, one finds modern hunter-gatherers who have persisted roughly in direct tradition of descent from ancient foragers. These groups include the aboriginal populations in Australia, northwestern parts of North America, the Southern tip of South America, as well as the pockets of similar hunter-gatherers in other parts of the world. Some current representatives of this first group comprise the Australian Pintupi, Arrernte and Warlpiri, the North American Eskimo, Shoshone and Cree, the South American Yamana, and the African Dobe Ju/'hoansi.

© Chris Christophersen/Shutterstock.com

As Lee and Daly see it, along the middle of the continuum, are the foragers who have consistently had close contact with sedentary farmers and herders throughout history (by means of trading forest products and similar exchanges). They include the South and Southeast Asian foragers, and the Central and East African hunter-gatherers. Indeed, the Batak in the Philippines (Eder 2004) and the Vedda in Sri Lanka (Seligmann 1911; Brow 1978; Stegeborn 2004) have maintained links with their agricultural neighbors for millennia; they bartered furs, honey, medicinal plants, and rattan for staple crops such as rice, provisions, and metal products. In much the same way, the Pygmy in Central Africa (Bahuchet 2004) have had a centuries old patron–client relationship with the neighboring sedentary farmers. Similarly, the Okiek foragers in East Africa (Kratz 1999) have traded with the Maasai and Kipsigis settlers by supplying honey and other forest products in exchange of provisions.

Per Lee and Daly, most of the tropical foragers in South America such as the Yamana in Tierra del Fuego archipelago (Vidal 2004), who plant gardens as one part of their annual trek represent another distinguishable category of hunter-gatherers (Lee and Daly 2004). With the advent of European colonialists in the sixteenth to eighteenth centuries, many of the indigenous groups in South America switched to foraging as a strategic secondary adaptation. These groups understood that the nomadic existence of foraging made them less vulnerable for colonial exploitation. Among certain tropical South American foragers, the above strategy had been in operation even before the European colonial times (Roosevelt 1999, 2004).

Mobility is a salient characteristic in most foraging societies. As they depend on naturally occurring, widely dispersed, and mostly seasonal food and water sources for sustenance, most foragers live fully or seminomadic life. Resource concentration or scarcity has been a decisive factor of foraging groups' movement. Every so often, groups with inadequate resources may move to regions where food sources are more abundant and concentrated. For example, temperate-climate foragers such as the Dobe Ju/'hoansi in the Kalahari, Southern Africa, and the Pintupi in the Gibson Desert, Australia, move great distances to gain access to a wide variety of plant food that the wet season usually bring in. They camp around seasonal and secondary water holes as it helps them to satisfy their daily water needs without difficulty. Additionally, seasonal water holes attract a vast array of migratory birds and game animals providing them with better hunting grounds. As the dry season set in with steadily rising temperature and drying out landscape, these foragers return to their territory and settle near the permanent water holes. This recognizable pattern of movement, in which foraging bands spend part of the year in small units while getting aggregated into larger units during the rest of the year, is characterized by anthropologists as one of concentration and dispersion (Lee and Daly 2004). By contrast, circumpolar foragers such as the Inuit in the Canadian Arctic and the Inupiat in the Alaskan Arctic who sustain by hunting sea mammals (whales, seals, and walruses) and catching fish choose to live along the coastal areas all year around. On occasions, foragers tend to move away from their camp settlements as a means of resolving conflicts as well (Lee and Daly 2004, 4).

Foragers keep guarding permanent water holes during the times of long drought, but willingly share them with others who comply with social conventions, and with the guests who ask for permission to use. When they move in search of seasonal food and water, foraging bands seek to limit their movement to a circumscribed area that they tacitly recognize as their home range. Nevertheless, the private ownership of land is almost absent in foraging societies. People do hold movable property individually. However, foragers keep only a few possessions, which they usually carry on their back. Their mobility throughout the year requires minimization of material possessions.

Foraging societies are known to have low population densities. Usually, population densities of hunter-gatherer societies do not exceed one person per 10 square miles (Lee 1968). As thinly dispersed population's demand for crucial resources is balanced with the time required for resource regeneration, foragers can avoid resource depletion.

Foragers live in small communities. The basic unit of social organization in most foraging societies is the band, a small-scale, informal, and autonomous political body held together mainly by kinship ties. Typically, a band comprises several foraging families. The band leadership is spontaneous, contextual, and nonpermanent. Moreover, the leadership is not driven by injunction but by example.

Postmarital residence among foragers tends to be matrilocal. This residential arrangement helps young mothers as they can get childcare support from their own mothers, who continue living next to them in the same camp.

Labor is typically divided by gender in foraging societies: Women do most of the gathering and men concentrate on big game hunting. The food gathered from a few hours of work on one day may be enough to feed a foraging woman's family for several days. She spends a few more hours to complete her daily chores at home, such as collecting firewood, fetching water, cracking nuts, and cooking food. This routine leaves her with plenty of time to do embroidery, visit other camps, to entertain visitors from nearby camps, and simply to unwind her. Foraging men's work schedule may be more uneven, although they tend to work more frequently than women do. They may work for a week overzealously seizing a rare opportunity to hunt a big game animal, yet they may not hunt at all for a few weeks afterward. Foraging men choose to visit friends, entertain, sing, and dance during these times (Lee 1968).

Age is an important criterion for foragers' task allocation. Both boys and girls do chores such as fetching firewood and water and tending to little ones. The elderly people do minor gathering, give some company to little kids, and repose themselves in their shelters. Generally, children and the aged spend considerably less time in food provision than adult members of the group.

Customarily, the people in foraging societies have egalitarian relationships. They are cooperative in collecting and sharing food and having access to resources such as foraging areas and water holes. The band members usually share plant food varieties that they gather, and small game that they hunt. In the same vein, they share occasional big game with everyone in the group, while prioritizing shares along the lines of kinship proximity (Marshall 1958).

The characteristics such as near absence of land ownership, cooperative food gathering and sharing practices, near gender equality, and the strong presence of generalized reciprocity, prodded some anthropologists to characterize foragers' way of life as something akin to primitive communism (Morgan 1881; Lee 1988). Marshall Sahlins believes that the hunter-gatherer society can be set apart from the rest, for it is the *original affluent society*. As he sees it, hunter-gatherers enjoy "affluence without abundance in the nonsubsistence sphere" (Sahlins 1972).

## Domestication of Plants and Animals

Archeological evidence suggests that the gradual transition of multiple human cultures from a nomadic lifestyle based on hunting and gathering to a nonnomadic or sedentary lifestyle based on domestication of plants and animals occurred at the end of the last ice age about 12,000 years ago.

Known as the **Neolithic Revolution** or the *Agricultural Revolution,* this process of adopting a set of food producing techniques (discussed below) eventually paved the way for the surplus production of food. Moreover, it led to other Neolithic developments such as

© jsp/Shutterstock.com

population expansion, the emergence of cities and urban centers, the depersonalized systems of knowledge (e. g., writing), the development of nonportable art and architecture, craft specialization, social stratification, and the rise of state systems.

Archaeological evidence indicates that, early humans, who subsisted from big game hunting (hunting Pleistocene megafauna) before the glacial retreat and the attendant substantial ecological change, have gradually learned the ways of efficiently locating and utilizing foraging patches within a heterogenous environment. The Agricultural Revolution indicates that humans have now begun to use that knowledge of **intensive foraging** for domesticating plants and animals.

**Domestication** is essentially a biological process occurring in plants or animals due to artificial selection or alteration by humans. During this process, organisms develop

© vanillaychile/Shutterstock.com

characteristics that increase their utility. The plant varieties that have been deliberately altered or selected by humans are recognized as *cultigens* (from the Latin *cultus*—cultivated, and *gens*—kind). Such man-made or anthropogenic plants usually provide larger seeds, fruits, and tubers suitable for human consumption than their wild progenitors.

The plants selected for domestication came from a wide range of families (or groups of closely related genera that share a progenitor). They included the grass (*Poaceae*), bean (*Fabaceae*), and nightshade or potato (*Solanaceae*). These plant families have produced a disproportionately large number of cultigens with features specifically amenable for domestication. For example, teosinte (*Zea mexicana*), the tall, stout grass of the *Poaceae* family, native to Mexico, Guatemala, Honduras, and Nicaragua was the most likely ancestor of corn or maize, domesticated in pre-Columbian times more than 6,000 years ago.

When domesticating wild animals, early humans evidently have concentrated on wild animals accustomed to group behavior—such species were favored for domestication over

© Eric Isselee/Shutterstock.com

wild animals that tend to live solitarily or exist alone. By breeding animal species that are social in the wild, early humans were able to gain control over them and increase the traits that are beneficial for people. Most domesticated animals are more docile than their wild counterparts. They have been helping humans by providing protection and companionship, assisting with traction and transport, controlling pests, and producing meat, milk, and wool for human consumption. What is more, they have been a reliable source of wealth for humans.

Animal species domesticated by early humans included the dog (*Canis lupus familiaris*), cat (*Felis catus*), sheep (*Ovis species*), goat (*Capra species*), cattle (*Bos species*), swine (*Sus species*), horse (*Equus caballus*), chicken (*Gallus gallus*), and duck (*Anatidae*). They are in plentiful domesticated breeds.

## Pastoralism

Raising and caring large herds of domesticated animals and using them and their products primarily as a way of sustenance is known as **pastoralism.** It is a food-getting strategy well-acclimatized to mountainous, semiarid, and tundra areas of the world, where extensive or intensive agriculture is difficult to practice due to insufficient water and terrain, yet herding is still possible due to modest availability of pasture lands and water for herd animals. Sizable pastoralist populations exist in places like Africa, Central Asia, Tibet, arctic Scandinavia, and Siberia.

Depending on environmental variables (e. g., climate and rainfall), population size (in relation to the available land), and their relationship with wider society, various pastoralists choose the types of animals for herding. These herd animals include sheep, goats, cattle, yak, llamas, alpacas, camels, and horses. Many pastoralists keep other herd animals yet identify themselves in respect to one type of animal. For example, East African herders, such as the Nuer, the Maasai, and the Samburu, often define themselves with cattle. In like manner, the Basseri who inhabit the Far Province of Southern Iran identify themselves as sheep and goat herders although they raise donkeys, horses, camel, and poultry as well.

The animals are herded for the most part for their meat, blood, eggs (in case of poultry), and dairy products (such as milk, cheese, butter, and yoghurt). The Nuer cattle herders of Southern Sudan, for example, consumed milk and blood of their animals regularly, while eating meat rarely when an animal is slaughtered on an occasion of ritual significance, or when an animal died of natural causes. Additionally, they used cow dung as an important source of fuel (Evens-Pritchard 1940).

In some instances, however, domesticated animals are raised for food, as well as for the products and services not related to food. On that account, cutting the wool off from animals to make clothes, and using the animals to carry the burden and to make traveling trouble-free, and using animals as highly mobile war-beasts in raiding and warfare become important reasons to raise certain varieties of animals. For example, the Navajo (Dine), Native American herders of the Southwestern United States, raised cattle, sheep, burros, mules, and horses, but only cattle were used solely as a source of food. Navajo herded sheep for meat and to use sheared wool from the animals for clothing simultaneously.

© Anndrzej Kubik/Shutterstock.com

The Navajo used sheep as a form of currency, and they used burros and mules for meat and to pull wagons. However, Navajo pastoralists raised horses only to use for raiding and warfare, and to exhibit their material wealth (Lamphere 2007; Downs 1964). Similarly, Plains Indian pastoralists, such as Blackfoot, Arapaho, Cheyenne, Lakota, Plains Apache, Stoney, and Plains Cree, raised horses to use for hunting the herds of bison that roamed the plains, for traveling great distances for intertribal trading, and for warfare, not for consumption. Likewise, the Basseri of Southern Iran herded horses, donkeys, and camels mainly for heavy transport and riding in the rocky terrain, and they raised dogs for keeping watch in camp sites.

Like foraging, pastoralism has mostly been a mixed subsistence strategy. Most pastoralists have been keen to combine livestock raising with other strategies of sustenance such as foraging, extensive farming, and trading animals or animal products for provisions with their sedentary agriculturalist neighbors. For instance, the Navajo pastoralists procured some of their food by collecting plant food, hunting game, and through extensive farming. Indeed, many Plains Indian groups hunted buffalo, did occasional fishing, cultivated some crops, and traded with neighboring tribes, in addition to raising herd animals. In like manner, the Nuer cultivated millet and maize in highland areas of the Nuer territory although they were pre-eminently pastoral (Evens-Pritchard 1940).

In a similar way to foraging, pastoralism is a subsistence strategy that demands extensive territory. This is because enough grazing land and water for herd animals are essential to maintain pastoralist way of life. The search of these two resources so crucial to their livelihood shape pastoralists' movement throughout the year. Accordingly, two patterns of movement occur with pastoralism: nomadic pastoralism and transhumance.

© Linda_K/Shutterstock.com

In **nomadic pastoralism,** the entire group of herders moves with their herd animals across a large area throughout the year seeking fresh pasturelands. They are horizontal migrants.

With **transhumance,** however, herders' movement becomes partial and seasonal. Only parts of the group (usually, men and boys) follow the herds to different pasturelands as they become seasonally available for grazing while the rest remain in home villages. With some transhumant pastoralists, the seasonal movements occur between winter and summer grazing lands. For example, among the Sami, traditional Finno-Ugric reindeer herders inhabiting in the northernmost parts of Norway, Sweden, Finland, and the far northwestern areas of Russia, movements between mountain pastures in summer and lower valleys in winter take place. The Sami herders have their permanent settlements in the valleys. During the months of summer, a certain number of Sami follow their flocks of reindeers to the fresh mountain pastures. As autumn approaches and grazing become insufficient, they bring back reindeers to the grazing lands in the lower valleys and join the rest of the family members in their homes (Paine 1994).

Among the transhumant herders who live in tropical or semitropical regions, however, the movements usually come about in accordance with the cycle of wet and dry.

© Anndrzej Kubik/Shutterstock.com

For instance, the Nuer, the Nilotic cattle herders in South Sudan, moves between villages located in the slightly elevated parts of the territory and cattle camping sites of the dry season. The two seasons, set apart by rain and drought, determine the movement pattern of the Nuer cattle herders. Much of the Nuer territory, located in the swamps of the upper Nile region, is flooded during the rainy season between April and October, so moving into higher grounds becomes imperative. Likewise, during the dry season between November and March, most members of the Nuer families settle near the cattle camps (kraals) as resources become extremely meager. During this time of the year, Nuer men and initiated boys sleep with their cattle in shelters made from local grass varieties. It is this seasonal pattern of movement makes Nuer people transhumant pastoralists (Evens-Pritchard 1940).

© John Wollwerth/Shutterstock.com

The movement from nomadic lifestyle to a more sedentary lifestyle is a tendency seen in many pastoralist groups in the world, including African herders in Kenya, Nigeria, Tanzania, and Sudan, and Scandinavian pastoralists such as the Saami in Norway. The life of permanent settlements, in turn, has been spawning notable changes in herders' living conditions, food habits, nutrition, and health (Ekpa, Omotayo, and Depeolu 2008).

Despite variations, in most pastoralist societies some form of division of labor based on gender and age exists. Typically, men and boys herd animals while women and children do the related activities such as milking and dairy processing. The existence of **age-sets** or the groups of individuals of similar age and same sex who together pass through some or all life stages shows how gender roles and age-based social categories are interconnected in certain pastoralist societies. For example, in the Maasai system of age-sets, *moran* warriors or young men (between the ages of about 14 and 30) collectively spend this life stage in isolation in the bush. Only after this rites of passage Maasai men can marry. The practice effectively lets older men to practice polygyny in Maasai society.

Pastoralism is generally associated with patrilineality. Many pastoral societies adhere to preinheritance, the father dispersing the herd among his male children prior to his death. The principle of patrilocality makes it certain that animals will remain in the same physical herd in most situations. Even in pastoral societies in which some animals go to daughters on the death of the household head due to the rules of Islamic inheritance, the herd is usually cared for by the women's male siblings. Men's ownership of the herds and the key role they play in moving and protecting animals in often difficult conditions indicate why pastoralist societies tend to favor patrilineality and patriarchy.

Pastoral organization is typically based on the clan, an extended unilineal kinship groups whose members believe them to be descended from an apical ancestor. However, the working kin group usually is the unilineal kin-ordered group known as the lineage in which tracing group members' genealogical links through several generations to a progenitor is possible.

Pastoral social organization is rank-based, and the form of political organization most pastoral societies prone to foster is either a tribe or chiefdom.

## Horticulture

**Horticulture** is the small-scale, rain-fed farming that uses basic techniques, simple tools (such as digging sticks, hoes, and machetes), and modest amounts of labor, in relation to the area of land being farmed. Horticulture may coexist with foraging, but horticultural societies are distinguishable from foraging societies by their use of domesticated plants as the main basis for sustenance. Likewise, horticultural societies differ technically from agrarian societies since horticulturalists do not rely on irrigation, draft animals, fertilizers, land improvement practices such as terracing, and the constant tending to farmland through sedentary living as intensive agricultural practitioners often do. The crop yield in horticulture is essentially contingent upon the factors such as the enough rainfall, the natural fertility of the soil, and the terrain that suits slash-and-burn farming.

The **slash-and-burn method** or swidden agriculture is the technique used by horticulturalists to modify wild vegetation or soil texture before planting crops. It involves cutting down brush and small trees using hand tools while leaving only the big trees in and around the farm plot. The vegetation is then allowed to dry out and burned. The resultant cluster of ash is the important nutrients on which crops are grown. As the soil productivity lasts only for a few growing seasons, the depleted land must be left fallow for several years to regenerate. Therefore, slash-and-burn cultivators must move on to clear new plots of uncultivated land every few years. For this shifting pattern of farming, slash-and-burn cultivation is sometimes referred to as shifting cultivation. Cultivating crops with a slash-and-burn method requires a reserve of uncultivated land and thus it is also known as extensive agriculture.

Horticulturalists commonly practice multicropping, cultivating a variety of different plants in the same farm plot. For example, Mesoamerican horticulturalists are known for planting corn, squash, and bean seeds in the same hole. The growing corn stalks in their farm plots provide support for the climbing bean plants while the squash plants that grow over the ground keep down the weed effectively. Cultivating many different species of plants helps horticulturalists' effort to protect their plots from soil erosion as the soil remain covered with vegetation throughout most of the growing season. Moreover, multicropping reduces the risk of the crops being literally wiped out by pests, insects, and fungal infections. Additionally, mixing plants minimizes the predicament of having to rely upon a single staple crop variety within a growing season.

Horticulture was a common subsistence strategy all over the world before high density of population forced people to adopt more intensive agricultural practices. Horticulture is still practiced in tropical forests of the Amazon Basin, mountainous regions of Central and South America, some parts of Central Africa, Southeast Asia, and Oceania.

© Muellek Josef/Shutterstock.com

The age-based maturity often generates respect and admiration in horticultural societies. The elders are treated as possessors of cumulated life experience and expertise invaluable for horticultural way of life. Therefore, the village elder, the medicine man/woman, the clan leader, and the likes can garner specific amounts of prestige levels in horticultural societies.

In horticulturalist societies, women contribute considerably to the activities of sustenance. Men may clear the land, and occasionally hunt and fish to supplement plant food procured from the farm plot, but women often tend to plants, the main source of sustenance of the extensive farmers.

As significant contributors to horticultural mode of subsistence, women play a central role in the social organization of horticultural societies. For example, among the Iroquois, the Native American horticulturalists that lived in what is now the Northeastern United

States, women elders could control clan structure as they elected tribal leaders who met in council. The female elders were also consulted when taking decisions that might affect tribal society. The Iroquois practiced matrilocality: When an Iroquois man married, he went to live with his wife's kin. Indeed, a lot of Native American horticulturalist societies were matrilineal. They include the Iroquois, the Lenape, the Hopi, and the Chickasaw. The prominence asserted to matrilineal descent by many horticulturalists indicates that female work in subsistence is especially important to such societies.

Still, most other horticultural societies are patrilineal. As women often become the principal source of food supply, many men tend to practice polygyny. For the most part, men in horticultural societies assume political and military roles. These tribal societies are centered on Tribal Chiefs, as in the instance of Polynesia or, the Big Men, as in the case of most societies in Melanesia (Sahlins 1963).

A host of questions was intensely debated by generations of anthropologists and archaeologists regarding the origins of agriculture. They include questions such as: Why did agriculture take place in various world regions nearly simultaneously? Did agriculture develop in places with rich natural resources (such as oases and river valleys), or in places where making a living from the land was more difficult?; Why and how had foragers come to adopt an agricultural way of life? and was the shift from foraging to agriculture a matter of choice or a matter of necessity?

## Intensive Agriculture

**Intensive agriculture** is a form of sedentary farming that employs draft animals, irrigation, nonsynthetic fertilizer, and terracing, and characterized by increasing labor intensity, and significant crop surpluses.

This strategy of crop production is intensive as its techniques permit the farmers to produce more than extensive agriculturalists could produce on the same amount of land while retaining their fields in incessant use. A large amount of labor is required for intensive farming under which main tasks of plowing, planting, weeding, caring for irrigation systems and terracing, as well as harvesting must be undertaken.

Intensive farmers use domesticated animals, sometimes referred to as the "beasts of burden," as machines of cultivation.

Draft animals are used to trample the fields, thresh the grains, and transport the produce to the storehouse or the market.

Additionally, their manure (animal excreta) is used to fertilize the fields while also utilizing the manure as a source of fuel.

Irrigation or the supply of water to help plant growth is a by-product of intensive agricultural practices. As most crop plants need water in a dry climate, intensive agriculturalists rely on irrigation to grow crops. In each growing season, water must be delivered to the fields at the right time in the right amount, and later it must be drained off the crops. Typically, a reservoir or an artificial lake is built by constructing an embankment or a dam across a perennial or seasonal water course and by housing the water behind the embankment. The water is then supplied to the fields through irrigation canals. The enough supply of

© ArtMari/Shutterstock.com

water, sound drainage, and well-drained soil being the most salient aspects of an effective irrigation system, intensive farmers tend to them delicately and consistently.

Intensive farmers have been innovative in storing, distributing, and draining water to grow crops for over several millennia. The mastery they achieved in irrigation technology may have largely contributed to the agricultural growth, and the resultant rise of civilizations in terrains such as Mesopotamia (along the Tigris and Euphrates rivers), Egypt (along the Nile river), the Indian subcontinent (along the Indus river), and China (along the Huang He or Yellow river and the Yangtze river) (Wittfogel 1957; Needham 1971).

© Ekkachai/Shutterstock.com

© Ksenia Ragozina/Shutterstock.com

© sleepingpanda/Shutterstock.com

Intensive agriculturalists continuously use land as they cultivate staple crops ceaselessly. Therefore, improving farmland to avoid any occurrence of soil exhaustion becomes a necessity. One innovative method used by intensive farmers to retain the fields replete with rich soil is **terracing.** It is a way of growing crops by planting on graduated terraces (a series of successively receding platforms) built by cutting into the slope of hilly or mountainous terrain. Terraced agriculture involves intensive labor. However, intensive farmers use terracing as an effective method to maximize arable land area in variable terrains. They also employ terracing to reduce soil erosion, the rapid surface runoff, and to enhance water efficiency when growing crops that require irrigation. Terraced fields are widely used to grow staple crops such as rice, wheat, rye, and barley by intensive farmers in South and Southeast Asia. Throughout the Mediterranean Basin, where drier climate exists, intensive farmers use terraced fields to plant grapevines, olive trees, and the likes. In the Andes of South America, intensive agriculturalists have used terraces to grow potatoes, maize, and other native crops. Likewise, terraced farms are used by intensive farmers in parts of Africa and Oceania to grow subsistence crops as well.

Intensive farmers grow a small number of staple crops in large quantities. In addition to cereal crops (e. g., rice, corn, and wheat), they also grow root and tuber crops (e. g., cassava, potato, sweet potato, taro, and yam), fruit crops (e. g., banana, breadfruit, and plantain), as well as pulses (e. g., bean, lentil, pea, and soybean).

© Tutti Frutti/Shutterstock.com

Unlike in horticulture, the long-term per capita yield per unit of land is greater and dependable in intensive agriculture. The improved production capabilities paved the way for the intensive agriculturalists in the ancient world to accumulate greater surpluses and to sustain larger sedentary populations in villages and urban centers. The ability to maintain reserve of staple crops from harvest to harvest also helped them to focus on specialized crafts, such as hydraulic engineering, urban planning, medicine, writing, trading, and warfare. As intensive farmers were getting acclimated to occupational specializations and sedentary living, society turned into a stratified one gradually.

Intensive agriculture is a family-centered subsistence strategy. Hence, it is sometimes known as *family farming* as well. Family farming has always been part of a larger economic system (Wolf 1966a). Nevertheless, the family members supply labor and resources to maintain family farm economy while playing the productive roles organized through gender and age-based division of labor.

## Industrial Agriculture

Of all twelve millennia known for agricultural growth, the last two centuries of industrial agriculture have been the most unprecedented. **Industrial agriculture** refers to contemporary, large-scale, and corporate farming practices, characterized by the increased use of capital in the form of money and property and the application of industrial technology for machinery, synthetic fertilizers, insecticides, fungicides, and herbicides to increase productivity. Today, industrial agriculture is practiced throughout the industrial world, where countries such as the United States, Canada, Great Britain, France, Germany, Russia, and Japan, are among the most noticeable. It is also being adopted in rapidly industrializing countries, such as China, India, and Brazil to an increasing degree. Additionally, some of the essential features of industrial farming are being absorbed with acceleration by almost every nation in the developing world as well.

Industrial agriculture is technology-dependent farming. It substitutes machinery for human and animal labor in every stage of food production, including plowing, planting, irrigating, weeding, pest controlling, and harvesting. Unlike intensive farming, which is depending on organic fertilizers (such as animal manure, compost, and crop residues), industrial agriculture relies on synthetic fertilizers (man-made inorganic compounds, usually derived from the by-products of petroleum industry) for yield enhancement. It also consistently utilizes the genetic research findings on new plant and animal varieties to strategize its farming practices.

© Suwin/Shutterstock.com

Industrial agriculture is capital intensive; it is a form of large-scale farming requiring huge investments on land, high efficiency farm machinery, seed supply, crop production, distribution, processing, agrochemicals, as well as marketing, and retail sales. An industry of its own, the capitalized industrial farming permits a handful of investors to produce massive amounts of food on vast stretches of land. Furthermore, it allows them to bring large portions of the supply chain into a single corporation through vertical integration. Therefore, the term industrial agriculture is often used synonymously with corporate farming or *agribusiness*. In corporate farming, huge companies not only own large farms and control selling of agricultural products, but also influence some of the main areas of agricultural practices (such as agricultural education, research, and public policy planning and implementation) through funding initiatives and lobbying efforts.

Corporate farming in North America relies almost entirely on migrant labor for its seasonal tasks and day-to-day operations, such as planting seeds, watering plants, and harvesting crops in the farmsteads. Along the same line, corporate farming depends on migrant labor for rounding up ruminants, mending fences, and tending to similar chores in the ranches. The labor demand being high during the planting and harvesting seasons of the year, a recurrent pattern of coming and going of migrant workers to the United States from Central America is observable. As anthropologist Leo Chavez observed, these undocumented immigrants, who come from places like Oaxaca, Mexico, work in corporate farms in Southern California as pickers of strawberries, oranges, lemons, and so on, while living temporarily in slum areas of cities such as San Diego (Chavez 1997).

The corporate farming practitioners do keep on producing crops extensively, yet they also pay keen attention to turning farm produce into food products. Although refined and neatly packaged oftentimes, food items such as grains, vegetables, and fruits are still sold in bulk in the market. Increasingly however, they are presented as food products, such as canned goods, dairy products, bakery products, snack food, and frozen food. For example, vegetable sorts are processed into packaged salads, vegetable chops, veggie burgers, and veggie drinks. Grain varieties are transformed into bakery products, such as bread, rolls, donuts, cakes, or snack items (i.e., cereal bars, pretzels, popcorn, and corn chips); nuts become honey-roasted or chocolate-coated products; fruit varieties are available as sugar-coated, chocolate-coated, or candy-coated dried fruit products, fruit pies, fruit cakes, and fruit beverages. The stress laid on food products by corporate farming indicates that, food is not merely a source of sustenance. Rather, it is a primary product of corporate food industry that can be bought and sold by using all-purpose currency. Succinctly put, food has become a commodity under industrial agriculture.

The unprocessed and edible agricultural items' transformation to refined or finished food products is a complex process, for which a vast amount of human and nonhuman energy is invested. For example, the process of changing raw potato to potato chips involves the following multiple areas of special expertise and tasks: destoning, mechanical washing, peeling, trimming, slicing, chemically treating to enhance color, frying, salting, adding flavors, cooling, sorting, packaging, and shipping. The process of transforming the meat produced in factory farms or concentrated animal feeding operations (CAFOs) into processed meat products (such as ham, sausages, and ground or canned meat) requires a host of special expertise and activities as well. They include the following meat processing technologies: cutting/chopping/comminuting (reducing size), mixing/tumbling, salting/curing, adding additional ingredients to processed meat, stuffing/filling into casings or other containers, fermenting, and drying. In short, food production has become a complex process.

© Studio Peace/Shutterstock.com

## Sustainability of Agriculture

Under industrial corporate agriculture, enormous amounts of staple crops production have become an ordinary occurrence. As industrial corporate farming spreads globally, a concurrent and dramatic weakening of foraging, pastoralism, and horticulture as modes of sustenance is noticeable. However, as this form of farming demands substantial capital and labor inputs, technology, and nonrenewable natural resources, its negative effects on the environment and society have become increasingly evident as well.

Anthropologists have examined some of the main features of industrial corporate agriculture and their impact on society. Accordingly, the expanded use of intricate technology (including machinery, chemicals, and genetic research) on new plant and animal species has played a decisive role in displacing small landholders and field laborers. For instance, the use of tractors for plowing instead of draft animals such as mules and horses in the American South during the 1930s enabled landowners to cultivate large swathes of land. However, it also effectively evicted small-scale sharecroppers from arable land. Likewise, the introduction of mechanical cotton picking accelerated the process of cotton production while also increasing the production volume. Nevertheless, it too, displaced the laborers who relied on cotton picking for living.

Moreover, capitalization creates opportunities for large-scale investors, yet it also generates risks for small-scale family farmers who cannot either invest capital heavily or absorb losses easily.

Furthermore, industrial corporate farming is essentially an energy-heavy mode of production. This makes farmers dependents on the global market of energy supplies (McWilliams 2000; Barlett 1993; and Barlett in Plattner 1989).

**Sustainable agriculture** is comprised of a set of innovative thoughts and related practices that seeks to produce food, fiber, and other plant and animal products while preserving environment, protecting public health, sustaining vibrant communities, and upholding animal welfare. It demotes the farming practices relying on petrochemicals-based pest control, synthetic fertilizers, genetically modified seed varieties, as well as the practices contributing to the degradation of water, soil, and other vital resources of nature. It promotes crop production and (pasture-based) livestock farming committed to protecting biodiversity and maintaining healthy ecosystems.

© JaffarAliAfzal123/Shutterstock.com

# Chapter Summary

This chapter concentrates on some of the main themes of economic anthropology. Specifically, it delves into the subsistence strategies through which people across cultures sustain themselves. It also investigates their patterns of exchange and distribution.

- The sphere of economics is consisted of production, exchange, and consumption.

- Mode of production refers to the way of organizing production. The means of production refer to the productive forces such as technology, land, and infrastructural and natural capital. The relations of production allude to the limited sets of socioeconomic and technological roles people find themselves in, that they must embrace for survival, as they take part in production activities.

- The notion of mode of subsistence was a predecessor to the concept of mode of production. The five basic types of subsistence strategy are foraging, pastoralism, horticulture, intensive agriculture, and industrial agriculture.

- Foraging is the mode of subsistence based on hunting, fishing, and gathering a broad range of wild foodstuffs. Foragers are a diverse group of people living in a broad range of conditions. While concentrating on foragers' movement or lack thereof, some researchers typify them into three distinct sets, namely, pedestrian, equestrian, and aquatic foragers. While emphasizing the link between environmental contexts and foraging, some anthropologists identify two dissimilar types of foraging, namely, the temperate-climate and circumpolar foraging. Moreover, by summarizing the historical trajectories of the world's foraging populations, Richard Lee and Richard Daly distinguish the following foraging categories: modern hunter-gatherers who have persisted in direct tradition of descent from ancient foragers, the foragers who have consistently had close contact with sedentary farmers and herders throughout history, and the people who have switched to foraging as a strategic secondary adaptation.

- Resource concentration or scarcity is crucial for foragers' movement. On occasions, they tend to move away from their camp settlements as a means of resolving conflicts as well.

- Most foragers live in small, band-based communities comprising several families. Most often, they incline to have matrilocal postmarital residential arrangements. Labor is typically divided by gender as foraging women do most of the gathering and men do big game hunting. Age is a significant criterion through which tasks are allocated. Cooperative in gathering and sharing resources, foragers customarily have egalitarian relationships.

- Raising and caring large herds of domesticated animals and using them and their products primarily for living is known as pastoralism. It is by concentrating on environmental variables, population size, and their relationship with wider society, various pastoralists choose the types of domesticated animals they want to herd. The animals are herded for food, as well as for products and services not related to food.

- Pastoralism has mostly been a mixed subsistence strategy. It is an extensive strategy as having enough grazing land and water for herd animals are crucial to maintain pastoralist way of life. Two patterns of movement occur with pastoralism: nomadic pastoralism and transhumance. In nomadic pastoralism, the entire group of herders move with their herd animals across a large area throughout the year seeking fresh pasturelands. With transhumance, herders' movement becomes partial and seasonal.

- In most pastoralist societies, some form of division of labor based on gender and age exists. Men and boys herd animals while women and children do the related activities such as milking and dairy processing. The existence of age-sets shows how gender roles and age-based social categories are interconnected in certain pastoralist societies.

- Pastoral social organization is patrilineal and clan based. The form of political organization most pastoral societies prone to foster is either a tribe or chiefdom.

- Horticulture is the small-scale, rain-fed farming that uses basic techniques, simple tools, and modest amounts of labor, in relation to the area of land being farmed. The slash-and-burn method is the technique used by horticulturalists to modify wild vegetation or soil texture before planting crops. Horticulturalists commonly practice multicropping, cultivating diverse plant varieties in the same farm plot.

- Age-based maturity often generates respect and admiration in horticultural societies. Gender-based division of labor is evident as women contribute more to the day-to-day activities of sustenance than men do. The prominence asserted to matrilineal descent shows that women play a core role in horticultural social organization. However, most other horticultural societies, in which men assume key political and military roles are patrilineal.

- Intensive agriculture is a form of sedentary farming that employs draft animals, irrigation, nonsynthetic fertilizer, and terracing, and characterized by increasing labor intensity, and significant crop surpluses. Intensive farmers grow a few staple crops in large quantities. Unlike in horticulture, the long-term per capita yield per unit of land is greater and dependable. Intensive agriculture is a family-centered subsistence strategy.

- Industrial agriculture refers to contemporary, large-scale, and corporate farming practices, characterized by the increased use of capital and the application of industrial technology for machinery, and petrochemicals to increase productivity.

- Corporate farming in North America relies almost entirely on migrant labor for its seasonal tasks and day-to-day operations.

- Under corporate farming, food has become a commodity. Moreover, food production has become a complex process.

- Sustainable agriculture is a set of innovative thoughts and related practices that seeks to produce food, fiber, and other plant and animal products while preserving environment, protecting public health, sustaining vibrant communities, and upholding animal welfare.

# Distribution: Probing the Aspects of Exchange and Processes of Circulation

© Matyas Rehak/Shutterstock.com

While customarily focusing on the industrial world, economists investigate economic behavior and institutions in strictly economic terms. Nonetheless, what customarily attracted anthropologists' attention has been the small-scale, nonindustrial economies of foragers, family farmers, and herders in which, modern economic features such as currency usage and market principle were either absent or not fully developed. They have been keen to look beyond impersonal monetized transactions and shed light on the interactions of culturally diverse people in economic processes.

# Economic Anthropology

The anthropological approach to economics is based on the premise that human activities are inseparable from their social and cultural contexts. Therefore, the analysis of economic behavior and institutions in stringent economic terms ignores the impact of salient cultural considerations on people's practical motives and decisions as they go about their daily lives. Expressed differently, sociocultural relationships play a pivotal role in shaping economic behavior. Understanding the issues of human nature that relate directly to the decisions of daily life and making a living requires an analytic space where economic perspectives and cultural approaches can coalesce (Wilk 1996; Wilk and Cliggett 2007; Rao and Walton 2004). The history of the dialogue between the students of anthropology and economics bespeak to the fact that, economic anthropology has been providing a useful analytic space in that regard.

Accordingly, **economic anthropology** examines economic activity and cultural relations wherever they may be found. Alternatively stated, economic anthropology offers a

© Gail Palethorpe/Shutterstock.com

perspective in which, cultural weight of economic processes around the globe is sought to ascertain. Since its inception as an anthropological subfield, economic anthropology has produced a corpus of rich ethnographies on economic activities practiced by people around the world who displayed a great deal of cultural variety. It was the ways with which, anthropologists dealt with this cultural diversity in theoretical terms that stimulated most debates within economic anthropology.

## Formalist versus Substantivist Debate

One of the main theoretical deliberations from which economic anthropology benefited immensely throughout a better part of the twentieth century was known as the **Formalist versus Substantivist debate.** This was a disciplinary debate carried on by economic anthropologists on the validity of using Western, capitalist model of rational economic behavior to analyze economic activities in non-Western precapitalist societies. The above model, derived from the school of thought known as *neoclassical economics,* rests on a set of suppositions.

The most salient among them is the notion that human decision making, and rationality is applicable to economics and other phenomena universally. Regardless of individuals' cultural orientation, the choices they make are rational, meant for happiness, and identifiable with whatever those individuals consider of being value. Put another way, human decision making and rationality is assumed to be driven by the pursuit of individual pleasure and happiness, which is proportionate to utility. Therefore, every individual is an economic man (*homo economicus*) who is bound to think and act as a utility maximizer; that is to say, individual economic actor always makes rational economic decisions that maximize wealth and minimize labor. Market exchanges are defined along the same line of thinking— they are the acts of simple trade between equally powerless economic men trying earnestly to maximize their individual pleasure or utility under the conditions of scarcity.

Accordingly, economics is the logic with which rational preferences among alternative means to alternative ends are made. The economic anthropologists such as Herskovits (1940), Goodfellow (1939), Firth (1939), and Schneider (1974) who drew from the aforementioned formalist model were known as *formalists.* They maintained that, as the principles of rational choice were attributable to all market relations, they were fundamental to human behavior and widely generalizable across cultures and phases of history.

The critics of the formalist views contended that economies of different societies were based on different logical processes and hence, would have comprehended on their own terms. As the livelihood of the people in non-Western, precapitalist, and nonindustrialized societies depended on redistribution and reciprocity (discussed below), and not on market exchange, analysis of such societies entailed a perspective with a substantive meaning of economics. The economic anthropologists who shared this alternative view were known as *substantivists.* Economic historian Karl Polanyi tried to explain the substantivist perspective through several key pieces of his writing (Polanyi 1944, 1957). In Polyani's view, the attempts to analyze noncapitalist economic systems through the concepts of capitalist market economics such as rational choice, supply and demand, and profit maximization were misleading and had led to misinterpretation and distortion. In noncapitalist societies based on subsistence provisioning, the above concepts were either meaningless or had different meanings. Taking trade as an example Polanyi pointed out that, like all other aspects of culture, it was a social construction and would not have meaningfully studied outside of its specific social setting.

Anthropologists Marshall Sahlins and George Dalton also debunked formalist analyses of economic life in noncapitalist societies as misrepresentations borne of "Neolithic prejudices" and "bourgeois ethnocentrism" (Sahlins 1972; Dalton 1969). By stepping away from Western notions of affluence based on the capitalist economic concept of bridging the gap between unlimited wants and insufficient means, Sahlins characterized foragers as members of the original affluent society in the world. According to Sahlins, as a society based on finite and few material wants, foragers were able to take the "Zen road to affluence."

The debates of the sorts underscore the tacit anthropological recognition that the economic activities such as the exchange of goods and services are at the core of the functioning of culture, as they form patterns of interaction, obligation, and mutuality among people. Anthropologists have identified three main modes of economic exchange: reciprocity, redistribution, and market exchange (Polanyi 1957). While it may be possible for several exchange patterns to function simultaneously, only a single mode of exchange usually becomes most prominent in any given society (See TABLE 9.1).

---

### TABLE 9.1   Main Modes of Economic Exchange

1. Reciprocity
    I.   Gifts or Generalized Reciprocity
    II.  Balanced or Symmetrical Reciprocity
    III. Negative or Market Reciprocity

2. Redistribution

3. Market Exchange

Source: Gajaba Naraddage

---

# Reciprocity

**Reciprocity** is the exchange of goods and services among people of relatively equal socioeconomic status. Found generally among foragers and horticulturalists, this mode of exchange involves gifting, receiving, and reciprocating activities of cultural variety. Three types of reciprocity may be distinguishable, depending on the extent to which exchange partners maintain distance from each other socially: generalized, balanced, and negative reciprocity (Sahlins 1972).

## Generalized Reciprocity

**Generalized reciprocity** is the reciprocal exchanges taking place among close kin and intimate friends. In this type of reciprocity, exchange partners do not keep track of what is given, its calculated value, or a period within which repayment must be made. Hence, it is also known as *delayed reciprocity.* This reciprocity type carries a moral obligation with it often reaching a level that may be characterized as almost altruistic. Parents' providing of goods and services for their children perhaps best fits this type of exchange. Their maintenance of overt accounts regarding the goods and services for the children is something generally unheard of as parents give food, clothes, shelter, education, care, and protection out of a sense of love, obligation, and social responsibility. In an extended family setting, parental care may continue even after the children become adults (and have their own children) and extend to the taking care of grandchildren. When the parents become incapable of taking care of themselves due to old age, the children usually look after them. Such transactions between parents and children suggest that even this most generalized reciprocal exchange is not entirely altruistic.

Generalized reciprocity is the predominant mode of exchange in small-scale societies, where family is the primary unit of economic organization. An economic strategy based on generalized reciprocity assists people in such societies to survive during harder times when resources are meager at best. For example, generalized reciprocity based on food distribution and sharing, common among foragers such as the Ju/'hoansi in the Kalahari, Africa, and the Inuit in the Canadian Arctic, helps them immensely to sustain all year around.

© gpointstudio/Shutterstock.com

## Balanced Reciprocity

**Balanced reciprocity** involves the exchange of goods and services of roughly equivalent value within a set time limit. This form of exchange mostly occurs between more distant relatives or social equals who are not considered as kin. In balanced reciprocity, the giver expects the gift to be accepted and reciprocated. Therefore, the recipient of the gift is obliged to reciprocate with a gift of equivalent value although it may not happen immediately. The absence of reciprocation is an act of straining the potential to build a useful social link. This tacit understanding helps the giver and the receiver to build an enduring trading relationship that can go beyond the immediate kin group. Indeed, the immediate repayment of the original gift may be a disinclination to establish a trading partnership in which "the obligation to give and the obligation to receive" are expected to endure (Mauss 1967, 10).

In contemporary North America, balanced reciprocity may be seen in a variety of formal and informal occasions, such as wedding ceremonies, birthday celebrations, religious holidays, baby showers (celebration of the pending or recent birth of a child by presenting gifts to the mother at a party), dinner parties, and taking turns in buying rounds for drinking friends at the bar.

## Negative Reciprocity

**Negative reciprocity** refers to the exchange of goods and services, in which each party seeks to gain more than it gives at the expense of others. If generalized and balanced reciprocity are based on relationships of familiarity, trust, and obligation, negative reciprocity is established through the links of unfamiliarity, distrust, and opposing interests. Therefore, negative reciprocal exchanges often occur between antagonistic, strange, and competitive trading partners who may not be hesitant to use manipulation, bargaining, and deception to minimize their cost and maximize the return. On occasions, such as plunder, this form of exchange may even extend to coercion and violence.

Negative reciprocity occurs often in contemporary North American society. For instance, credit card companies lure customers (such as college students) by offering credit cards at higher percentage rate (APR) that the card holder cannot afford to repay, ultimately forcing the card holder to spend a sizable chunk of his or her monthly earning as the credit card premium on a regular basis. Likewise, Wall Street investment managers tempt clients to invest on the prospects of high returns while eventually sucking up to their clients' money. In the same vein, there are instances in which online racketeers manage to extract bank information from their targeted email recipients by promising to share a fortune with them.

© diy13/Shutterstock.com

## Redistribution

Whereas reciprocal exchange lays stress on establishing a relationship *between* two distinct parties with their own interests, redistribution draws attention to a *within-group* relationship based on centralized collection and redivision. **Redistribution** is the mode of exchange in which goods are collected from or contributed by members of a group and then redivided among those members in a different pattern. The goods, services, and their equivalents are brought from the local level to a center, before reallocating among members of the society. The pooling of goods and services essentially requires the presence of a social center. Depending on the form of social organization in which redistribution occurs, the social center may take varying forms ranging in size and scope from the chief's storehouse in a chiefdom to the capital of a central administration.

The inward and outward flow of goods involves a hierarchy of officials who may consume some of them in the process. However, the existence of leveling mechanisms usually ensures that the goods eventually flow down through the hierarchy to the lower tier of the community.

## Leveling Mechanism

**Leveling mechanisms** are the practices and organizations functioning to maximize the collective socioeconomic well-being of a society through reallocation of resources. Leveling mechanisms act to discourage more prosperous members' attempt to put themselves above others of the community by pressurizing such individuals to host public feasts, give away goods, provide services, and thereby show generosity. Leveling mechanisms serve to lessen social inequality.

**Potlatch,** the ceremonial feast held by the Kwakiutl in the Pacific Northwest region, is a classic ethnographic example for the ceremonial practices of redistribution (Boas 1966; Suttles 1991). The potlatch is a feast and a redistribution ceremony simultaneously: it is an elaborate feasting ceremony as relatives of the hosting chief, his community members, as well as the high-ranking chiefs in neighboring chiefdoms are invited as guests and served with the best food available (such as fish, seal meat, berries, and nuts) in abundant quantities; it is also a redistribution ceremony, in which material goods (such as carved wooden boxes, hand-woven mats, embroiled blankets, and even canoes) are redistributed broadly among the group members, and generously presented as gifts to the neighboring chiefs, the other invited guests. The more the hosting chief gives, the more he increases his chances to earn social prestige, and the more his guests feel obliged to reciprocate. The chief's generosity is also a calculated measure with which pressure is applied on his guests to reciprocate in similar manner, or even better in a later potlatch. In this sense, potlatch is a strategic investment of community resources as well (Boas 1966).

Marshall Sahlins considered chiefly redistribution as a well-organized form of kinship-rank reciprocity. As he saw it, a starting mechanism for a more general hierarchy may be found in the acts of generalized reciprocity within families by elders. The French Marxist anthropologist Claude Meillassoux (Saul 2013) also thought that the lineage mode of production seen in chiefdoms and kingdoms in Western Africa was associated with the growth of ranked kin distribution from generalized reciprocity (Meillassoux 1978, 127–57).

Some forms of redistribution are evident even in economic systems in which modern market economies prevail. The practice of collecting taxes from citizens based on their earnings and property is one such instances of redistribution facilitated by the state. Redistribution takes place when the money raised from taxation is indirectly given back to citizens through the provision of public services or directly through welfare benefits.

## Market Exchange

**Market exchange** is the mode of economic exchange in which goods and services are bought and sold at a money price essentially decided by the market forces of supply and demand (Narotzky 1997; Plattner 1984). In this act of simple trade, ideally all participants turn into potential buyers or sellers. They are equally powerless economic men who may be able to make rational choices to maximize their individual pleasure or utility under the conditions of scarcity. Just as a seller's willingness to sell (supply) is directly proportional to price increases, a buyer's willingness to buy (demand) is directly proportional to price decreases. When the supply of goods and services matches demand, it leads the market to the state of price equilibrium. The forces of supply and demand become relatively equal in the market.

The classical political economist Adam Smith in his well-known capitalist manifesto *The Wealth of Nations* (1776) used the metaphor of "invisible hand" to highlight the unobservable force of market that assists the demand and supply of goods in a free market to reach equilibrium naturally. Smith believed that the market system must be unhindered by government restrictions such as regulations, privileges, tariffs, and subsidies. When the economy is freed or liberated from government interference, Smith maintained, it is quite capable generating free trade, enterprise, and competition, and thereby, unleashing human potential. Smith's advocacy for *laissez-faire* (hands-off) economics became the cornerstone of capitalist economics.

An economic system based on the above principle is considered a capitalist market economy. It promotes the capitalist market economy. The goal of the capitalist mode of production is to amass wealth in the form of money to gain control of the means of production, and then use that control to accumulate even greater wealth. The above goal is achievable due to the existence of **surplus value,** the amount of value produced by workers that is greater than the wage paid to them.

This system began in earnest with **mercantile capitalism**, a social system based on competition for control of natural resources and trade in external markets. The rise of mercantile system was significant in the development of European colonialism in the seventeenth and the eighteenth centuries (See Chapter 12).

## Commodities

Under the capitalist mode of production, products have become commodities. **Commodity** is a sellable or exchangeable product or service in return of money, other products, or services.

## Commodity Fetishism

In an oft-cited passage in *Das Kapital* (Capital), Karl Marx used the image of the fetish or an object which is believed to possesses spiritual power to illustrate the way in which people misapprehend the true nature of commodities by obsessively treating them as persons, thus attributing power and agency to things, while treating people who really do have agency, mere repositories of labor power for sale in the market. Marx characterizes this tendency as **commodity fetishism** (Marx, *Capital*, Vol. 1, Chapter 1, section 4).

For Marx, capitalism is tied to the *alienation* of workers from the means of production. Alienation is the contention that workers will essentially lose control over their lives under the conditions of capitalist industrial production (For a discussion of alienation, see Chapter 10).

A sharp distinction between objects and people occurs in commodity exchange. The notion of private property is central to this distinction as being able to sell means none other than the ability to transfer ownership rights fully to the new owner. Once sold, the object comes to be alienated from its first owner. Therefore, commodities are alienable; their ownership rights can be taken away from or given away by the owner. In commodity exchange, the seller and the buyer are in a state of reciprocal independence, because every exchange is fragmented at each instance of the exchange of objects (Gregory 2015). Commodity exchange gives rise to alienation, control, and dominance.

## Money as Means of Market Exchange

Commodities are bought or sold for money that comes mainly in the form of paper and coin, but also in other forms, sometimes. The other forms of money include precious metals, gem, or other material objects. It is also increasingly common today for people to use virtual money in e-commerce transactions, that is, when buying and selling is done fully electronically. Money serves for several functions: it is a universally recognized medium of exchange; it measures the value of goods and services; it allows wealth to be preserved over time; it is a measure of debt; it is usable in nonmarket situations to pay off debts. Differentially put, **money** is a recognizable, divisible, interchangeable, movable, and durable means of market exchange (Dalton 1971). Money came into prominence as a main medium of economic exchange in many parts of the globe with the advent of merchant capitalism (Davis and Davis 2005; Wolf 1982).

The recognition of money as the universal medium of exchange necessitates the maintenance of financial stability in a money-based economy. Usually, during a period of monetary crisis, two possible outcomes may be anticipated, depending on the context involved. One possibility is currency devaluation causing hyperinflation. The other is the short supply of money, and in that case, money itself turns into an item of barter rather than a means of economic exchange (Humphrey 1985).

Unlike in noncash economies, in which people may be able to compensate their providers of goods and services through time and labor, in money-based economies, such as current industrial settings, consumers must rely almost totally on their access to cash or some virtual form of money (e-currency). Indeed, **e-currency** or currency in electronic form is increasingly gaining prominence as Internet-based commerce or e-commerce is on the rise. Electronic cash reached new heights in 2009 with the introduction of Bitcoin, a type of digital currency that uses state-of-the-art cryptography, and has a decentralized distribution system.

Writing in 1907, sociologist Georg Simmel pointed out the seductive dangers associated with the development of money economy and the "objective culture" in the modern world (Simmel [1907] 1978). In the commodified world, today, money is a primer—it is a stimulus that fires through people's brains, changing their behavior subconsciously. Indeed, mere reminders of money can influence people's attitudes and behavior in a substantial way. This is known as the **money priming** (Frick 2012).

# Gift

It is almost like an unspoken agreement: the parents give the gift of life to their children, feed them, clothe them, and raise them. Although at first this gift is without conditions, it comes back around so children may return the favor—it is usually expected to be returned—when the parents are old, and the children are grown and attained maturity. This common scenario shows us that the gifts are anything, but spontaneous and without obligation. The thought that gifts bear obligations is instilled early in our lives. Accordingly, we get accustomed to the feeling that, the gifts are subtle bonding experiences between people that reflect an exchange of respect and ensure cooperation and alliance.

We also tend to think that the act of generosity is innately related to benignity and benevolence. It may be used to benign activities such as forming new relationships and strengthening the existing ones, so people can assist the needy in the alliances while also keeping expectations high whenever help is required to them. Indeed, anthropologist Carol Stack refers to such a robust tradition of benevolent exchange known as **swapping** existed in an Illinois ghetto region of the Flats (a pseudonym) during her time of ethnographic fieldwork (Stack [1974] 2003).

Still, no act of giving is fully generous or free of calculation, as anthropologist Richard Lee learned from the !Kung, his hosts in the Kalahari, Africa, when he gifted them a healthy and fat ox for the feast during Christmas. Lee learned further that, ridiculing gifts was the !Kung foragers' way of diminishing the expected return. Moreover, it was their way of enforcing humility on the donor who would otherwise use gifts to raise his or her own status within the group (Lee [1969] 2000, 27–30).

Richard Lee's story tells us that the gifts may be used to place the receiver in debt, so the donor can control the receiver and demand loyalty. By belittling Lee's generous gift, the !Kung people showed Lee that gifts come with strings attached and they may exert influence on how people and groups relate to each other. The point is well grounded not only in the context of an American anthropologist and a Kalahari foraging community were the involving parties but also, within the context, in which affluent donor countries offering foreign aid packages to impoverished nations.

Gifts may be used for antagonistic purposes as well. For the Big Men in Papua New Guinea, the **Moka** was a highly ritualized feasting ceremony, in which reciprocal gifts of pigs

and food (e.g., sweet potato) were exchanged. The Moka participants knew that, by giving more, they could earn greater prestige (than their actual or potential rivals). In brief, the Moka was an opportunity for achieving social status, gaining prestige, as well as shaming rivals.

Likewise, for the Kwakiutl Indians in the Pacific Northwest, Potlatch was not merely a ceremonial feast, during which hosts distributed a large quantity of food and goods that had been collected over many months or even years (See above in this chapter). It was an occasion, in which the old war of blood may be replaced with a new war of wealth.

Fighting with gifts is not uncommon among enemies and rivals, as seen in the following sequence of the film *The Godfather* (1972) directed by Francis Ford Coppola: A group of men are seen chatting by the dinner table of the Corleone family home. A man (Tessio) brings in Luca Brasi's bulletproof vest, delivered with a fish inside. Visibly annoyed, the group leader (Sonny Corleone) reacts with these words: "what the hell is this?" This sequence tells us that, in a society where power, violence, blood ties, and family loyalty intermixed, sending a dead fish as a gift by a crime family boss to the heir apparent of another crime family competing for power and political supremacy can be a powerful symbolic message of revenge.

Figuratively, antagonistic generosity is killing with kindness. By showing kindness to a party who has wronged, one may insight frustration (or even animosity) as one did not respond in a manner consistent to the attacking party. Think about the following scenario, for example, the husband and the wife are arguing (over a family matter), and the husband may choose to say as a response to the wife's barrage, "I love you," before walking away!

© Laszlo Mates/Shutterstock.com

## The Spirit of the Gift

According to the French anthropologist Marcel Mauss, the author of the seminal essay *The Gift* or *Essai sur le don* (1925), a gift may appear as something given (to one party by another) or a service rendered (by one party to another) spontaneously, disinterestedly, and voluntarily. However, it is something given, or a duty performed, obligatorily. Therefore, gifting is an act of fulfilling an obligation, in strict sense of the term. The obligation to repay gifts received implies obligation to give and receive as well. Marcel Mauss called the forms of contract and exchange as a system of "total prestations" (Mauss, [1925] 1967, 3, 10). **Prestation** is paying in money, in goods, or in service as a way of fulfilling an obligation. The contract to give, receive, and reciprocate imposes reciprocal prestations (prestations and counterprestations) upon the parties.

Marcel Mauss was addressing a question raised by anthropologist Bronislaw Malinowski in his well-known ethnography on the Trobriand islanders, *Argonauts of the Western Pacific* (Malinowski [1922] 1984). Referring to the network of exchanging bracelets and necklaces across the Trobriand Islands, which he carefully traced and identified as part of a system of the **Kula ring,** Malinowski raised the following question: "Why would men risk life and limbs to travel across huge expanses of dangerous ocean to give away what appear to be worthless trinkets?" Malinowski noted that, among the Trobriand Islanders, the exchange of goods was essentially between individuals, not among groups. Moreover, their nonaltruistic motives in giving (expectation for a return of the goods of equal or greater value) was evident to him. Trobriand gifting, according to Malinowski, implied reciprocity, not generosity. There were no giveaways.

"Why anyone would give gifts (food, women, children, charms, land, labor, services, religious offices, and rank) away?" asked Marcel Mauss. The gifts of all sorts were things that needed to be given away and repaid. Therefore, Mauss continued in answering the above question, the gifts pass and repass between clans and individuals, ranks, sexes, and generations in an interminable interchange of spiritual matter. The spirit of the practice of gifting was the source of reciprocity in exchange. It involved, as in the Maori concept of *Hau*, belief in a force binding the giver and the receiver, Mauss contended. The exchange of gift and counter-gift keep the relationship between the giver and the receiver, as well as the pledge for future gifts alive (Mauss 1967).

At the core of Mauss's analysis was the ambivalence generated by the gift–It brought into being desirability and disinterestedness. It gave rise to sociability and nonsociability. It was the source of sacrifice and acquisition. It created inequality while mystifying it. All simultaneously! The ambivalence of the practice of gifting was conspicuously evident when Mauss pointed out that the gift was a form of self-deception by which domination is mostly disguised. Reciprocity neutralized power, whereas commodity exchange has forgotten the theme of the ambiguity of the gift (Mauss 1967).

## The Paradox of the Gift: Keeping While Giving

Exchange acts fuel tension, for all exchange is based on the universal paradox of "how to keep while giving," contends anthropologist Annette Weiner (Weiner 1992). According to Weiner, the motivation for reciprocity indeed stems from its opposite: "the desire to keep something back from the pressures of give and take" (Weiner 1992). As certain things/objects become saturated with intrinsic qualities of their owners in a community closely knitted by kinship, descent, and marital ties, they "assume a subjective value that places them above exchange value" (Weiner 1992). Hence, such objects become *inalienable possessions*, unlike alienable goods or commodities that may be bought, sold, or given up.

For instance, when a Maori woman puts on a Maori cloak, she becomes more than herself as she begins to be her ancestors as well. The cloak now acts as a conduit for the woman's *Hau* or life-giving spirit, source of energy and strength, and origination of potential knowledge. Additionally, she may be having the risk of losing her *Hau*. Therefore, the cloak now stands for the Maori woman's own persona. In other words, the cloak has become her inalienable possession. "What makes a possession inalienable," contends Weiner, "is its exclusive and cumulative identity with a particular series of owners through time." Its history is validated by fictive

© Gina Smith/Shutterstock.com

or true lines of descent, origin myths, sacred ancestors, and divine beings. In this way, certain things acquire biographies inseparable from people's memories, and that makes such things inalienable possessions or "transcendent treasures" (Weiner 1992, 33).

Let's try to understand Weiner's thesis by focusing on a scenario in the American realist novel *The Grapes of Wrath*, written by John Steinbeck (Steinbeck 1939). Set during the Great Depression (1929–1941), the novel concentrates on a poor family of tenant farmers driven from their Oklahoma home by drought, poverty, and the changes in agricultural industry. They decided to set out for California and seek a better life there. However, the members of the family—women, in particular—faced the dilemma of sorting their belongings to carry with them in their small truck while discarding the rest. How can these women live without the things they've gathered and kept for generations, because these things have biographies deeply and persistently embedded in the memories of the women? Then, how can the women discard these inalienable possessions?

> "When everything that could be sold was sold—still there were piles of possessions; The women sat among the doomed things, turning them over and looking past them and back. This book. My father had it. He liked a book—Got his name in it. And his pipe—still smells rank—Think we could get this china dog in? Aunt Sadie brought it from the St. Louis Fair. See? Wrote right on it—Here's a letter my brother wrote the day before he died—No, there isn't room.
>
> How can we live without our lives? How can we know it's us without our past?" (Steinbeck 2006 [1939]).

© Rolf_52/Shutterstock.com

Weiner cogently explains the paradox inherent in the process of keeping-while-giving. The need to keep something transcendent and out of circulation is driven by the fear of loss and the desire to defeat it, even though the pressures to give transcendent treasures to others is constant and acute. Therefore, the process of keeping-while-giving is a burden and a responsibility at the same time. Although not always attainable, it is also a masterly accomplishment simultaneously.

Moreover, Weiner argues, the act of keeping-while-giving is an effort to bring permanence into a social world that is consistently in the process of change. Although inalienable possessions are the most powerful force in the efforts of unsettling change, they are also the agents in sowing and nurturing "the seeds of change" (Weiner 1992, 8).

Weiner's discussion on the process of keeping-while-giving and power sheds new lights on the ambiguous nature of inalienable possessions. Subjectively, each inalienable possession is unlike anything else. Therefore, it can elevate the social persona of its owner. By echoing German literary critic Walter Benjamin's usage of the term (Benjamin [1936] 1968) Weiner points out that, the "aura" of the possession/sacred object pervades every aspect of owner's social life (including, social identity, rank, and status) while legitimizing them. In this way, the ownership of an inalienable possession confirms difference rather than equivalence. Consequently, the process of keeping-while-giving begins to be fundamental in setting up difference (Weiner 1992).

Taking most of her ethnographic examples from Polynesia, as well as from the Trobriand Islands, Weiner underscores the salient role women play in the production and the use of economic, political, and religious power in such societies.

In Polynesia, Weiner indicates, a greater part of valuables held as clan treasures are the goods either produced for women, by women, or over which women maintain exclusive individual rights. Such valuables may be ranging from symbols of a rank or title to gifts and counter-gifts associated with birth, marriage, and death rituals. Moreover, Weiner notes, the Polynesian woman enjoys a higher rank as the sister than her male counterpart, the brother— she is on a par with ancestors, the gods, and the sacred. The brother–sister relationship is treated with the sacred, so women and the feminine are present in earnest at the core of Polynesian institutions, just as they can be seen in intimate relations (Weiner 1992).

The strategic role brother–sister relations play in forming the social sphere and setting up power motivates Weiner to reject the well-known anthropological formula by Levi-Strauss: the basis of kinship is the "exchange" of women among men (Strauss [1949] 1969). Mindful of Polynesian brother–sister relations, Weiner contends that, a sister given as a wife may be considered as the equivalent of a wife received in place of that sister (Werner 1992; Godelier 1999, 33–35).

Among the Trobriand Islanders, Weiner points out, the gifts exchanged by males during their periodic Kula ring expeditions serve to draw countergifts. Therefore, they may be treated as movable goods. Weiner contrasts them with immovable goods such as landed property held by Trobriand women. She also indicates further; inheritance is passed through the female lines as descent is reckoned matrilineally in the Trobriand society (Weiner 1992).

## The Enigma of the Gift

Traditional theories of gift giving, both old and recent, are fundamentally flawed because they concentrate only on exchangeable gifts, argues French anthropologist Maurice Godelier

(Godelier 1999). Reexamining gift exchange and rereading Mauss, Levi-Strauss, Weiner, and many others, Godelier contends that, there exists certain nonexchangeable things in any given society. Despite the value they possess, such items are never exchanged, since they "must not be given" and "must not be sold" (Godelier 1999, 8). What makes such objects sacred, Godelier contends further, is "the authoritative conferral of power associated with them." Godelier's work stresses the salient role gifts play in social life while drawing attention again to the traditional anthropological theme of gift exchange simultaneously.

## Spheres of Exchange

What Mauss meant by the "spirit of the gift" may have led some anthropologists to conclude that market economies are at variance with gift economies, fully. The two categories are often shown as distinct spheres of exchange, treatable as opposites. Accordingly, commodity exchange involves an immediate exchange of alienable objects between reciprocally independent parties. It is a quantitative relationship established between the objects exchanged. This exchange gains prominence in class-based societies. In contrast, gift exchange calls for a delayed exchange of inalienable goods between reciprocally dependent people. Gift exchange is a qualitative relationship established between the trans-actors. This exchange prevails in clan-based societies (Gregory [1982] 2015) (See TABLE 9.2).

### TABLE 9.2 Gift Economies versus Market Economies

| Gift Exchange | Commodity Exchange |
|---|---|
| • Clan-based societies | Class-based societies |
| • Boundness between gifts and people during exchange | Strict distinction between commodities and people during exchange |
| • Gift exchange engages and links giver and receiver magically, morally, religiously | Commodity exchange separates individuals judicially and morally |
| • Every gift exchange embodies some coefficient sociability | Fragmented at each instance, every commodity exchange embodies alienation, dominance, and control. |
| • Gift exchange mystifies and neutralizes inequality/power relations | Commodity exchange sanctifies and reinforces inequality/power relations |
| • Gifts are inalienable, and hence, they are possessions | Goods and services that can be bought and sold are alienable, and hence, they are commodities. |

Source: Gajaba Naraddage

Anthropologists such as Marilyn Strathern (Strathern 1988) have discouraged seeing these distinct exchange spheres as opposites. In his classic study of Haitian market women, anthropologist Sidney Mintz also demonstrated how buyers and sellers in the market were connected by deep-rooted and personal relationships, and not by the minute changes of supply and demand (Mintz [1961] 1986).

© Sandra Foyt/Shutterstock.com

Nevertheless, the link between systems of market exchange and nonmarket exchange prevalent in many indigenous economic systems has been an intriguing theme for many anthropologists who tried to conjecture unalike exchange spheres emerging in societies newly merged into the market. The pattern of "dual economy" in Indonesia observed by Clifford Geertz (1963) and the model of "moral economy" in lower Burma (Myanmar) and Vietnam in the 1930s proposed by James Scott (1976) are fine examples to the point. Geertz viewed colonialism as the stabilizer as well as the accentuator of the dual economic pattern in Indonesia as it allowed the capital intensive western sector to thrive while letting the labor-intensive eastern sector to languish. Geertz used exchange sphere to make sense of peasant complacency in the face of exploitation. Scott tried to show how the capitalistic, market economy intruded into traditional agrarian societies, undermining the intricate networks of peasant subsistence. He used exchange sphere to explain peasant resistance and rebellion.

# Commodity Flows and Singularization

**Commoditization** makes goods and services indistinguishable from similar products and services. Commoditization seems an irresistible force, yet it has its counter drive, known to anthropologists as **singularization.** This latter process singularizes objects by making them transcendent treasures that can be withdrawn from the market. Whereas commoditization homogenizes value, singularization essentially discriminates objects through culture. It not only resists commoditization, but also resingularizes what has been already commoditized sometimes. For example, a wedding ceremony can transform a ring purchased from the jewelry shop (which is, technically a commodity) into a priceless heirloom, the only one of its kind for a family.

Examining how the objects of specific sorts are traded in restricted spheres of exchange has been the traditional anthropological approach. However, some anthropologists began to pay attention to how objects flowed between the spheres of exchange. The focus on culturally defined aspects of exchange and socially regulated processes of circulation shifts attention away from the nature of human relationships built through exchange. Moreover, an approach based on the flow of commodities paves a way for making better sense of the "social life of things" (Appadurai 1986).

By seeing a commodity not as a thing, but as one phase in the entire life cycle of the thing, anthropologist Arjun Appadurai draws on the works of several fellow anthropologists, most notably on those of Igor Kopitoff (1986) and Nancy Munn (1986). They indicate that, to understand a commodity's full value, one must analyze its entire trajectory. Nicholas Thomas' account of historical anthropology also takes a similar tack (Thomas 2009).

Igor Kopitoff views commoditization as a cultural and cognitive process; an object goes through different contexts, hands, and uses while gathering a biography, or a series of

© GUDKOV ANDREY/Shutterstock.com

biographies (Kopitoff 1986). In her discussion of the kula system in Gawa, a small island off the Southwest coast of mainland Papua New Guinea, Nancy Munn also expresses a similar view. For example, she contends that "to understand what is being created when Gawans make a canoe, we have to consider the total canoe into other objects" (Munn [1986] 1992). In his study of Western and non-Western gifts and commodity transactions in the Pacific, Nicholas Thomas lays emphasis on the shared history of colonial entanglement. In so doing, Thomas shows how, during their encounter in the last two centuries, Pacific Islanders and the colonial visitors have fashioned identities for themselves and for each other by appropriating and exchanging goods (Thomas [1991] 2009).

## The Paradox of Debt: Morality and Menace

There is no denial that the law of quid-pro-quo or tit-for-tat may be the basis of much of human life, but social scientists have been too quick to reduce the transactions based on it—both moral and material—to the principle of reciprocity, contends anthropologist David Graeber. What informs everything humans do, he argues further, is not barter, not money, but debt (and, by inference, credit). Graeber's argument is the opposite of the narrative given in standard economic texts dating back to the classical capitalist economic theorist Adam Smith. Graeber cites numerous historical, archeological, and anthropological accounts to support his claim that barter transactions never preceded money, and money itself appeared after debt, the oldest means of trade (Graeber 2011).

© Marzolino/Shutterstock.com

History of debt and money is also a history of war and violence, Graeber asserts. According to him, debt has been the basis of all human sociability. Social relations are ultimately based on the "communism of senses" or "the shared conviviality" (Graeber 2011, 385). Formerly, economic life was based on social currencies, and they were closely connected to routine nonmarket interactions. The social and economic life was based on mutual expectations and responsibilities among individual members of the community. Graeber characterizes this as a society founded upon "everyday communism." Graeber maintains that, the introduction of reciprocal exchange paved the way for the hierarchies, and consequently, for institutionalized forms of inequality such as customs and castes. Early "human economies," in which informal, imprecise, community-building indebtedness prevailed, were replaced by mathematically precise and firmly enforced debts, argues Graeber. It was by introducing state-sponsored violence this was done, he contends further (Graeber 2011).

Alluding to its "paradox" (in this context, Graeber uses the term euphemistically) Graeber indicates that, debt is a promise to repay. Moreover, it is a promise that can be quantified; typically, debt is an obligation to pay certain amount of money according to certain conditions, often at a certain rate of interest by a certain time. According to Graeber, even though we despise debt, and dislike those who are in the habit of lending as menaces, we tend to think that debt must be repaid—it is our moral obligation. Indeed, debt is the basis/logic behind all morality, Graeber claims. Debt is a promise, so it is sacred. He points

© hecke61/Shutterstock.com

out that, great religious texts and traditions have readily utilized the language of debts. For example, Graeber argues, the story of Nova shows the biblical roots of a nation in debt: Nova's covenant with God in the aftermath of the flood is to be understood as Nova was in God's debt!

It is indeed possible to make relations of power more palatable by dressing them up in the language of debt, states Graeber. However, he insists that the above trick tends to fail spectacularly in the event of excessive popular indebtedness causing unrest, insurrection, and revolt. Throughout human history, Graeber contends, the struggle between the rich and the poor has largely transpired into the conflict between the creditors and the debtors. He refers to the revolutionary movements that led to the Athenian and Roman rebellions, as well as to the more recent turmoil of the Arab Spring, claiming that popular insurrections in the last 5,000 years have begun in the same way with the ritual destruction of the debt records (Graeber 2011).

# Chapter Summary

This chapter also focuses on some of the main themes of economic anthropology. Specifically, it deals with social and cultural relations pertaining to the practices of exchange and distribution.

- Economic anthropology examines economic activities and cultural relations.

- The Formalist versus Substantivist debate was an economic anthropological discussion on the validity of employing Western, capitalist model of rational economic behavior to analyze economic activities in non-Western, precapitalist societies.

- Reciprocity is the exchange of goods and services among people of relatively equal socio-economic status. Three distinct types of reciprocity are generalized, balanced, and negative reciprocity. In generalized reciprocity, exchange partners do not track of what is given, its calculated value, or the period within which repayment must be made. In balanced reciprocity, goods and services of roughly similar value are exchanged within a set time limit. In negative reciprocity, each exchange party tries to gain more than it gives at the expense of others.

- Redistribution refers to the mode of exchange in which goods are collected from or contributed by members of a group and then redivided among those members in a different pattern.

- A classic ethnographic example for the ceremonial practices of redistribution is potlatch, the ceremonial feast held by the Kwakiutl in the Pacific Northwest.

- Market exchange is the mode of economic exchange in which goods and services are bought and sold at a money price decided by the market forces of supply and demand.

- Commodity is a sellable or exchangeable product or service in return of money, other products, or services.

- Marx's notion of commodity fetishism refers to the attribution of power and agency to commodities, treating people who do have agency as mere repositories of labor power for sale in the market.

- Money is a recognizable, divisible, interchangeable, movable, and durable means of market exchange.

- Gifts may be given sympathetically or softheartedly. They may be given however, unsympathetically, or even worse, antagonistically.

- According to the French anthropologist Marcel Mauss, a gift may appear as something given (to one party by another) or a service rendered (by one party to another) spontaneously, disinterestedly, and voluntarily. However, it is something given, or a duty performed, obligatorily.

- According to American anthropologist Annette Weiner, all exchange is based on the universal paradox of "how to keep while giving." The motivation for reciprocity, she maintains, stems from its opposite: "the desire to keep something back from the pressures of give and take."

- Seemingly irresistible force, commoditization makes goods and services indistinguishable from similar products and services.

- Singularization, the counter drive of commoditization, is a process that singularizes objects by turning them into transcendent treasures (that can be withdrawn from the market).

- According to anthropologist David Graeber, what informs everything humans do is not barter, not money, but debt, the oldest means of trade.

# Stratification: Exploring Culturally Institutionalized Inequality

© Gajus/Shutterstock.com

As persistent interdependence is central to their survival, human beings have become a species adapted to collective way of life. They live in social groups known as societies. A human **society** is an aggregate of individuals living together while sharing a distinct pattern of social relations. Anthropologists believe that different human societies may assume different forms in different places and times owing to the form of economic (See Chapters 8 and 9) and political (See Chapter 11) organization under which society is structured. In addition to these parallel features, they refer to another correlated characteristic that sets apart societies from one another, which is the extent to which people have equal access to wealth, power, and prestige. When some members or component groups of society have more and stable access to above categories of economic, political, and cultural resources than the others, it generates hierarchical relationships among different groups as if they were organized in layers or strata—in a word, **stratification**. A typical and potent structuring force in many societies around the globe, social stratification is tantamount to culturally institutionalized inequality.

## Egalitarian Society

Although some form of social stratification is found almost universally, most contemporary anthropologists differentiate human societies on the basis of the existing levels of social inequality. Following the early lead of anthropologist Morton Fried (Fried 1967), they identify three types of societies: egalitarian, rank, and stratified. In an **egalitarian society**, all members or component groups have near equal access to wealth, power, and prestige. Usually found among small groups of foragers and horticulturalists, egalitarian societies tend to have economic activities based on reciprocity and social relations in which political role specialization is either insignificant or absent altogether.

© franco lucato/Shutterstock.com

Still, there exist possible inequalities based on certain individual traits, such as intelligence, aptitude, industriousness, and personality, as well as attribute inequalities, such as age and gender. In spite of such forms of inequality, a variety of positions people occupy in egalitarian social settings is likely to remain within the bounds of individual and situational spaces (Berreman 1989, 8).

## Rank Society

In a **rank society,** every person has nearly equal access to wealth and power but some who are ranked above others in the social hierarchy have unequal access to prestige or social honor. In this social system organized on the basis of rank, some clans and lineages may be considered superior due to their genealogical proximity to the chief while other such kin groups are rank ordered in terms of their genealogical distance from the chiefly line. Individuals and kin groups hold distinct positions hierarchized in respect to all others.

In systems of rank, people obtain status positions partly by heredity. The ability to inherit title, office, and privilege makes the acquisition of a rank position an **ascribed status,** or a position assigned to an individual at birth. For instance, chiefs in many rank societies inherit their position according to the *rule of primogeniture,* the principle with which the eldest child is given priority and privilege over younger children to represent the family by holding position, title, and privilege.

© Aerial-motion/Shutterstock.com

In most rank societies in which only men can occupy status position, the eldest male child may obtain a position of rank. However, in some rank systems, the eldest female child might inherit and hold a status position.

In systems of rank, one might come into possession of a status position, in part, by one's own merits as well. The obtainability of a rank position partially through the qualities such as demeanor and charisma of the person makes it an **achieved status,** or a position that is earned through skill, ability, and effort.

Individuals who hold superior status positions in rank societies are likely to enjoy high degree of social honor or privilege over others. Their remuneration for holding high office is amply shown socially as they are treated with respect and as their influence in life affairs is readily acknowledged by people of lower rank. Nevertheless, high-rank positions are unlikely to help individuals to gain disproportionate access to wealth and power. For example, the chief in rank societies may be designated the owner of the land, but as he is only the titular owner, people of lower rank have the right to use the land. More to the point, the annual produce from the land may be housed in the chief's storehouse but these accumulations are mostly given away in the process of redistribution and the rest is used for feasts. The chief's privileged position is not dependent on his capacity to impose will over others as he possesses no real enforcement ability. Rather, chief's office attains its privileged status primarily through the chief's own persuasive ability, generosity, and his overall proficiency to lead by example (Sahlins 1958, 80–81).

© Keith Michael Taylor/Shutterstock.com

In most societies with social ranking, such as the native inhabitants in the northwest coastal regions of North America, and various native populations in Oceania (Polynesia, Melanesia, and Micronesia), people practice horticulture or herding for sustenance. Extremely dynamic and even potentially volatile of the sorts, social organization in these societies exhibit the conditions in which enduring patterns of social stratification have not yet been fully emerged regardless of the erosion of egalitarian social relations that have been well under way. Maybe that is why anthropologists generally agree on the premise that perhaps totally stratified social systems may have stemmed at some point from rank societies.

## Stratified Society

Whereas the most distinct feature in a rank society is the unequal access to prestige, what sets apart a **stratified society** from the rest is the unequal access to all forms of social dividends, namely wealth, power, and prestige. In stratified social systems, the individuals or component groups who constitute the top layer or strata of society are able to gain immoderately higher and perpetual access to economic, political, and cultural resources than the people of the lower layers who have to get by with fewer financial dividends, less power, and lower social status. The resultant inequality manifested in every sphere of social life ranging from wealth, access to power, and standard of living to lifestyle is formally acknowledged by most members of stratified society. Therefore, social stratification has become a typical and dominant structuring force in many societies around the world.

## Caste

Anthropologists usually characterize **caste** as a closed system of social stratification in which hierarchical social status is ascribed at birth and fixed for life. A term of European origin, caste is mostly used to describe social hierarchy in India, regarded as its original and longest survivor, as well as the social groupings in other South Asian societies. Anthropologists have been using the term to describe stratified societies resembling caste system elsewhere in the world as well.

### Social Grouping Based on Ritual Purity: *Jaati* ("kind")

Caste in traditional India comprises an intricate system of hereditary ranking with which social groupings are made on the premise of ritual purity. *Jaati* (literally meaning "kind"), a term derived from classical South Asian language Sanskrit, is used to refer to these groupings or castes which number in the thousands. Each specific group is ranked within the caste hierarchy and caste boundaries are maintained through endogamous marriages or the practice of marrying within (See Chapter 7 for details), occupational groupings, dining practices such as commensality or eating together, and styles of dress. Ranking differences among the castes are traditionally legitimized by the Hindu concept of *karma,* the belief that individual's position in this life is predestined by individual's action, good or bad, in previous births.

© Nila Newsom/Shutterstock.com

## Occupational Grouping Based on Ritual Purity: *Varna* ('colors')

All caste groups are classified into four ranked orders known as *varna* (literally meaning "colors"), differentiated largely with reference to the associative links between castes and traditional occupations. Each occupation and the caste identified with it, is ranked in accordance with descending ritual purity. Consequently, the *Braahman* or priests and scholars are considered the purest and therefore the highest ranked *varna.*

The *Kshatria,* the next highest are the warriors and kings. Third ranked are the *Vaisya* or commoners, including merchants, farmers, and herders. And, the fourth are the *Sudra* or menial workers and artisans. Below these four *varna* are the fifth group of people, considered as "God's children" (*Harijan*) by Indian nationalist leader Mohandas Gandhi, are the untouchables or *Dalit* (literally meaning "oppressed" or "crushed").

The members of this Pariah caste are supposed to collect garbage, remove animal carcasses, clean roads, dispose sewage, dung, and waste, and similar work, considered as ritually impure.

© Donald Yip/Shutterstock.com

## Caste and Its Economic Links: The *Jajmani* System

Some of the early anthropological researchers would argue that caste was primarily an agrarian economic system of nonmonetary, nonmarket exchange in rural India. Writing in 1936, William Wiser noted that this pattern of reciprocal economic exchanges, or in his words *jujmani system*, had been active in a north Indian village where he conducted fieldwork (Wiser 1936). According to him, under jujmani system, the members of the landholding castes and occupational service castes such as Washermen, Barbers, Carpenters, Potters, and Blacksmiths hereditarily involved in a symmetrical order of mutual economic transactions in which grain for the services were exchanged. Influenced partly by Marxian thought, a later generation of researchers critiqued Wiser's rendition that the exchanges between landholders (*jujman*) and occupational castes were mutual and symmetrical. On the contrary, they maintained, there was every reason to believe that such transactions had been coercive and asymmetrical, and intended to bring about most benefits for economically and politically powerful groups or dominant castes. Still, these researchers shared the view that the jujmani system was a nearly bounded, mutually dependent, and self-sustaining village network of exchanges that existed among hereditary occupational castes on a long-term basis (Gould 1958; Beidelman 1959; Harper 1959).

## Purity, Pollution, and Caste Hierarchy

Whereas the above researches concentrated on caste and its economic links, several anthropological studies sought to take a different path stressing association between caste and religion. These anthropologists focused on analyzing caste essentially as a religious mode of social organization. The most well-known and influential theorist to put forward this analytical model of caste was Louis Dumont (1911–1998). He contended that Indian society, in spite of its enormous cultural diversity—linguistic, regional, ethnic, caste-related, or any other—is fundamentally hierarchical and built on a single-most important principle, namely "the opposition of the pure and the impure" (Dumont 1970). This being the framework for hierarchy, castes are ranked along the scale of purity and pollution—the higher the caste status, the purer the individual or the group become by virtue of hereditary occupation, diet, and custom (See the above description of *varna* or four ranked orders). Dumont's analysis of caste, together with his notion of pan-Indian ideological whole, gained attention of some Indian scholars.

However, a score of others joined in criticizing Dumont for his exclusive reliance on Sanskritic sources, uncritical acceptance of the views of ancient Brahman literati, his ahistorical approach to Indian society and culture, and conspicuous relegation of Indian Muslims, Christians, and other minorities.

## Critical Perspectives on Caste Studies

Although the presence of caste within modern India is often interpreted conventionally as evidence for the persistence of the traditional within the modern, caste is a historically constructed variable, and changing reality. Indeed, a main critique leveled against some of the anthropological studies of caste is the apparent readiness on the part of anthropologists to treat caste-related ideas as perpetual sets of meaning. According to the contributors for the above critical perspective, the reliance on the elite factions' views in Hindu society, such as textual, Brahmanical analyses of caste have led many anthropologists to adopt a strangely ahistorical approach, almost as if nothing worthwhile had happened to Indian society between the Vedic times and the British arrival, or even thereafter. As Bernard S. Cohn (Cohn 1996) indicates, in their effort to control native population in colonial India, the British colonizers had given caste a tangible form by treating it as an unalterable set of ranked social groups. Consequentially, such ranked groups became actual categories in social and political domains within which Indians had to function. Whereas Louis Dumont's analysis concluded caste as a "traditional" religious system, the historical anthropology of caste has bespoken how understandings of the caste system by both anthropologists and the state are connected to the administrative and knowledge practices of the colonial state (Dirks 2001; Appadurai 1986).

The critiques of the sort also came from those scholars receptive to **subaltern studies,** a field that concentrates on nonelite perspectives and histories. According to them, by adopting aforementioned models of caste as their primary sources, anthropologists have refused to acknowledge the existence of possible alternative perspectives stemming from the nonelite (Dube 1998; Kapadia 1995; Trawick 1988).

Caste distinctions are not as sharp-cut as they seem. The specific ranking of a caste can gradually change as time passes, and may be at variance in different geographical regions. Moreover, only a limited number of castes correspond to occupational groupings, and even in such cases people may and do engage in occupations other than the ones traditionally designated for their caste. Notwithstanding the fact that endogamy and commensality are still very much observed by the members of specific castes, especially those in the higher echelons of society, people in urban India today are increasingly flexible in making marriage choices and in dealing with dining taboos (Mines and Lamb 2010). Studies have made it abundantly clear that the borderlands of distinct castes have expanded lately, allowing some degree of intercaste interactions to occur (Fuller and Narasimhan 2008). For example, as an untouchable Pariah caste woman's first-person account of caste relations in her village in South India shows, caste hierarchy is still structured through the rules and practices pertaining to marriage, occupation, and food exchange. However, the aforementioned Dalit woman's narrative also reveals the growing politicization of caste in her community. Even more, it discloses the emerging possibilities of upward class mobility even for an individual or a group in the lowest rung of caste hierarchy. Accordingly, the likelihood of gaining "high" status in terms of affluence and power while being "low" in terms of caste purity concurrently has increased in rural Indian villages in recent years (Viramma, Racine, and Racine 2010, 171–79).

Anthropologists have increasingly recognized the need to move beyond the tradition-modernity dichotomy that characterizes the ways with which caste has been conventionally apprehended. Accordingly, Vivek Dhareshwar suggests that caste has to be understood as a relational identity marker situated within concrete institutional and ideological formations (Dhareshwar 1993). Taking a similar tack and examining everyday cultural politics of caste identities in the South Indian state of Kerala, Ritty Lukose maintains that caste is a complicated and messy product of the secular and the modern. In justifying her position, Lukose presents some compelling ethnographic evidence from a college setting where participation of caste and religion in the making of "modern" citizen is starkly evident, yet the salient presence of caste and religion within the public space of the college (therefore, in contemporary, "secular" life) is ambiguously left unacknowledged (Lukose 2010, 206–18).

## Caste and Contemporary Politics in India

Over the last several decades, the association of caste and contemporary political life became noticeable to an increasing extent in many South Asian societies in general, and in Indian society in particular. As caste identity has come to be defined as political identity, parallel changes have taken place in terms of redefining caste membership and redrawing caste boundaries, and thereby making caste alliances possible (Bayly 1999; Metcalf and Metcalf 2006). On this point, the transformation of the *Dalit* from the people relegated in the Indian caste hierarchy as untouchables or outcastes to a salient social and political movement has been a considerable development. The Dalit, renamed as *harijan* or "people of God" by Hindu nationalist leader Mahatma Gandhi, have struggled against caste-based inequalities in Indian society or what has been called India's "hidden apartheid" for more than a century (Moon 2001; Omvedt 1994). In the 1950s, the Indian social reformer B. R. Ambedkar (1891–1956) facilitated mass conversion of Dalits to Buddhism as Buddha's message of eternal bliss (*nirvana*) for everybody was appealing to their cause. Dalit people, some 200 million in number, dispersed across India's vast territories, have now grown into a social and political movement which must be reckoned with.

© StockImageFactory.com/Shutterstock.com

# Social Class

For the nineteenth-century political economist Karl Marx, the analysis of social class, class structures, and modifications in those structures are central to apprehending capitalist system (which is based on capitalist mode of production) and the other social systems that preceded it. For Marx, the **classes** are defined and structured by the ownership or nonownership of the means of production, the social relationships involved in work and labor, and the control of the surplus human social labor can produce. Whereas the objective situation of a class does exist due to its place in the production process, in Marx's view, what is salient in defining class is its relationship to other classes.

As society is structured around contradictions, the relationship of a class to other classes is essentially contradictory. Accordingly, class is always defined by its potential for conflict. For example, in capitalist society, profit-making through capital investment becomes possible due to the exploitation of the labor of the workers—the recruitment of wage laborers and turning their labor into surplus value.

## Alienation

In capitalist society, it is the capitalists who employ the workers—they own the workers' labor time. Additionally, the capitalists own the means of production, such as the production tools and raw materials. What is more, they own the products, the ultimate result of the workers' labor. As the workers' labor (manual or intellectual labor) is not their own, the workers are forced to work for the capitalists for wages (the workers are coerced to sell their labor time to capitalists). Therefore, in capitalist society, the workers are effectively reduced to things or tools, and they are not treated as individuals. It is this condition, the condition under which the estrangement of individuals from their own labor and their species-being (or true human nature) takes place, what Marx considered as **alienation** (*Entfremdung*) (Marx 1964 [1932]).

According to Marx, alienation or estrangement has four basic components. First, in capitalist mode of production, the workers are alienated from their production activity. The unmediated relation between the workers' productive labor and what is paid to them as the compensation (by reducing that labor power to wages) alienate the workers physically and psychologically. Wage compulsion, as well as the production content, form, and direction imposed on them by the capitalists, make the workers unhappy and less energetic. In capitalist mode of production, maintained Marx, labor does not belong to the worker's essential being.

Second, the workers are alienated from their product. In capitalist system of production, workers' manual and intellectual labor is reified in concrete terms as "work" or job. It is for "getting the work/job done" wages are paid. The product, the ultimate result of workers' labor does not belong to them. It is the capitalists' private property, and it is treated as a commodity. The conversion of labor into an activity, as well as the exclusion of the workers from the design and production protocol alienate workers from their product.

Third, in capitalist mode of production, the workers are alienated from their fellow workers. As capitalism reduces the labor of the workers to a commodity, it is traded in the competitive labor market. It is not treated as a constructive and cooperative force usable for individual and collective well-being of society. Therefore, in capitalist economic system, cooperation and collective efforts are discouraged and disrupted while individual competition and rivalry is promoted. Workers—strangers and familiar folks alike—are forced to work alongside for the capitalists. Moreover, even if the workers on the factory assembly line or office cubicles share camaraderie, the nature of technology generates a considerable isolation and the desire to work only for personal survival.

Finally, the workers in capitalist mode of production are alienated from their innate human potential that Marx termed as species-being (*Gattungswesen*). The workers are simply reduced to a mass of alienated people who are incapable of expressing their essential human qualities.

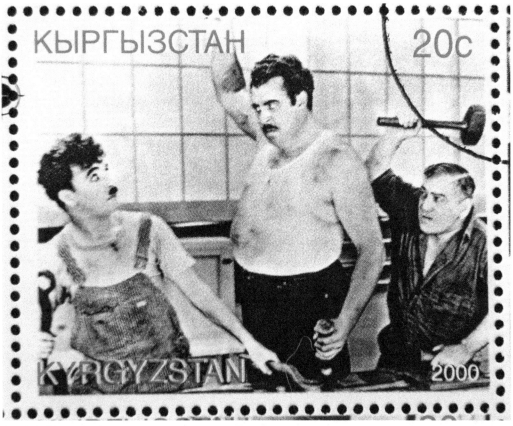
© neftali/Shutterstock.com

The surplus value of labor, Marx suggested, is the portion of workers' labor that is retained as profit by those who control the means of production. Marx believed that it is this underlying contradiction that leads to class conflict, which will bring forth the capitalist system to its eventual end.

## Class-in-Itself versus Class-for-Itself

For Marx, the genuine existence of a class begins when a class is in active pursuit of its interests as an organized stratum of society. Marx characterized it as a *class–for-itself*. When people become members of a class-for-itself, they may refuse to accept the definition of reality imposed upon them by the dominant class, and begin to construct a counter worldview intended for the well-being of their own class. Marx identified the above potential of a subordinate class as *class consciousness*. A class may merely exist as a category of people having a common relation to means of production as well. Marx distinguished it as a *class-in-itself*. As members of such a class are unaware of their common class position, interests, and their conflicting relation to other classes, they usually accept the dominant ideology that portrays the privileged position of the dominant class as legitimate. Marx characterized this condition as *false consciousness*.

## Two Primary Classes in Capitalism: *Bourgeoisie* and *Proletariat*

According to Marx's analysis, there exist two primary classes in capitalism: bourgeoisie and proletariat. The *bourgeoisie* or the capitalists own capital and the means of production, purchase and exploit labor power, and use the surplus value created from employment of labor power to accumulate and expand their capital. By contrast, the *proletariat* or the workers own nothing but the ability to work, with their bodies and minds. In order to sustain themselves, these property-less workers must sell their physical and mental labor to a capitalist-employer.

The social relationship between the capitalists and the workers is inherently exploitative, contradictory, and antagonistic: It is exploitative as capitalist-employers who hire wage laborers make profit and accumulate wealth by keeping wages low and by making workers work more intensively; it is contradictory as the wage laborers have a set of interests totally incompatible to that of the capitalists; it is antagonistic as the capitalists and the wage laborers act in the interests of their own class, and therefore, in antagonistic terms toward each other's class.

Despite their exploitative, contradictory, and antagonistic relationship, these two classes are also partners! They are partners in the sense that capital investment and the supply of labor are prerequisites for production. Likewise, they are partners to an exploitative relationship in which one is the exploiter and the other is the one being exploited. The bourgeoisie could not exist without the proletariat, and vice-versa. As Marx explained however, this unity in partnership is essentially a unity of the opposites, since the interests of the two classes in relationship are diametrically opposed to each other.

© Gambarini Gianandrea/Shutterstock.com

## Other Classes: Landowners, *Petty Bourgeoisie*, Peasantry, and *Lumpen Proletariat*

In addition to the above classes, Marx referred to several other classes: class of landowners, petty bourgeoisie and middle class, peasantry, and lumpen proletariat.

While situating within the context of Europe's (especially, Great Britain's) Industrial Revolution and the growth of capitalism, Marx discussed about the class of landowners or landlords which was once considered powerful and dominant. During the advent of capitalism, some segments of the landowner class managed to transform their wealth in land into landed capital—they used their land as a means for capital expansion. However, having lost their key role in production and the organization of society, most members of this class were now experiencing their economic and social marginalization. Quite appropriately, they were considered by Marx to be a marginal class.

Petty bourgeoisie or the lower middle class constitutes the small-scale property owners who still work their own means of production. This class does own some property, but does not have enough resources to get all work completed by recruiting workers. Therefore, in order to sustain, the members of the petty bourgeoisie must themselves do some of their production-related work. In this sense, they are owner-cum-workers. Its dual existence, together with the resultant dual role it performs, makes the petty bourgeoisie a class of divided interests as well. As it shares the interests of the capitalist class, it may want to preserve private property and property rights. At the same time, it may also be having interests often opposed to those of the capitalist class. In the same vein, the petty bourgeoisie may be politically conservative, and indeed, reactionary. Concurrently, this class may have radical and reformist elements in its fold, so small-scale property owners and employers may be inclined to criticize large entrepreneurs and monopolies for trying to eliminate small businesses. Marx believed that the petty bourgeoisie class would disappear as capitalism developed, with some members' ascension to the capitalist class, and most others' descension into the rank of the proletarian.

For Marx, peasantry is an insignificant class as it is not having the necessary strength or organizational ability to carry out change. He believed that this class of displaced farmers would eventually cease to exist; as the likelihood of most of them becoming members of the proletariat class was greater. He also thought that the more successful members of the peasantry would transform themselves to landed capitalists.

The lumpen proletariat class is made up of people such as ruined and adventurous offshoots of the bourgeoisie, vagabonds, discharged soldiers, beggars, pickpockets, gamblers, tricksters, and brothel-keepers—they are the ragged proletarians. Marx largely downplayed this class's revolutionary potential while characterizing it as the refuse of all classes or a class of the social scum (Marx [1852] 1970). As they have dissociated from their actual class origin and come to form a free-floating mass instead, the members of this class often find conservative ideologies and reactionary movements particularly attractive, especially when capitalist society is going through crisis situations (Bottomore 2001). Marx referred to the class of lumpen-proletariat within the context of describing how capitalism uses, misuses, and casts aside people of all variety without letting them accomplish their true human potential. The homeless people, the slum-dwellers, and the other segments of urban underclass are often considered to be the present representatives of the lumpen-proletariat.

# Race

Anthropologists consider **race** as a culturally constructed concept rather than a conclusive statement on human biological reality. It is through race humans are categorized into different groups with the assumption that the boundaries of each population category correspond to a specific set of biological attributes. In other words, the concept of race alleges that a group of people's evident traits such as anatomical and physiological features or *phenotypical* characteristics dovetail with the group members' actual genetic makeup or *genotypical* traits. In the context of race, the above peculiarities are then allegedly affiliated with individuals' cultural traits, personality, character, intelligence, and morality that are innate, immutable, and ascribed.

© Jason Stitt/Shutterstock.com

Many of the current ideas of race originated during the era of European colonization of the world. When Europeans travelled overseas to gain access to natural resources and monopolize global trade, they came across native inhabitants in Africa, Asia, and the Americas who markedly mismatched their own kind's physical appearance, ways of communication, and behavioral traits. These differences were gradually sorted into systems by naturalists and scientists, and they became the basis for today's notion of race. The consequential rise of "race science" legitimized European colonialism by reinforcing the widely held belief that people of nonwhite origin were biologically inferior.

The efforts of systematizing human differences were benefited from the research of the late nineteenth-century anthropologists as well. Indeed, the notion of race and its deepseated association with the very origin of anthropology as a discipline was conspicuously evident. For instance, Johann Blumenbach (1752–1840), one of the pioneers of physical anthropology, came up with a typology of race with which he divided the human species into five racial groups, namely, the Caucasian or White race, the Mongolian or Yellow race, the Malayan or Brown race, the Ethiopian or Black race, and the American or Red race. By analyzing sixty human crania (skulls), Blumenbach concluded that the original human ancestors were of Caucasian race and the other races have come about due to degeneration caused by environmental factors such as geography and dietary practices, as well as cultural factors such as customs and mannerism.

The early twentieth-century anthropologists such as Franz Boas stayed the course in exposing the shortcomings of such attempts. Contending against the projects aimed at establishing a causal relationship between racial hierarchies and cultural traits, they pointed out that culture, a defining feature of being human, is not something human species inherit genetically, but a set of beliefs and practices that they learn and share as a species accustomed to social life.

## Colorism

**Colorism,** sometimes also referred to as *pigmentocracy,* is a term adopted by anthropologists and other social scientists to identify the hierarchies of social status and wealth constructed primarily on skin color. It is a loosely structured and flexible system of hierarchies in which situational negotiation of social identities is possible along a continuum of skin colors between white and black (Lehman 2001). Derived from the larger system of racism, and promoted through global media images and the industries such as skin bleaching and cosmetic surgery, this system of skin color stratification does offer more opportunities for individuals with fair skin complexion over dark-skinned people in areas such as wealth, education, occupation, and the marriage market. As colorism allows the gray areas to exist in between the boundaries, individuals find possibilities to negotiate their color identity position afresh whenever they enter into a new social situation.

Anthropologist Roger N. Lancaster's analysis of skin colorism in Nicaragua offers a fine example to the point. According to Lancaster, three types of color identity classification exist in Nicaragua: phenotypic, polite, and pejorative/affectionate (Lancaster 1991, 339–53). The phenotypic color identity hierarchy is the first of such classificatory systems. It has the following subcategories: *blanco* (white), *moreno* (brown), and *negro* (black). They reflect people's long-standing perceptions on the skin tone variations among mestizos or the Spanish-speaking people who mostly live in the West sector of Nicaragua. As linguistic, cultural, and ethnic mestizoization or blending had been occurring long before the beginning of the twentieth century, mestizo culture has emerged as the Nicaraguan national culture. In terms of the physical features however, most Nicaraguans can be considered as typical morenos. Given this reality, the phenotypic color hierarchy allows to identify people with reference to their physical traits regardless of their cultural associations. For instance, in the phenotypic system, negros may be classified either as people of African descent or indigenous origin.

© Anton_Ivanov/Shutterstock.com

The color racial categories based on physical characteristics may be inflated under the second system, which Lancaster characterizes as the polite identity hierarchy. The usage of gracious terms often occurs when the individual to whom speaker is referring is present. Accordingly, a person of Caucasian descent is courteously referred to as *chele*, stressing the blue eyes, a physical feature stereotypically attributed to that racial category. Likewise, moreno people may be identified as blanco even though most morenos in Nicaragua are brown-skinned people. Similarly, a black-skinned individual is never addressed as a negro in that person's presence as it is considered offensive. Indigenous people are not referred to as *indios* either; rather, they are called as *mestizos*.

The third color identity hierarchy, according to Lancaster, permits to use the terms *chele* (fairer skin complexion and lighter hair) and *negro* (darker skin and black hair) both to insult and to show friendliness, depending on the situation. Hence, he characterizes this system as pejorative/affectionate system (Lancaster 1991, 339–53).

© Anton_Ivanov/Shutterstock.com

## Racism

**Racism** is the methodical discrimination of one or more culturally constructed races by another culturally defined race affirming the biocultural pre-eminence of the latter over the former. Racism may take a number of forms. When discrimination or favoritism occurs within individuals on the basis of race, it is regarded as *interpersonal racism*.

© pathdoc/Shutterstock.com

Prejudiced behavior toward specific races can occur in institutions such as public administrative bodies, private business corporations, educational institutions, and the mass media. Such are the instances of *institutional racism*.

© Magda;ema Rydz/Shutterstock.com

Anthropologists consider *structural racism* as the most potent and ubiquitous form of racism for all other forms such as interpersonal and institutional racism stem from it. It is a system of hierarchy and inequality, primarily marked by preferential treatment, privilege, and power for one culturally constructed and supposedly superior race at the expense of the other allegedly inferior racial groups. Its main indicators may range from inequalities in power, opportunity, admittance, treatment, to policy adoption, and policy outcome. As structural racism involves the strengthening effects of diverse institutions and cultural conventions, previous and current, repeatedly producing new, and reproducing old forms of racism, locating its presence is always a more strenuous task.

Focusing on homeless heroin injectors in the city of San Francisco, anthropologists Philippe Bourgois and Jeff Schonberg discuss how divisions based on skin color are kept in force through everyday interactions to produce a form of racism. Bourgois and Schonberg dub it provocatively as "intimate apartheid" to highlight the fact that this form of racism is in existence among the whites, blacks, and Latinos regardless of the addiction and destitution that they share together with their physical proximity (Bourgois and Schonberg 2007).

© a katz/Shutterstock.com

© Martina Badini/Shutterstock.com

# Ethnicity

**Ethnicity** refers to a sense of identity and membership in a group that shares common cultural, linguistic, and ancestral links, and that imagines itself to be distinguishable from other groups. Therefore, ethnicity is a powerful force that unifies the group membership while dividing and excluding those who are not considered as group members.

The conventional notions of seeing ethnicity as a primordial bond or a link existing since time immemorial is misleading, says Norwegian anthropologist Fredrik Barth. According to Barth, ethnic identities are sustained by the maintenance of the "boundaries" or the lines drawn to separate or distinguish one group from another. He stresses the cogency of focusing on the interface or the point where two groups meet, interact, and negotiate boundary marking. By zooming in on the boundaries Barth believes, one can learn on the interconnectedness of ethnic identities, the interdependency of ethnic groups, as well as the processes through which ethnic distinctions are constructed and maintained. Put another way, ethnic boundaries involve social processes of inclusion and exclusion, the processes appropriate to recognize group membership and to draw off distinctions. The cultural elements used to distinguish one ethnic group from another vary. Moreover, they usually constitute only a small part of a specific group's cultural repertoire (Barth 1969; Jenkins 2008).

A cultural belief and related practice (such as shared ancestry, food habits, language use, racial identity, or religious affiliation) may be singled out to highlight group members' similarity, and their distinctiveness from others outside the group. The pervasion of the above acts is powerful to the extent that the group members begin to imagine

© dron ba/Shutterstock.com

themselves to be different from others. The sense of belonging to the group is indeed at the heart of ethnocentrism or the tendency to judge the aspects of other cultures from the vantage point of one's own culture. Ethnicity may be fluid and flexible, but the construction and maintenance of ethnic boundaries can even lead to **ethnic cleansing,** the mass expulsion or killing of one ethnic group by the members of another in a specific geographic location.

# Sexuality and Gender

Anthropologists investigate the links between sex, sexuality, and gender, and how they are culturally constructed.

## Sex and Sexuality

The term **sex** refers to the biological and physiological characteristics with which males are distinguished from females. These characteristics include primary differences in genitalia, reproductive organs, and sexual chromosomes, as well as secondary differences in breasts, distribution of body hair, body shape, the size of the bones, average weight and height, and voice. **Sexuality** refers to people's preference or orientation, and experience in the context of sexual activity. Influenced mainly by French philosopher and social critic Michel Foucault's work on sexuality (Foucault 1979), most contemporary anthropologists incline to see sexuality in plural terms. They focus on a wide variety of approaches and discourses concerning human sexual activity while also acknowledging how sexual desires and pleasures have always been fashioned by cultural, social, and political structures of the larger societies in which humans inhabit.

## Gender

**Gender** refers to the culturally constructed roles assigned to males and females which may vary substantially from society to society. The anthropological understanding and research of the cultural construction of gender were significantly invigorated by the upswing of feminist anthropology in the second half of the twentieth century. Feminist anthropologists have been highly critical of what they believed to be the androcentric or the male-oriented point of view prevailed within the discipline. According to them, what ethnographic field data concerning women existed in the body of anthropological writing was in fact accounts of male informants passed on mostly by elite males using androcentric language. In the past, even women ethnographers had been playing down female perspectives and analyzing the societies they studied from a male perspective instead, feminist anthropologists have pointed out. Ethnographic engagement on women-related themes had been customarily reduced to the contexts such as kinship, family, and marriage since anthropologists relied on the notion that women were "living in the shadows of men—occupying the private rather than the public sector of society" (Weiner 1988, 4–7).

Margaret Mead's study of gender in three New Guinea cultures, *Sex and Temperament in Three Primitive Societies* (1935) was a widely known exception in the study of gender roles.

Referring to the ways with which the three cultures she studied shuffled things around, Mead maintained that although gender-based division of labor and other differences between genders were the cross-cultural rule, there wasn't worthwhile ethnographic evidence to suggest the existence of interdependence between biological sex and culturally expected behavior of men and women.

In spite of Mead's early exposure of the complexity, anthropological interest on gender did not become widespread until, by the early 1970s, feminist anthropologists made a convincing case to carefully scrutinize taken-for-granted views about the roles of women and men in human society. The exploration of questions on the roles of women in diverse societies became a primary focus within this context. As Michelle Rosaldo and Louise Lamphere explained in the volume on the study of gender they have coedited, a thorough understanding of human society "will have to incorporate the goals, thoughts, and activities of the second sex" (Rosaldo and Lamphere 1974, 2).

Feminist anthropologists such as Michelle Rosaldo (1974) and Sherry Ortner (1974) attempted to analyze the asymmetry in gender roles through universal binary oppositions such as public versus domestic, production versus reproduction, and nature versus culture. Some feminist anthropologists also preferred the Marxist theoretical framework stemming from the early writings of Karl Marx and Friedrich Engels concerning the status of women in capitalist economic systems and the historical origins of female subordination. In his influential work *The Origin of the Family, Private Property, and the State* (Engels 1970), Engels attributed the oppression of women to shifts in the mode of production which occurred during the Neolithic Revolution. According to Engels, men's desire to transfer their land and domesticated animals to male offspring via patrilineal inheritance was achieved by dismantling matrilineal inheritance and related defense mechanisms.

© Kudryashova Vera/Shutterstock.com

This overthrow, maintained Engels, led to the "world historical defeat of female sex" (Engels 1970, 120–21). Feminist anthropologists with Marxist theoretical leanings believed that the subordination of women in capitalist societies, both in terms of their reproductive role, as well as their value as unpaid or underpaid labor, stemmed from historical trends predating capitalism itself.

It is within this context American anthropologist Annette B. Weiner commenced her fieldwork among the Trobriand islanders in 1971. Reportedly, she went to this Melanesian island to study woodcarvings made for the tourist trade, but decided to explore the salient economic role played by Trobriand women in its stead. As it became gradually evident to Weiner, this was a theme neglected by her esteemed predecessor Bronislaw Malinowski who conducted ethnographic fieldwork among the islanders some sixty years prior to her own research. According to Weiner, a systematic investigation into Trobriand women's productive activities helped her to understand the centrality of women's own wealth in every sphere of the Trobriand economy. Moreover, the above understanding has aided Weiner to revise a number of Malinowski's assumptions about Trobriand men, because women and their wealth were at the core of men's role within the Trobriand matrilineal family, as well as within the extensive cycles of exchanges which defined the strength of their relationships (Weiner 1988, 4–7).

The growth of feminist anthropology in the 1970s forced anthropologists to re-examine the prevailing perceptions on women's role in foraging societies as well. During the first wave of post-World War II studies of the foragers in the Kalahari, Africa, anthropological attention had been concentrated on the model of "man the hunter," as evidenced from the influential work bearing the same title, coedited by Richard Lee and Irvin DeVore in 1968, as well as from the equally influential ethnographic film which upheld the same theme *The Hunters,* directed by John Marshall in 1957. However, as Richard Lee's later research (Lee 1979), Marjorie Shostak's study (Shostak 1981), and the likes (Dahlberg 1981) demonstrated, discussion on hunter-gatherers' subsistence strategies expanded to accommodate the model of "woman the gatherer" acknowledging that foraging women in the Kalahari had been gathering more food than the men ever had with the precarious work of big game hunting.

Shostak's work *N!ai: The Life and Words of a !Kung Woman* (1981), was a collaborative endeavor, which had come to pass during her fieldwork in Botswana from 1968 to 1971. It offered a Ju/'hoan woman's perspective on themes such as love,

© Silent O/Shutterstock.com

© franco lucato/Shutterstock.com

marriage, and family, previously known to anthropological readers only through the views of Ju/'hoan men. In this notable ethnography, the Ju/'hoan woman named Nisa reveals Shostak that boys and girls interacted with each other as equals, and there were ample opportunities to experiment with sex; marriages were usually arranged for girls by age ten or twelve, for boys some ten years later. Although intense, marital relationships rarely turned into lifelong commitments among the Ju/'hoansi. And, Ju/'hoan women, who considered themselves attractive, were not hesitant to have complicit relationships with lovers, if opportunity arose to do so:

> "When you are a woman, you just don't sit still and do nothing—you have lovers. You don't just sit with the man of your hut, with just one man. One man can give you very little. One man can give you only one kind of food to eat. But when you have lovers, one brings you something and another brings you something else. One comes at night with meat, another with money, and another with beads. Your husband also does things and gives them to you" (Shostak 1981).

Nisa's autobiographical narrative and Shostak's anthropological complements which accompanied it, brought to light how women viewed at a culture that had been mainly known to anthropological audiences for men's unrelenting resolve to find game hunting in the unforgiving landscape of the Kalahari and the aptitude they display in doing so.

As noted earlier, Annette Weiner acknowledged the considerable extent to which her concentration on women's economic role assisted her when she attempted to make better sense of men's role in Trobriand society (Weiner 1980). Ethnographic studies of the sorts conducted on diverse cultural settings have made it abundantly clear that women's gender roles could not be explored meaningfully apart from the gender roles of men and vice versa. Some of the recent ethnographic accounts on South Asian female migrants to the Middle East offer fine illustrative evidence in this regard.

For instance, anthropologist Michele Ruth Gamburd explains how female and male gender roles and power relations change in Sri Lankan villages as women move out into the international labor market (Gamburd 2000). According to Gamburd, men whose wives have gone to the Middle East as domestic workers are often represented in village stories stereotypically as emasculated and lazy spendthrifts while women are depicted as promiscuous and selfish pleasure-seekers. Gamburd describes the strategies with which village men associated with female migrants have sought to grapple with the aforementioned local representations while reasserting the male power and respect lost in the face of the new role embarked on by women as the breadwinners for the family. Village men, the former breadwinners, only rarely and reluctantly subscribe to anything close to a reversal of their gender role: becoming the home-maker in the home a migrant woman leaves behind. In its stead, most of the times, men prefer to delegate the bulk of the house chores to female relatives while taking care of the bare minimum of the duties and responsibilities by themselves.

© Paul Cowan/Shutterstock.com

Gaining membership in drinking groups and spending lavishly remittances from migrant women have become some of the salient means with which men attempt to restore their masculine image. Each of the three village men in Michele Gamburd's illustrative cases asserted his masculinity in a distinct way: one with idleness and alcohol, another through work and wealth accumulation, and the last through "a playful self-parody of his feminizing house-keeping role" (Gamburd 2010, 122). Gamburd's ethnography also shows how female migration and their prolonged absence from the everyday affairs of family have changed not only men's social position but also their own. Migrant women periodically return to their home villages and families with accumulated wealth and find that they no longer fit into village society the same way they had before they left. Ambivalent about assuming the traditional housewife's role in their Sri Lankan homes, many migrant women choose to stick to their new economic role and go back to the Middle East (Gamburd 2000).

As cross-cultural variations of gender diversity and gender alternatives became more and more evident through ethnographic examples, and as previously stigmatized sexual preferences in Western societies such as lesbian, gay, bisexual, and transgender (LGBT) categories gradually earned some form of public acceptance, many anthropologists set about to stress the necessity to discuss sexuality and gender roles in more accommodative terms. The supposition that heterosexuality is the only natural form in which sex and gender roles were assorted was put into question within this context.

Anthropologists such as Marilyn Strathern tried to push the boundaries of thought on gender even further toward complex gendered social relations. Analyzing field data collected among Hagen people in Papua New Guinea, Strathern pointed out that various societies regularly relied on gender imagery as a resource when classifying people, events, and things of different sorts. Therefore, she stressed the need to adopt an expansive approach than the ones being used when making sense of gender (Strathern 1980).

Speaking of complex gender relations, some of the recent studies carried out by anthropologists like Ann Laura Stoler stand out for showing the historical links between the matters of the intimate and the politics of the European colonialists (Stoler 2002). Analyzing colonial Indonesian society in the late nineteenth and early twentieth centuries, Stoler observed how European supremacy was asserted in terms of gender-specific sanctions established and enforced along the line of racial virility. Accordingly, "white" colonizer's masculinity was always treated as superior and powerful than the feminized inferiority of "non-white:" the colonized males—indigenous men were regarded as not manly enough to defend their land and protect their women. To this end, any sexual contact between local men and European women was highly discouraged and severely punished, whereas European men sexually conquered local women of their own choosing freely (Stoler 2002).

## Chapter Summary

This chapter concentrates on social stratification based on class, caste, race, ethnicity, gender, and the like in the contemporary world. It examines how hierarchical relationships commensurate with culturally institutionalized inequality.

- Stratification or the hierarchical relationships among different groups in society is commensurate with culturally institutionalized inequality. Based on the existing levels of social inequality, anthropologists identify three distinct types of societies, namely egalitarian, rank, and stratified. In an egalitarian society, all members or component groups have near equal access to wealth, power, and prestige. The most distinct feature in a rank society is the unequal access to prestige. The unequal access to all forms of social dividends, namely wealth, power, and prestige, is what sets apart a stratified society from the rest.

- Caste is a closed system of social stratification in which hierarchical social status is ascribed and fixed for life. It is mostly used to describe social hierarchy in India and the social grouping in other South Asian societies. In traditional India, caste is a complex system of hereditary ranking based on the premise of ritual purity and maintained through endogamous marriages, occupational groupings, dining practices, and the style of dress.

- The early twentieth-century anthropological researchers held the view that caste was primarily an agrarian economic system of nonmonetary, nonmarket, reciprocal exchange in rural India. Several later researchers, including the influential theorist Louis Dumont (1970), stressed the association between caste and religion (Hinduism). In recent years, some of the dominant anthropological models of caste were critiqued for their ahistorical approach, exclusive reliance on elitist textual materials, nonrecognition of the possible alternative perspectives, and the apparent readiness to treat caste-related ideas as perpetual sets of meaning.

- According to Karl Marx, the classes are defined and structured by the ownership or non-ownership of the means of production, the social relationships involved in work and labor, and the control of the surplus human social labor can produce. As society is structured around contradictions, the relationship of a class to other classes is essentially contradictory.

- In capitalist society, the exploitation of the workers' labor by the capitalists generates the condition Marx termed as alienation. It is the condition under which the estrangement of individuals from their own labor and their species-being (or true human nature) takes place.

- Marx characterized a class that actively pursues its interests (as an organized stratum of society) as a *class-for-itself* while differentiating it from a *class-in-itself* or a category of people having a common relation to means of production.

- According to Marx, the two primary classes in capitalism are the *bourgeoisie* or the capitalist class and the *proletariat* or the working class. For Marx, the social relationship between these coexisting two classes is inherently exploitative, contradictory, and antagonistic. In addition to the above classes, Marx referred to several other classes: class of landowners, *petty bourgeoisie* and the middle class, peasantry, and *lumpen-proletariat*.

- Anthropologists see race as a culturally constructed concept rather than a conclusive statement on human biological reality. It is through race humans are sorted into distinct groups with the assumption that boundaries of each population category correspond to a set of biological attributes, as well as to individual cultural traits, personality, character, intelligence, and morality.

- Colorism or pigmentocracy is a loosely structured and flexible system of hierarchies in which situational negotiation of social identities is possible along a continuum of skin colors between white and black. Anthropologist Robert N. Lancaster's analysis of skin colorism in Nicaragua offers a fine example to the point. According to him, three types of color identity classification exist in Nicaragua: phenotypic, polite, and pejorative/affectionate.

- Racism is the methodical discrimination of one or more culturally constructed races by another culturally defined race affirming the biocultural pre-eminence of the latter over the former. Racism may take interpersonal, organizational, and structural forms. Anthropologists consider *structural racism* as the most potent and ubiquitous form of racism for all other forms such as interpersonal and institutional racism stem from it.

- Ethnicity refers to a sense of identity and membership in a group that shares common cultural, linguistic, and ancestral links, and that imagines itself to be distinguishable from other groups.

- The term sex refers to the biological and physiological characteristics with which males are distinguished from females. Sexuality refers to people's preference or orientation, and experience in the context of sexual activity. Gender refers to the culturally constructed roles assigned to males and females which may vary substantially from society to society.

- The anthropological understanding and research on gender were considerably invigorated by the upswing of feminist anthropology in the second half of the twentieth century. Feminist critique was leveled against anthropology's supposed male-oriented point of view, androcentric language, and the customary reduction of the roles of women to the themes such as kinship, marriage, and family in ethnographic engagements. Theoretically, feminist anthropologists drew inspiration mainly from structuralism and Marxian Thought.

## CHAPTER 11

# Political Anthropology: Probing the Exercise of Social Power

© Ron Ellis/Shutterstock.com

The specialization known as **political anthropology** focuses on politics and power, stressing context, process, and scale. Some political anthropologists adopt an approach based on structural framework, as they tend to see power and the role of political behavior and institutions in social reproduction as systemic. Others favor a more processual approach, highlighting conflict, contradiction, and change, instead. All political anthropologists are known for their stark emphasis on themes such as political transformation, dynamics of political institutions, and social inequality, as well as for their general sidelining of "culture" as a main analytic category.

# Types of Political Systems

The efforts of developing a framework for political classification were very much evident in the mid-twentieth-century political anthropology. With a political typology capable of providing a common parlance for sociopolitical difference, anthropologists hoped to communicate across cultural areas and to measure the similarities and dissimilarities between their ethnographic findings (Lewellen 2003). After the Second World War, for example, a number of anthropologists showed keen interest in investigating and classifying preindustrial political systems in Africa (Fortes and Evans-Pritchard [1940] 1968; Gluckman 1954; Turner 1957), South and Central Asia (Barth 1959; Leach 1961), Southeast Asia (Leach 1954), Central America (Redfield 1941), and North America (Wallace 1957).

The culmination of such attempts was the four-part typology of political systems proposed by political anthropologist Elman Service: band, tribe, chiefdom, and state (Service 1962). This typology, although intermittently used today, gained terminological acceptance and influenced the thinking of many political anthropologists in the latter half of the twentieth century. In distinguishing preindustrial political forms, Elman Service concentrated on means of political integration and cohesion, access to leadership positions, and methods of decision-making. His position, which he shared with other neo-evolutionary political anthropologists of his time such as Morton Fried (Fried 1967), was that political systems naturally progressed through a series of steps, beginning with egalitarian societies, then stratified societies, and finally class-based state societies. In this process, Service proposed, societies evolved from less integrated to more integrated, and political leadership gradually transformed from weaker to stronger (Service 1962).

Elman Service's typology of political systems was critiqued for being too simplistic, and consequently, for being incapable of apprehending the intricacy and diversity of political institutions and the related practices. The existence of certain bands, tribes, and chiefdoms that have not been influenced by colonialism, state power, or the forces of globalization was one such point highlighted by the critics. Some critiques came from the opposite direction, however. Accordingly, the supposed existence of the bands, tribes, and chiefdoms as autonomous, homogeneous, and isolated sociopolitical entities was nothing more than a fallacy proposed by early and mid-twentieth-century social scientists and anthropologists. Anthropologist Eric Wolf for example, rebuked this practice as the "atomization of the world" (Wolf 1982).

## Band, Tribe, and Chiefdom

The basic social unit in many foraging societies, the **band** is a relatively small, loosely organized, and kin-based group of nomadic people who hunt and gather for a living over a specific territory.

© DevonJenkin Photography/Shutterstock.com

Generally larger than the band, the **tribe** is a form of political organization found mostly among a range of kin-ordered groups of horticulturalists or pastoralists who share a common ancestry, culture, language, and territory.

© Marzolino/Shutterstock.com

Composed of a multitude of villages and communities and held together by the heredi-tary office of a paramount chief, the **chiefdom** is an autonomous political body, in which a redistribution-based economy and hierarchy based on social ranking exist.

© ChameleonsEye/Shutterstock.com

## State

The **state** is a centrally, bureaucratically, and hierarchically organized, autonomous struc-ture of political, legal, and military power that administers a territory and populace as the ultimate authority. Anthropologist Robert Carneiro defines the state as "an autonomous political unit encompassing many communities within its territory, having a centralized government with the power to collect taxes, draft men for work or war, and decree or enforce laws" (Carneiro 1970, 733). Accordingly, the state is known for its following specialized functions:

- controlling population through fixing and maintaining territorial boundaries, categoriz-ing citizenry, and taking periodic censuses,
- raising and maintaining state revenues through systemic tax collection,
- upholding judiciary through laws, legal procedure, and judges, and
- enforcing law and order through permanent military and political forces.

## Origin of the State

In a better part of the twentieth century, anthropological studies about the state were dominated by several main concerns. The archeological fascination and interest on the conditions that led to the rise of earliest states (archaic states) in Fertile Crescent or Mesopotamia, the Nile Valley, Yellow River Valley, Indus River Valley, Andean region, and Mesoamerica (Childe 1936; White 1959; Wittfogel 1957; Murphy 1957; Needham 1971; Coe 1966; Lanning 1967; Silverblatt 1978; Service 1975) was one of them.

© Evdoha_spb/Shutterstock.com

Anthropologists were also intrigued by those indigenous polities still functioning in the early decades of the twentieth century. The postwar anthropological gaze was shifted into the affairs of postcolonial states then known as the "new nations" (Geertz 1980; Nandy 1983; Comaroff 1991). In recent years, anthropologists and other social scientists have begun to pay

a considerable attention to the predicaments of the modern nation-state in the age of globalization (Giddens 1985; Appadurai 1996; Robbins 1999; Nagengast 1994; Ong 2003; Gupta and Ferguson 2002; Tsing 2005; Ferguson 2006).

Whereas many theories have been suggested for the origin of the state, all of them may be sorted into two general types: voluntaristic and coercive. Voluntaristic theories hold that people surrendered their individual sovereignties voluntarily and steadfastly to form the larger political structure of the state,

© Muhammad Qadri Anwar/Shutterstock.com

believing in the benefits they may be able to reap in so doing. These benefits include the possibilities for increased food production, the prospects for resolving intra- and intergroup disputes more effectively, and the aspirations for sociopolitical stability in general.

In the first half of the twentieth century, one of the leading arguments for voluntaristic origin of the state was made by the Australian-born British archeologist Vere Gordon Childe (1892–1957). According to his theory, Agricultural Revolution or the growth of intensive agriculture (prodded by the use of more sophisticated tools, metallurgy, draft animals, and irrigation) automatically brought into being a surplus of food, making it possible for some segments of the populace to focus on occupations other than food production, such as pottery, blacksmithing, masonry, weaving, scribing, and trading. This extensive occupational specialization initiated the process by which small, kin-based, and nonliterate villages were transformed into large, socially and economically complex, urban societies. As a result, social integration increased exponentially uniting previously discrete communities into the political structure of the state (Childe 1936).

Another voluntaristic theory of state origins was proposed by the German-American historian and sinologist Karl August Wittfogel (1896–1988). His thesis, known as the **irrigation theory** or the *hydraulic hypothesis,* stresses three main points:

- the central role played by the large-scale irrigation works in economic and social growth,
- the centralized bureaucratic structures required to build and maintain them, and
- the resultant formation of the absolutist managerial state.

Wittfogel maintained that, at some point, the small-scale irrigation farmers in arid and semiarid regions of the world decided to set aside their individual autonomies and merge their small communities into a single larger political entity capable of bringing off extensive irrigation. The body of officials they built to devise and oversee such large-scale irrigation works brought the state into being. As irrigation played the causal role in state formation, Wittfogel considered such early states to be "hydraulic civilizations." He cited ancient China, India, Mesopotamia, as well as pre-Columbian Mexico, and Peru as main areas exemplifying his thesis of hydraulic hypothesis (Wittfogel 1957).

Cultural ecological anthropologists such as Marvin Harris (See Chapter 4) took up Wittfogel's thesis of hydraulic society (Harris 1991). However, some critics have been arguing against the notion that Sri Lanka and Bali were hydraulic societies in Wittfogel sense (Leach 1961; Lansing 1991; Barker and Molle 2004). Moreover, as archaeological evidence suggest, in Mesopotamia and China (cited by Wittfogel), full-fledged states developed well before the introduction of large-scale irrigation (Kraeling and Adams 1960). Furthermore, the first states emerged in Mexico were antecedent to massive irrigation systems.

© J. Lekavicius/Shutterstock.com

In contrast to all voluntaristic theories of state origin emphatic on social integration, theories based on Marxian thought focus on social conflict. One leading theory taking the tack of conflict is American anthropologist Robert Carneiro's **conflict theory**, sometimes known as the theory of *environmental circumscription*. Carneiro holds that war played a pivotal role in the rise of the state. While recognizing war as the mechanism of state formation, he focuses on specifying the conditions under which it paved the way for the state to emerge.

## Nation-State

The **nation-state**, a more recent type of political organization, is a set of institutional forms of governance with which an administrative monopoly over an economic, political, legal, social, and cultural territory is established and maintained. It is a form of state functioning to provide a sovereign territory for a particular nation, a collectivity aptly characterized by anthropologist Ben Anderson as an "imagined political community" (Anderson 1983). It is from the above function that the nation-state acquires its legitimacy. Hence, an ideal of congruence between cultural (nation) and political (state) units always exists within a nation-state. To put it differently, the nation-state is bound to construct a national identity in its own formation. As the space in which the premodern states inhabited was culturally and politically heterogeneous, none of the state forms existed before the emergence of the nation-state (such as monarchical states, theocracies, or premodern empires) was associated with the concept of the nation. "In the older imagining where states were defined by the centers," mentioned Ben Anderson, "borders were porous and indistinct, and sovereignties faded imperceptibly into one another" (Anderson 1983).

The rise of the nation-state, classical social theorists such as Karl Marx and Max Weber readily observed, was simultaneous to the advent of capitalism. Industrial Revolution, the period of European history generally regarded as occurring in the late eighteenth-century, was marked by a shift in production from agriculture to industrial goods, urbanization, and factory system, transforming premodern or traditional societies into modern ones. Moreover, it paved the way for the establishment of capitalistic socioeconomic order. As Marx viewed it, during the Industrial Revolution, the capitalist class (or the *bourgeoisie*) gained the control of the means of production and established their position of control over the working class (or the *proletariat*).

© Everett Historical/Shutterstock.com

This was accomplished through repression and manipulation of ideology. Max Weber also contended that, by providing an entrepreneurial personality type that capitalism demanded, the protestant reformations helped to promote the growth of modern industrial capitalism (Weber 1958). By the eighteenth century, the rulers were beginning to view trade as the ultimate source for economic well-being. As a new partnership developed between the ruling elites and the merchant class, the nation-state became the building block of an emerging global economic network (Wolf 1982, 109).

Many of the functions that the earlier states used to fulfill, such as controlling the population within its territory, maintaining armed forces and order, along with collecting tributes and/or taxes are carried out by the modern nation-state as well. However, unlike the premodern state forms, the nation-state is meant to be the guardian of the national economy. As it functions largely to advance the economic life of its citizens, the nation-state's influence and control over trade and commerce is considerable. Therefore, constructing a nation or groups of people who believe that they share a common culture, language, and history, and who, therefore, identify themselves as members of the collective body of the nation, is paramount among the activities of the nation-state.

The construction of national identity involves several systematic tasks. One of them is the creation of some "Other." This other consists of individuals or groups excluded from the nation-state, who in turn create boundaries between those persons or groups who are legitimate members and those who are not. The criteria for creating others may include racial (physical features of individuals and groups), linguistic, religious, and other cultural affilia-

tions. The construction of the others is an integral part of the nation-state's project of social integration in its attempt to bind together often disparate and conflicting groups into one collectivity or the nation. The **Southern strategy** used by conservative American political strategists in the recent past is a fine example to the point. It was used to increase political support among white voters in the South by appealing to racism against African Americans.

To this end, the systematic disintegration of alternative categories begins in earnest. This is carried out through concerted and combined efforts of the integrative categories or the forms within which difference cannot be adequately expressed and *prima facie* (apparent) equality can be made manifest. The members of the "nation," the citizens of the state, or the voters of the constituencies are some of such integrative categories. The negation of alternative categories is also done through the routines and rituals of rule. Under this scheme, ordinary procedures of the state are inflated, so official routines become the simply given or common-sense boundaries of the possible, occupying the domain of social perception.

© Michael Candelori/Shutterstock.com

Constructing a nation-state also requires an infrastructure that serves to integrate all members of the state into a common bureaucracy. It also requires building a national education system to train and socialize children to identify themselves as members of the nation-state.

While the symbolic barriers of excluded others, infrastructure, and education are essential for nation-state formation, the threat of using coercive force and the actual use of it remains key instruments in constructing and maintaining the nation-state (Nagengast 1994, 119–20).

© gmeland/Shutterstock.com

There is a growing anthropological interest over the nation-state's ability to remain autonomous within the increasingly globalized world where national boundaries have increasingly become irrelevant. The salience of the nation-state as the undisputed, unifying entity is evidently decreasing since the process of globalization intensifies the level of inter-action and interdependence between individuals, societies, and states. Globalization is the rapid transformation of local cultures around the world in response to the economic and other influences of a dominant culture (See Chapter 13). Sociologist Anthony Giddens characterizes globalization as "time–space distanciation," a profound reorganizing of time and space in social life. He views the development of global networks of production and exchange as weakening any control people have over local circumstances, resulting in the extraction of micro and macro socioeconomic decision making from local interests of inter-action. This is a situation in which, according to Giddens, "disembedding of social relations" takes place (Giddens 1990).

The expansion of international regimes and international regulatory systems undermine the competence of the nation-state. Similarly, with an internationalization of the state through a vast increase in the amount of international organizations, and the rise of qua-si-supranational bureaucratic regimes of power such as the European Union, the endurance of the nation-state as a form is seriously challenged. By the same token, nation-state's ability to control its own destiny is constrained. In addition, the nation-state's authority or its abil-ity to handle any internal or external constraints in its own domain is reduced sharply. The existence of international regimes further challenges the authority of the nation-state mak-ing it looks like a local authority governed by globally structured regional and national governing bodies.

Given these circumstances in which phenomenal worlds are truly becoming global, some social scientists contend that the process of globalization is gradually dissolving the core structures of the nation-state. Some scholars even suggest that the nation-state is enter-ing a terminal crisis (Appadurai 1996; Robbins, 1999).

## Social Power and State

**Power** is the ability to command others and secure their compliance. This generalized "trans-formative capacity" (Giddens 1979, 88) is seen when one's will over other individuals is exer-cised by commanding them to do certain things and getting their compliance even against their wishes. However, power does not merely operate among the individuals—it is obvi-ously operative among societies as well. Moreover, power does not limit itself to coercion or the use of (mostly physical) force. Sometimes, others' compliance may be gained by convinc-ing or by persuading them. Succinctly stated, social and political compliance is often secured through persuasion or coercion, or by using a mechanism that combines both strategies.

When power is institutionalized, it is manifested as **authority**—it evolves into the socially approved use of power. Therefore, it is distinguishable from **influence** or the ability to persuade others to comply with one's lead.

Anthropologist Eric Wolf has discussed about social power (and ideology) substantially (Wolf, 1982, 1994, 1999, 2001). Wolf described three distinct modes of social power: interpersonal power, organizational power, and structural power. Accordingly, the ability of one person to impose his/her will on another person is referred to as *interpersonal power*. Furthermore, the ability of a group of people or social units to limit or control the actions of other people in a specific social settings and domains is what Wolf characterized as *organizational power*. Moreover, the ability to organize social settings themselves, as well as the ability to control social labor is known as *structural power*. Wolf described structural power as follows:

"By this I mean the power manifest in relationships that not only operates within settings and domains but also organizes and orchestrates the settings themselves, and that specifies the direction and distribution of energy flows" (Wolf 1982).

Accordingly, the extensive and increasingly global division of labor among regions and groups, their dissimilar relations, and the way such relations are retained and altered over time must be understood through structural power. For example, one can understand the patterns of structural power by examining how clothing is manufactured currently in places like Bangladesh, Dominican Republic, Mexico, and Indonesia for the buyers in affluent places such as the United States, Canada, Europe, and Japan. The people who work in apparel and garment factories must work long hours for extremely low wages under appalling conditions. Usually, the workers cannot afford to buy the clothing that they produce, even if it were available for purchase in the local market!

Anthropologists tend to highlight the state's deep-seated connection with social power as the state is considered the ultimate authority. The spatialization of the state (Gupta and Ferguson 2002) or the perception that the state can saturate a specific space while simultaneously encompassing every facet of culture and socially reigning supremely has turned the state to the ultimate authority or the hegemon.

## Hegemony

The concept of **hegemony** is a theoretical perspective on the exercise of power originally opened by an Italian revolutionary named Antonio Gramsci (1891–1937). According to Gramsci, hegemony is the ability of a dominant or potentially dominant group or class to articulate the interests of the other social groups or classes to its own while still retaining its own privileged position. Focusing on the fascist nation-state of Italy in the 1930s and relying on Marxist analytic framework, Gramsci argued that the dominant groups strengthen their hold of power not by coercive measures alone, but through persuasive tactics of an ideology that could lead the dominated or subordinate classes to accept the supremacy of the ruling bloc as legitimate. For Gramsci, hegemony entails the accommodation of the interests and partialities of the classes over which it is to be exercised (Gramsci 1971, 216).

© Alessandro Giordano 1981/Shutterstock.com

What is pivotal to Gramsci's arguments is his recognition of hegemony as a continuous and open-ended process rather than a fixed state of affairs. It is precisely this recognition that has given the concept its analytical strength and vitality (Ariyaratne 2000). Always intrinsically unstable and vulnerable to challenges, hegemony is to be understood as something, which is realized through the "balancing of competing forces, not the crushing calculus of class domination" (Comaroff and Comaroff 1991, 20). The struggle for hegemony, Gramsci maintained, is a continuous process in which the interests of the other groups are coordinated with those of a dominant or potentially dominant group, through the creation of "not only a unison of economic and political aims, but an intellectual and moral unity" (Gramsci 1971, 181).

According to Gramsci, hegemonic struggle takes place through the ideological processes that he has characterized as the *education of "consent."* Gramsci is extremely particular when he states that consent is not to be generic and vague as it is expressed in the instance of elections or in opinion polls. The capitalist nation-state and its associated civil institutions that represent the interests of the ruling classes, usually play an instrumental role in the education of consent (Gramsci 1971, 259). In reality, therefore, the nation-state is first and foremost an "educator." It "never stops talking" (Corrigan and Sayer 1985, 3). It works to bring about new cultural configurations while working to restructure and reorganize economic forces and relations concurrently.

© Joseph Sohm/Shutterstock.com

The consent of the masses is produced through the *reshuffling of the inventory of "common sense"* or what for Gramsci, the "uncritical and largely unconscious way of perceiving and understanding the world that has become 'common' in any given epoch" (Gramsci 1971, 322). Gramsci makes it crystal clear that, for this reason, "to refer to common sense as a confirmation of truth is nonsense" (Gramsci 1971, 423). Nevertheless, he continues, common sense is an essential and vital part of the education of consent and the construction of everyday forms of rationality which inform that consent. Therefore, common sense can be seen as a cultural product of the ideological struggle over subjectivity. According to Gramsci, in order to produce a particular form of subordination or a particular form of consent, common sense should always be reconstructed. Put in other words, hegemony necessitates the dominant classes to present their worldview in such a way that it is preferred by dominated classes as the only sensible way of seeing the world—common sense.

In the articulation of a form of hegemony, Gramsci states that the nation-state never rules out the reinforcement of consent through repressive sanctions. Institutions such as schools are to fulfill positive educative functions (i. e., persuasive power) while institutions like courts, military, and police are to meet the negative educative functions (i. e., coercive power). In reality, however, a multitude of such "initiatives and activities tend to the same end—initiatives and activities which form the apparatus of the political and cultural hegemony of the ruling classes" (Gramsci 1971, 258). In the end, Gramsci maintained, hegemonic dominance relies upon what may be called *consented coercion.* In an instance of authority crisis, the masquerades of consent disappear, and it may bring out into open the true face of hegemonic dominance, which is the clutch of force.

Gramsci did not consider hegemony to be a solely ideological or cultural phenomenon. According to him, it is a phenomenon which is based on different modalities of organized and educated consent and activating through multiple forms. Ideological and cultural dominance, though crucial, is to be understood as only one form of hegemony. Thus, the ideological instance within a hegemony is not unitary, and as such, the consciousness or consent that it produces takes differing and complex forms.

Scholars who integrate the analysis of structural constraints with that of human agency, and who believe in the openness of any given historical process have been inspired by Gramsci's writings. Anthropologists have been moved by his concept of hegemony as it reinforced the recognition that persistence of cultural forms may be ascribed as much to the pursuit of power as to an instinctive consensus about values.

## Neo-Gramscianism

Influenced by the writings of Antonio Gramsci to a great degree, **neo-Gramscianism** focuses on investigating the interface of ideas, institutions, and material capabilities as they give shape to the contours of state formation. Stepping away from the perspective of seeing hegemony as the "predominant power of a state or a group of states" (Cohn 2005, 130–31), the contributors to the approach of neo-Gramscianism indicate the validity of seeing the sovereignty of the state as a power relegated to sidelines by the emergence of a transnational financial system and a corresponding system of transnational production. In this global economic system, the neo-Gramscian scholars contend, the international financial institutions, such as the World Bank (WB) and International Monetary Fund (IMF), have developed into a *transnational historic bloc* capable of acting as the global hegemon. This historic bloc gains the consent of the governed population mainly through the methods of intellectual, cultural (and coercive) persuasion. The neo-Gramscian scholars, coming mainly from the disciplines of critical theory, the global political economy, and international relations, believe that the state formation and the interstate politics have to be examined in the context of the "transnational dynamics of capital accumulation and class formation" (Overbeek and Hank 2000, 168–69).

© Simon Roughneen/Shutterstock.com

The forces who may form counterhegemonies to challenge the above transnational historic bloc (as part of an open-ended class struggle, and to establish themselves as a new historic bloc) might include a multitude of actors, such as the neo-mercantilists, the alliances of lesser-developed countries, the feminists, the environmentalists, and the likes (Cox 1983, 162–75).

## Governmentality

French philosopher Michel Foucault (1926–1984) discusses his concept of governmentality within the context of his discussion of *biopower* (a new form of power, according to him, emerged in the nineteenth century). Biopower relates to modern nation-states' regulation of people through a variety of techniques for accomplishing "the subjugation of bodies and the control of populations" (Foucault 1976, 140).

Foucault does not concentrate on the state per se. Instead, he focuses on the "practices and rationalities that compose the means of rule and government" (Dean 1994, 153). What is truly important, he maintains, is not so much the State-domination of society, but the "governmentalization of the state" (Foucault 1979, 20). To this end, Foucault examines how bodies are regulated, the conduct is governed, and how the self is constructed (Foucault 1977). **Governmentality** is the art of governing in which the willing participation of the governed (usually against their own well-being and interests) takes place.

© Eugene Ivanov/Shutterstock.com

## Chapter Summary

This chapter on political anthropology probes the exercise of social power. It discusses how a state exercises power, referring to related concepts such as structural power, hegemony, and governmentality.

- The basic social unit in many foraging societies, the band is a relatively small, loosely organized, and kin-based group of nomadic people who hunt and gather for a living over a specific territory.

- Generally larger than the band, the tribe is a form of political organization found mostly among a range of kin-ordered groups of horticulturalists or pastoralists who share a common ancestry, culture, language, and territory.

- Composed of a multitude of villages and communities and held together by the hereditary office of a paramount chief, the chiefdom is an autonomous political body, in which a redistribution-based economy and a hierarchy based on social ranking exist.

- The state is a centrally, bureaucratically, and hierarchically organized, autonomous structure of political, legal, and military power that administers a territory and populace as the ultimate authority.

- A more recent type of political organization, the nation-state is a set of institutional forms of governance with which an administrative monopoly over an economic, political, legal, social, and cultural territory is established and maintained. It is a form of state functioning to provide a sovereign territory for a nation.

- According to Antonio Gramsci (1891–1937), hegemony is the ability of a dominant or potentially dominant group or class to articulate the interests of the other social groups or classes to its own while still retaining its own privileged position. Hegemonic struggle takes place through the ideological processes that Gramsci has characterized as the *education of "consent."* He stated further, the consent of the masses is produced through the *reshuffling of the inventory of "common sense."*

- Influenced vehemently by the writings of Antonio Gramsci, Neo-Gramscianism focuses on investigating the interface of ideas, institutions, and material capabilities as they give shape to the contours of state formation.

- Foucault's notion of governmentality is the art of governing in which the willing participation of the governed (usually against their own well-being and interests) takes place.

# CHAPTER 12

# The World System: Examining the Growth of Modern World Order

© AlexanderZam/Shutterstock.com

The links that created the conditions for a fully integrated global economy and the concurrent sociocultural changes by the latter half of the twentieth century were originally established by European economic powers some 500 years ago. The Europeans were certainly not the originators of **colonialism,** ascertainable as political conquest of a territory, and subsequent economic and sociocultural domination of its people by another nation. Nor were they peerless in profiting from transoceanic trade and commerce that eventually made them the most salient economic powers of the world. Since the growth of state systems roughly 5,000 years ago, state societies in different parts of the globe ranging from China, India, Mexico, and the Middle East, have conquered the adjacent territories while incorporating the people in such subjugated lands into their broadening empires. At the minimum, Indian Ocean–based trade and commerce, led by China, India, and Islamic powers in the Middle East kept Asia, Africa, and Europe connected for two millennia (Braudel 1982; Wolf 1982; Frank 1998; Abu-Lughod 1989). When seeking to establish links with the Old World and the New World in the fifteenth century, European elites were well aware that they had been standing in the periphery.

## The Growth of Modern World Order and the Colonial Legacy

A host of reasons may have stimulated the Europeans, including the adventurous and intriguing experience of sailing to explore exotic lands of the globe and Christian zealotry for proselytizing the native inhabitants of such lands. The primary motivation for European expansion, however, was the thirst to accumulate wealth by controlling external resources and trade. This motive was strongly driven by Europe's growing population within the context of the stagnant economy caused by the long-term feudal crisis (Wallerstein 2011 [1974]; Wolf 1982). The intent to appropriate global wealth also reflected the aspirations of Europe's rising class of merchants and bankers. The European expansion was aided by technological advances in the spheres of navigation, ship building, cartography, and welfare, as well as by the diseases European colonizers carried for which, oftentimes, indigenous populations found to have no immunity (Diamond 1999). The tactics such as warfare, plunder, and enslavement had been employed by all previous colonial empires in dealing with subjugated people, so the use of them by European colonial powers was not unexpected. Nevertheless, in terms of the heights they were able to reach up by embarking on such tactics, the European colonial empires easily surpassed all empires of the past. During the first phase of European expansion that lasted roughly a little more than two centuries from the mid-fifteenth century to the late seventeenth century, Europe was able to shed the economic scars inherited from the feudal crisis and being the march toward world supremacy slowly but surely. During the second and the most potent phase, which spanned approximately from the second half of the nineteenth century until the end of Second World War when European colonies began to secure independence, European powers became the colonial masters for much of the world population. Led by Great Britain, France, Spain, Portugal, Netherlands, and Belgium, driven by economic reasons, they adopted an innovative course of action from the aforementioned antiquated set of tactics when acquiring colonies in far-off lands.

## Plunder

Accordingly, they seized large tracts of land from colonized people on regular basis, for several reasons. One of the most salient reasons for capturing land was to extract resources such as precious metals (e.g., gold, silver, and copper) and minerals (e.g., gem).

© Vadim Nefedoff/Shutterstock.com

© tateyama/Shutterstock.com

When conquering territories in the Caribbean and the Americas, acquisition of metals and minerals was at the top of colonial agenda. Under this scheme, the Mayan, the Aztec, and the Inca kingdoms were systematically plundered, and the extracted gold and silver in large quantities were swiftly sent off to Europe.

As happened in silver mines in Peru, native populations were forced to extract minerals from the mines under colonial supervision. As a consequence, within a century (from 1500 to 1600), Spanish colonies in the Americas were able to dispatch a massive 300 tons of plundered gold and 25,000 tons of silver to Spain (Scammell 2003 [1989], 133). During this same period, Europe experienced an unprecedented eightfold increase in the supply of silver in circulation.

European merchant class needed access to gold and silver for one other important reason as well. China, their main trading competitor in Asia, has been insisting that all trade deficits be paid off in gold and silver. In fact, it was the intense rivalry to acquire prized metals and minerals that set the stage for the first Opium War in 1839 and China's agreement to accept opium grown in British plantations in India in lieu of silver in the aftermath of that war (Frank 1998).

The act of looting in wartime was neither limited to metals and minerals. Indigenous work of art and craft, artifacts, as well as a wide variety of objects, which were capable of arousing public interest by being novel, unique, and exotic (curiosities) were ransacked and sent off to Europe to meet the growing demand from art-loving elites, private collectors, and museum curators. Nor did pillaging confined just to the New World. For example, after the British East India Company (BEIC) assumed dominance over the Indian subcontinent in 1858, it raided the treasury of Bengal and shipped the looted wealth to stockholders of the company in Britain (Wolf 1982, 244).

## Cash Cropping

Another reason of considerable import for appropriating lands of the colonized people was to convert them to large-scale farms for **cash cropping,** sometimes also referred to as

© Everett Historical/Shutterstock.com

© Everett Historical/Shutterstock.com

© Maciej Czekajewski/Shutterstock.com

*mono-crop plantations.* Single crop varieties such as sugar and cotton produced in the Americas and spices such as cinnamon, clove, mace, and nutmeg grown in the Indian Ocean islands were exported to Europe where consumer demand for them was steadily rising.

Sugarcane was originally grown in the South Pacific, and the early merchants indeed had carried sugar as luxury trade good to the Mediterranean, the Middle East, India, and to the Far East via Oceanic and land-based trade routes. Through the nineteenth century however, the Spanish and the Portuguese converted sugar into a powerful commodity in the industrial world by establishing a plantation economy in the Caribbean and South America to produce and export it in stunningly large quantities. Between 1650 and 1800, sugar consumption increased in massive 2,500 per cent in Great Britain alone. The upsurge of demand was met with an equally sizable production hike. Between 1800 and 1890, sugar production grew 2,500 per cent, making it the single most important cash crop. Its importance grew even further as people began to use sugar for sweetening three other stimulant commodities introduced by European planters as cash crops—coffee, tea, and cocoa (Mintz 1986).

## Forced Labor

European colonial powers heavily relied on transatlantic slave trade to supply their labor requirements. On most occasions, local populations in the Caribbean and South America were simply incapable of sustaining plantations as they perished in large numbers by either

© Everett Historical/Shutterstock.com

exposure to European diseases or failing to adapt to strenuous conditions of uncompensated, **forced labor**, also known as *corvee labor*. Trading African people for servitude had been in existence long before the European expansion (Lovejoy 2011; Alexander 2001), but it was the Europeans who practiced it with an immensity never seen before. As European planters and the slave shippers found slavery to be enormously profitable, the exportation of African people for enslavement in the Americas began in earnest. The overwhelming majority of those enslaved were either bought from the collaborators in Western and Central parts of Africa or captured directly by the European forces themselves. Considered as cargo and shipped across the Atlantic Ocean as quickly and cheaply as possible, these slave immigrants landed in the New World in great numbers to labor in sugar, coffee, and tobacco plantations, gold and silver mines, as well as in constructional projects in the new European colonies. Millions of Africans may have died during the horrendous sea passage, as well as under dire conditions in servitude (Coquery-Vidrovich 1988). The demand for slavery was invigorated even further when in the nineteenth century supplying slave labor became essential for the plantations located in the American South that supplied cotton for Great Britain's thriving textile industry. Transatlantic slave trade drained productive labor out of Africa considerably. By the same token, uncompensated African slave labor invested in the lands appropriated from the native populations in the Americas by colonial planters contributed to the economic prosperity and industrialization in Europe.

## Joint-Stock Companies

Despite the fact that the European pursuit of amassing global wealth was based mostly on an age-old course of action comprising warfare, pillage, and servitude, to a considerable extent, its success was also hinged on the deployment of a tactic never used before in such pursuits: **joint-stock company.** It was a firm administered by a centralized board of directors, but was owned jointly by its shareholders. While the stockholders received annual dividends according to the value of the money they invested in the company, they were equally liable for company debts as well. The emergence of joint-stock trading companies was a clear indication of the influential economic role assumed by Europe's rising class of bankers and merchants. The joint-stock companies were quite useful for the Europeans in accomplishing the goals of merchant capitalism. For instance, during the early centuries of European expansion, the joint-stock companies were the most reliable sources of funding required for exploration of foreign territories and subsequent colonization of them. As launching large-scale business ventures became possible with their swift fund raising ability from a large numbers of shareholders, joint-stock companies turned out to be a true game changer in European expansion. Even more importantly, unlike the elites in European states who oftentimes considered the pursuit of prestige and the elevation of missionary zeal as equally valuable motives, joint-stock companies were consistently working to accomplish their single most important objectives—the pursuit of profit for their shareholders. It was the strategies and practices pertaining to this objective that made European expansion distinct from previous empires as it was eventually able to connect the entire world into a single world-system based on capitalist economies (Wallerstein 2011).

The Dutch East India Company (DEIC, or after initials in Dutch for *Vereenigde Oostindische Companie,* VOC) was the world's first joint-stock company; it was established in 1602.

© SamanWeerafunga/Shutterstock.com

The DEIC was chartered by the Dutch government to monopolize trade in the waters between the Cape of Good Hope and the Straits of Magellan. The company operated almost as a government as it possessed the power and ability to build strategic fortresses, maintain armed forces, wage war, establish colonies, as well as imprison those who resist the company's orders, and carry out executions of the convicts. In addition, it was able to negotiate and conclude trade treaties with local rulers and strike its own coins (Scammell 2003).

The DEIC soon displaced the Portuguese, the European pioneers who came to the East in search of trade in the closing years of the fifteenth century. When the DEIC commenced its trading activities in the East Indies, the Portuguese has established themselves as serious rivals to the Arabs for the trade of Asia. Unlike the Portuguese who showed a great zeal not only for trade, but also for making converts, the DEIC was mostly interested in controlling trade. By seizing control of seaports and maritime regions in a number of key islands in the Indian Ocean, such as Java (a part of what is now Indonesia), Ceylon (currently, Sri Lanka), and Malacca (presently, State of Malacca in Malaysia), the DEIC effectively established its control over the production and trade of spices (such as cinnamon, cloves, nutmeg, and cardamom) in the region. During the first half of the seventeenth century, the DEIC was also capable of defeating the British fleet. The company prospered through such successes and went onto become the dominant force of the Indian Ocean trade. For example, during the period of 1602 to 1796, 4,785 ships owned by the DEIC carried nearly a million Europeans for trading activities in Asia and netted 2.5 million tons of Asian trade goods consequentially. During this same period, the fleet of the BEIC, the nearest competitor of the DEIC, managed to transport just one-fifth the tonnage of the trade merchandise delivered by the

© Jordan Tan/Shutterstock.com

DEIC ships. During much of the seventeenth and eighteenth centuries, the DEIC stockholders received annual dividends of 18 percent approximately.

Toward the end of the eighteenth century however, the company's fortunes began to dwindle due to fierce competition from other European companies such as the BEIC, as well as corruption and inefficiency that plagued the company administration. The DIEC's continual involvement in local welfare and the brutal violence it perpetrated became disastrous as well. In the absence of definite military advantage, the company often chose to assist different functions of native principalities, but its claim for commercial privileges went unheeded. In instances of war, native principalities inclined to form strategic partnerships in the interest of defeating the DIEC, their common foreign enemy. Although the DEIC was dissolved by the Dutch government in 1799, and its assets were turned over to the Batavian Republic, a Dutch client state of France, it was instrumental in building and maintaining the Dutch commercial empire for nearly two centuries (Wolf 1982; Ricklefs [1981] 2008).

The BEIC, the oldest among several European East India Companies of similar origin, received Royal Charter from Queen Elizabeth of Great Britain to manage trade and commerce in the Indian Ocean and the Far East in 1600. The company was mostly associated with trade in basic commodities such as cotton, silk, salt, tea, and opium. In the eighteenth century, Britain turned into a dominant power in the Indian and Pacific Oceans.

298 Key Concepts of Cultural Anthropology

© Ranjith Kumar Ravindran/Shutterstock.com

Before asserting the British Crown's direct rule over the Indian subcontinent in 1858, the British wielded imperial control to a considerable degree through the BEIC. The company's primary interests were commercial; British cultural imperialism was never an official policy of the BEIC. Moreover, since the caste system in India facilitated imperial policy, the BEIC did not promote Christian missionary activity until the 1830s and 1840s. As the company administrators directly involved in exploiting land revenues, introducing agrarian reforms, and implementing peasant settlement policies, the economic impact of the company rule was extensive.

For example, the BEIC policies promoted cash cropping in arable and pasturable lands at the expense of farming and herding for sustenance in the territories over which it had controlling power. Likewise, the company encouraged massive logging operations undertaken by British and other European entrepreneurs, as the clearing of jungle land was an important part of the British effort to pacify indigenous peasant populations. Indeed, by transforming native peasants and pastoralists into a more homogeneous farming society through policies and practices of the above sorts, the BEIC provided a better base for the subsequent colonial administration. However, such policies and practices irritated even the segments of small but powerful, educated classes of Indian elite who were positively exposed to Christian and secular values associated with the European Enlightenment. For instance, Ram Mohan Roy (1772–1833), an influential member of Indian elite in the nineteenth century, campaigned against the company's unfair and autocratic commercial practices while defending reforms.

As the seventeenth century unraveled, more British joint-stock companies linked to trade and commerce of North America followed suit. For example, the Hudson's Bay Company (HBC), one of the oldest commercial corporations in North America, was incorporated to English Royal Charter in 1670, and had been functional ever since until it was finally dissolved in 2012. In the same vein, the Virginia Company of London (VCL) was founded with a charter from King James I in 1606. Its main goal was to extend commercial assistance to establish colonial settlements on the coastal areas of North America. However, the company's prospects were short-lived as it was dissolved in 1624. Similarly, the Massachusetts Bay Company (MBC) was formed in 1629, but its charter was revoked by King Charles II in 1684.

© Tethys Imaging LLC/Shutterstock.com

© ValeStock/Shutterstock.com

By the mid-century, French, German, Swedish, and Danish joint-stock companies were also formed. The share ownerships of these companies typically represented a cross section of European aristocracy and the wealthy merchant class.

The era of joint-stock trading companies ended in the nineteenth century, when European governments commenced their direct involvement in colonization by acquiring, administering, and exploiting foreign territories. Although they eventually became defunct, the trading companies played the key role in accumulating world wealth and placing in the hands of European elites. The elite class invested that wealth in many areas, such as art and architecture, as well as science and industry. As a matter of fact, the extraordinary affluence brought to the continent of Europe by the joint-stock trading companies became a main source for the Industrial Revolution and the simultaneous advent of capitalism.

## Colonialism and Its Legacy

As indicated earlier, the most potent phase of European expansion began approximately by the second half of the nineteenth century, and lasted until the end of the Second World War. The conquest of the New World (the Caribbean and the Americas) during the first phase of European colonialism heralded the coming of the next phase that ultimately touched every corner of the world. What mainly caused the actual possession and administration of foreign territories by European governments was the **Industrial Revolution:** the rapid growth of machine-based manufacturing that occurred in Great Britain and quickly spread in other European countries in the late eighteenth and the nineteenth centuries. The new industries heavily depended on the colonized territories' supply of raw materials and cheap labor. In addition, the colonies became favorable markets for the mass-manufactured, European factory goods.

Driven by the intention to fulfill the above requirements of the Industrial Revolution, European powers began to decisively restructure the geopolitical landscape of the world through massive colonization projects. Throughout the nineteenth and the twentieth centuries, Great Britain, France, the Netherlands, Belgium, Germany, Russia, the United States, and Japan played a leading role in turning nonindustrial regions into colonial territories, and thereby securing their own economic and political well-being. For example, during the period of 1815 to 1914, France acquired or dominated as protectorates the following countries: Algeria, Morocco, and Tunisia in the Near East and North Africa; Benin, Burkina Faso, Central African Republic, Chad, Djibouti, Ivory Coast, Madagascar, Mali, Mauretania, and Niger in Africa; Cambodia, Laos, and Vietnam in Asia; and New Caledonia, and Tahiti in the Pacific. Similarly, during this same period of time, Great Britain acquired or dominated as protectorates in the following territories: Aden (in Yemen), Bahrain, Cyprus, Egypt, Kuwait, Oman, and the United Arab Emirates in the Near East and North Africa; Botswana, Ghana, Kenya, Lesotho, Malawi, Nigeria, Somaliland, Sudan, Swaziland, Uganda, Zambia, Zanzibar, Zimbabwe, and Zululand (in South Africa) in Africa; Brunei, Hong Kong, Malaysia, Myanmar (Burma), Nepal, Papua, and Singapore in Asia; and Fiji, Tonga, and Solomon islands in the Pacific. Indeed, when French and British empires were at their heights around 1914, European powers commanded nearly 85 percent of the world.

During this period, colonial powers were able to establish a system of *spheres of influence* in Africa, Asia, and the Pacific, by which they could intervene the economic and political affairs of the colonized countries. In some cases, the spheres of influence were simply meant for political claim (by a colonizing country) to exclusive control over foreign territories. For example, from 1885 to 1908, the African country Congo (Zaire) was a property of the Belgian King Leopold II (1865–1909). On occasion, the spheres of influence referred to a legal agreement by which other colonial powers pledge themselves desist from interference within the sphere. For instance, in 1884 to 1885, representatives from fourteen countries, including Germany, Portugal, France, Great Britain, Spain, Belgium, Turkey, Russia, and the United States assembled at the Berlin Conference in Germany to arrive at a negotiated settlement in the

© Everett Historical/Shutterstock.com

competition to control trade and natural resources in Africa. All colonial powers at the Berlin Conference agreed to carve up the continent of Africa into fifty colonies.

In the same vein, the military might of the European colonial powers in the Far East forced China into a series of unequal territories, through which countries such as Great Britain, France, Germany, and eventually the United States could enjoy special privileges and indemnity within China. The eighteenth-century commercial activities between Britain and China (with which British goods to colonial India, Indian cotton to China, and Chinese tea to Britain were traded) was largely in China's favor. As the silver flowing into China from this trade spurred monetization of Chinese markets, the British in the 1820s took action to reverse the balance of trade by replacing cotton with Indian opium. Chinese government reacted by banning opium trade altogether in 1836. This was what led to the First Opium War in 1839 and lasted until 1842. It proved that Chinese forces were no match for the advanced military weaponry and strategies of the British, developed through decades of continental warfare and naval battles. The resultant Nanjing treaty granted Britain the island of Hong Kong, together with security and protection against a loss or other financial burden. The Nanjing treaty also opened five ports: Fuzhous, Guangzhou (Canton), Ningpo, Shanghai, and Xiamen (Armory). In 1856, a second war was broke out, and in 1860, the British were able to capture Beijing. A number of new unequal treaties were to follow. These treaties mandated low tariffs for imports from European countries to China, while legalizing

© milosk50/Shutterstock.com

opium trade and sanctioning European diplomats' presence in Beijing. The new treaties also provided for the opening of eleven new ports. Such treaty ports were little enclaves of privilege and security under the rule of foreign consuls, where European finances were safe from confiscation, and the trade was hugely favorable for colonial powers.

Although a late arriver to the systematic colonization of spatial regions, during the height of its existence in the Second World War, the Japanese Empire had a quite large sphere of influence spread over most of East Asia, including Taiwan, Korea, Vietnam, and the eastern seaboard of China. Likewise, Russia acquired Amur territories (from China), Central Asia, and Chechnya while the United States gained possession of the Philippines in Asia, Guam, Hawaii, Midway, and Wake in the Pacific.

When justifying colonization of foreign territories to the people in their home countries, European elites relied on the idea of the Caucasian race's superiority over other races. Many racist notions were in circulation at the time. One such version, which was mostly appealing to Christian zealotry, stressed white man's destiny as the messenger of gospel to the world of heathens. Another variant stemmed from social Darwinism. Accordingly, white Europeans were considered more fit and versatile than everyone else in the struggle for survival. Another powerful variation was articulated by Rudyard Kipling (1865–1936), an English poet born in colonial India. It referred to the idea of the "white man's burden." White man had a burden of delivering the blessings of advanced European civilization to the non-European world, which was yet to be made civilized. The imbrication of ideas of

IF THEY 'LL BE GOOD.

UNCLE SAM — You have seen what my sons can do... now see what my daughters can do in peace.

the above sorts generated an ideological justification for Eurocentric racism and Western aspiration to dominate the non-Western world.

The stress laid on the ideology of social betterment proved to be even more useful in justifying colonial enterprise for subject populations. Focusing exclusively on educational policies in colonized territories, European rulers invested a significant ideological capital to convince that their inherent inferiority shown in moral, intellectual, and cultural behavior. For instance, the British system of education, which was introduced to colonial India in 1835, encouraged Indian children to follow their role model, the Englishman (Viswanathan 1988). Indians were generally portrayed as backward heathens in need of the civilizing influences of English culture, religion, political system, law, and education. In much the same way, France's colonial project in Africa was portrayed as a civilizing mission (*mission civilisatrice*). By treating individuals educated and assimilated to French culture as evolves, or evolved people, French structure of education augmented the position of the colonizer in colonial Africa augmented the position of the colonizer while simultaneously constructing a subservient educated class persuaded of its superiority. As a matter of fact, under the social engineering project of colonial education, the colonized people were "learning to be marginal" (Kelly 1986; Bodley 2008; Cumming 2006; Cole and Raymond 2006).

On some occasion, the inadequacy of knowledge on local traditions and lower administrative costs had motivated colonial powers to prefer indirect rule through native

leaders instead of direct political control. The subservient class of educated colonial subjects was mostly helpful in establishing indirect rule in colonized territories. Prospects of education, employment, and ascendency in social hierarchy were specifically appealing to social outcasts and ethnic minorities in many precolonial societies; they inclined to be among the most unreserved supporters of colonial rule. As Patrick Harries has pointed out in regard to colonial Africa, at times, colonial powers and missionaries have collaboratively crafted totally new collective identities by combining colonized groups stemming from various cultural, linguistic, and ethnic traditions (Harries 1987). Oftentimes, indirect rule was also established through some segments of local elites who were ready to pledge allegiance to European colonizers as it enabled them to retain wealth, power, and prestige to a notable degree.

## Anticolonial Struggles, Decolonization, and Neocolonization

In both continents of the Americas, independence movements had engendered substantial changes in the eighteenth and the nineteenth centuries. The United States declared independence from Great Britain in 1776, ultimately gaining independence through the Revolutionary War, which was formally ended in 1783. The impact of the American Revolution, as well as the French Revolution (1789–1799) on the French, Spanish, and Portuguese colonies in the Americas was profound. In 1804, Haiti, a French slave colony in the Caribbean became the first colony to follow the United States to independence, while also becoming the first

© Sylvie Corriveau/Shutterstock.com

independent former colony to be governed by people of African descent. In Latin America, the Portuguese colony Brazil drifted into independence in 1822, as the Constitutionalist Revolution broke out in Portugal in the 1820s. The spread of independence movements across Hispanic America was very much evident during this time as well. For example, Spanish colonies such as Argentina, Venezuela, and Colombia had declared their autonomy in 1816, 1819, and 1820, respectively. By 1825, most of Spain's colonies in South America gained some form of independence.

The Second World War (1939–1945) generated conditions more favorable for national independence movements and the disintegration of the colonial system in Asia and Africa. As Japanese occupation destroyed colonial infrastructure in Asia to a considerable degree, European colonial powers were substantially weakened. Moreover, the war-scarred European home economies and political institutions were no longer capable of sustaining colonial operations as usual, especially against the ascending movements of organized civil disobedience and resistance.

Given the circumstances, the five decades that followed the end of the war also turned out to be the decades, in which almost all regions of the world were seen assuming some form of native governance. In 1945, Indonesia, the largest country in Southeast Asia and the largest archipelago in the world by size, proclaimed independence by formally ending the colonial rule of the Dutch East Indies. In the following year, the Philippines, another archipelago in the region of insular Southeast Asia, gained independence from the United States.

306 Key Concepts of Cultural Anthropology

In 1947, India and Pakistan, the two main countries in South Asia (after the partition), as well as Burma in mainland Southeast Asia declared formal independence from the British Crown. In the following year, the island of Ceylon, located just the southern tip of India, gained independence from Great Britain as well. The decolonized nations in the subsequent years included constituents of the region known as Indo China: Cambodia (1953), Laos (1954), and Vietnam (1954). In addition, Malaysia (1956) in the insular region of Southeast Asia, Sudan (1956), Ghana (1957), and Guinea (1958) in the continent of Africa, and many others became sovereign territories. When the United Nations General Assembly adopted Resolution 1514 in December 1960 by granting independence to colonial countries and peoples, the course of action for independence was already advancing in earnest in most of the former colonies. During the next three decades, African countries such as Congo (1960), Kenya (1963), Angola (1975), Mozambique (1975), Zimbabwe (1980), and many others became independent nation-states.

The process of decolonization continued throughout the 1990s as well. For example, despite the fact that South Africa became an independent nation-state in 1961, its rule of apartheid ended only in 1994. Likewise, the constituencies of the Soviet Union became sovereign nation-states only immediately before or after the union's fall in 1991. In another instance, the transfer of sovereignty over Hong Kong from Great Britain to China took place in 1997. Similarly, the returning of Portugal-controlled Macau to China did not happen until December 1999.

© Nataly Reinch/Shutterstock.com

© byvalet/Shutterstock.com

By the dawn of the new century, the historical process of colonialism, under which dominant Western countries were able to conquer and rule weaker countries, territories, or people, seemed to have reached its end. A handful of colonies do exist even today however. For instance, Great Britain still has some fourteen colonies or "overseas territories" in its possession, including the Pitcairn Islands in Oceania, Bermuda in the North Atlantic Ocean, and Gibraltar in the European continent. In much the same vein, France maintains as "overseas departments" of its own, including Martinique in the Caribbean Sea and French Guiana located in the North Atlantic coast of South America. Likewise, the United States has its "organized unincorporated territories," which include American Samoa and Guam in Oceania.

More importantly, the profound, as well as exploitative socioeconomic links that had kept colonies tied to their colonial rulers continue to exist despite political independence. It is this persistence, with which former colonial rulers are still capable of putting socioeconomic pressure upon their former colonies that anthropologists (and other social scientists) consider as **neocolonialism.** Indeed, many colonies which had gained independence in the aftermath of the Second World War are among the most impoverished countries in the world today.

## Critiquing the Modern World Order: Dependency Theory and the World-System Analysis

Globalization, according to the dependency theorists and the contributors to the world-system analysis, is neither a novel phenomenon, nor a process that warrants extolment.

## The Dependency Theory

Arose as a reaction to the modernization theory, the **dependency theory** was an analytic framework based on its ideological preference: critiquing the growth of world capitalist system. Articulated during the late 1950s and the 1960s by Latin American liberal economic reformists and Marxist intellectuals, this theory attempted to explain the persistent poverty existing in much of the underdeveloped world amid the extraordinary affluence in a handful of advanced industrial countries. The dependency theorists offered a critical perspective for the divergent development patterns in the current era of globalization. Dismissing the claim that globalization brings wealth and prosperity to the poor countries, they argued that, as a matter of fact, globalization perpetuates the asymmetric linkage between the opulent core nations by serving the needs of the former at the expense of the latter (Ferraro 2008, 58–64). According to its core propositions, dependency is a structurally interrelated, capitalist, and exploitative process known for its deep historical roots.

All dependency theorists regarded dependency as a structurally interrelated and interdependent process. Marxist economist Andre Gunder Frank (1929–2005), one of the early proponents of the dependency theory was most explicit on this point. Writing in 1966 in his paper entitled *The Development of Underdevelopment*, Frank maintained that the world capitalist system is organized as a series of metropolis-satellite relations within which economic surplus flows to the metropolis continuously (Frank 1966). Frank attempted to explain the structural interrelationship between the metropolis and the satellite by using the Marxian process of reasoning known as dialectics. In this process, the contradiction between conflicting forces is seen as the causal factor in their continuing interaction. According to Frank's assertion, the dominant-dependent relationship between the metropolis and the satellite contributes directly to the development of underdevelopment in the satellite. Stated another way, the underdevelopment in the satellites or peripheral areas is the outcome of the linkage between the metropolis and the satellites, ever renewed and refreshed in the process of surplus transfer and ever reinforced by the perpetual dependency of the satellites on the metropolis.

The dependency theorists viewed the incessant poverty existing in much of the peripheral world as a result of capitalist exploitation. As capitalism is the driving force behind the

© Fabio Lotti/Shutterstock.com

relationship between the poor nations and the rich ones, that uneven relationship is seen by the dependency theorists as essentially capitalist and exploitative. They often described this linkage as one of dominant-dependent, center-periphery, or metropolitan-satellite, stressing it capitalist, exploitative, and asymmetric nature. What causes the disparity of resource allocation among the two sets of states, held the dependency theorists, is the way the poor nations are integrated into the capitalist world-system by perpetuating a state of dependency between them and the rich nations. Under an unyielding international division of labor imposed by the capitalist system, the dependent states are made to conform to the resource usage patterns that serve the interests of the dominant states. Accordingly, the poor nations serve as suppliers of raw materials, repositories of unskilled labor and obsolescent technology, and markets for the products coming from wealthy nations. Stated succinctly, by structuring the dominant-dependent nexus through an international division of labor, capitalist exploitation always rewards the core and penalizes the periphery.

As the dependency theorists characterized, the relationship between the dominant and dependent states is acute, dynamic, and collaborative since maintaining the unequal patterns of resource diversion is not only among the prime interests of the dominant states, but also among the elites in the dependent states. Stated differently, the perpetual dependency is ensured through the collaborative efforts of the dominant states and the elites in the dependent states as the former's involvement coincides with the class interests of the latter. The uneven, yet collaborative relationship between the dominant states and the

© Tero Hakala/Shutterstock.com

dependent polities makes "metropolitan capitalism" and "peripheral capitalism" distinctive within the growth of world capitalist system, the dependency theorists argued (Baran 1957; Amin 1976).

As noted earlier, for the dependency theorists, the central feature of the global economy throughout the entire era of modernity has been the persistence of poverty in the peripheral regions of the globe. Regardless of the specific identity of the state(s) which was in control, they contended, a dependent relationship always existed between the dominant and the dependent states. Therein lays the dependency theorists' critique of the modernist position that the nation-states have to be treated as autonomous, discrete, and primordial entities that can be hierarchized from the backward or underdeveloped nation-states of the bottom tier to the advanced or developed countries at the zenith. From the perspective of the dependency theory, individualistic analyses of the above sorts ignore the fact that nation-states are the products of history. All dependency theorists agreed on the premise that dependency is a deep-seated historical process. Some even argued for the existence of world-systems well before the European dominance of the world and the concurrent rise of capitalism.

For instance, Andre Gunder Frank who earlier stated that the modern world-system was born some 500 years ago later suggested that some form of world-system may have been in existence even some 5,000 years ago (Frank 1978 and 1998). Likewise, geographer Janet Abu-Lughod argued cogently for a world-system existed in the thirteenth century before European hegemony. That world-system, according to Abu-Lughod, was centered in the subcontinent of India and linked Western Europe, Southeast Asia, and East Africa via land and ocean based trade (Abu-Lughod 1989). The general proposition shared by many dependency theorists was that the capitalist world-system has been in place since the sixteenth century. The underdevelopment existing in many parts of the world today is the direct consequence of these specific and ongoing series of relationships to the international system (Bodenheimer 1971, 157).

Traceability of the peripheral nations' contemporary predicaments through their historical roots (Lappe and Collins 1977, 99–111) is highly relevant to the following argument of the dependency theorists: *underdevelopment* is fundamentally different from *undevelopment*. The dependency theorists considered underdevelopment as a condition in which the resources available in the dependent states are being used mainly for the benefit of the dominant states. They also treated undevelopment as a condition in which the use of available resources is either lacking or minimal. Once again, Frank was right on the mark in this regard when he pointed out that "underdevelopment is not just the lack of development" and "before there was development, there was no underdevelopment" (Frank 1969 and 1975, 1). The above distinction places the peripheral nations in a historical context starkly different from that of the core nations. This analytical strategy helped Frank and other dependency theorists to repudiate the modernist argument that poverty in the peripheral countries is due to their failure to keep pace in adopting scientific transformations or absorbing enlightenment values of the European core. Furthermore, the above analytical strategy assisted the dependency theorists to forcefully present their position, which was, the incessant poverty in the countries of the peripheral world is due to the coercive integration of them into the capitalist world-system advantageous for the now-developed core countries.

## The World-System Analysis

The strength of the dependency theory lies in its critique of the modernization theory and associated paradigms of development, which were in vogue in the 1950s, the 1960s to 1970s. By pointing out that the success of the advanced industrial nations was an exceedingly contingent and particular incidence in global economic history, the dependency theory was able to take out some of the steam out of the suggestion that the peripheral nations should emulate the paths previously taken by the core nations on their march to achieve developmental goals.

However, being a theory zoomed in for the most part on economies, the dependency theory did not pay adequate attention to the fact that the affluent core states actively exert dominant influence on the peripheral states by a variety of means, and the nature of dependency may be multifaceted. For example, the dependency models such as Frank,s metropolitan-satellite theory (Frank 1966; Dos Santos 1971) were primarily concentrating on economic dominance, placing much less emphasis on cultural dimensions of dominance. The dependency theorists were also critiqued for ignoring the complex internal character of the peripheral societies (Laclau 1971).

Toward the 1980s, it was broadly agreed on by anthropologists that, in critiquing the growth of world capitalist system, the dependency theory had largely failed to grasp the intricacies of that historical process. Its successor, the **world-system analysis** is also based on the Marxist critique of capitalist colonialism as well as the structural functionalist approach (For structural functionalism, see Chapter 4) adopted by historians such as Fernand Braudel. This analytic framework offered a perspective of great breadth to the world-system while also stretching out and strengthening the related themes earlier brought to the forefront by the dependency theory.

## Fernand Braudel's Approach to History

The ideas of Fernand Braudel (1902–1985), the postwar French historian and the culminating figure of the *Annales School of History*, can be attributed to the world-system analysis. Braudel insisted on viewing historical time over long historical periods and large geographical spaces. According to Braudel, the complex totality of human experience has to be captured by focusing on the long-term, slowly evolving, and practically immobile *structures*, as well as medium-term, fluctuating, cyclical movements or *conjunctures*. Therefore, focusing on the long-term structures and the cyclical processes is essential for historical inquiry. Braudel critiqued contemporary historiography for its sole reliance on short-term and highly visible events or *evenements* whose significance he downplayed vehemently. Surface events are nothing but the mere dust of history as the long-term and large-scale socioeconomic structures lie beneath the ephemeral and discrete events of princess, generals, civil servants, and diplomats, contended Braudel. His conceptualization of historical time influenced Immanuel Wallerstein, the leading contributor for the world-system analysis, as evident in Wallerstein's concentration on long-term movements and geoecological regions as units of his analysis.

In his three-volume study *Civilization and Capitalism, 15th – 18th century* (1981, 1982, and 1992), Braudel used the world-system analysis in developing the theme of three-tiered hierarchy of economic life. Accordingly, the lowest layer is made up of everyday life or material foundations, the middle layer is formed of economic functioning, and the top layer is composed of capitalist monopolies and constraints. This three-layered arrangement is metaphorically significant as it helps to recognize modern history as a constant struggle between the two lower layers and the highest layer of capitalist monopolies and constraints.

## Immanuel Wallerstein's Analysis of the Modern World-System

Sociologist Immanuel Wallerstein is the most well-known and articulate contributor to the world-system analysis. He holds that globalization is a form of discourse advanced by powerful groups to highlight old features of the capitalist world-economy with an optimistic gloss. According to him, this is done while ignoring the terminal structural crisis the world-system is currently experiencing. As Wallerstein puts it, the ideological celebration of globalization is in actuality "the swan song of our historical system" which has been in existence since the late-fifteenth and the early-sixteenth century (Wallerstein 1998, 32).

Wallerstein's innovative approach motivates him to apply the structural functionalist frame of reference to analyze the modern world-system. He concentrates on two of the core conflicts of capitalist world order: bourgeois versus proletariat and core versus periphery, in an effort to describe both the cyclical rhythms and secular transformations of capitalism, perceived as a singular world-system. The focus on cyclical rhythms or short-term economic fluctuations and cyclical crises that bring about the end of the system shows Wallerstein's notable leaning on the fellow world-system analyst Fernand Braudel in this regard.

According to Wallerstein, unlike world empires of the past that had relied on a single political authority to contain all of their wide-stretched territories, the modern world-system holds together its constituent parts solely by economic means. Hence, first and foremost, the modern world-system is a world-economy. Second, since the driving force of the world-economy is amassing private wealth through exploitative production and profit-oriented sale in a market, the modern world-economy is, and only can be, a *capitalist world-economy*. During the 500 years of its longevity and flourish, the existence of multiple political entities within its radius has enabled the modern world-system to offer opportunities for the capitalists to bring into being structurally based maneuvering (Wallerstein 2011; Goldfrank 2000). The absence of a single political center also has strengthened the modern world-system making continual economic expansion within the system possible. Moreover, as the capitalist economic mode functions within the expanse larger than that which any single political authority is capable of governing fully, the system has ensured the unequal distribution of economic dividends within the world-economy. Therefore, in its continuous process of growth, the capitalist world-economy tends toward expanding economic and social disparity among its numerous areas.

Notwithstanding that it contains many nation-states and cultures, the modern world-system consists a single division of labor within one world market (Wallerstein 2011). The international division of labor is divided among functionally established and geographically distinguishable parts arranged in a hierarchy of occupational tasks. What this means in actuality is that the tasks requiring higher levels of skills and greater financing are kept secured for higher-ranking areas. Consequently, the division of labor not only enhances the capability of certain groups within the world-system to exploit the labor of the rest, but also legitimizes such exploits.

In keeping with the role they play within the world-system's international division of labor, Wallerstein sorts the nation-states into several categories. Accordingly, the **core** is constituted by the most powerful states which are capable of focusing on higher-skill and capital-intensive production, appropriating much of the world-economy's surplus, and maintaining a strong military. The core states are meant to serve the interests of the economically powerful classes, assist to maintain the peripheral states' dependence on the core, and suck in any economic losses that the system must endure occasionally.

The **semiperiphery** has stronger states with diverse economies, and their dependence on the core is minimal. A crucial buffer between the core and the periphery, these states are to fend off the real and potential resistance primarily coming from the peripheral groups, thwart unified opposition, and assist the core as a moderator to keep the system's hierarchical structure intact.

Finally, the **periphery** is consisted of the states which are militarily weak and economically dominated by the capitalist core. Located in the regions historically dominated by powerful wealthy nations as colonial rulers, these peripheral states are only capable of focusing on low-skill, labor-intensive production and raw material exportation. Not necessarily isolated from one another geographically, the features of the core and the periphery may coexist, Wallerstein contends. The existence of wealthy collaborators with the core within the world's poor peripheral regions, and the presence of impoverished ghettos in the core's opulent city neighborhoods or the rural countryside are conspicuous examples to the point.

© vichie81/Shutterstock.com

© Oleksly Mark/Shutterstock.com

© Sylvie Corriveau/Shutterstock.com

As Wallerstein sees it, among other reasons, two salient factors tend to serve as an "ideological mask" (Wallerstein 2011) in camouflaging the economic and social disparity generated by the capitalist world-economy. One of them is the building of powerful state machinery and its embedment with national culture in core states. As a result, the people in affluent nation-states incline to believe that socioeconomic polarization is gratifying and justifiable. The other factor which is likely to mask the ever-widening socioeconomic gap is the technological advances that the world-economy's process of growth brings forth while precipitating certain changes in semiperipheral and peripheral areas.

According to Wallerstein's analysis, specific regional actors may change their structural role in the world-economy as such switchovers become advantageous to them. For instance, the peripheral region of one century may become the semiperipheral region or the core area of the next century. In the same vein, the core states can fall into the semiperiphery as well. At random, a specific state may assume the role of the hegemon or the dominant leader and begin to lead other states by means of technology and wealth. However, Wallerstein insists, as the modern world-system is a capitalist world-economy in which states are under necessity to compete with each other, no single state could dominate the system. For example, during the first centuries of the modern world-system's growth, Northwestern Europe comprised the core, the Mediterranean region the semiperiphery, and Eastern Europe, Western hemisphere, as well as the Asian region the periphery (Wallerstein [1974] 2011). In the mid-seventeenth century, the Netherlands was a hegemon, but in the mid-nineteenth century the hegemonic power of the United Kingdom was clearly evident. By the mid-twentieth century, the advanced industrial states still constituted the core. However, the core shifted dominance once again, this time from wealthy European states to the United States. Furthermore, the long-independent, non-Western countries came to be known for their role in the semiperiphery and many impoverished, recently independent colonies constituted the periphery. The shift in dominance from one power to another, according to Wallerstein, is a result of several intertwining factors, including gains in productivity, monopolistic fragility, and success in war.

According to Wallerstein, the world-system reached its geographic terminal point in regard to the global expansion of capitalist markets and the state system in the twentieth century. The core dominance remains unshaken on the face of antisystemic resistance from communist regimes and postcolonial states throughout this time, but it was toward the end of 1960s the economic and political power of the world-system began to decline. Wallerstein believes that the modern world-system is in its last legs, and experiencing what he calls "crises of contraction" which, unlike in previous crises that the system had experienced and recovered from, cannot be resolved by exploring new markets. As a historical consideration, the capitalist world-economy is destined to be antiquated (Wallerstein 1998).

## Eric Wolf's Critique of the "Atomization of the World"

The impact of the world-system analysis on anthropology has been considerable. American anthropologist Eric Wolf (1923–1999), an early adherent to the world-system analysis, made an important critique of anthropological practice and offered some insights for the directions cultural anthropologists ought to take. Writing in 1982 in his most well-known work entitled

*Europe and the People without History,* Wolf singled out Andre Gunder Frank and Immanuel Wallerstein from the rest of the contemporary social scientists to commend them for paying attention to the "capitalist world-system and the arrangements of its parts" (Wolf 1982, 22–23). However, according to Wolf, in their intense focus on the macro processes at work in mercantile and capitalist development, both Frank and Wallerstein have not given enough space in their analyses to the effects of the above processes on the micropopulations, the sorts of topics traditionally studied by anthropologists and ethnohistorians (Wolf 1982, 23). Wolf harshly criticized the academic practitioners of social sciences for turning a blind eye on the reality that the world of humankind is a "totality of interconnected processes." In his view, the practice of treating nations, societies, and cultures as internally homogenized and externally bounded entities, or what he characterized to be the "atomization of the world," has turned social sciences into nothing but an antidote for sociopolitical change. As the quest for pristine and primitive cultures frozen in time is remaining as a main paradigm for ethnographic pursuits, cultural anthropology is equally culpable in this regard, Wolf argued.

In his own historical ethnography, Wolf took a path leaning toward the systematic narrative of modern history provided by Wallerstein and the likes while probing into local situations and life ways of local populace. In doing so, he tried to show that the European peasantry were not an obscure group "without history," supposedly living for centuries in isolation, but people who were maintaining contact and connections with the outside world as an active participants of producing regional and microgeographic social histories.

The critiques and insights by the likes of Eric Wolf have not gone unnoticed. Today, cultural anthropologists of all sorts are receptive to the fact that global interconnections are undeniably present in any culture on which they conduct ethnographic research. However, their approaches to study such relationships tend to be varied greatly. For instance, some cultural anthropologists prefer to carry out their ethnographic fieldwork on a group of inhabitants in a specific locality while concentrating on how and to what extent global processes and institutions affect the life ways of that local population. Some cultural anthropologists primarily focus on the predicaments of certain populations as global politicoeconomic forces and processes make them uproot from their native lands and life ways, and force to reorient elsewhere as workers, refugees, and immigrants. Keen to capture the dynamics of such human movements and the realities they generate, some ethnographers follow the moving groups, displaced populations, and their new settlement sites across cities, nation-states, and continents. Anthropologist George Marcus considers the shift from single-site probing of local situations and peoples to multisited ethnography as an emergent "methodological trend" in anthropological research (Marcus 1995, 95–117). In his view, multiple-sites based fieldwork is capable of traversing the "local"/the "global" polarity, and capturing interconnections and sociocultural landscapes that single-site based ethnographic inquiry would have glossed over in the past. As Marcus notes, when tracing a cultural construction across and within multiple field sites, the ethnographer has to go after the people, the conflicts, and the objects, including those objects which may be traced within the realm of discourse or mode of thought such as metaphors, plots, stories, and allegories. Transcendence from the "three supposedly distinct arenas" of society/ economy/politics and the acknowledgment that these categories are indeed interconnected

(Wallerstein 2011; Wolf 1982), are adhered to by many contemporary cultural anthropologists. Accordingly, historical ethnographic studies on the dynamics of international political economy are continuously carried out as well.

## Chapter Summary

The chapter examines the growth of the modern world order over the course of last five centuries. It investigates into the motives for European expansion and the methods used to accomplish it, exploring its impact on native populations around the world from the sixteenth through the eighteenth centuries. The chapter proceeds to delve into colonialism of the nineteenth and the early twentieth centuries, the decolonization process in the aftermath of the Second World War, and the predicaments borne of neocolonialism. The chapter also critically examines the critiques of modern world order, primarily focusing on the theoretical positions of the dependency theorists and the subscriptions to the world-system analysis.

- The relationships that constructed the conditions for an entirely mingled global economy and the simultaneous sociocultural changes by the latter half of the twentieth century were initially established by the European colonial powers some 500 years ago. The hunger for amassing wealth by controlling external resources and trade was the primary motive for the European expansion.

- The European colonial powers seized large tracts of land from the indigenous people to gain possession of metals and minerals and to convert native lands to large-scale farms for cash cropping. To supply uncompensated and forced labor for the above tasks, they relied heavily on transatlantic slave trade. The most reliable sources of funding (required for exploration of foreign territories and subsequent colonization), and the most committed ally for profit making they found in joint-stock companies.

- Globalization is neither a novel phenomenon, nor a process that vindicates glorification, assert the dependency theorists. While relying heavily on the Marxist critique of capitalist colonialism, the dependency theorists were focusing on critiquing the growth of the modern world-system. They contend that globalization keeps the asymmetrical relationship between the wealthy and the impoverished nations alive by serving the needs of the former at the expense of the latter. According to the core assertions of the dependency theorists, dependency is structurally interrelated, capitalist, and exploitative process, which is also known for its deep historical roots. Andre-Gunder-Frank, one of the early proponents of the dependency theory, contended that the capitalist world-system is organized as a series of metropolis-satellite relations within which economic surplus flows to the metropolis continuously. According to Frank, the dominant-dependent relationship between the metropolis (core) and the satellite (periphery) contributes directly to the development of underdevelopment in the satellite. As Frank and the other dependency theorists saw it, the perpetual dependency is ensured through the collaboration between the dominant states and the elites in the dependent states because the former's involvement coincides with the class interests of the latter.

- The dependency theory is critiqued mostly for its inadequate attention to the following areas: the multiple ways with which the core states exert dominant influence on the peripheral states, cultural dimensions of dominance, and the complex internal character of the peripheral societies.

- The world-system analysis, the successor to the dependency theory, is based on the analytic framework of the Marxist tradition and the structural functionalist approach.

- The ideas of the French historian Fernand Braudel are attributable to the world-system analysis. Historical inquiry, insisted Braudel, ought to zoom in on the long-term structures and the cyclical processes or conjunctures, not on ephemeral, surface events. He also characterized the economic life of capitalist society as a hierarchical one, in which the following three echelons are the most salient: material foundations, economic functioning, and the capitalist monopolies and constraints.

- Sociologist Immanuel Wallerstein, a leading contributor to the world-system analysis, holds that globalization is a form of discourse promoted by powerful groups to highlight old features of the capitalist world-economy with an optimistic gloss. According to him, amid the ideological celebration of globalization, the modern world-system is experiencing a terminal structural crisis currently. Applying the structural functionalist frame of reference innovatively, and constraining on two of the core conflicts of the capitalist world order, namely, the bourgeoisie versus the proletariat, and the core and the periphery, Wallerstein describes the modern world-system as a broad economic entity, uncircumscribed by political and cultural boundaries. The system has a single division of labor, which is divided among functionally established and geographically distinguishable hierarchy of occupational tasks. In keeping with the role they play within the system's international division of labor, Wallerstein classifies the world's nation-states into three categories: the core, the semiperiphery, and the periphery. As he sees it, the economic and social disparity generated by the capitalist world-economy is camouflaged through the embedment of state machinery with national culture in core states, as well as through the technological advances that precipitate certain changes in semiperipheral and peripheral areas.

- Anthropologist Eric Wolf criticized the academic practitioners of social sciences for treating societies, cultures, and nations, as internally homogenized and distinct entities. Although their approaches to global interconnections tend to be varying, the presence of such interconnections in every culture that they study is broadly accepted by cultural anthropologists today.

## CHAPTER 13

# Globalization: Making Sense of the Culture of Capitalism

© Annnna_11/Shutterstock.com

The intensified interaction and increased movement of natural resources, trade goods, human labor, information, technology, and finance capital within and across national borders of the globe, as well as the simultaneous proliferation of global organizations and institutions that structure such processes have come to be known as **globalization.**

## Cultural Dimensions of Globalization

As mentioned in Chapter 3, anthropological and other scholarly analyses on the complex processes that lead to cultural globalization derive roughly from two theoretical approaches—one lays stress on homogeneity while the other on its opposite, heterogeneity. Despite the apparent polarity, both of these approaches are based on the premise that culture, in its various forms, has become a salient agent of globalization. "The central problem of today's global interaction," argues anthropologist Arjun Appadurai, "is the tension between cultural homogenization and heterogenization" (Appadurai 1996).

## Cultural Homogenization

**Cultural homogenization** is seen as the transnational expansion of a rich array of common cultural codes and practices that causes an overwhelming uniformity and erasure of cultural diversity. As the forces of globalization—above all, mass migration and time–space compression—make traditional boundaries increasingly irrelevant, cultural homogenization is regarded as a process, by which indigenous cultures are either absorbed or altered by a dominant alien culture. In the context of the dominant role played by Europe and North America in spreading colonialism and capitalism in recent centuries (See Chapter 12), cultural homogenization is customarily used to acknowledge cultural domination of *the West* over the rest of the world. The terms such as *Americanization* and *Westernization* have come into being within the aforementioned discursive terrain. Cultural domination is especially evident in the areas such as popular culture, food and cuisine, entrepreneurial practices, political fabric, civic engagement, and technology.

© Alla-Berlezova/Shutterstock.com

# Cosmopolitanism

The most upbeat assessments of cultural homogenization often prefer to discuss globalization with reference to cosmopolitanism. At its most basic, **cosmopolitanism** refers to the frame of mind with which one may be able to synthesize both universality and cultural difference (Appiah 1998). Derived from the Greek conjunction of "world" (*cosmos*) and "city" (*polis*), a cosmopolite or cosmopolitan (an individual who adheres to the idea of cosmopolitanism) is meant to be the one who is free from local, regional, national, or any other particularistic attachments—a "citizen of the world." A cosmopolitan is capable of reaching out "across cultural differences through dialogue, aesthetic enjoyment, and respect; of living together with difference" (Werbner 2008, 2).

As globalization embraces the cross-cultural spread of people, money, technology, mass media, and ideas, cosmopolitanism has increasingly become relevant in debates and discussion of globalization. According to the scholars who argue for its relevance in this day and age, cosmopolitanism offers a unique perspective capable of analyzing the themes of globalization meaningfully than the viewpoints offered by most other notions, such as civil society, globalism, transnationalism, hybridity, cultural pluralism, and diaspora. They find cosmopolitanism to be a salient perspective on matters of social policy as it proposes a useful dialogue between community membership and the loyalty to tradition, while also acknowledging the power of individual agency in charting individuals' own destinies. Moreover, the cosmopolitan scholars contend, cosmopolitanism is a theme through which the seemingly daunting task of bringing together a host of conceptually, methodologically, and empirically diverse points of views could be accomplished.

The emergence of a host of anthropological researches stressing the need for a new cosmopolitan anthropology was observable in recent years. The most of such researches have referred to an innate affinity existing between cosmopolitanism and anthropology. Cosmopolitanism focuses on microcosmic individual life with the aim of drawing attention to its inexorable association with universal human life. This theme, new cosmopolitan anthropologists observe, unmistakably corresponds with anthropological holism, which is seeking to explore connections and interdependencies between individual life, cultural beliefs and practices, structure of society, and natural environment in the broadest possible way. Moreover, anthropology's keenness to study social and cultural relations in global perspective aptly connects with the cosmopolitan ideal of pursuing the unyielding linkage between what is considered to be the local and its counterpart, the global.

Indeed, both cosmopolitanism and anthropology have derived their origin from Enlightenment Thought, a complex movement of intellectual and cultural forces in the eighteenth-century Western Europe, which emphasized human reason and innovation, rather than tradition and authority. The above concepts were introduced as modern projects by the Enlightenment thinker Immanuel Kant (1724–1804) by emphasizing the symbiotic relationship between anthropology, a science focusing on human similarity and variety, and cosmopolitanism, an endeavor of perceiving humanity through every day diversity and global historical community (2006 [1798]). According to new cosmopolitan anthropologists, identifying cosmopolitanism within an anthropology agenda, in which humanity may be seen over and above the identity markers of proximity (such as nation, ethnicity, gender, class, and locale), might be appreciated as a thoughtful step for returning to anthropology's Enlightenment origin.

Writing in 1994, anthropologist Adam Kuper argued for a place of cosmopolitanism within anthropology based on collectivity, discourse, comparison, and intellectual engagement (Kuper 1994). According to most such researches, in the era of globalized modernity, multiple cosmopolitan practices (with specific histories and world views of their own) coexist, and that makes concentration on vernacular (Bhabha 1996) and working class forms of cosmopolitanism (Werbner 1999) justifiable. Accordingly, Ulf Hannerz distinguishes cosmopolites or those who are "willing to engage with the other" (Hannerz 1992, 239) aesthetically from locals or the "representatives of more circumscribed territorial cultures" (Hannerz 1992, 252). Deviating from the conventional usage of the term, in which cosmopolites have been referred to as the urban elites and the professionals who travel widely and interact comfortably with culturally diverse people, Hannerz also acknowledges the increasing presence of nonelite cosmopolites in the globalized world (Hannerz 2004, 77). Similarly, Lila Abu-Lughod describes a nonelite form of cosmopolitanism that she has observed during her ethnographic fieldwork in Egypt. She investigates the salient role being played by television dramas in crafting the identity of the new Egyptian citizen. This is done so, contends Abu-Lughod, by nudging the rural poor to move beyond the parochial bounds of local culture within the context of globalization. Although the poverty limitations inevitably bar many rural Egyptians from fully participating in global consumer culture, they are undoubtedly touched by the features of cosmopolitanism (Abu-Lughod 2005).

Meanwhile, disputing the view that cosmopolites are essentially the members of elite, the cultural studies and globalization scholar James Clifford questions the grounds for treating migrant workers, tour guides, assistants, carriers, translators, companion-servants, and the likes as equals to privileged travelers in terms of the power they possess. Taking a somewhat different tack from others who promote the notion of a vernacular and working class forms of cosmopolitanism, Clifford argues for a project of comparing and translating a variety of traveling cultures without basing on the criteria such as class or ethnicity. Accordingly, he characterizes today's cosmopolitanism as plural and "discrepant" (Clifford 1992).

Not all global travelers, including many members of diverse diaspora communities existing around the globe are cosmopolites, although they may be heterogeneous (Werbner 1999). Indeed, as anthropologist Aihwa Ong's account of affluent Chinese elites who engage in overseas trading while holding multiple passports and multiple homes in Asia and North America strongly suggests, many such Chinese cosmopolites do not seem to be attuned to cultural openness and empathy generally attributed to cosmopolitanism (discussed later).

Despite the recent research of the sorts which have been promoting the alternative cosmopolitanism of the nonelites, admitting anthropology to a cosmopolitan constitution has not been resolved fully.

As anthropologist-cum-historian George Stocking pointed out a while ago, throughout its history, anthropology has been swinging uncertainly between two conflicting ideals: the universalism rendered by *anthropos* and the diversitarianism (the notion that grants priority to variety or diversity) delivered by *ethnos* (Stocking 1992). According to the critics, the traditional loyalty of anthropological practice for localized identities seems to be running counter to the universalistic ideals of expanding horizons through reaching out across cultural differences globally. Anthropologists' current effort of constructing a space for cosmopolitan ideals within anthropological discourse, as well as cosmopolitan advocates' espousal of universal human rights, global justice, and world citizenship have come under scrutiny as well. Accordingly, above efforts do not acknowledge Western imperialist societies' key role in generating cosmopolitan scholarship, as well as anthropological knowledge and practice. Nor do they display a genuine interest of moving beyond a language of comparative world cultures or utopian cosmopolitanism. To the contrary, anthropologists and cosmopolitan advocates are merely engaged in a project of legitimizing "the dominance of the West over the rest" (Werbner 2008).

The critiques of the sort are reminiscent of the scathing remarks on Orientalist scholarship made by literary theorist Edward Said some time ago. In Said's view, the patronizing attitudes and fictitious portrayals of "the East" or the Orient (the peoples and cultures in the Middle East, Africa, and Asia) were inextricably linked to the Western imperialist societies that produced them (Said 1978). In anthropology *per se,* the internal critique of the discipline's colonial upbringing began in the 1970s (Asad 1973). It gathered further momentum with the intellectual trends of interpretive anthropology and postmodernism in the 1980s (Clifford and Marcus 1986; Clifford 1988). Contemporary anthropology's central problem, indicated George Marcus and Michael Fischer, was "representing social reality in a rapidly changing world." The authors proposed to adopt a more politically and historically sensitive approach as a way of dealing with the aforementioned crisis of representation in anthropology. Therefore, anthropology ought to be a *cultural critique* (Marcus and Fischer 1986, vii–xii).

Today, even this argument seems largely outdated as the contributors to the "writing against culture" trend of critical anthropology (See Chapter 4) charge that the historically constructed and maintained distinction between the Western self and the non-Western other firmly rests on the concept of culture (Abu-Lughod 1991; Gupta and Ferguson 1997; Ariyaratne 2012).

## Cultural Imperialism

The tendency toward Western cultural homogeneity is sometimes seen favorably under the rationale that benefits of homogenization may exceed the worth of cultural diversity (Tomlinson 1991). For some conservative commentators, Western cultural homogenization is an irrefutably beneficial and inevitable process that everyone has to be reckoned with—it is the only game in town.

However, for some others, such as the left-leaning scholars of media studies, it is a clear testimony to the presence of **cultural imperialism,** cultural domination exerted on the rest of the world by the core countries like the United States and other affluent Western nations through mass-produced food, brand name merchandise, and mass media, with a specifically forceful imposition on peripheral countries—it is essentially a one way street (Schiller 1976; Mattelart 1983, 1991).

According to the arguments for the notion of cultural imperialism, the affluent Western countries possess the economic means and the structural capability to make the people in economically less prominent countries feel overwhelmed with intense commodification and mediatization. Accordingly, societies in weaker countries are forced to surrender their own cultural distinctiveness. The scholarly analyses which rendered the above viewpoint began to appear from the 1960s onward.

For example, in an early Marxist critique of globally spreading cultural forms of American consumer capitalism, the impact of comic books featuring the Walt Disney Duck cartoon characters, such as Donald Duck and Scrooge McDuck were scrutinized. In this analysis, the Duck comic books are branded as manifestations of imperialist ideology while also characterizing them as mirror images of American corporate exploitation in Latin American countries (Dorfman and Mattelart 1991 [1971]). According to such analyses made for the cultural imperialism argument, cultural homogenization is not an innocent process through which various cultures keep exchanging cultural components concurrently (Hamelink 1983; Mattelart 2000, 2010). Rather, it is a process, in which Western exertion of cultural dominance on non-Western cultures around the globe transpires without any notable reciprocation.

© David Herraez Calzada/Shutterstock.com

Anthropologists have critiqued the notion of cultural imperialism citing several reasons: For one, it is based on a simplified understanding of culture change; it patronizingly assumes that non-Western cultures are on the brink of losing their authenticity due to the onslaught of inauthentic and synthetic cultural forces of the West. The above assumption presupposes that cultures may retain their originality intact as long as they remain without outside contact. Anthropologists know that such pristine cultures do not exist in the world, and most likely, had never existed in the past either. "Authenticity," at least in its popular sense, becomes a problematical concept in the context of culture, as it is based on the erroneous view that cultures from the past were monolithic, bounded, unchanging, and hence, "authentic."

© maxwindy/Shutterstock.com

Moreover, the idea of cultural imperialism does not seem heeding to the fact that, in various occasions, cultural forms circumvent the West in their movement from one part of the non-Western world to another. The favorable reception India's Bollywood movies have been getting from audiences in the Caribbean, the Middle East, and sub-Saharan Africa is a fine example to the point. The popularity of Latin American telenovela (a type of limited-run serial drama) and Japanese anime (a cartoon television series or movies) among non-Western TV and movie fans are among similarly top-notch examples.

© Pixel-Shot/Shutterstock.com

Instances of the above sort indicate that the notion of cultural imperialism effectively denies agency to the people in non-Western societies by treating them as passive recipients of Western cultural forms.

Similarly, by overemphasizing the salience of external determinants (cultural forces coming from various Western metropolises), the notion of cultural imperialism is underrating the internal dynamics within local cultures (Inda and Rosaldo 2002, 22–24).

The studies of globalization focusing on themes such as the growth of the new means of consumption and McDonaldization (succinctly discussed below) came into being within the theoretical approach of cultural homogenization.

## The New Means of Consumption

In recent years, some scholarly analyses on how the rapidly globalizing world functions have begun to focus on the rise of the new means of consumption. According to them, the **new means of consumption** are highly rationalized new innovations, such as fast-food franchises, shopping malls, megamalls, cybermalls, superstores, discounters, cruise lines, Las Vegas-styled casino hotels, Disney-type theme parks, that have come into existence in the second half of the twentieth century and have been continuously booming ever since. The Marxian emphasis on production still remains relevant, yet the calls for shifting focus from the means of production to the means of consumption have increasingly gotten louder as well (Zukin 1991; Ritzer 1999).

Although he had discussed consumption at length, notably in his work on commodities, Marx focused mainly on production (Marx 1991 [1884], 471). However, several recent analyses have attempted to highlight the importance in distinguishing consumer goods from the means of consumption (such as shopping malls and cruise ships). According to them, this was an area of capitalism that had escaped Marx's otherwise unparalleled scrutiny, perhaps owing to the fact that culture of consumerism was not even a fledgling phenomenon during his time. The aforementioned analyses have tried to shed light on this area and show the "parallel in the realm of consumption to the mediating and expediting role played by the means of production" (Goodman and Ritzer 2004, 555; Baudrillard 1998 [1970]).

## George Ritzer's Model of Fast-food Restaurant: "McDonaldization"

One of the most well-known among the current theories of globalization that focuses on the new means of consumption and stresses cultural homogenization is the McDonaldization thesis by sociologist George Ritzer (2000). **McDonaldization** is the global spread of Western consumerism through a variety of U.S. dominated channels of corporate culture and the resultant increasing rationalization of everyday routine tasks. For Ritzer, the fast-food restaurant embodies this mode of rationalization. According to him, many of the fundamental elements with which fast-food chains were constructed stemmed from the modern system of speedy mass production known as **Fordism,** introduced to North America by Henry Ford chiefly through the creation of automobile assembly line.

McDonaldization retains Fordism's emblematic features: homogenization of production process, products, labor, and consumption. Consequently, McDonaldized systems also share several related characteristics associated with Fordism, such as deskilling or making the workers' skills obsolescent, managing workflows through adoption of standardized work routines (Taylorism), and the use of inflexible technologies.

In Ritzer's view, Fordism has been transmogrified into McDonaldization. Ritzer identifies four key dimensions of McDonaldization—efficiency, calculability, predictability, and control.

*Efficiency* refers to the pursuit for the optimum means to the end. In McDonaldized systems, following the steps in a predesignated process is required as it is meant for keeping workers as well as customers functionally effective. The introduction of the drive-through window in fast-food franchises is a fine example in this regard. The shopping mall where all shops are found literally in one location is another instance. In the shopping mall, the workers become a part of a highly efficient selling machine while the consumers assume the form of merchandise purchasers.

*Calculability* is laying stress on the quantitative aspects of the products sold (such as the portion, the size, and the cost) and the service offered (such as the time spared to get the product to the customer). It is highly appropriate for McDonaldized systems to disregard quality in favor of quantity. For example, in fast-food restaurants, customers are led to believe that they can buy large quantities of fast (and fresh) food, for incredibly low prices.

© Everett Collection/Shutterstock.com

Similarly, in discount department stores like Walmart, quantifiable features of low price, large quantity, and wide variety are emphasized to attract customers.

*Predictability* is offering predictable and uniformed products by the workers who behave in predictable ways in McDonaldized systems. For instance, in fast-food chains, the store design and ambience, the menu, the taste of the food, and even the decorum of the servers are nearly identical. In like manner, upscale store chains bring forth uniformed and predictable high design to the mass market.

*Control* is controlling workers and customers through programmed methods in McDonaldized systems. For example, in fast-food restaurants, workers are kept in check through detailed directions, speed, as well as assembly-line methods of food preparation and serving; customers are also restrained through programmed methods such as drive-through windows, lines, limited menus, and impersonal service. Relatedly, in shopping malls, customer behavior is kept under control by technologically controlling temperature, lighting, merchandise, and events within the mall space. In order to manage the emotions of customers, shopping malls are transformed into windowless, timeless (clocks are not often displayed), brightly lit, uniformed, sprightly, and cheerful spaces. In such spaces, even

© Yaoinlove/Shutterstock.com

© Fachral/Shutterstock.com

greater control is exerted on workers, so they are metamorphosed into "mall prisoners" (Ritzer and Goodman 2004, 557).

As Ritzer sees it, the phenomenal growth of McDonaldization (Barber 1996) has been spawning global homogeneity while drenching local distinctiveness with an overwhelming uniformity.

Ritzer's thesis of local cultural erosion due to the global flow of Western consumer cultural forms is thrown into question by some studies stem from anthropological and other perspectives. For example, John Fiske, a scholar of communication studies, points out the salience of focusing on a multitude of meanings existing beneath the surface of various cultural artifacts, such as shopping malls, pop music, and forms of mass media. Fiske also refers to people's creative, and even subversive,

© Settawar Udom/Shutterstock.com

ways of reading these "cultural texts," while discrediting the notion that people mindlessly consume every product offered to them by global consumer capitalism (Fiske 2011).

A volume of ethnographic essays on McDonald's restaurants in diverse Asian settings, such as Tokyo, Taipei, Hong Kong, Seoul, and Beijing take a similar approach (Watson 1997). According to the scholars who contribute to this volume, McDonald's (along with Coca-Cola or Pepsi, Microsoft, Nike, and similar products of Western capitalist consumer culture) has a notable presence in Asia. What attracts anthropological attention the most however, is how McDonald's has been forced to localize its products, service philosophy, and marketing strategies in its effort to reach local consumers in Asian societies.

For instance, by accommodating local preference on slow-paced dining out experience in a leisurely atmosphere of family gathering, McDonald's has sidelined its emblematic *fast-food* philosophy, which is equivalent to nothing less than *eat quickly and leave*. Accordingly, McDonald's restaurant managers in many Asian settings, modify the usual pace of service to let on for a slower turnover of tables. In the same vein, McDonald's provides separate areas of dining for single men, and delivers its products to single women who cannot enter a McDonald's restaurant as such acts go against local custom in Saudi Arabia. McDonald's has localized its products to suit local taste and food preferences as well; for example, in India, it serves Indianized version of pizza—*paneer salsa* and *chicken tikka,* as well as chili and garlic sauce with veggie burgers. McDonald's assimilation into various Asian societies

© Radu Bercan/Shutterstock.com

offers a compelling portrayal of how local cultures indigenize global cultural forms through accommodation, compromise, and change (Watson 1997).

# Cultural Heterogeneity

Anthropological studies of the aforementioned sort are not merely casting a critical eye on the notion that the global dissemination of Western cultural forms is threatening the existence of local cultures, if not delivering a deathblow. They are also highlighting the instances, in which global and local cultural forms exist side-by-side, actively compromise (in order to serve local objectives), and intermingle with each other producing a distinctive blend. This complex process of cross-cultural interaction, generally known as **cultural heterogeneity,** is articulated by some anthropologists through the concepts such as indigenization (Appadurai 1996), cultural hybridization (Pieterse 1995), and creolization (Hannerz 1992). By employing the above concepts, they have been attempting to offer a more nuanced analysis of globalizing processes and flows than what is brought to bear on the side of the homogenization argument.

## Indigenization

As shown in previously mentioned study of McDonald's ascendency in Asia (Watson 1997), the borrowing of cultural forms by a particular culture frequently involves adoption of

© BojBos/Shutterstock.com

© Danny Ye/Shutterstock.com

what is borrowed to suit local purposes. In the process of modification to be in harmony with local culture, cultural forms tend to become indigenized (or as some scholars prefer to characterize, *customized* or *domesticated*). Therefore, **indigenization** is the modified borrowing of cultural forms that is in harmony with local culture. Such indigenized cultural forms could be found in spheres as diverse as art, architecture, science, terrorism, spectacles, and constitutions (Appadurai 1996).

Anthropological literature is dense with ethnographic examples of indigenization. The Japanese practice of indigenizing the foreign without changing its cultural core is one such fine example. Japan has been borrowing various forms and practices from Western consumer culture, but Japan's localization strategy has repackaged them with Japanese flavor for local (and, by extension, Asian) consumption (Yoshimoto 1989; Iwabuchi 2002).

The portrayal of the Virgin of Guadalupe or Our Lady of Guadalupe in Mexico is another case in point. The syncretism of the Virgin Mary, mother of Jesus, with the indigenous Aztec goddess Tonantzin occurred as a part of a strategy employed by the members of Christian clergy who were keen of proselytizing Indians, so the Brown Virgin miraculously appeared in 1531 in Guadalupe, Mexico. Today, the Virgin of Guadalupe has become a powerful symbol of the imagined community of Mexican nation across national boundaries of the United States and Mexico. This is vividly illustrated in the annual pilgrimage of carrying a lit torch and a portrait of the Virgin from Mexico City to New York by Mexican Catholic devotees. In this long and arduous journey, they walk across the vast United States–Mexico border, pass through the neighborhoods of large Mexican immigrant communities in the Southeastern United States, and finally reach New York City to join thousands of Mexican Catholic immigrants who walk in procession to St. Patrick's Cathedral in Fifth Avenue for the annual celebration of the Feast Day of Our Lady of Guadalupe. It has truly become an event that blends religious devotion and the struggle for citizenship rights among Mexican immigrants (Galvez 2009). Succinctly put, Mexican Catholics have indigenized a feature they borrowed from Roman Catholicism, (which is, the worship of Virgin Mary) to fit local culture and purposes.

## Cultural Hybridization

When the elements of global and local cultural forms fuse or synthesize while producing new cultural forms, it is referred to as **cultural hybridization** or *hybridity*. According to globalization theorist Jan Nederveen Pieterse, seeing globalization as the world becoming uniformed and standardized due to cultural synchronization originating from the West is a narrow assessment in that it is critical in intent. In like manner, viewing globalization as a culminating phase of modernity is equally incapacious as it is an ambiguous assessment at best. Both of these interpretations are variations of the notion that connects globalization with Westernization. In Pieterse's view, globalization is a process of hybridization, which gives rise to a global mélange. For Pieterse and other social scientists that use the concept of hybridity, it is a useful interpretative device, with which cultural dimensions of globalization can be better understood (Pieterse 1995, 2003; Canclini 1995).

## Creolization

Swedish anthropologist Ulf Hannerz introduces the term creolization, which he adopted from the linguistic analogy of creole languages (See Chapter 5) in order to give broader social and cultural insights into the speedy, extensive, and global flow of people, capital, information, and cultural objects. He believes that the biological metaphor of hybridization/hybridity used by many social scientists is insufficient for appreciating the constant activity of contact and transformation evident in the process of cultural encounter and intermingling, which is what **creolization** actually is (Hannerz 1987, 1992). A creole is a full-fledged and stable language "that evolved out of the contact of diametrically distinct linguistic elements" of European and non-European languages in the Caribbean, American South, and elsewhere in the world (Glissant 1989). Much the same way, a creole culture comes out of the mixing of cultural elements in two or more highly unalike cultures in new and innovative manners. The sort of cultural mixture a creole culture brings forth, argues Hannerz, is not necessarily atypical, of lesser quality and coherence, or lacking worth, as hybridity metaphors often seem to suggest. Mindful of the deep-seated link between the concepts concerning mutual permeation of cultural spheres and power relations, Hannerz acknowledges that the core components of creole culture, such as a coalescence of diversity, interconnectedness, and innovation, have to be discussed "in the context of center-periphery relations" (Hannerz 1992). The point is particularly relevant to the notion of creolization as creole cultures arose in the historical context of European colonialism in peripheral regions of the world and the use of slave labor for cash-crop production by the colonizers (See Chapter 12). Indeed, at the innermost part of creole cultures one always finds a variety of contentious encounters between oppressors and oppressed. In spite of the aforesaid recognition however, Hannerz refuses to characterize creolization through the polar opposites of exploitative center and the exploited periphery alone. Taking a different tack, Hannerz prefers to indicate the confluence of distinct historical currents within the framework of center-periphery, while highlighting the creative interplay and cultural transformation such instances of contact produce (Hannerz 1992).

The concepts such as indigenization, cultural hybridization, and creolization give prominence to cultural creativity and accomplishment while sidelining the concerns over dependency and cultural loss. They recognize the agency of the borrowers of cultural forms and take rug out from under on the notion of cultural authenticity. Overall, the above concepts labor the point that cultural intermingling is to be seen in positive light.

## The Complexity of the New Global Cultural Economy

Anthropologist Arjun Appadurai discusses the complexity of the new global cultural economy in his oft-cited work *Modernity at Large: Cultural Dimensions of Globalization* (1996). According to him, the theoretical models that appraise globalization either as homogenization or as heterogenization are incapable of capturing a certain dialectic movement existing within the process of globalization, namely the constant production and continuous dissolution of locality affected by this very same process (For dialectics, see the discussion on Dependency Theory in Chapter 12). As Appadurai sees it, the homogenization argument, ever more uniformed with the arguments about McDonaldization, Americanization, and commoditization, fails to recognize how the forces of globalization process gravitate toward indigenization as swiftly as they are brought into new societies from the various modern metropolises. Likewise, the heterogenization argument does not offer anything more than an essentialization of locality.

In the globalized world, argues Appadurai, one has to keep away from assuming that sites are fully equivalent to communities, or localities are necessarily geographical locations. Although traditionally viewed as a form of national geography secured by borders, checkpoints, transitions, and the likes, locality has now become an increasingly inconspicuous or contested phenomenon. It is a "complex phenomenological quality," which has to be understood primarily as *relational* and *contextual,* not as scalar and spatial. For example, whereas localities (and journeys to reach them) remain actual and burdensome to highly vulnerable groups such as prisoners, refugees, and asylum-seekers, for some other groups such as global financiers, scientists, arms-dealers, and drug-traffickers, geographical/national boundaries have become increasingly irrelevant. From Appadurai's perspective, sites have largely faded from being secured localities for the ordinary affairs of everyday life. In contrast, neighborhoods are to be considered as *situated communities* distinguishable through their spatial or virtual activity, as well as their potential for social reproduction. The translocal migrant communities, the new virtual neighborhoods, and the likes, are some of such instances. Neighborhoods are, therefore, the existing social forms, and in them, locality is every so often realized as a dimension or as a value.

## Arjun Appadurai's Model of Global Cultural Flows: "Landscapes"

According to Appadurai, the theories based on the traditional spatial models, even those which form the foundation of the best Marxist analyses of global capital, have largely unsuccessful in capturing the complexity of the new global cultural economy. Here, Appadurai's critique is leveled against the center–periphery models used in the analyses such as the dependency theory and the world-systems analysis. In such analyses, the association between economy, society, and subjectivity is established through the reliance on some type of spatial or territorial stability. Appadurai offers a contextual and relational alternative to the theoretical models.

A set of five **"landscapes"** or basic conditions constitutes the core of Appadurai's model of global cultural flow: ethnoscapes, technoscapes, financescapes, mediascapes, and ideoscapes (Appadurai 1996, 33). The use of the suffix "scape'" makes room for Appadurai to stress his point that the above global flows are irregular, fluid, overlapping, and perspectival constructs or disjunctive forces, and therefore, the traditional spatial models are not helpful in making sense of how these different spheres relate to each other.

By *ethnoscapes* Appadurai refers to the global circulation of persons as seen in the moving groups and individuals such as tourists, guest workers, exiles, and refugees that play an increasingly significant role in the globalized world. The landscape of mass migration obviously takes into account actual human movement, but it also involves fantasies of wanting to move (Appadurai 1996, 33) (See the reference to imagined places and actual localities in Chapter 6, discussed within the ethnographic context of urban youths in Kathmandu, Nepal).

© Cristina Conti/Shutterstock.com

By *technoscapes* Appadurai means the ever-fluid, new global technological configurations and their speedy and peculiar movement across various types of boundaries which were earlier known for their impenetrability (Appadurai 1996, 35).

The movement of global capital "through national turnstiles at blinding speed" and the involvement of "currency markets, national stock exchanges, and commodity speculations" in such processes are what Appadurai calls *financescapes* (Appadurai 1996, 34–35).

*Mediascapes* pertain to the "distribution of the electronic capabilities to produce and disseminate information (newspapers, magazines, television stations, and film-production studios," as well as to the actual dissemination of the images of the world generated by these media. Depending on the mode and hardware use to produce them, the audiences that they reach, and the interest of the people who own and control them, these images associate with many complicated inflections (Appadurai, 1996, 35).

Appadurai considers *ideoscapes* as the transfer of images which are directly political and deeply rooted in the ideologies of states and the "counter ideologies of movements explicitly oriented to capturing state power or a piece of it" (Appadurai 1996, 36).

According to Appadurai, the landscapes are the constituent parts of what he calls *imagined worlds.* He defines them as the "multiple worlds that are constituted by the historically situated imaginations of persons and groups" disseminate across the globe (Appadurai 1996, 33). Key to all forms of agency, imagination has developed into an organized field of social practice. Thus it has now emerged as the central element of the new global order.

## Disjunctures

Global flows transpire through the above landscapes, but what's more, they occur increasingly in and through the *disjunctures* among them. Appadurai insists that the global linkage among these landscapes is "deeply disjunctive and profoundly unpredictable." As each of them is susceptible to its own constraints and incentives (political, informational, and techno-environmental), each functions to curb the other global flow's mobility while also acting as a guideline for movements in the other landscape at the same time. Free flow in some landscapes may be at variance with hindrances in the others. As such, the disjunctures have ripened into the central factor in the politics of global culture (Appadurai 1996, 37). For example, the Japanese may be friendly to ideas (ideoscapes), and may be tech-savvy (technoscapes), but they are also notoriously inhospitable toward immigration (ethnoscapes). And, for that matter, they are more like the Swiss, the Swedes, and the Saudis, who accommodate migrant populations as guest workers, and thereby, create a labor diaspora of Turks, Italians, other circum-Mediterranean groups, and South Asians (Appadurai 1996, 37).

© DeGe Photos/Shutterstock.com

Within the above context, Appadurai highlights several new features which he considers as fundamental to current global cultural politics: production fetishism, the fetishism of the consumer, deterritorialization, and the role of the nation-state.

Appadurai believes that Marx's concept of the fetishism of the commodity has been supplanted by two new, mutually supportive descendants: production fetishism and the fetishism of the consumer. To recap Marx's original concept, **the fetishism of the commodity** is the consideration of products as dissociated from their production. That is to say, it inclines to reify commodities as autonomous objects by forgetting their true origin as the products of human labor. By obsessively treating them as persons, commodity fetishism attributes power and agency to things while treating people who do have agency as mere repositories of labor power for sale in the market.

## Production Fetishism

Appadurai changes the focus of the above fetishism to the act of production and the consumer.

He defines *production fetishism* as the condition in which "the locality (both in the sense of the local factory or site of production and in the extended sense of the nation-state) becomes a fetish that disguises the globally dispersed forces that actually drive the production process." The globally dispersed forces (cloaked by the locality) comprise translocal capital, transnational earning flows, global management, and faraway workers who engaged in various types of high-tech putting out operations (Appadurai 1996, 42).

© RossHelen/Shutterstock.com

## The Fetishism of the Consumer

By the *fetishism of the consumer* Appadurai means to point out that the consumer has been transformed through the flow of commodities and the accompanying mediascapes into a sign. It is a "mask for the real seat of agency, which is not the consumer but the producer and the many forces that constitute production" (Appadurai 1996, 42). He cites global advertising as a primary medium which conceals the true source of agency, in addition to prolonging that obscurity. In global advertising, contends Appadurai, the consumer is consistently led to believe in his or her seat of agency. Even so, that false sense of agency flies in the face of the consumer as he or she is no more than a commodified pawn manipulated and used by the producer and the process of production. Appadurai's point is conspicuously evident in many television commercials that the U.S. television audience is accustomed to watch. A television commercial is a representation, in which a number of selected shots are delicately blended, edited, and represented to alter consumer perception in favor of a certain product. Therefore, it is often in conflict with reality.

Take, for example, the cigarette commercials of anthropomorphic Joe Camel, an animal designed to depict human characteristics. The presence of Joe Camel in various settings ranging from the Middle-eastern deserts to Vegas-style-casino-hotels make cigarette smoking look exotic and fashionably attractive at the same time. The influence of such ads for purchase of cigarettes is echoing the consumer's affectionate response to the Joe Camel presentation, more than a conscious decision-making process on the part of the consumer. In like manner, the Nature-as-backdrop ads frequently use landscape scenery, flowers, trees, animals, and the likes in order to promote products that do not share either straight or palpable link with the features of the natural world presented (Corbett 2006). The advertisements specifically designed to target green consumers (consumers who want to buy products that are produced in a way that protect the natural environment) exploit nature by blending the artificial with the natural, and thereby, turning environment into a commodity. As advertisements such as the Coca-Cola nature commercial of 2009 vividly illustrate, the global beverage giants are among the companies at the forefront of promoting green consumerism primarily for the purpose of selling their brand of products. In the global gluttony of ideas and images of consumer agency, as Appadurai argues, the consumer believes that "he or she is an actor," but in reality, "he or she is at best a chooser" (Appadurai 1996, 42).

## Deterritorialization

Appadurai views *deterritorialization* as one of the primary forces of the globalized world as it brings various laboring populations into lower-class quarters and spaces of relatively well-to-do societies. Therefore, the politics of deterritorialization bespeaks the larger sociology of displacement. It is in the rich terrain of deterritorialization, in which finance capital, commodities, and people are engaged in an endless chasing of each other across the globe, the ideoscapes and imagescapes locate their fragmented mate. Appadurai stresses the dominant role which is being played by social imagination in the highly globalized and deterritorialized world while also disclosing how it and today's massive use of electronic media

© MITstudio/Shutterstock.com

generate *diasporic public spheres* or *translocal communities*: "As Turkish guest workers in Germany watch Turkish films in their German flats, as Koreans in Philadelphia watch the 1988 Olympic in Seoul through satellite feeds from Korea, and as Pakistani cabdrivers in Chicago listen to cassettes of sermons recorded in mosques in Pakistan or Iran, we see moving images meet deterritorialized viewers" (Appadurai 1996, 4) (See a discussion on deterritorialization in Chapter 6).

## The Weakening Role of the Nation-State

The discussion on deterritorialization particularly helps Appadurai to focus on another significant and new feature in global cultural politics: the weakening role of the nation-state. Throwing spotlight on that front, he claims that the state's ability to capture and dominate the ideas about nationhood is now seriously undermined. The ideas of nationhood have increasingly grown into a political sentiment separated from territoriality and statehood. The nation-state, which is seeking to monopolize the moral resources of community (Gramsci 1971; Corrigan and Sayer 1983; Ariyaratne 2000), finds itself dealing with translocal communities and transnational diaspora who attempt to ignite action in nation-state's own domain of micropolitics. In Appadurai's pithy characterization, now "state and nation are at each other's throat" (Appadurai, 1996, 39).

In Appadurai's view, the dwindling and uncertain role of the nation-state is directly related to the disjunctive relationships among various global flows or landscapes occurring in a way partly or fully independent from any nation-state. Around the world, states' accommodation of travel, technology, financial circulation, and mass media intensify

consumerism while also increasing the desire to consume. Consequentially, the craving for new commodities may bring in not only new ethnoscapes and mediascapes, but also ideoscapes countering state ideologies, and thereby, threatening to occupy the space of nationhood or peoplehood earlier dominated by the state. In similar fashion, as a result of the state's mediation of imagescapes, images of well-being disseminate across national boundaries. They, in turn, generate public imagination for well-being that can hardly be satisfied by national standards of living and consumer capabilities. To put succinctly Appadurai's position, as the state assumes the role of mediating global forces, it is having difficulty in saturating subjectivity of its citizens (Appadurai 1996).

## Globalization and Changing Modalities for Governance

Whereas seeing transnational patterns in the core dynamics of social, cultural, and economic life have been a subject of growing interest in social sciences, treating transnationality as necessarily detrimental to the nation-state is erroneous, contends anthropologist Aihwa Ong. In her view, previous studies on globalization that adopted the above position and prophesized the nation-state's terminal crisis (Appadurai 1996), as well as "the clash of civilizations" (Huntington 1996) in the rapidly homogenizing world, have failed to acknowledge the efficacy of individual agency in the large-scale global flow of people, images, and cultural forces.

Focusing on the life ways of the people she studied, such as population segments in Malaysia and Indonesia who are being subjected to differential treatments by the state, overseas Chinese elites navigating multiple immigration regimes in Asia and North America, and Cambodian refugees in California attempting to cope with the disciplinary regimes that socialize them, Ong points out that such transnational subjects have come to embody the fluidity of capital, as well as the straining link between national and political identities. Ong's views are mainly articulated through the themes such as graduated sovereignty, flexible citizenship, and the disciplinary regimes of citizen-subject making.

## Graduated Sovereignty

Aihwa Ong examines the shifting links between market, state, and society in the globalized world and how the state deals with such fluctuating relations by flexibly experimenting with sovereignty. She uses the model of graduated sovereignty in this context. According to Ong, **graduated sovereignty** refers to the different modalities with which the state governs segments of its own population regardless of the extent of connection such population segments maintain with the global market. In addition, the model is useful in exploring the different combinations of legal compromises and control tailored to fulfill the needs of special production zones (Ong 2006).

Ong focuses on East and Southeast Asian states such as Malaysia and Indonesia where neoliberalism (the socioeconomic approach supposedly seeking to create a *laissez-faire* atmosphere for economic growth through minimization of state intervention) itself is not among the general features of governing technologies. The admittance of the states of the above sorts into the global economy has needed strategic adoption of neoliberal features for managing populations to meet corporate demands. According to Ong, graduated sovereignty provides a frame of reference for such selective neoliberal interventions.

In Malaysia, Ong observes, the state makes different types of biopolitical investments in different sectors of population. Accordingly, the indigenous Muslim majority people known as Malays enjoy state favoritism in gaining political rights and economic benefits over the ethnic Chinese and Indians who have descended from immigrant populations. Whereas Malay elites and middle-class people are given state incentives to become competitive Muslim professionals in global capitalism, immigrant workers (who provide cheap labor for Malaysian factories) are constantly subjected to legal and social control through various forms of surveillance and methods of induced self-discipline (Ong 1987). Malaysian state justifies the privileged status of the Malay by linking adherence to Islam with allegiance to the state and treating that linkage as a rationale for national economic ascendency. In this case, the state's governmentality (Foucault 1979) based on naturalization of racial/ethnic differences and racialized/ethnicized class formation has enmeshed well with economic globalization.

Ong observes another governing modality of the state, with which certain population segments are made more competitive and productive, while marginalizing those who resist

© mysyaraafiq/Shutterstock.com

such efforts. Accordingly, Malaysian aborigines are granted special affirmative-action rights and ushered to give up aboriginal way of life to become agricultural producers, as they are a potential source in augmenting the Malay race and attracting foreign currency from tourists. However, resistant groups are evicted, and their resource-rich land areas are readily utilized for commercial purposes.

Ong finds that, in the archipelagic state of Indonesia, governance primarily takes the form of military coercion. As industrial workers are rarely protected by labor rights, systematic marginalization of a sizable part of working population is routinely carried out by this New Order regime under the pretext of strengthening the polity and the growth of national economy. According to Ong, the state policies and practices that favor the spread of Javanese people, the inhabitants of the densely populated island of Java, are meant to displace other ethnically and culturally distinct groups from their enclaves while strengthening Javanese dominance in population. Moreover, Indonesian state's favoritism for Javanese elite that controls corporations, monopolizes the food and fuel distribution, and protects agricultural products from foreign interests has been a strategic move to divert public attention from front-burner issues stemming from social divisions, such as class, ethnicity, and religion.

Ong also brings to light another significant aspect of graduated sovereignty: the flexibility shown by the above and similar states when making various legal compromises in national sovereignty to meet the requirements of the special production zones.

As Ong's examples demonstrate well, graduated sovereignty involves gradations in governing, such as managing sectors of populace through surveillance and supervisory strategies, military coercion, as well as through maintenance of areas where state's presence is nearly absent. In other words, in graduated sovereignty, populations segments are disciplined differentially, granted privileges and protections discriminatingly, and thereby, inserted into the processes of global capitalism diversely.

## Flexible Citizenship

The re-engineering of political spaces and populations as a governing technology has broad implications not only for the practices of sovereignty, but also for the form and the meaning of citizenship. In an era of globalization, neoliberal exceptions cause mutations in sovereignty, as well as in citizenship (Ong 2006). Ong maintains that, the traditional views of citizenship based on membership of political rights and participation within a nation-state have been largely replaced by the ideas representing an emerging new form of "disembedded citizenship." She identifies it as **flexible citizenship.** It is an ideology, in which one most likely to consider economic concerns as the central contributing factor in choosing citizenship, not the reasons such as political rights, engagement, or an allegiance one owes to the residing nation-state.

In identifying flexible citizenship arisen over the past few decades, Ong concentrates on new affluent and privileged Asian immigrants who choose to relocate their families and wealth to North America, while maintaining business and entrepreneurial interests in Asia (Ong 1999).

© rawf8/Shutterstock.com

## The Disciplinary Regimes of Citizen-Subjects Making

Having examined the flexible ways, with which elite Asians redefine citizenship (by shuttling across the Pacific), Aihwa Ong then explores the experiences of what she considered to be the "other Asians"—Cambodians who managed to escape the repressive Pol Pot regime in the 1970s and eventually settled in California's inner city and high-tech enclaves (Ong 2003). For the affluent Asian globetrotters, citizenship may simply be a matter of acquiring multiple passports or identifying business, educational, or other elitist opportunities in global metropolises. For these newcomers from Indochina however, it is a matter of "figuring out the rules of coping, navigating, and surviving the streets and other public spaces of the American city." In her work entitled *Buddha Is Hiding* (2003), based on ethnographic fieldwork conducted in Oakland and San Francisco, California, Ong discusses how the institutional apparatuses of health care, welfare, law, police, church, and industry participate in the American project of making the above immigrants "particular kinds of ethnic minorities, laboring subjects, and moral beings."

© Mekong Photography/Shutterstock.com

## Friction: Awkward Interconnection across Difference

Anthropologist Anna L. Tsing utilizes Arjun Appadurai's analytic framework of global landscapes as the basis to develop her discussion on today's messy global capitalism, which she metaphorically characterizes as **friction** or "the awkward, unequal, unstable aspects of interconnection across difference" (Tsing 2005, 4). She dismisses the claim that the processes of globalization homogenize the world, because "universal claims do not actually make everything everywhere the same." In making sense of the different and incompatible social interactions that make up the contemporary world, Tsing seeks to stress the validity of focusing on specific situations arising from the specialty of global connections (Tsing 2005, 1–2).

Shifting away from the focus on localities, yet concentrating on one specific "zone of awkward engagement," Tsing investigates the issues pertaining to environment and political engagement in Kalimantan, Indonesia's rain forest industry in the 1980s and the 1990s, the time when she conducted her ethnographic fieldwork there. She attempts to find answers for the questions of the following sorts: "Why is global capitalism so messy? Who speaks for nature? And, what kinds of social justice makes sense in the twenty-first century" (Tsing 2005, 2).

© Syarief_Rakh/Shutterstock.com

By way of exploring these questions, Tsing proceeds to detail how commodification of tropical rain forests in Indonesia involved a variety of internal and external forces (such as private and foreign corporate investors, and government policy makers) with divergent motives ranging from large-scale logging, international commercial interests, to nation-building. Notably, Tsing points out, the collaboration of such disparate forces was not exclusively guided by a corporate design. Rather, it came to pass through an awkward chain of legal and illegal investors, and their pursuit of generating resources for far-flung markets. The biologically diverse tropical rain forests were traditionally managed by the forest dwellers themselves. However, tropical rain forests were later transformed into biologically monotonous or "simplified" forests, usually favored by commercial loggers. As Tsing's ethnographic account vividly reveals, the above transformation was a result of the steps taken by the state such as illegalization of shifting cultivation and the creation of "wilderness" through industrial tree plantation. Moreover, the construction of such anthropogenic landscapes (landscapes created by human intervention) received state patronage in view of the fact that the state was largely banking on revenue from selling forest permits to favored political cronies. The state justified its action by linking commodification of rain forests to its hegemonic project of nation-building (Tsing 2005).

© Dimash38/Shutterstock.com

The environmental movement that arose to successfully defend the rainforests and the erosion of indigenous rights came to pass through a "forest of collaborations" as well, points out Anna Tsing. This noncentralized Indonesian movement did not exactly borrow a page from Western environmental activism. It was a movement grew out through relationships formed by unlikely groups with unalike goals such as nature preservation, student activism, financial accountability, good governance, and protection of indigenous rights.

Anna Tsing refers to Appadurai's theory of landscapes in analyzing this context. For example, by touching on Appadurai's financescape, she views the increasing capitalist interests in Indonesia during the 1980s and the 1990s as the imagined "economy of appearance," richness made apparent through sheer financial speculation and misinterpretation. Furthermore, this endeavor was fully in concert with the "global dreamscape" or the universal claim for a united Indonesia, propagated by the regime of President Suharto at the time. It was through the ideoscapes of the sorts that the knowledge pertaining to the promotion of capitalism and neoliberal economic policies were conveyed to local people. Moreover, Tsing herself contributed to spread information on the environmental movement's triumph of forest conservation over investors and commercial loggers through her travels while narrating her circuitous association with the movement. This steady flow of information or mediascape, according to Tsing, has provided an additional incentive for global nature lovers.

Anna Tsing concludes her analysis with an optimistic note on the processes that lead to globalization. "Globalization," she claims, "is not delivered whole and round like a pizza." In the grip of worldly encounter, peculiar cultural differences may be messy and unpredictable, but they may be creative and capable of producing desired effects as well. Friction makes one think that "heterogeneous and unequal encounters can lead to new arrangements of culture and power" (Tsing 2005, 5).

# Chapter Summary

This chapter concentrates on the complex processes that lead to globalization. It provides an overview of the theoretical approaches to cultural globalization that lay stress on homogeneity and heterogeneity, and takes up the complexity of the new global cultural economy recently analyzed through anthropological models such as new means of consumption, global cultural flows or landscapes, changing modalities of governance, and friction or awkward interconnection across difference.

- The heightened interaction and the stepped-up movement of natural resources, trade goods, human labor, information, technology, and finance capital within and across national borders of the world, as well as the concomitant and rapid growth of global organizations and institutions that structure such processes are referred to as globalization.

- Anthropological and other scholarly analyses on the complex processes of globalization derive roughly from two theoretical approaches—one lays stress on homogeneity while the other on its opposite, heterogeneity. Both approaches are based on the premise that culture, in its various forms, has become a salient agent of globalization.

- The transnational expansion of a vast array of common cultural codes and practices that causes an overwhelming uniformity and erasure of cultural diversity is considered as cultural homogenization.

- The new means of consumption are exceedingly rationalized and new innovations, such as fast-food franchises, shopping malls, megamalls, cybermalls, superstores, discounters, cruise lines, Las Vegas-styled casino hotels, Disney-type theme parks. They have come into existence in the second half of the twentieth century and have been continuously booming ever since.

- As sociologist George Ritzer sees it, McDonaldization is the global dissemination of Western consumerism through diverse U.S.-dominated channels of corporate culture and the increasing rationalization of everyday routine tasks concomitantly. For Ritzer, the fast-food restaurant has come to symbolize this mode of rationalization. The remarkable growth of McDonaldization, argues Ritzer, has been spawning homogeneity across the globe while saturating local discreteness with overwhelming uniformity.

- According to anthropologist Arjun Appadurai, the traditional, spatial theoretical models that apprised globalization either as homogenization or heterogenization have failed to capture a certain dialectic movement existing in the process of globalization, namely the constant production and continuous dissolution of locality. He offers a contextual and relational alternative. The core of Appadurai's model constitutes a set of five landscapes or cultural flows: ethnoscapes or human movements, technoscapes or technological flows, financescapes or transfer of capital, mediascapes or information and image dissemination, and ideoscapes or transfer of images pertaining to state ideologies and counter-ideologies of movements.

- Global flows transpire not only through the five landscapes, but also, in and through the disjunctures among them increasingly. Appadurai puts emphasis on several new features which, in his view, are central to global cultural politics today. They are the following: production fetishism, the fetishism of the consumer, deterritorialization, and the role of the nation-state.

- Anthropologist Aihwa Ong studies transnational subjects such as overseas Chinese elites navigating multiple immigration regimes in Asia and North America, population segments in Malaysia and Indonesia who are being subjected to differential treatments by the state, and Cambodian refugees in California who are trying to figure out the rules of coping, navigating, and surviving the streets and other public spaces of the American city. According to Ong, these transnational subjects have come to embody the fluidity of capital, as well as the straining links between national and political identities. Ong articulates her views mainly through the themes of graduated sovereignty, flexible citizenship, and the disciplinary regimes of citizen-subject making.

- Anthropologist Anna Tsing metaphorically characterizes today's messy global capitalism as friction or "the awkward, unequal, unstable aspects of interconnection across difference."

# GLOSSARY

## A

**acculturation:** the process of the intermingling of cultures in which firsthand contact and forced borrowing take place generating profound changes in either or both involving cultures.

**achieved status:** a position that is earned through skill, ability, and effort.

**aesthetics:** the theories about nature and value in art, and sensations associated with beauty.

**affinity:** kin links based on marriage.

**agency:** individual actions, both personal and collective, that make it possible for individuals to take some measure of control over their own lives.

**the age-sets:** the groups of individuals of similar age and same sex who together pass through some or all life stages.

**alienation:** the estrangement of individuals from their own labor and their species-essence or true human nature in capitalist society.

**anthropocene:** the age in which human activity or anthropogenic disruptions has been the dominant influence on global climate, ecosystems, and sociocultural environment.

**anthropology:** the study of humankind in all its facets, times, and places.

**anthropological linguistics:** the subfield of anthropology concerned with the systems of human communication and languages in time and space.

**applied anthropology:** the use of existing anthropological knowledge to determine, evaluate, resolve problems in the contemporary world while fashioning and accomplishing policy objectives.

**arbitrariness:** a design feature of language that highlights the nonintrinsic relationship between the sounds associated with the word and the physical object, action, or idea that the word signifies.

**archaeological sites:** locations where material evidence of past human activity is present.

**archaeology:** the reconstruction, distribution, and interpretation of human lifeways and patterns through the study of material remain of prehistoric populations.

**arranged marriage:** a marriage that places the interests of parents, guardians, or kin groups above the emotional interests and desires on spousal selection.

**arrival trope:** the central theme on ethnographic entry.

**art by appropriation:** the host of objects that grew to be art because they were held as such at certain historical moments by certain people and institutions.

**art by intention:** objects which were made to be art by their original creators.

**artifacts:** anything made or altered by past humans.

**art world:** the individuals and the institutions involved in the processes of transforming diverse objects into art.

**ascribed status:** a position assigned to an individual at birth.

**assimilation:** the process by which individuals of foreign or minority origin become integrated with the standards of the dominant culture.

**authority:** the socially approved use of power.

**avunculocal residence:** the residence pattern in which marital partners live with the husband's mother's brother (maternal uncle).

# B

**balanced reciprocity:** the exchange of goods and services of roughly equivalent value within a set time limit.

**the band:** a relatively small, loosely organized, and kin-based group of nomadic people who hunt and gather for a living over a specific territory.

**bilateral descent:** cognatic descent system under which an Ego may be able to recognize all consanguineal kin traced through both the mother's side, and the father's side of the family.

**bilocal residence:** the residence pattern in which marital partners live alternatively and flexibly with or near the husband's and wife's relatives, depending on the resources available.

**biological anthropology:** the subfield of anthropology that studies human biology from an evolutionary perspective, with a stress laid on the interaction between biology and culture.

**the blended family:** the family unit that takes place when previously divorced individuals remarry and bring the children they have inherited from previous marital affairs into a new household.

**bound morpheme:** an affix morpheme, which is incapable of operating independently unless attached to a free morpheme.

# C

**cash cropping:** single-crop varieties, such as sugar, cotton, tea, coffee, and tobacco, grown in large-scale farms for global market; monocrop plantations.

**caste:** an intricate system of hereditary ranking in traditional India, with which social groupings are made on the premise of social purity.

**the chiefdom:** an autonomous political body, composed of a multitude of villages and communities and held together by the hereditary office of a paramount chief, a redistribution-based economy, and hierarchical social ranking.

**chronemics:** the perception and uses of time by humans as species accustomed to learned behavior.

**civilization:** a society's reach toward an advance stage of sociocultural development and organization, as certain cultural traits make that society distinguishable from other kinds of society.

**clan:** an extended unilineal kinship group whose members believe them to be descended from a progenitor even though they may not be able to demonstrate their common progeny through known kin.

**the class:** defined and structured by the ownership or nonownership of the means of production, the social relationships involved in work and labor, and the control of the surplus human social labor can produce.

**cognates:** the words in different languages identifiable as terms derived from the same word in their ancestral language.

**cognatic descent:** reckoning genealogical links without unilineal restrictions.

**colonialism:** the political conquest of a territory, and the subsequent economic and sociocultural domination of its people by another society.

**colorism:** a term adopted by anthropologists and other social scientists to identify the hierarchies of social status and wealth constructed primarily on skin color.

**commoditization:** a process that makes goods and services indistinguishable from similar products and services.

**commodity:** a sellable or exchangeable product or service in return of money, other products, or services.

**commodity fetishism:** the way in which individuals misapprehend the true nature of commodities by obsessively treating them as persons, thus attributing power and agency to things, while treating people who really do have agency, mere repositories of labor power for sale in the market.

**common fieldwork situations:** the instances in which ethnographers consistently face intertwining issues, concerns, and problems common to all ethnographic fieldworkers.

**comparative analysis in historical linguistics:** the comparison of earlier and later forms to reconstruct how languages change over time.

**the comparative method:** the methodological approach in examining data for the purpose of noting similarities and differences.

**conflict theory:** a theory based on the position that war played a pivotal role in the rise of the state.

**consanguinity:** kin links based on descent.

**the core:** the most powerful states in the world, which can focus on higher-skill and capital-intensive production, appropriating much of the world economy's surplus, and maintaining a strong military.

**core vocabulary:** a small set of primary nouns (such as basic numerals, basic color taxonomy, and words for common anatomical features), pronouns, common adjectives, and primary verbs.

**cosmopolitanism:** the frame of mind, with which one may be able to synthesize both universality and cultural difference.

**creole:** a full-fledged and stable language with its own phonetic, semantic, and grammatical features despite its pidgin origin.

**creolization:** the constant activity of contact and transformation evident in the process of cultural encounter and intermingling.

**cross-cousins:** mother's brother's children and father's sister's children.

**cross-cultural scope:** the application of comparative method to cultures to ferret out the components that are shared and panhuman, as well as those that are not shared and culture specific.

**cultural aesthetics:** culturally specific notions about nature and value in art, as well as such notions associated with beauty.

**cultural anthropology:** the study of similarities, differences, and change among contemporary and recent human societies across the globe as they are fashioned by culture.

**cultural consultants:** the networks of friends and contacts through which cultural anthropologists gather ethnographic data.

**cultural ecology:** an anthropological theory that assumes cultural evolution as a process, potentially taking multiple paths simultaneously due to the force exerted by the primary factors of evolution, such as ecology and economics, as well as the secondary factors such as political system, ideologies, and world views.

**cultural heterogeneity:** the complex process of cross-cultural interaction, in which global and local cultural forms actively compromise (in order to serve local objectives), exist side-by-side, and intermingle with each other while producing a distinctive blend.

**cultural homogenization:** the transnational expansion of a wide array of common cultural codes and practices that causes an overwhelming cultural uniformity and a reduction of cultural diversity.

**cultural hybridization:** fusion or synthesis of the elements in global and local cultural forms and the resultant production of new cultural forms.

**cultural imperialism:** cultural influence exerted on the rest of the world by the core countries like the United States and other Western nations through mass-produced food, brand name merchandise, and mass media, with a specifically forceful imposition on peripheral countries.

**cultural materialism:** a theoretical perspective that lays stress on examining material conditions in order to arrive at causal explanations for diversity in thought and behavior found among the members of various cultures around the world.

**cultural relativism:** the apprehension of beliefs and behavior of another culture within the context of that culture, and not within the cultural setting of one's own; the position that any assessment of a specific culture warrants only its own standards.

**cultural resource management (CRM):** identification, conservation, and management of archeological sites and monuments of cultural value threatened by current human activity.

**cultural transmission through learning:** the passing of cultural knowledge and skills (including communicative skills) from one generation to the next through the broad and complex process of learning and sharing known as enculturation.

**culture:** a series of beliefs and practices humans acquire as constituent parts of society through learning and sharing.

# D

**deductive approach:** developing observations through general explanations.

**the dependency theory:** an analytic framework articulated in the 1950s and 60s by Latin American liberal economic reformists and Marxist intellectuals to highlight that the opulent, core countries thrive at the expense of the impoverished, peripheral countries.

**descent group:** an assemblage of kin who consider themselves as lineal descendants of a progenitor (founding, apical, or common ancestor) or progenitress (founding, apical, or common ancestress) stretching back over two generations.

**deterritorialization:** the process of severing art objects, forms, and traditions from their places of origin and populations, as this process gains intensity from mediatization, migration, and commodification.

**diachronic analysis in historical linguistics:** the investigation of earlier and later forms of a single language to glean how change has occurred in that language, or a group of languages to understand their historical relationship.

**diffusion:** the transmission of discrete cultural traits in the form of objects, ideas, and behaviors from its original culture to another through migration, trade, intermarriage, warfare, or other means of contact and interaction.

**discourse:** a stretch of utterance in which diverse voices, styles, and worldviews intermingled to form a complex unity.

**displacement:** language's ability to make known about things, people, or beings that are not physically present, as well as events that are not happening at the moments of interactive engagement.

**domestication:** a biological process occurring in plants or animals due to artificial selection or alteration by humans.

**doublespeak:** the pervasive use of language to deliberately mislead others through the practices such as euphemism, jargon, gobbledygook (bureaucratese), and inflated language.

**duality of patterning:** language's ability to produce and transmit an infinite number of meaning units by combining a finite number of meaningless sound units in specific orders.

# E

**eco-facts:** a variety of objects found in natural environment ranging from animal bones, plant seeds, and wood, to the remains of insects and animal pests.

**economic anthropology:** the examination of economic activity and cultural relations in societies around the world.

**economic system:** an organized arrangement of production, exchange, and consumption in a specific population.

**e-currency:** currency in electronic form.

**egalitarian society:** a society in which all members or component groups have near equal access to wealth, power, and prestige.

**elderspeak:** a form of English speech reflective of society's negative attitudes toward the elderly and aging.

**eliciting devices:** the activities and objects used to persuade people and intimate them to recollect and share information.

**emic approach:** the perspective based on the views of the native cultural actors; the research strategy with which ethnographers use the cultural concepts and categories that are relevant and meaningful to the culture under investigation.

**enculturation:** the complex process with which culture is gradually learned and transmitted across generations.

**endogamy:** the rule whereby individuals are supposed to find marital partners within the social groups to which they belong.

**ethnic art:** the production of specific types of art works by artists and craftsmen representing their cultural heritage and ethnic identity.

**ethnicity:** a sense of identity and membership in a group that shares common cultural, linguistic, and ancestral links, and that imagines itself to be distinguishable from other groups.

**ethnic cleansing:** the mass expulsion or killing of one ethnic group by the members of another in a specific geographic location.

**ethnocentrism:** the tendency to judge the aspects of other cultures from the vantage point of one's own culture.

**ethnographic audio recording:** the documentation of the aspects of culture and communication in audio format.

**ethnographic data gathering:** the investigative strategy centered on enduring personal observation and social participation.

**ethnographic fieldwork:** the method of research data gathering that emphasizes on-site engagement in fieldwork and experiential learning.

**ethnographic filmmaking:** filmic documentation of the life ways of the people being studied.

**ethnographic interview:** the primary method of interview used by cultural anthropologists to gain insights on the lifeways of a specific group, while taking extra care to build mutual trust and understanding.

**ethnographic mapping:** the data gathering technique that focuses on culturally distinctive, geographically relevant, and ethnographically specific features of local landscapes.

**ethnographic photography:** recording images for ethnographic fieldwork.

**ethnographic videography:** video documentation of lifeways of the people being studied.

**ethnography:** the data collection through extended, up close, and personal fieldwork, as well as the anthropological monographs produced in written, visual, or virtual forms by basing on the evidence collected.

**ethnology:** the comparative study of two or more cultures.

**ethnosemantics:** the area of anthropological linguistics, in which the meaning of words, phrases, and sentences in specific cultural contexts are studied.

**ethos:** the emotional communality that the members of a culture share.

**etic perspective/approach:** the perspective based on the anthropologist's own, observer-oriented views; the research strategy that stresses the cultural concepts and categories stemming from the ethnographer's own perspective and culture.

**event analysis:** the documentation of notable episodes in a cultural landscape such as rituals, ceremonies, and festivities.

**exogamy:** the rule whereby individuals are supposed to find marital partners outside of the social groups in which they are members.

**the extended family:** a family unit which is consisting of three or more generations of kin, such as the parents, the children, and the grandchildren.

# F

**the family by choice:** the family type seen among the individuals who moved away from his or her consanguineal kin, as well as among the individuals who haven't committed to a marital relationship.

**the family of orientation:** the family in which one is born and grows up.

**the family of procreation:** the family in which one becomes, or one is having the probability of becoming, a procreator (a parent).

**the family of same-sex partners:** two people of the same gender sharing a lasting sexual relationship and cohabitation while also sharing legal, economic, social, and other responsibilities of the family (such as parenting children).

**features:** the objects of human manufacture or modification that cannot be readily removed from the archeological sites and carried away to laboratory for further study.

**the feminization of poverty:** the increase of poverty in households that are headed by women.

**the fetishism of the commodity:** the consideration of products as dissociated from their production.

**fieldwork-based data collection:** gathering primary evidence in natural field contexts.

**the formalist versus substantivist debate:** a twentieth-century disciplinary debate carried on by economic anthropologists on the validity of using Western, capitalist model of rational economic behavior to analyze economic activities in non-Western, precapitalist, and nonindustrial societies.

**flexible citizenship:** a new form of "disembedded citizenship" in which one most likely to consider economic concerns as the central contributing factor in choosing citizenship.

**foraging:** the mode of subsistence primarily based on hunting, fishing, and gathering a variety of wild foodstuffs.

**forced labor:** uncompensated labor required by a governing authority; *corvee* labor.

**fordism:** the modern system of speedy mass production introduced to North America by Henry Ford chiefly through the creation of automobile assembly line.

**fossils:** hardened remains and impressions of ancient life forms including humans preserved under conditions favorable for fossilization.

**free morpheme:** a morpheme which can operate independently.

**friction:** the awkward, unequal, unstable aspects of interconnection across difference.

# G

**garbology:** the study of garbage middens to explore the links between material culture and social behavior.

**gender:** the culturally constructed roles assigned to males and females, which may vary substantially from society to society.

**genealogical method:** the system of notation and symbols with which kin ties are traced.

**general anthropology:** the holistic field of study comprising anthropology's four main subdisciplines (biological, archeological, cultural, and linguistic anthropology), as well as applied anthropology.

**generalized reciprocity:** a form of reciprocity in which exchange partners do not keep track of what is given, its calculated value, or a period within which repayment must be made.

**gestures:** the movements of the body, such as movements of head, arms, hands, and face, with which various culture-specific ideas, opinions, and emotions are expressed.

**globalization:** the intensified interaction and increased movement of natural resources, trade goods, human labor, information, technology, and finance capital within and across national borders of the globe, as well as the simultaneous proliferation of global organizations and institutions that structure such processes.

**governmentality:** the art of governing in which the willing participation of the governed (usually against their own well-being and interests) takes place.

**graduated sovereignty:** the different modalities with which the state governs segments of its own population, regardless of the extent of connection such population segments maintain with the global market.

**the great vowel shift:** a massive shift that has taken place in vowel pronunciation during the fifteenth to the eighteenth centuries in English language.

**greetings:** one of the first and notable routines all humans perform in social encounters by combining features of speech and nonverbal communication.

**group interview:** the ethnographic interview for which more than two individuals participate.

# H

**haptics:** the study of the ways with which humans use touch in communication.

**hegemony:** the ability of a dominant or potentially dominant group or class to articulate the interests of the other social groups or classes to its own while still retaining its own privileged position.

**(cultural) heterogeneity:** the process in which many global and local cultural inputs interact to generate a distinctive blend.

**high culture:** the elitist space of culture in which, according to some, artistic consummation and epistemic perfection prevail.

**historic archaeology:** deals with the past human societies that left behind historical records.

**historical linguistics:** the study of the links between earlier and later forms of language.

**holistic approach:** seeing human conditions in its broadest possible context.

**horticulture:** the small-scale, rain-fed farming that uses basic techniques, simple tools (such as digging sticks, hoes, and machetes), and modest amounts of labor, in relation to the area of land being farmed.

**human biological variation:** the field of inquiry on the factors contributing to generate variation in human biology.

# I

**incest taboo:** the categorical prohibition against having sex with each other by close relatives or primary kin.

**indigenization:** the modified borrowing of cultural forms that is in harmony with local culture.

**inductive approach:** gathering specific data before arriving at generalizations.

**industrial agriculture:** contemporary, large-scale, and corporate farming practices, characterized by the increased use of capital in the form of money and property and the application of industrial technology for machinery, synthetic fertilizers, insecticides, fungicides, and herbicides to increase productivity.

**industrial revolution:** the rapid growth of machine-based manufacturing that occurred in Great Britain and quickly spread in other European countries in the late eighteenth and the nineteenth centuries.

**influence:** the ability to persuade others to comply with one's lead.

**informed consent:** obtaining voluntary assistance by truthfully disclosing the aims, nature, and anticipated consequences of the research projects.

**intensive agriculture:** a form of sedentary farming that employs draft animals, irrigation, nonsynthetic fertilizer, and terracing, and characterized by increasing labor intensity, and significant crop surpluses.

**intensive foraging:** efficiently locating and utilizing foraging patches within a heterogenous environment.

**invention/innovation:** the emergence of qualitatively advanced and ideologically or technologically oriented cultural forms (such as material objects, thoughts, or behavioral patterns) as a result of a synthesis taking place in between such existing features within a culture.

**the irrigation theory:** a theory that stresses the central role played by the large-scale irrigation works in economic growth, the centralized bureaucratic structures required to build and maintain them, and the resultant formation of the absolutist managerial state.

# J

**joint family:** the family made up of a married couple, unmarried daughters, their married sons, their sons' wives and children, and even grandsons' wives and great-grandchildren living in one household.

**joint-stock company:** a firm administered by a centralized board of directors but was owned jointly by its shareholders.

# K

**key cultural consultants:** the individuals who display knowledge about their society and culture, coherence, and articulation when ethnographers seek their consultation.

**the kindred:** a network of relatives, traceable through bilateral descent, and linked to Ego and Ego's siblings.

**kinesics cues:** the forms of nonverbal communication based on body language.

**kinship:** the system of meaning and power that cultures construct on the basis of biology, marriage, and choice to ascertain relatedness, mutuality, rights, and responsibilities.

**kin term:** a word used in a language to primarily classify a relative.

**the kula ring:** the network of exchanging bracelets and necklaces across the Trobriand Islands

# L

**landscapes:** global cultural flows, characterized as irregular, fluid, overlapping, and perspectival constructs or disjunctive forces.

**language family:** a group of languages, which have descended from the same protolanguage.

**leveling mechanisms:** the practices and organizations functioning to maximize the collective socioeconomic well-being of a society through reallocation of resources.

**levirate:** the spousal preference rule in which a widow marries her deceased husband's brother (the spousal preference rule in which a man marries the wife of his deceased brother).

**life history research:** a technique used by ethnographic fieldworkers to gain an in-depth understanding about the life of an individual and the culture in which the individual is a member.

**lineage:** a unilineal kin-ordered group whose members can clearly demonstrate their common progeny, tracing genealogical links through several generations to a progenitor.

**lineality:** the relatives connected to Ego through a lineal relative.

**lingua franca:** a vehicular or bridge language used by various speech communities to communicate with each other.

**linguistic anthropology:** the subfield of anthropology concerned with the systems of communication and languages in time and space.

**loanwords:** the words "borrowed" or adopted by the speakers of one language from a different or source language.

**love marriage:** a marriage that places individual's emotional interests and desires on spousal selection above the interests of parents, guardians, or kin groups; the marriage between two or more individuals who are in love.

# M

**market exchange:** the mode of economic exchange in which goods and services are bought and sold at a money price essentially decided by the market forces of supply and demand.

**marriage:** a socially binding, culturally sanctioned, status transforming, enduring, sexual, companionate, and frequently procreative union between two or more individuals that establishes a set of reciprocal rights and obligations between the married partners, their offspring, and their kin groups.

**matrilineal descent:** establishing kin connection exclusively through females from a progenitrix; a descent group, which is consisted of a female Ego, her mother, the mother's mother, the mother's siblings, the mother's sister's children, the siblings, the sister's children, Ego's own children, and the children of her daughters.

**matrilocal residence:** the residence pattern in which marital partners live with or near the wife's mother.

**McDonaldization:** the global spread of Western consumerism through a variety of U.S.-dominated channels of corporate culture and the resultant increasing rationalization of everyday routine tasks.

**the means of production:** the technological knowledge and the materials used in production, such as technology, land, and capital (infrastructural and natural).

**mercantile capitalism:** a social system based on competition for control of natural resources and trade in external markets.

**the mode of production:** a way of organizing production.

**the moka:** a highly ritualized feasting ceremony held by the Big Men in Papua New Guinea, during which reciprocal exchange of gifts of pigs and food were exchanged.

**money:** a universally recognized medium of exchange that measures the value of goods and services and allows wealth to be preserved over time.

**monogamy:** the form of marriage whereby the union between a pair of individuals take place.

**morphemes:** the smallest units of sounds that carry meanings.

**morphology:** the study of the forms in which sounds combine to form morphemes or the smallest units of sounds that carry meanings.

**multisited ethnography:** conducting ethnographic fieldwork in multiple localities.

# N

**nation-state:** a form of state functioning to provide a sovereign territory for a nation or a collective sociopolitical body characterized by anthropologist Ben Anderson as an imagined political community.

**negative reciprocity:** the exchange of goods and services, in which each party seeks to gain more than it gives at the expense of others.

**neo-evolution:** an anthropological theory based on the premise that the driving force of evolution has been cultural systems' increasing capacity to harness energy or their advancing level of technology, or both.

**neo-Gramscianism:** a critical theory approach, which is investigating the interface of ideas, institutions, and material capabilities as they shape the contours of state formation.

**the Neolithic revolution:** the process of adopting a set of food producing techniques that eventually paved the way for the surplus production of food.

**neolocal residence:** the residence pattern in which marital partners set up an independent household in a location apart from either the husband's or wife's kin.

**the new means of consumption:** highly rationalized new innovations, such as fast-food franchises, shopping malls, megamalls, cybermalls, superstores, discounters, cruise lines, Las Vegas-styled casino hotels, Disney-type theme parks, that have come into existence in the second half of the twentieth century and have been continuously booming ever since.

**nomadic pastoralism:** the movement of the entire group of herders with their herd animals across a large area throughout the year seeking fresh pasturelands.

**the nuclear family:** a kin unit consisting of a pair of parents accustomed to neolocal, monogamous living, and their unmarried children.

## O

**openness:** language's ability to blend, analogize with, and transform previous linguistic messages to generate inexhaustible amount of novel and creative expressions, which are meaningful and comprehensible to the other speakers of the same language.

## P

**paleoanthropology:** the study of the complex course of human evolution, specifically as evidenced in the fossil record.

**paralanguage:** voice effects that accompany utterances.

**parallel cousins:** mother's sister's children and father's brother's children.

**participant-observation:** gaining insights on people's way of life through personal observation and social participation.

**pastoralism:** raising and caring large herds of domesticated animals and using them and their products primarily as a way of sustenance.

**patrilineal descent:** establishing kin connection exclusively through males from a progenitor; a descent group comprised of a male Ego, his father, the father's siblings, the father's brother's children, the siblings, the brother's children, Ego's own children, and the children of his sons.

**patrilocal residence:** the residence pattern in which partners in marriage live with or near the husband's father.

**the periphery:** the states, which are militarily weak and economically dominated by the capitalist core.

**phoneme:** a minimal, meaningless, and distinctive unit of speech sound (a sound contrast) that differentiates meaning in a specific spoken language.

**phonology:** the area in linguistics that studies speech sound systems in specific languages.

**pidgin:** an elemental language with starkly simple syntactic rules and a limited lexicon.

**political anthropology:** a subfield of cultural anthropology that focuses on politics and power, stressing context, process, and scale.

**polyandry:** the form of marriage in which the union between a woman and multiple men is permitted.

**polygamy:** the form of marriage in which the union between multiple partners is possible.

**polygyny:** the form of marriage in which the simultaneous union between a man and multiple women is permitted.

**popular culture:** lifeways of the ordinary folks.

**positivism:** a school of modern Western thought that advocated the pursuit of explainable, predictable, empirically verifiable, value-neutral, and universal knowledge through the unity of scientific method.

**postmodernism:** a style and movement in architecture, art, literary criticism, and many other fields, as well as related theoretical perspective that came into being as a severe critique of modernist enterprise and its ideals such as scientific objectivity and the scientific method.

**potlatch:** a ceremonial feast existed among the Kwakiutl Indians in the Pacific Northwest, during which hosts distributed a large quantity of food and goods that had been collected over many months or even years.

**power:** the ability to command others and secure their compliance.

**prehistoric archaeology:** the study of preurban societies in the world for which historical records literally do not exist.

**prestation:** paying in money, in goods, or in service as a way of fulfilling an obligation.

**prevarication:** the design feature of language that provides the means to equivocal utterances ranging from trivial lies, intentionally vague and ambiguous statements, to deliberate fabrications.

**primatology:** the study of nonhuman primates such as prosimians, monkeys, and apes in their habitats or in captivity.

**project Camelot:** an aborted research program funded by the U.S. Army to study possible causes for civil unrest and violence in developing countries.

**project Minerva:** a project launched in the 1980s to seek the expertise of social scientists to counter actual and potential threats to the U.S. national security.

**protolanguage:** a common ancestral form from which a group of languages have descended.

**proxemic analysis:** the study of the ways with which people in different cultures perceive and use space.

**proxemics:** the perception and the uses of space by humans as species accustomed to learned behavior.

# R

**race:** a system of hierarchy, in which humans are categorized into different groups with the assumption that the boundaries of each population category correspond to a specific set of biological attributes.

**racism:** the methodical discrimination of one or more culturally constructed races by another culturally defined race affirming the biocultural pre-eminence of the latter over the former.

**rank society:** a society in which every person has near equal access to wealth and power, but some who are ranked above others in the social hierarchy have unequal access to prestige or social honor.

**reciprocity:** the exchange of goods and services among people of relatively equal socioeconomic status.

**redistribution:** the mode of exchange in which goods are collected from or contributed by members of a group and then redivided among those members in a different pattern.

**the relations of production:** the totality of socioeconomic and technological relationships into which people should enter to sustain themselves and to engage in various production activities.

**restudies:** fieldwork research carried out in previously researched communities.

**reterritorialization:** the restructuring process, in which territorial relocalizations of old art forms, institutions, and activities, as well as new art productions emphatic of locality and culture takes place.

# S

**the Sapir–Whorf hypothesis:** a hypothesis formed by linguists Edward Sapir and Benjamin Lee Whorf with the belief that, by influencing the way people think and behave, language effectively shapes culture.

**semanticity:** associative links between linguistic signals and features in the physical and sociocultural world of a linguistic community.

**semantics:** the study of meaning that concentrates on the nexus of signifiers (words, phrases, signs, and symbols) and what it denotes for most speakers of a specific language.

**the semiperiphery:** the stronger states (with diverse economies and powerful militaries), which serve as a crucial buffer between the core and the periphery.

**serial monogamy:** the form of monogamy whereby individuals are permitted to remarry any number of partners successively.

**sex:** the biological and physiological characteristics with which males are distinguished from females.

**sexual cohabitation:** cohabitation of two people of the opposite sex sexually on a long-term basis and share economic, social, and other responsibilities of family (such as child rearing) without getting married to each other.

**sexuality:** the people's preference or orientation and experience in the context of sexual activity.

**sign language:** a form of nonverbal communication primarily based on deliberate hand movements.

**silence:** a form of nonverbal communication with its own specific cultural values and meanings.

**the single-parent family:** a family with underage children headed by a parent who is widowed, separated and not remarried, or by a parent who has never married.

**singularization:** the process, which is singularizing objects by making them transcendent treasures that can be withdrawn from the market.

**the slash-and-burn method:** the technique used by the practitioners of rain-fed agriculture to modify wild vegetation or soil texture before planting crops.

**social Darwinism:** the school of thought based on the belief that Darwin's theory of evolution may be applicable to society and culture.

**society:** an aggregate of individuals living together while sharing a distinct pattern of social relations.

**sociolinguistics:** the study of language and its social and cultural context.

**sororate:** the spousal preference rule in which a widower marries his deceased wife's sister (the spousal preference rule in which a woman marries her deceased sister's husband).

**sound:** a vocalic feature used by humans in combination of spoken language and kinesics cues, or alone to express emotions, convey impressions, construct links, pass judgments, as well as to make others convinced or deceived.

**the Southern strategy:** a strategy used by conservative elements in American politics to increase political support among white voters in the South by appealing to racism against African Americans.

**speech sounds:** phonetically distinct units of speech.

**the state:** a centrally, bureaucratically, and hierarchically organized, autonomous structure of political, legal, and military power that administers a territory and populace as the ultimate authority.

**stratification:** hierarchical relationships existing among different groups in society, as if they were organized in layers or strata.

**stratified society:** a society, which is marked by the unequal access to all forms of social dividends, such as wealth, power, and prestige.

**street theater:** a theatrical form adopted by the actors ranging from buskers (street performers who perform for gratuities such as food, drink, or little money) to theater practitioners who, either want to experiment with performance spaces, or to promote a cause of sociopolitical significance.

**structural functionalism:** a theoretical paradigm that identifies sociocultural institutions as functional and integrated parts of a social system.

**structural linguistics:** the field of study in which structural features of language are documented, described, and analyzed.

**structured interview:** the interview in which the ethnographer maintains considerable control over the interviewing process.

**subaltern studies:** a field that concentrates on nonelite perspectives and histories.

**subculture:** the carving of notably different collective cultural identities within the same space in a society where the core culture inhabits.

**surplus value:**  the amount of value produced by workers that is greater than the wage paid to them.

**sustainable agriculture:**  a set of innovative thoughts and related practices that seeks to produce food, fiber, and other plant and animal products while preserving environment, protecting public health, sustaining vibrant communities, and upholding animal welfare.

**swapping:**  a robust tradition of benevolent exchange existing in the ghetto regions of Chicago.

**symbolic and interpretive anthropology:**  an anthropological approach seeking to explore the way human beings ascribe meanings to symbols and related processes (such as myth and ritual) for giving their lives direction, order, and coherence.

**symbolic representation:**  a pervasive mode of thought that has fashioned and streamlined every aspect of human intellect, including mode of communication.

**syntax:**  language rules by which words are structured to make phrases and sentences to convey linguistic messages.

## T

**terracing:**  a way of growing crops by planting on graduated terraces (a series of successively receding platforms) built by cutting into the slope of hilly or mountainous terrain.

**the theater of the oppressed:**  A set of interactive and politically expressive theatrical forms and techniques created by a Brazilian theater practitioner named Augusto Boal (1931–2009).

**thick description:**  the deciphering of a cultural text while placing primacy on the detailed, contextualized, and empirical description.

**transhumance:**  pastoralism in which herders' movement becomes partial and seasonal.

**the transnational family:**  the family unit maintaining sustained links of family members and networks of relatives across the borders of multiple nation-states.

**the tribe:**  a form of political organization found mostly among a range of kin-ordered groups of horticulturalists or pastoralists who share a common ancestry, culture, language, and territory.

## U

**unilineal cultural evolutionism:**  the evolutionary scheme in which different cultural status is aligned in a single line that moves from the most primitive to the most advanced or civilized.

**unilineal descent:**  specifying descent group affiliation by establishing a direct line from a progenitor or progenitress (progenitrix) exclusively through Ego's male or female ancestors, but not both.

**unstructured interview:**  the interview in which the ethnographer maintains minimum control over the interviewing process.

# V

**versatility:** the ability to adapt.

**vocabulary:** the body of words used in a specific language.

**vocalics:** the uses of sound and silence in communication.

# W

**the world-system analysis:** an analytical framework which recognizes the current system as a historically produced, socially and politically salient, global economic system based on wealth and power differentials, with a division of labor that is not circumscribed by political or cultural boundaries.

# BIBLIOGRAPHY

Aboidun, Roland. "Verbal and Visual Metaphors: Mythical Allusion in Yoruba Ritualistic Art of Ori." *Word Image* 3, no. 3 (1987): 252–70.

Abu-Lughod, Janet Lila. "Writing against Culture." In *Recapturing Anthropology*, edited by Richard G. Fox, 137–54. Santa Fe, NM: The School of American Research, 1991.

——————. *Before European Hegemony: the World System A.D. 1250–1350*, 6th ed. New York, NY: Oxford University Press, 1989.

——————. *Dramas of Nationhood: the Politics of Television in Egypt.* Chicago, IL: University of Chicago Press, 2005.

Alexander, J. Islam, Archeology, and Slavery in Africa. *World Archeology* 33 (2001): 4460.

——————. *Before European Hegemony: The World System A. D. 1250–1350.* New York, NY: Oxford University Press, 1989.

Allan, Derek. *Art and Time.* Newcastle upon Tyne, UK: Cambridge Scholars Publishing, 2013.

Alland, Jr., Alexander. *The Artistic Animal: An Inquiry into the Biological Roots of Art.* New York, NY: Anchor Books, 1977.

Amin, Samir. *Unequal Development: An Essay on the Social Formations of Peripheral Capitalism.* New York, NY: Monthly Review Press, 1976.

Anandavardhana, and Abhinavagupta. *The Dhvanyaloka of Anandavardhana with the Locana of Abhinavagupta* (Harvard Oriental Series, vol. 49). Edited and translated by Daniel H. H. Ingalls, J. M. Masson, and M. V. Patwardhan. Cambridge, MA: Harvard University Press, 1990.

Anderson, Benedict. *Imagined Communities: Reflections on the Origin and Spread of Nationalism.* New York, NY: Verso Books, 1983.

Anderson, Richard. *Calliope's Sisters: A Comparative Study of Philosophies of Art.* Upper Saddle River, NJ: Pearson Education, 2004.

Anzaldua, Gloria E. *Borderlands/La Frontera: The New Mestiza.* San Francisco, CA: Aunt Lute Books, 1987.

Appadurai, Arjun. *Modernity at Large: Cultural Dimensions of Globalization.* Minneapolis, MA: University of Minnesota Press, 1996.

_____. *The Social Life of Things,* edited by Arjun Appadurai and Carol A. Breckenridge. Cambridge, MA: Cambridge University Press, 1986.

_____. "Disjunctures and Difference in the Global Cultural Economy." In *Global Culture,* edited by Mike Featherstone, 295–310. London, UK: Sage, 1990.

Applebaum, Kalman D. "Marriage with the Proper Stranger: Arranged Marriage in Metropolitan Japan." *Ethnology* 34, no. 1 (Winter 1995): 37–51.

Ariyaratne, Ari. Spring 2012, "You Are What You Eat: Anthropological Pedagogy and Popular Cultural Discourses of the Other." *Teaching Anthropology: SACC Notes* 18, no. 1 (Spring 2012):13–17.

_____. *Nation-State, Development, and Community in a Rural Sinhalese Setting.* Ph. D. Dissertation, Urbana-Champaign, IL: Graduate College, University of Illinois, 2000.

Arnold, Matthew. *Culture and Anarchy,* edited by Jane Garnett. Oxford, NY: Oxford University Press, 1869.

Asad, Talal. *Anthropology and the Colonial Encounter,* edited by Talal Asad. Ithaca, NY: Ithaca Press, 1973.

Bahuchet, Serge. "Language of African Rainforest 'Pygmy' Hunter-gatherers: Language Shifts without Cultural Admixture." In *Historical Linguistics and Hunter-gatherers Populations in Global Perspective.* Leipzig, Germany: Max-Planck Institute, 2004.

Bhabha, Homi. "Culture's in Between." In *Questions of Cultural Identity,* edited by S. Hall and P. Du Gay. London, UK: Sage, 1996, 53–60.

Bakhtin, M. M. *The Dialogic Imagination: Four Essays,* edited by Michael Holquist. Translated by. Caryl Emerson and Michael Holquist. Austin, TX: University of Texas Press, 1981.

Baran, Paul A. *The Political Economy of Growth.* New York, NY: Monthly Review Press, 1957.

Barber, Benjamin R. *Jihad vs. McWorld: How Globalism and Triabalism are Reshaping the World.* New York: Ballantine Books, 1996.

Barker, Randolph, and Francois Molle. *Evolution of Irrigation in South and Southeast Asia.* Colombo, Sri Lanka: Comprehensive Assessment Secretariat, 2004.

Bartlett, Albert A. "Reflections on Sustainability, Population Growth, and the Environment." *Population and Environment* 16, no. 1 (September 1994): 5–35.

Barth, Fredrik. *Ethnic Groups and Boundaries.* Long Grove, IL: Waveland Press, 1969.

_____. *Political Leadership among Swat Pathans.* London School of Economics Monographs on Social Anthropology, No. 19. London, UK: Athlone Press, 1959.

Barthes, Roland. *Elements of Semiology.* New York, NY: Hill and Wang, 1968.

Basso, Keith H. *Portraits of "the Whiteman:" Linguistic Play and Cultural Symbols among the Western Apache.* Cambridge, MA: Cambridge University Press, 1972.

Bateson, Gregory, and Margaret Mead. *Balinese Character: A Photographic Analysis.* New York, NY: New York Academy of Sciences, 1942.

Baudrillard, Jean. *Simulacra and Simulation.* Ann Arbor, MI: University of Michigan Press, 1995.

_____. *The Consumer Society.* London, UK: Sage, 1998 [1970].

Baugh, Alfred C., and Thomas Cable. *A History of the English Language.* Eaglewood Cliffs, NJ: Prentice-Hall, 1983.

Bayly, Susan. *Caste, Society, and Politics in India from the Eighteenth Century to the Modern Age.* Cambridge: Cambridge University Press, 1999.

Becker, Howard S. *Art Worlds,* 25th Anniversary ed. Oakland, CA: University of California Press, 2008 [1982].

Beeston, Laura. "The Ballerina and the Bull: Adbusters' Micah White on 'the Last Great Social Movement.'" *The Link* 32, no. 7 (October 11, 2011).

Beidelman, Thomas O. "A Comparative Analysis of the Jajmani System." *Monographs of the Association of Asian Studies* 8 (1959).

Benjamin, Walter. "The Work of Art in the Age of Mechanical Reproduction." In *Illustrations,* edited by Hannah Arendt. London, UK: Fontana, 1968 [1936], 214–18.

Berreman, Gerald. *Social Inequality: Comparative and Developmental Approaches.* New York, NY: Academic Press, 1989.

Bharata Muni. *Natya Shastra of Bharata Muni: Text, Commentary of Abhinava Bharati by Abhinavaguptacarya,* edited by Pushpendra Kumar. Translated by Manmohan Ghosh, 3 vols. Delhi, India: New Bharatiya Book Corporation, 2006 [1st Century BC—3rd Century CE].

Boal, Augusto. *Theatre of the Oppressed.* London, UK: Pluto Press, 1979.

Boas, Franz. *Handbook of American Indian Languages,* Vol. 1, Bureau of American Ethnology, Bulletin 40. Washington, DC: Smithsonian Institution, 1911.

_____. *Kwakiutl Ethnography,* edited by Helen Codere. Chicago: Chicago University Press, 1966.

Bodenheimer, Suzanne. "Dependency and Imperialism: the Roots of Latin American Under-development." *Politics and Society* 1, no. 3 (1971): 327–57.

Bodley, John H. *Victims of Progress,* 5th ed. New York, NY: Altamira Press, 2008.

Boellstroff, Tom. *Coming of Age in Second Life: An Anthropologist Explores the Virtual Human.* Princeton and Oxford, MA: Princeton University Press, 2008.

Bonvillain, Nancy. *Language, Culture, and Communication,* 4th ed. Upper Saddle River, NJ: Prentice Hall, 2003.

Bourdieu, Pierre. *The Logic of Practice.* Translated by Richard Nice. CA: Stanford University Press, 1990.

Bottomore, Thomas B., ed. *A Dictionary of Marxist Thought.* Malden, MA: Blackwell Publishers, 2001 [1983].

Bourgois, Philippe, and Jeff Schonberg. "Intimate Apartheid: Ethnic Dimensions of Habits among Homeless Heroine Injectors." *Ethnography* 8, no. 1 (2007): 7–31. Los Angeles, CA: Sage Publications.

Braudel, Fernand. *Civilization and Capitalism,* vol. 1. London, UK: Collins, 1981.

_____. *Civilization and Capitalism,* vol. 2. London, UK: Collins, 1982.

_____.1984 *Civilization and Capitalism,* vol. 3. London, UK: Collins, 1984.

Brazell, Karen. *Traditional Japanese Theater: An Anthology of Plays.* New York, NY: Columbia University Press, 1998.

Brow, James. *Vedda Villages of Anuradhapura: the Historical Anthropology of a Community in Sri Lanka.* Seattle, WA: University of Washington Press, 1978.

Brown, Donald. *Human Universals.* Philadelphia, PA: Temple University Press, 1991.

_____. 2004, "Human Universals, Human Nature, and Human Culture." *Daedalus* 133, no. 4 (2004): 47–54.

Bryceson, D., and U. Vuorela. Transnational Families in the Twenty-first Century. In *The Transnational Family: New European Frontier and Global Networks,* edited by D. Bryceson and U.Vuorela. Oxford, MA: Berg, 2002.

Canclini, Nestor Garcia. *Hybrid Cultures: Strategies for Entering and Leaving Modernity.* Minneapolis, MN: University of Minnesota Press, 1995.

Carneiro, Robert. "A Theory of the Origin of the State." *Science,* (August 1970): 733–38.

Carsten, Janet. *After Kinship.* Cambridge, MA: Cambridge University Press, 2004.

Carter, Janis. "Lucy, Me, and the Chimps." *Reader's Digest* (August 1982): 99–103.

Chandler, Susan Meyers. "Family Structures and the Feminization of Poverty: Women in Hawaii." *The Journal of Sociology and Social Welfare* 16, no. 2 (June 1989): Article 12.

Chavez, Leo et. al. 7, "Undocumented Latina Immigrants in Orange County, California: A Comparative Analysis." *International Migration Review* 31, no. 1 (1997): 88–107.

Childe, Vere Gordon. *Man Makes Himself.* London, UK: Watts, 1936.

Chomsky, Noam. *Aspects of the Theory of Syntax.* Cambridge, MA: MIT Press, 1965.

_____. *Syntactic Structures.* The Hague/Paris: Mouton, 1957.

_____. *Reflections on Language.* New York, NY: Pantheon Books, 1975.

Clifford, James. *The Predicament of Culture: Twentieth-century Ethnography, Literature, and Art.* Cambridge, MA: Harvard University Press, 1988.

Clifford, James, and George E. Marcus, eds. *Writing Culture: the Poetics and Politics of Ethnography*. Berkeley, CA: University of California Press, 1986.

Cohen, Margot. "A Search for a Surrogate Leads to India." *The Wall Street Journal* (October 8, 2009): I–D.

Cohen, Yehudi A. *Man in Adaptation: the Institutional Framework*. New York, NY: Routledge, 1971.

_____. *Man in Adaptation: the Institutional Framework,* 2nd ed. Chicago, IL: Aldine Transaction, 1974.

Cohn, Bernard S. *Colonialism and Its Forms of Knowledge: The British in India*. Princeton, NJ: Princeton University Press, 1996.

Cole, Alistair, and Gino Raymond. *Redefining the French Republic*. Manchester: Manchester University Press, 2006.

Comaroff, Jean, and John L. Comaroff. *Of Revelation and Revolution, Vol I: Christianity, Colonialism, and Consciousness in South Africa*. Chicago, IL: University of Chicago Press, 1991.

Coontz, Stephanie. *The Way We Never Were: American Families and the Nostalgia Trap*. New York, NY: Basic Books, 1992.

Coquery-Vidrovitch, Catherine. *Africa: Endurance and Change South of Sahara*. Berkeley, CA: University of California Press, 1988.

Corbett, Julia B. *Communicating Nature*. Washington, DC: Island Press, 2006.

Corrigan, Philip, and Derek Sayer. *The Great Arch: English State Formation as Cultural Revolution*. New York, NY: Blackwell, 1985.

Dalton, Gregory. *Economic Anthropology*. New York, NY: Basic Books, 1971.

_____. 1969 "Theoretical Issues in Economic Anthropology." *Current Anthropology* 10, no. 1 (1969): 63–102.

Darwin, Charles. *On the Origin of the Species*. New York, NY: Dutton, 1958 [1859].

Das, Shrimati, and Asha N. Raab. "Street Theatre—The Third Theatre: Agents for Social Engineering in India." *Humaniora* 24, no. 2 (2012): 168–74.

Davis, Timothy S., and Timothy Davis. *Ricardo's Macroeconomics: Money, Trade Cycles, and Growth*. Cambridge, MA: Cambridge University Press, 2005.

Deacon, Terrence. *The Symbolic Species: The Co-evolution of Language and the Brain*. New York, NY: W. W. Norton & Co, 1997.

Dean, Mitchell. *Critical and Effective Histories: Foucault's Methods and Historical Sociology*. London, UK: Routledge, 1994.

Deleuze, Gilles, and Felix Guattari. 1972, *Anti-Oedipus*. Translated by Robert Hurley, Mark Seem, and Helen R. Lane. London, UK: Continuum 2004 vol. 1 of Capitalism and Schizophrenia (2 vols., 1972–1980).

Dharmasiri, Kanchuka. *Streets Ahead With Haththotuwegama,* edited by Kanchuka Dharmasiri. Colombo, Sri Lanka: Ravaya Publishers, 2012.

Diamond, Jared. "The Worst Mistake in the History of the Human Race." *Discover* (May 1987): 64–66.

_____. *Guns, Germs, and Steel: Tanchukahe Fates of Human Societies.* New York, NY: Norton, 1999.

Dil, Anwar S. *Language Structure and Language Use/Essays by Charles A. Ferguson; Selected and Introduced by Anwar S. Dil.* Stanford, CA: Stanford University Press, 1971.

Dissanayake, Ellen. *Homo Aestheticus: Where Art Come From and Why?* Seattle, WA: University of Washington Press, 1995.

Dirks, Nicholas B. *The Hallow Crown: Ethnohistory of an Indian Kingdom.* New York, NY: Cambridge University Press, 1987.

Dobson, E. J. *English Pronunciation 1500–1700,* 2nd ed., vol. 2. Oxford, NY: Clarendon P., 1968, 594–713.

Dominguez, Martin, and Pasko Rakic. "Language Evolution: The Importance of Being Human." *Nature* 462 (2009): 169–70.

Dorfman, Ariel, and Armand Mattelart. 1991, "How to Read "Donald Duck:" Imperialist Ideology in the Disney Comic." In *International General,* 4th ed. Translated by David Kunzle, 17.

Dos Santos, Theotonio. "The Structure of Dependence." In *Readings in the U.S. Imperialism,* edited by K. T. Kan and Donald Hodges. Boston, MA: Horizon, 1971.

Douglas, Mary. *Purity and Danger.* New York, NY: Penguin Books, 1966.

Downs, James F. 1964, "Animal Husbandry in Navajo Society and Culture." *Anthropology* 1, no. 1 (University of California 1964).

Dube, Saurabh. *Untouchable Pasts: Religion, Identity, and Power among a Central Indian Community, 1780–1950.* Albany, NY: State University of New York Press, 1998.

Duranti, Alessandro. *Linguistic Anthropology.* Cambridge, MA: Cambridge University Press, 1997.

Durkheim, Emile. *The Rules of Sociological Method.* New York, NY: Free Press, 1982 [1895].

Dumont, Louis. *Homo Hierarchicus: The Caste System and Its Implications.* Chicago, IL: University of Chicago Press, 1970.

Eck, Diana P. *Darsan: Seeing the Divine Image in India.* New York, NY: Columbia University Press, 1981.

Eliot, T. S "Towards the Definition of Culture." In *T. S. Eliot: the Contemporary Reviews,* edited by Jewel Spears Brooker, 497–514. Cambridge, UK: Cambridge University Press, 2004

[1948, 1949]; online publication is available at e-mail link http://dx.doi.org/10.1017/CBO9780511485466

Engels, Friedrich. *Origins of Family, Private Property, and the State.* New York, NY: International Publishers, 1884.

Errington, Shelly. *The Death of Authentic Primitive Art and Other Tales of Progress.* Berkeley, CA: University of California Press, 1998.

Evans-Pritchard, E. E. *The Nuer: A Description of the Modes of Livelihood and Political Institutions of a Nilotic People.* London, UK: Oxford University Press, 1968 [1940].

Farinelli, L. "The Sounds of Seduction." In *The Nonverbal Communication Reader,* edited by Laura K. Guerrero and Michael L. Hecht, 160–68. Long Grove, IL: Waveland Press, 2008.

Farrell, James. *One Nation Under Good: Malls and the Seductions of American Shopping.* Washington, DC: Smithsonian Books, 2002.

Ferguson, James. *Global Shadows: Africa in the Neoliberal World Order.* Durham, NC: Duke University Press, 2006.

Ferraro, Gary, and Susan Andreatta. *Cultural Anthropology: An Applied Perspective.* Belmont, CA: Wadsworth, 2012.

Ferraro, Vincent. "Dependency Theory: An Introduction." In *The Development Economic Reader,* edited by S. Giorgio, 58–64. London, UK: Routledge, 2008.

Firth, Raymond. *Primitive Polynesian Economy.* London, UK: Routledge and Kegan Paul, 1939.

Fiske, J. *Reading the Popular,* 2nd ed. New York, NY: Routledge, 2011.

Flaherty, Robert. *Nanook of the North.* Ethnographic Film, 1922.

Foucault, Michael. *Discipline and Punish: The Birth of the Prison.* New York, NY: Vintage, 1979.

————————. 1982, "The Subject and Power." *Critical Inquiry* 8, no. 4 (1982): 777–95. Chicago, IL: University of Chicago Press.

Fouts, Rogers S., and Stephen T. Mills. *Next of Kin: My Conversations with Chimpanzees.* New York, NY: William Morrow and Co., 1997

Fox, Robin. *Kinship and Marriage: An Anthropological Perspective.* New York, NY: Cambridge University Press, 1983 [1967].

Frank, Andre-Gunder. *Reorient: Global Economy in the Asian Age.* Berkeley, CA: University of California Press, 1998.

————————. *Dependent Accumulation and Underdevelopment.* London, UK: Macmillan Press, 1978.

_____. *On Capitalist Underdevelopment.* Bombay, India: Oxford University Press, 1975.

_____. *The Development of Underdevelopment.* New York, NY: Monthly Review Press, 1966.

_____. *Latin America: Underdevelopment or Revolution.* New York, NY: Monthly Review Press, 1969.

Franklin, Donna L. "Feminization of Poverty and African American Families: Illusions and Realities." *Sage Journals* (1992).

Frazer, James G. *The Golden Bough: A Study in Magic and Religion.* New York, NY: The Macmillan Company, 1951 [1922].

Freire, Paulo. *Pedagogy of the Oppressed.* New York, NY: Continuum, 2000 [1970].

French, Hillary. *Vanishing Boarders: Protecting the Planet in the Age of Globalization.* New York, NY: W. W. Norton, 2000.

Frick, Bob (Senior Editor). How Money on the Mind Changes Our Behavior? In kiplinger. com, June 1, 2012.

Fried, Morton H. *The Evolution of Political Society: An Essay in Political Anthropology.* Random House Studies in Anthropology AS 7. New York, NY: Random House, 1967.

Friedman, Jonathan. *Cultural Identity and Global Processes.* London, UK: Sage, 1994.

Galvez, Alyshia. *Guadalupe in New York: Devotion and the Struggle for Citizenship Rights among Mexican Immigrants.* New York: New York University Press, 2009.

Gamburd, Michelle Ruth. "Breadwinners No More: Identities in Flux." Pp. 110-123. In *Everyday Life in South Asia, 2nd ed.,* edited by Diane P. Mines and Sarah Lamb. Bloomington, IN: Indiana University Press, 2010.

_____. *The Kitchen Spoon's Handle: Transnationalism and Sri Lanka's Migrant Housemaids.* Ithaca, NY: Cornell University Press, 2000.

Gaonkar, Dilip P. *Alternative Modernities.* Durham, NC: Duke University Press, 2001.

Gardner, R. A., B. T. Gardner, and T. E. Van Cantfort, eds. *Teaching Sign Language to Chimpanzees.* Albany, NY: SUNY Press, 1989.

Geertz, Clifford. *Interpretation of Culture.* New York, NY: Basic Books, 1973.

_____. *Negara: The Theater State in Nineteenth Century Bali.* Princeton, NJ: Princeton University Press, 1980.

Ghosh, Manomohan, ed. *Natyasastra.* Kolkata, India: The Asiatic Society, 2002 [1950].

Giddens, Anthony. *The Consequences of Modernity.* Stanford, CA: Stanford University Press, 1990.

_____. *The Nation-State and Violence: Volume Two of a Contemporary Critique of Historical Materialism.* Cambridge, UK: Polity Press, 1985.

Glissant, Edourd. *Caribbean Discourse*. Charlottesville, VA: University Press of Virginia, 1989.

Godelier, Maurice. *The Enigma of the Gift*. Chicago, IL: University of Chicago Press, 1999.

Gluckman, Max. *Custom and Conflict in Africa*. Oxford, UK: Blackwell, 1954.

Goldfrank, Walter L. "Paradigm Regained? The Rules of Wallerstein's World-System Method." *Journal of World-Systems Research* 6, no. 2 (2000): 150–95.

Gonzalez, Laura. "Who Are You?" February 1, 2013. http://modernarrange.marriage.blog-spot.com/

Goodall, Jane. *The Chimpanzees of Gombe: Patterns of Behavior*. Boston, MA: Bellknap Press of the Harvard University Press, 1986.

Goodfellow, David Martin. *Principles of Economic Sociology: The Economics of Primitive Life as illustrated from the Bantu Peoples of South and East Africa*. London, UK: Routledge, 1939.

Goodman, Douglas J., and George Ritzer. *Sociological Theory*, 6th ed. New York, NY: McGraw Hill, 2004.

Gordon, Peter. "Numerical Cognition without Words: Evidence from Amazonia." *Science* 306 (2004): 496–99.

Gould, Harold A. 1958, "The Hindu Jujmani System: A Case of Economic Particularism." *Southwestern Journal of Anthropology* 14 (1958): 428–37.

Graeber, David. *Debt: The First 5000 Years*. New York, NY: Melville House, 2011.

Gramsci, Antonio. *Selections from the Prison Notebooks*. Translated by Q. Hoare and G. N. Smith. New York, NY: International, 1971.

Gregory, Chris A. *Gifts and Commodities*, foreword by Strathern, Marilyn (2nd ed.). Chicago, IL: Hau Books, 2015 [1982].

Guest, Kenneth J. *God in Chinatown: Religion and Survival in New York's Evolving Immigrant Community*. New York, NY: NYU Press, 2003.

Gupta, Akhil, and James Ferguson. "Beyond "Culture": Space, Identity, and the Politics of Difference." *Cultural Anthropology* 7, no. 1 (February 1992): 6–23, American Anthropological Association: Blackwell Publishing.

——————————————. *Anthropological Locations: Boundaries and Grounds of a Field Science*, edited by Gupta, Akhil and James Ferguson. Berkeley, CA: University of California Press, 1997.

——————————————. "Spatializing States: Toward an Ethnography of Neoliberal Governmentality." *American Ethnologist* 29, no. 4 (2002): 981–1002.

Gutierrez Garza, Ana P. *Care for Sale: An Ethnography of Latin American Domestic and Sex Workers in London*. New York, NY: Oxford University Press, 2019.

Hall, Edward T. *The Silent Language*. New York, NY: Anchor Books, 2013 [1959].

_____. *The Hidden Dimension.* Garden City, NY: Doubleday, 1966.

Hamelink, Cees J. *Cultural Autonomy in Global Communications.* Longman Publishing Group, 1983.

Hannerz, Ulf. "Cosmopolitans and Locals in World Culture." In *Global Culture: Nationalism, Globalization and Modernity,* edited by Mike Featherstone. London, UK: Sage, 1990.

_____. *Cultural Complexity: Studies in the Social Organization of Meaning.* New York, NY: Columbia University Press, 1992.

_____. 1987, "The World in Creolization." *Africa IAI* 57, no. 4 (October 1987): 546–59. (Published online by Cambridge University Press: December 07, 2011).

_____. *Soul side: Inquiries into Ghetto Culture and Community.* Chicago, IL: University of Chicago Press, 2004.

Harmon, Amy. "Sperm Donor Father Ends His Anonymity." *The New York Times,* February 14, 2007.

Harper, Edward B. 1959, "A Hindu Village Pantheon." *Southwestern Journal of Anthropology* XV (Autumn 1959): 227–34.

Herrera Lima, Fernando. *Transnational Families: Institutions of Transnational Spaces.* London, UK: Routledge, 2001.

Harries, Patrick. "The Roots of Ethnicity: Discourse and Politics of Language Construction in Southeast Africa." *African Affairs* 87 (1987): 25–52.

Harris, Marvin. *Cultural Materialism: the Struggle for a Science of Culture.* New York, NY: Random House, 1979.

_____. "The Cultural Ecology of India's Sacred Cattle." *Cultural Anthropology* 7, no. 1 (1966): 51–56.

_____. *Cows, Pigs, Wars, and Witches: the Riddles of Culture.* New York, NY: Vintage, 1974.

_____. *Good to Eat: Riddles of Food and Culture.* IL: Waveland Press, Inc., 1985.

_____. *Our Kind: Who We Are, Where We Came From, Where We Are Going.* New York, NY: Harper & Row Publishers, 1990.

Hernandez, Gil Manuel i Marti. *The Deterritorialization of Cultural Heritage.* Journal of Contemporary Culture, No. 1, 2006, 92–107.

Herskovits, Melville. *The Economic Life of Primitive Peoples.* New York, NY: Knopf, 1940.

Herzfeld, Michael. *Cultural Intimacy: Social Poetics in the Nation-State.* New York, NY: Routledge, 1997.

Hess, Elizabeth. *Nim Chimsky: The Chimp Who Would Be Human.* New York, NY: Bantam Dell, 2008.

Hirsch, Jennifer S., and Holly Wardlow, eds. *Modern Loves: The Anthropology of Romantic Courtship and Companionate Marriage.* Ann Arbor, MI: University of Michigan Press, 2006.

Hobsbaum, Eric J. "The Future of the State." In *Social Futures, Global Visions*, edited by Cynthia Hewitt de Alcantara. Oxford, MA: Blackwell, 1997.

Hockett, Charles Francis. *Universals of Language.* Cambridge, MA: MIT Press, 1963.

Hoebel, E. A. *Men in the Primitive World: an Introduction to Anthropology,* 2nd ed. New York, NY: McGraw-Hill, 1958.

Holm, Bill, and Bill Reid. *Indian Art of the Northwest Coast: A Dialogue on Craftsmanship and Aesthetics.* Seattle, WA: University of Washington Press, 1975.

Huntington, Samuel P. *The Clash of Civilizations and the Remaking of World Order.* New York, NY: Simon and Schuster, 1996.

Humphrey, Caroline. "Barter and Economic Disintegration." *Man* (New Series) 20, no. 1 (March 1985): 48–72. Royal Institute of Great Britain and Ireland.

Hymes, Dell H. "Toward Linguistic Competence." *Working Papers in Sociolinguistics*, No. 166 (1973).

Illouz, Eva. *Consuming the Romantic Utopia: Love and the Cultural Constructions of Capitalism.* Berkeley, CA: University of California Press, 1997.

Inda, Jonathan Xavier, and Renato Rosaldo. "Introduction: A World in Motion." In *The Anthropology of Globalization,* edited by Jonathan Xavier Inda and Renato Rosaldo, 1–34. Malden, MA: Blackwell, 2007.

Iwabuchi, Koichi. *Recentering Globalization: Popular Culture and Japanese Transnationalism.* Durham, NC: Duke University Press, 2002.

Jacknis, Ira. *Carving Traditions of Northwest California.* Berkeley, CA: Phoebe Hearst Museum of Anthropology, 1995.

Jankowiak, W. R., and E. F. Fischer. 1992, "A Cross-Cultural Perspective of Romantic Love." *Ethnology* 31 (1992): 149–55.

Jameson, Fredric. *Postmodernism, or the Cultural Logic of Late Capitalism.* Durham, NC: Duke University Press, 1991 [1984].

Jenkins, Richard. *Rethinking Ethnicity: Arguments and Explorations.* Newbury Park, CA: SAGE, 2008 [1997].

Jolly, Allison. *The Evolution of Primate Behavior.* New York, NY: MacMillan, 1972.

Kant, Immanuel. *Anthropology from a Pragmatic Point of View,* edited by Robert B. Louden. Cambridge, UK: Cambridge University Press, 2006 [1798].

Kapadia, Karin. *Siva and Her Sisters: Gender, Caste, and Class in Rural South India.* Boulder, CO: Westview Press, 1995.

Kaplan, Caren. "Deterritorializations: The Rewriting of Home and Exile in Western Feminist Discourse." *Cultural Critique,* no. 6 (The Nature and Context of Minority Discourse 1987): 187–98. Minneapolis, MA: University of Minnesota Press, 1987.

Karp, Ivan, and Steven D. Lavine. *Exhibiting Cultures: The Poetics and Politics of Museum Display*. Washington, DC: Smithsonian Institution, 1991.

Kelly, Gail P. "Learning to Be Marginal: Schooling in Interwar French West Africa." *Journal of Asian and African Studies* 21 (1986): 171–84.

Kemper, S., and T. Harden. "Experimentally Disentangling What's Beneficial About Elderspeak from What's Not." *Psychology and Aging* 14 (1999): 656–70.

Kendon, Adam. *A Sign Language of Aboriginal Australia: Cultural, Semiotic, and Communicative Perspectives*. Cambridge, MA: Cambridge University Press, 1988.

Kilbride, Philip L. *Plural Marriage for Our Times: A Reinvented Option?*, 1st ed. West Point, CT: Bergin and Garvey, 2006.

Kopytoff, Igor. "The Cultural Biography of Things: Commoditization as Process." In *The Social Life of Things*, edited by Arjun Appadurai, 64–91. Cambridge, MA: Cambridge University Press, 1986.

Kottak, Conrad Phillip. *Mirror for Humanity: A Concise Introduction to Cultural Anthropology*. New York, NY: McGraw-Hill, 2008.

Kratz, Corrine A. "Okiek of Kenya." In *Foraging Peoples: An Encyclopedia of Contemporary Hunter-Gatherers*, edited by Richard Lee and Richard Daly. Cambridge, UK: Cambridge University Press, 1999.

Kroeber, Alfred, and Clyde Kluckhohn. *Culture: A Critical Review of Concepts and Definitions*. New York, NY: Random House, 1952.

Kruisel, Richard. *Seducing the French: The Dilemma of Americanization*. Berkeley, CA: University of California Press, 1993.

Kuper, Adam. *Culture: the Anthropologists' Account*. Cambridge, MA: Harvard University Press, 2000.

—————. "Culture, Identity, and the Project of a Cosmopolitan Anthropology." *Man* (1994): 537–54. London, UK: Royal Anthropological Institute of Great Britain and Ireland.

Labov, William. "The Social Motivation of a Sound Change." *Word* 19 (1963): 273–309.

Lamphere, Louise. "Migration, Assimilation, and the Cultural Construction of Identity: Navajo Perspectives." *Ethnic and Racial Studies* 30, no. 6 (2007): 1132–151.

—————. "The Effect of Social Mobility on Linguistic Behavior." In *Explorations in Sociolinguistics*, edited by S. Lieberson, 186–203. Bloomington, IN: Indiana University Press, 1966.

—————. 1972, "Some Features of the English of Black Americans." In *Varieties of Present-Day English*, edited by R. W. Bailey and J. L. Robinson, 236–55. New York, NY: MacMillan, 1972.

Laclau, Ernesto. "Feudalism and Capitalism in Latin America." *New Left Review* 1/67, May–June 1971 at web address: http://newleftreview.org/I/67/ernesto-laclaufeudalism-and-capitalism-in-latin-america.

Lancaster, Roger N. "Skin Color, Race, and Racism in Nicaragua." *Ethnology* 30, no. 4 (1991): 339–53.

Lanning, Edward P. *Peru Before Incas.* Englewood Cliffs, NJ: Prentice-Hall, 1967.

Lansing, Stephen J. *Priests and Programmers: Technologies of Power in the Engineered Landscape of Bali.* Princeton, NJ: Princeton University Press, 1991.

Lappe, Frances Moore, and Joseph Collins. *Food First: Beyond the Myth of Scarcity.* Ballantine Books, a division of Random House, Inc., 1977, 99–111.

Larsen, Clark Spencer. *Essentials of Physical Anthropology: Discovering Our Origins.* New York, NY: W. W. Norton & Co., 2010.

Lash, Scott. "Introduction." In *Post Structuralist and Postmodernist Sociology,* ix–xv. Andershot, UK: Edward Elgar, 1991.

Leach, Edmond. *Pul Eliya: A Village in Ceylon: A Study of Land Tenure and Kinship.* Cambridge, UK: Cambridge University Press, 1961.

——————. *Political Systems in Highland Burma: A Study of Kachin Social Structure.* Cambridge, MA: Harvard University Press, 1954.

Leathers, Dale G. *Successful Nonverbal Communication: Principles and Applications,* 3rd ed. Boston, MA: Allyn and Bacon, 1997.

Lee, Richard B. *Eating Christmas in the Kalahari (postscript: People of /Xai/xai/ Thirty Years On).* 2000 [1969], 27–30. Laulima.hawaii.edu.

——————. *Kung San: Men, Women and Work in a Foraging Society.* New York, NY: Cambridge University Press, 1979.

——————. *Man the Hunter,* edited by Lee, Richard B. and Irven Devore. Piscataway, NJ: Transaction Publishers, 1968.

Lee, Richard B., and Richard Daly. *The Cambridge Encyclopedia of Hunters and Gatherers.* New York, NY: Cambridge University Press, 2004 [1999].

Levi-Strauss, Claude. *Structural Anthropology.* New York, NY: Basic Books, 1963.

Strauss, Claude Levi. *Elementary Structures of Kinship.* Boston, MA: Beacon Press, 1969 [1949].

——————. *The Elementary Structures of Kinship,* 2nd ed. Boston, MA: Beacon Press, 1969 [1949].

——————. *The Raw and Cooked: Mythologiques,* vol. 1. Chicago, IL: University of Chicago Press, 1983.

——————. *From Honey to Ashes: Introduction to a Science of Mythology,* vol. 2. New York, NY: Harper and Row, 1973.

Levy, B. R., M. D. Slade, and S.V. Kasl. "Longitudinal Benefit of Positive Self-perceptions of Aging on Functional Health." *The Journal of Gerontology,* Series B, Psychological Sciences and Social Sciences 57, no. 5 (2002): 409–17.

Lewis, M. Paul, Gary F. Simons, and Charles D. Fennig, eds. *Ethnologue: Languages of the World,* 16th ed. Dallas, TX: SIL International, 2009. Online version: http://www.ethnologue.com.

_____. *Ethnologue: Languages of the World*, 17th ed. Dallas, TX: SIL International, 2013. Online version: http://www.ethnologue.com.

Liechty, Mark. "Out Here in Kathmandu: Youth and the contradictions of Modernity in Urban Nepal." In *Everyday Life in South* Asia (2nd ed.), edited by Diane P. Mines and Sarah Lamb, 40–49. Bloomington, IN: Indiana University Press, 2010.

Lilleker, Darren. *Key Concepts in Political Communications.* London, UK: Sage, 2008.

Liu, Siyuan. *Routledge Handbook of Asian Theater.* New York, NY: Routledge, 2016.

Lloyd, C. B., ed. *Growing Up Global: The Changing Transitions to Adulthood in Developing Countries.* Committee on Population, National Research Council, and the Institute of Medicine of National Academies, Washington, DC: National Academies Press, 2005, 450–53.

Lovejoy, Paul E. *Transformations in Slavery: A History of Slavery in Africa*, 3rd ed. New York, NY: Cambridge University Press, 2011.

Lukose, Ritty. "Recasting the Secular: Religion and Education in Kerala, India." Pp. 206-179, In *Everyday Life in South Asia* (2nd ed.), edited by Diane P. Mines and Sarah Lamb. Bloomington, IN: Indiana University Press, 2010.

Lutz, William D. "Language, Appearance, and Reality: Doublespeak in 1984." *ETC: A Review of General Semantics* 44, no. 4 (1987): 382–91.

Macleod, Arlene E. *Accommodating Protest: Working Women, the New Veiling, and Change in Cairo.* New York, NY: Columbia University Press, 1991.

Malinowski, Bronislaw. *Argonauts of the Western Pacific.* Prospect Heights, IL: Waveland Press, Inc., 1984 [1922].

_____. *Sex and Repression in Savage Society.* London, UK: Kegan Paul and Co., 1927.

Mankekar, Purnima. *Screening Culture, Viewing Politics: An Ethnography of Television, Womanhood, and Nation in Postcolonial India.* Durham, NC: Duke University Press, 1999.

Maquet, Jacques. *The Aesthetic Experience: An Anthropologist Looks at the Visual Arts.* New Haven, CT: Yale University Press, 1988.

Marcus, George. "Ethnography in/of the World-System: The Emergence of Multi-sited Ethnography." *Annual Review of Anthropology* 24 (1995): 95–117.

Marcus, George, and Michael F. Fisher. *Anthropology as Cultural Critique: An Experiment Moment in Human Sciences.* Chicago, IL: University of Chicago Press, 1986.

Marcus, George, and Fred Myers. *The Traffic in Culture: Refiguring Art and Anthropology.* Berkeley, CA: University of California Press, 1995.

Marshall, John. *The Hunters.* Ethnographic Film (1958).

Martha, Chen, Joann Venek, and James Heintz. 2005, "Informality, Gender, and Poverty: A Global Picture." *Economic and Political Weekly* 41, no. 21: 2131–139.

Marx, Karl. *The Origin of the Family, Private Property, and the State.* 2010 [1884], online version: Marx/Engels Internet Archive (Marxists.org): http://www.marxists.org/archive/marx/works/1884/origin-family/.

_____. *Capital,* vol. 1. London, UK: Penguin Books, 1990 [1867].

_____. *Capital,* vol. 2. New York, NY: Vintage Books, 1991 [1884].

_____. *The Economic and Philosophic Manuscript of 1844,* edited by Dirk J. Struik. New York, NY: International Publishers, 1964 [1932].

_____. "The Eighteenth Brumaire of Louis Bonaparte." In *The Marx-Engels Reader,* edited by R. C. Tucker, 436–525. New York, NY: W. W. Norton, 1970 [1852].

Mattelart, Armand. *The Globalization of Surveillance.* Polity Press, 2010.

_____. *Networking the World 1794–2000.* Minneapolis, MA: University of Minnesota Press, 2000.

_____. *Advertising International: The Privatization of Public Space.* New York, NY: Routledge, 1991.

_____. *Transnationals and the Third World: The Struggle for Culture.* Santa Barbara, CA: Bergin and Garvey, 1983.

Mauss, Marcel. *The Gift: Forms and Functions of Exchange in Archaic Societies.* Translated by Ian Cunnison. New York, NY: W. W. Norton, 1967 [1925].

Mead, Margaret. *Sex and Temperament in Three Primitive Societies.* New York, NY: W. Morrow and Company, 1935.

Mehrabian, Albert. *Silent Messages: Implicit Communication of Emotions and Attitudes,* 2nd ed. Belmont, CA: Wadsworth, 1981.

Mehta, Suketu. "Bollywood Confidential." *New York Times Magazine,* November 14, 2004, 66ff.

Meillassoux, Claude. In *Relations of Production: Marxist Approaches to Economic Anthropology,* edited by David Seddon, 127–57. London, UK: Frank Cass, 1978.

Metcalf, Barbara D., and Thomas R. Metcalf. *A Concise History of Modern India,* 2nd ed. Cambridge, UK: Cambridge University Press, 2006.

Miles, H. Lyn White. "Language and the Orangutan: The Old 'Person' of the Forest." In *The Great Ape Project,* edited by P. Cavalieri and P. Singer, 45–50. New York, NY: St. Martin's Press, 1993.

Miller, Laura. "Those Naughty Teenage Girls: Japanese Kogals, Slang, and Media Assessment." *Journal of Linguistic Anthropology* 14, no. 2 (2004): 225–47.

Mines, Diane P., and Sarah Lamb, eds. *Everyday Life in South Asia,* 2nd ed. Bloomington, IN: Indiana University Press, 2010.

Mintz, S. W. *Sweetness and Power: The Place of Sugar in Modern History.* London, UK: Penguin, 1986.

_____. "Pratik: Haitian Personal Economic Relationships." In *Proceedings of the* 1961 *Annual Spring Meeting of the American Ethnological Society,* 54–63. Seattle, WA: University of Washington Press, 1961.

Montagu, Ashley. *The Human Significance of the Skin.* New York, NY: Harper Collins Publishers, 1978.

Montes, Leonidas, and Eric Schliesser, eds. *New Voices on Adam Smith.* London, UK: Routledge, 2006.

Moon, Vasant. *Growing Up Untouchable in India: A Dalit Autobiography.* Translated by Gail Omvedt. New York, NY: Rowman and Littlefield, 2001.

Morgan, Lewis Henry. *Ancient Society.* Cambridge, MA: Belknap Press, 1963 [1877].

_____. *House and House-Life of the American Aborigines.* U.S. Government Printing Office, 1881.

Morphy, Howard, and Morgan Perkins, eds. *The Anthropology of Art: A Reader.* Hoboken, NJ: Wiley-Blackwell, 2006.

Mountford, Charles P. *Aboriginal Art (The Art in Australia).* London, UK: Longmans, 1961.

Munn, Nancy D. "The Fame of Gawa: A Symbolic Study of Value Transformation in a Massim Society." In *The Social Life of Things,* edited by Arjun Appadurai. Cambridge, MA: Cambridge University Press, 1986.

_____. "The Cultural Anthropology of Time: A Critical Essay." *Annual Reviews in Anthropology* 21 (1992): 93–123.

Murdock, George Peter. "The Common Denominator of Culture." In *The Science of Man in the World Crisis,* edited by Ralph Linton. New York, NY: Columbia University Press, 1945.

_____. *Social Structure.* New York, NY: Macmillan, 1949.

Nagengast, C. "Violence, Terror, and the Crisis of the State." *Annual Review of Anthropology* 23 (1994): 109–36.

Nanda, Serena. "Arranging a Marriage in India." In The Naked Anthropologist. edited by Philip R. DeVita, 1992, 34–42. (1992).

Nandy, Ashis. *Intimate Enemy: Loss and Recovery of Self Under Colonialism.* New York, NY: Oxford University Press, 1983.

Narotzky, Susana. *New Directions in Economic Anthropology.* Chicago, IL: Pluto Press, 1997.

Needham, Joseph. *Science and Civilization in China,* vol. 4, Part 3, Civil Engineering and Nautics. Cambridge, UK: Cambridge University Press, 1971.

Obeyesekere, Ranjini. *Sri Lankan Theater in a Time of Terror: Political Satire in a Permitted Space.* New Delhi, India: Sage Publications, 1999.

Omvedt, Gail. *Dalits and the Democratic Revolution: Dr. Ambedkar and the Dalit Movement in Colonial India.* New Delhi, India: Sage, 1994.

Ong, Aihwa. "The Pacific Shuttle: Family, Citizenship, and Capital Circuits." In *The Anthropology of Globalization*, edited by Jonathan Xavier Inda and Renato Rosaldo, 172–97. Malden, MA: Blackwell Publishers, 2002.

_____. *Spirit of Resistance and Capitalist Discipline: Factory Workers in Malaysia*. Albany, NY: State University of New York Press, 1987.

_____. *Buddha Is Hiding: Refugees, Citizenship, the New America*. Berkeley, CA: University of California Press, 2003.

_____. *Flexible Citizenship: the Cultural Logic of Transnationality*. Durham, NC: Duke University Press, 1999.

Ong, Aihwa, and Stephen J. Collier, eds. *Global Assemblages: Technology, Politics, and Ethics as Anthropology Problems*. Malden, MA: Blackwell Publishing, 2005.

_____. *Neoliberalism as Exception: Mutations in Citizenship and Sovereignty*. Duke University Press, 2006.

Ortner, Sherry. "Sexual Meanings: The Cultural Construction of Gender and Sexuality." In *Gender and Sexuality in Hierarchical Societies*, edited by Harriet Whitehead and Sherry Ortner. New York, NY: Cambridge University Press, 1981.

_____. "Is Female to Male as Nature Is to Culture?" In *Woman, Culture, and Society*, edited by Michelle and Louise Lamphere, 68–87. Stanford, CA: Stanford University Press, 1974.

Ottenheimer, Martin. *Forbidden Relatives: the American Myth of Cousin Marriage*. Urbana, IL: University of Illinois Press, 1996.

Overbeek, Henk. "Transnational Historical Materialism." In *Global Political Economy: Contemporary Theories*, edited by Ronan Palan, 168–69. New York, NY: Routledge, 2000.

Paine, Robert. *Herds of the Tundra: A Portrait of Saami Reindeer Pastoralism*. Washington, DC: Smithsonian Institution Press, 1994.

Paterson, "Penny" Francine. *Koko: A Talking Gorilla* (French: *Koko: le gorille qui parle*), 1978. Directed by Barbet Schroeder.

Pieterse, Jan N. 1995, "Globalization as Hybridization." In *Global Modernities*, edited by Mike Featherstone, Scott Lash, and Roland Robertson. London, UK: Sage, 1995.

_____. *Globalization and Culture: Global Mélange*. Lanham, MD: Rowman and Littlefield, 2003.

Pinker, Steven. *The Language Instincts: How the Mind Creates Language*. New York, NY: Collins Publishers, Inc., 2000.

_____. *The Blank Slate: The Modern Denial of Human Nature*. New York, NY: Penguin Putnam, 2002.

Plattner, Stuart. "Economic Decision Making of Marketplace Merchants: An Ethnographic Model." *Human Organization* 43, no. 3 (1984): 252–64.

Polanyi, Karl. *The Great Transformation.* New York, NY: Farrar & Rinehart, 1944.

_____. *The Great Transformation.* Boston, MA: Beacon Press, 1957.

Potts, Rick, and Chris Sloan. *What Does It Mean To Be Human?* Washington, DC: National Geographic, 2010.

Redfield, Robert. *The Folk Culture of Yucatan.* Chicago, IL: University of Chicago Press, 1941.

Reed, Susan A. *Dance and the Nation: Performance, Ritual, and Politics in Sri Lanka.* Madison, WI: University of Wisconsin Press, 2010.

Ricklefs, Merle C. *A History of Modern Indonesia: Since ca. 1300 to the Present,* 4th ed. New York, NY: Palgrave Macmillan, 2008 [1981].

Ritzer, George. *Expressing America: A Critique of the Global Credit Card Society.* Thousand Oaks, CA: Pine Forge Press, 1995.

_____. *Enchanting a Disenchanted World: Revolutionizing the Means of Consumption.* Thousand Oaks, CA: Pine Forge Press, 1999.

_____. *The McDonaldization of Society,* New Century ed. Thousand Oaks, CA: Pine Forge Press, 2000.

_____. *The Globalization of Nothing: Why So Many Make So Much Out of So Little.* Thousand Oaks, CA: Pine Forge Press, 2004.

Ritzer, George, and Douglas J. Goodman. *Sociological Theory,* 6th ed. New York, NY: McGraw-Hill, 2004.

Roa, Vijayendra, and Michael Walton, eds. *Culture and Public Action.* Stanford, CA: Stanford University Press, 2004.

Robbins, Richard H. *Global Problems and the Culture of Capitalism.* Upper Saddle River, NJ: Pearson Allyn & Bacon, 1999.

Robertson, Roland. *Globalization, Social Theory, and Global Culture.* London, UK: Sage, 1992.

Roosevelt, Anna C. "Archaeology." *The Cambridge Encyclopedia of Hunters and Gatherers,* edited by Richard B. Lee and Richard Daly, 86–91. Cambridge, UK: Cambridge University Press, 1999 [2004].

Rosaldo, Michelle, and Louise Lamphere, eds. *Woman, Culture, and Society.* Stanford, CA: Stanford University Press, 1974.

Rosaldo, Renato. *Cultural Citizenship in Island Southeast Asia: Nation and Belonging in the Hinterlands.* Berkeley, CA: University of California Press, 2003.

Rumbaugh, Duane M. *Language Learning by a Chimpanzee: The Lana Project.* New York, NY: Academic Press, 1977.

Ryzik, Melena. "A Bare Market Lasts One Morning, Art and Design Column." *The New York Times,* August 1, 2011.

Sahlins, Marshall. *Stone Age Economics.* New York, NY: Routledge, 1972.

_____. "Rich Man, Big-Man, Chief: Political Type in Melanesia and Polynesia." *Comparative Studies in Society and History* 5, no. 3 (April 1963): 285–303. Cambridge, UK: Cambridge University Press.

_____. *Social Stratification in Polynesia* (A publication of the American Ethnological Society). Seattle, WA: University of Washington Press, 1958.

Said, Edward W. *Orientalism.* New York, NY: Random House, 1978.

Salzmann, Zdenek. "Explorations in Linguistic Relativity (Review)." *Language* 77, no. 4 (2001).

Sapir, Edward. *Language: An Introduction to the Study of Speech.* London, UK: Rupert Hart-Davis, 1921.

_____. "The Status of Linguistics as a Science." In *Culture, Language, and Personality,* edited by D. G. Mandelbaum. Berkeley, CA: University of California Press, 1958 [1929].

_____. *Culture, Language, and Personality: Selected Essays.* Berkeley, CA: University of California Press, 1949 [1912].

Saul, Mahir. "Claude Meillassoux." In *Theory in Social and Cultural Anthropology: An Encyclopedia* (vol. 2, 8th ed.). Newbury Park, CA: Sage, 2013.

Sarachchandra, E. R. *The Folk Drama of Ceylon.* Colombo, Sri Lanka: Ceylon University Press, 1953.

Saussure, Ferdinand de. *Course in General Linguistics,* edited by Charles Bally and Albert Reinlinger. New York, NY: McGraw-Hill, 1966 [1916].

Scammell, Geoffrey V. *Imperial Age: European Overseas Expansion c. 1400 – 1715.* New York, NY: Routledge, 2003 [1989].

Schiller, Herbert I. *Mass Communications and American Empire.* International Arts and Sciences Press, Inc., 1976.

_____. "Communication and Cultural Domination." *International Journal of Politics* 5, no. 4 (Winter 1975/1976).

Schneider, David M. *American Kinship: A Cultural Account.* Upper Saddle River, NJ: Prentice Hall, 1968.

Schneider, Harold. *Economic Man.* New York, NY: Free Press, 1974.

Seligmann, Charles Gabriel, and Brenda Seligmann. *The Veddas.* Cambridge, UK: Cambridge University Press, 1911.

Semic, Beth. "Vocal Attractiveness: What Sounds Beautiful Is Good." In *The Nonverbal Communication Reader (3rd ed.),* edited by Laura K. Guerrero and Michael L. Hecht, 153–68, Long Grove, IL: Waveland Press, 2008.

Sengupta, Somini. 2006, "'India's Idol' Recipe: Mix Small-Town Grit and Democracy." *New York Times,* May 25, 2006, A–4.

Service, Elman. *Primitive Social Organization: An Evolutionary Perspective.* New York, NY: Random House, 1962.

_____. *Origins of the State and Civilization.* New York, NY: W. W. Norton, 1975.

Schroeder, Ulrich von. *Buddhist Sculptures in Sri Lanka.* Weesen, Switzerland: Visual Dharma Publications, 1990.

_____. *Buddhist Statutes in Tibet: Evolution of Tibetan Sculptures.* Chicago, IL: Serindia Publications, 2008.

Shahd, Laila S. "An Investigation of the Phenomenon of Polygyny in Rural Egypt." *Cairo Papers in Social Science* 24, no. 3 (2005).

Shostak, Marjorie. *Nisa: The Life and Words of a !Kung Woman.* New York, NY: Vintage, 1981.

Silverblatt, Irene. "Andean Women in the Inca Empire." *Feminist Studies* 4 (1978): 7–61.

Smith, Adam. *An Inquiry into the Nature and Causes of the Wealth of Nations,* vol. 1. New York, NY: E. P. Dutton & Co., 1776.

Spencer, Jonathan, and Alan Barnard, eds. *Encyclopedia of Social and Cultural Anthropology.* London, UK and New York, NY: Routledge, 1996.

Stack, B. Carol. *All Our Kin: Strategies for Survival in a Black Community.* New York, NY: Basic Books, 2003 [1974].

Stegeborn, Wiveca. "The Disappearing Wanniyala-Aetto ('Veddahs') of Sri Lanka: A Case Study." *Nomadic Peoples (New Series)* 8, no. 1 (2004): 43–63.

Steinbeck, John. *The Grapes of Wrath.* London, UK: Penguin Publishing Group, 2006 [1939].

Stiglitz, Joseph E. *Globalization and Its Discontents.* New York, NY: W. W. Norton, 2002.

Stocking Jr, George W. "The Ethnographer's Magic." In *The Ethnographer's Magic and Other Essays in the History of Anthropology,* 12–59. Madison, WI: Wisconsin University Press, 1992.

Stoler, Ann Laura. "Colonial Archives and the Art of Governance." *Archival Science* 2 (2002): 87–109.

Strathern, Marilyn, and Carol MacCormack, eds. *Nature, Culture, and Gender.* Cambridge, UK: Cambridge University Press, 1980.

Suttles, Wayne. *The Economic Life of the Salish in the Northwest Coast.* Ph. D. Dissertation, Seattle: University of Washington, 1991.

Sutton, R. Anderson. *Calling Back the Spirit: Music, Dance, and Cultural Politics in Lowland South Sulawesi.* New York, NY: Oxford University Press, 2002.

Terrace, Herbert S. *Nim, A Chimpanzee Who Learned Sign Language.* New York, NY: Columbia University Press, 1987.

Therborn, Goran. *Between Sex and Power: Family in the World, 1900–2000.* New York, NY: Routledge, 2004.

Thomas, Nicholas J., Mark Adams, James Schuster, and Lyonel Grant. *Rauru: Tene Waitere, Maori Carving, Colonial History.* Dunedin, FL: University of Otago Press, 2008.

Thompson, Richard H. "Assimilation." In *Encyclopedia of Social and Cultural Anthropology* (vol. 1), edited by David Levinson and Melvin Ember, 112–15. New York, NY: Greenwood, 1996.

Thompson, Robert Farris. *African Art in Motion: Icon and the Act in the Collection of Katherine Coryton White.* Los Angeles, CA: University of California Press, 1973.

_____. *Black Gods and Kings: Yoruba Art at UCLA*, 1st ed. Los Angeles, CA: University of California Press, 1971.

Tiger, Lionel, and Robin Fox. *The Imperial Animal.* Dumfries, NC: Holt, Rinehart, and Winston, 1971.

Tomlinson, John. "Cultural Imperialism: A Critical Introduction." *Continuum* (1991): 45–50, 108–13.

Thornton, Sarah. *Seven Days in the Art World.* New York, NY: W. W. Norton, 2008.

_____. *33 Artists in 3 Acts.* New York, NY: W. W. Norton, 2014.

Trawick, Margaret Egnor. "Spirits and Voices in Tamil Songs." *American Ethnologist* 15 (1988): 193–215.

Trivedi, Bijal P. "Scientists Identify a Language Gene." *National Geographic News*, October 4, 2001. http://news.nationalgeographic.com/news/2001/10/1004_Tvlanguagegene.html.

Trudgill, Peter. *Sociolinguistics: An Introduction to Language and Society.* New York, NY: Penguin Books, 1983.

Tsing, Anna L. *Friction: An Ethnography of Global Connection.* Princeton, NJ: Princeton University Press, 2005.

Turner, Victor. *The Forest of Symbols: Aspects of Ndembu Ritual.* Ithaca, NY: Cornell University Press, 1967.

_____. *Schism and Continuity in an African Society: A Study of Ndembu Village Life.* Oxford, UK: Berg Publishers, [1957] 1996.

Tylor, Edward B. *Primitive Culture: Researches into the Development of Mythology, Philosophy, Religion, Art, and Custom.* 2 volumes. London, UK: Bradbury: Evans, and Co., 1871.

Vidal, Hern N. J. "Yamana." In *The Cambridge Encyclopedia of Hunters and Gatherers*, edited by Richard B. Lee and Richard Daly, 114–18. Cambridge, UK: Cambridge University Press, 2004.

Viramma, Josiane Racine, and Jean-Luc Racine. "High and Low Castes in Karani." In *Everyday Life in South Asia*, edited by Diane P. Mines and Sarah Lamb, 171–79. Bloomington, IN: Indiana University Press, 2010.

Wadley, S. Susan. "One Straw from a Broom Cannot Sweep: The Ideology and Practice of the Joint Family in Rural North India." In *Everyday Life in South Asia* (2nd ed.), edited by Diane P. Mines and Sarah Lamb, 14–25. Bloomington, IN: Indiana University Press, 2010.

Wallerstein, Immanuel. *Modern World-System I: Capitalist Agriculture and the Origins of the European World Economy in the Sixteenth Century.* Berkeley, CA: University of California Press, 2011 [1974].

_____. *Utopistics: Or Historical Choices of the Twenty-First Century.* New York, NY: New Press, 1998.

_____. *World-Systems Analysis.* Durham, NC: Duke University Press, 2004.

Wallman, Joel. *Aping Language.* Cambridge, MA: Cambridge University Press, 1992.

Watson, James L. ed. *Golden Arches East: McDonald's in East Asia.* Stanford, CA: Stanford University Press, 1997.

Weber, Max. *The Protestant Ethic and the Spirit of Capitalism.* New York, NY: Scribner, 1958.

Weiner, Annette B. *Inalienable Possessions: The Paradox of Keeping While Giving.* Berkeley, CA: University of California Press, 1992.

_____. *The Trobrianders of Papua New Guinea: Case Studies in Cultural Anthropology.* New York, NY: Holt, Rinehart, and Winston, 1988.

Werbner, Pnina. *Anthropology and the New Cosmopolitanism: Rooted, Feminist, and Vernacular Perspectives*, edited by Pnina Werbner. Oxford, NY: Berg, 2008.

White, Leslie. *The Evolution of Culture: the Development of Civilization to the Fall of Rome.* New York, NY: McGraw-Hill, 1959.

Whorf, Benjamin L. *Language, Thought, and Reality,* edited by J. B. Caroll. Cambridge, MA: Cambridge University Press, 1956 [1940].

Wichmann, Elizabeth. "Tradition and Innovation in Contemporary Beijing Opera Performance." *TDR* (TDR 1988–) 34, no. 1 (1990): 146–78.

Wilk, Richard. *Economies and Cultures: Foundations of Economic Anthropology.* Boulder, CO: Westview Press, 1996.

Wilk, Richard, and Lisa C. Cligget. *Economies and Cultures: Foundations of Economic Anthropology.* New York, NY: Avalon Publishing, 2007.

Williams, Raymond. "Culture is Ordinary." In *Resources of Hope: Culture, Democracy, and Socialism.* London, UK: Verso, 1989 [1958].

Wiser, William H. *The Hindu Jajmani System.* Lucknow, India: Lucknow Publishing House, 1936.

Witherspoon, Gary. *Navajo Kinship and Marriage.* Chicago, IL: University of Chicago Press, 1975.

Wittfogel, Karl A. *Oriental Despotism.* New Haven, CT: Yale University Press, 1957.

Wolf, Eric. *Europe and the People without History.* Berkeley and Los Angeles, CA: University of California Press, 1982.

_____. *Envisioning Power: Ideologies of Dominance and Crisis.* Berkeley, CA: University of California Press, 1999.

_____. "Kinship, Friendship, and Patron-Client Relations in Complex Societies." *The Social Anthropology of Complex Societies* (1966).

_____. *Building an Anthropology of the Modern World* (with Sydel Silverman). Berkeley, CA: University of California Press, 2001.

Yoshimoto, Mitsuhiro. "The Postmodern and Mass Images in Japan." *Public Culture* 1, no. 2 (Spring 1989): 8–25.

Zukin, Sharon. *Landscapes of Power: From Detroit to Disney World.* Berkeley, CA: University of California Press, 1991.

# INDEX

CPSIA information can be obtained
at www.ICGtesting.com
Printed in the USA
JSHW060801140123
36242JS00005B/88

9 781792 407642